THE WISCONSIN SYNOD LUTHERANS

A History of the Single Synod, Federation, and Merger

Edward C. Fredrich

NORTHWESTERN PUBLISHING HOUSE
Milwaukee, Wisconsin

Third printing, 2017
Second printing, 2000

All rights reserved. No part of this publication may be reproduced stored in a retrieval system, or transmitted in any form or by any means—electronic, mechanical, photocopy, recording, or otherwise—except for brief quotations in reviews, without prior permission from the publisher.

Library of Congress Card 91-68217
Northwestern Publishing House
1250 N. 113th St., Milwaukee, WI 53226-3284
© 1992 by Northwestern Publishing House.
Published 1992
Printed in the United States of America
ISBN 978-0-8100-0423-8

15N0541
ISBN 978-0-8100-0423-8

Contents

Foreword and Acknowledgments v

Chapter One: Roots That Reach the Rhine 1

Chapter Two: First the Stalk 9

Chapter Three: Good Neighbors 18

Chapter Four: Turn to the Right 27

Chapter Five: Early Interchurch Relations 37

Chapter Six: In the Synodical Conference 49

Chapter Seven: Silver Anniversary Perspective 62

Chapter Eight: Fifteen Good Years: 1876-1891 78

Chapter Nine: The Federation Years: 1892-1917 93

Chapter Ten: Doctrinal Concerns at the
    Turn of the Century 106

Chapter Eleven: From Federation to Merger 119

Chapter Twelve: Merger Beginnings in War Years 132

Chapter Thirteen: Focus on Education 143

Chapter Fourteen: Protes'tant Controversy 154

Chapter Fifteen: Missions Old and Missions New 164

Chapter Sixteen: Significant Intersynodical Developments 175

Chapter Seventeen: In The Great Depression and
    World War II 186

Chapter Eighteen: Break with Missouri	198
Chapter Nineteen: Into All the States	209
Chapter Twenty: Into All the World	219
Chapter Twenty-One: Three Decades of Progress and Problems in Education	234
Chapter Twenty-two: Synodical Administration	250
Chapter Twenty-three: The Mischke Years and Beyond	260
Endnotes	269
Index	295
Photo History	308

Foreword and Acknowledgments

Much of the writing was done in 1985 and 1986 when an Aid Association for Lutherans grant, an Oscar J. Naumann fellowship, resulted in a writing sabbatical. Wisconsin Lutheran Seminary also contributed generously to the venture. To both I am deeply grateful.

After a lapse of several years the remaining third of the book was completed. The manuscript was delivered to Northwestern Publishing House on the last full day of the 1990-1991 school year, my last at Wisconsin Lutheran Seminary. "At the time of this writing" does not always mean the same thing when it appears on the following pages.

There are many who aided the writing project. The library staff and the librarian, Martin Westerhaus, at the Seminary were always helpful. My fellow church history teachers served as readers and correctors while the work was in process. Students in their research papers over the years provided much information, some acknowledged in the book and more not mentioned because it could not be sorted out after the passing of years.

Two people, above all others, are owed a great debt of thanks. They are Mrs. Kathie Fredrich—no relative—and Mrs. Nell Baczanski, faculty secretaries. To them fell the unenviable assignment of deciphering my longhand and putting it into readable form. Without them and their special skill there would be no book. The writer has never been able to master even the typewriter, to say nothing of word processors and even more complicated tools.

Another great boon for me and the writing was the help of the book editor, Roland C. Ehlke of the Northwestern Publishing House staff. He waited patiently and worked diligently and skillfully.

A special thank-you goes to my wife Elaine for helping see me through the writing process.

The "Photo History" at the end of the book is certainly not meant to be exhaustive. Rather, it is a small, representative taste of WELS history in pictures.

The content of the book rests primarily on the printed record. It is a record of the grace of God who loves a little church body dearly. May the Lord of the church, to whom the greatest gratitude is due, bless the book and its readers.

Written at Watertown on March 24, 1992.

E. C. Fredrich

CHAPTER ONE

Roots That Reach the Rhine

THE WISCONSIN EVANGELICAL LUTHERAN SYNOD, alphabetized WELS, in its present structure came into being in 1917 through a merger of the Wisconsin, Michigan, Minnesota, and Nebraska Synods. Each of these synods had its own history with roots running back into the middle decades of the previous century. The longest and strongest of these roots are those that link the present church body to the original Wisconsin Synod formed on May 27, 1850 at Granville, Wisconsin under the official designation, "The German Evangelical Ministerium of Wisconsin."[1]

While it is the purpose of this writing to focus attention on the merged synod from 1917, it will supply some review of the story of the original Wisconsin Synod, as well as that of its three partners in the merger. This resumé will lean heavily on the definitive writing by J. P. Koehler, *The History of the Wisconsin Synod* to which the interested reader is referred for a more ample record of Wisconsin Synod history up to the 1920s.[2]

A German Synod

The chapter heading seeks to emphasize the German character of the old Wisconsin Synod that held sway throughout its history from 1850-1917. Almost to a man the first pastors were German. German was their mother tongue and Germany was the place where they were born and, for the most part, received their theological training. When the synod began to train its own pastors at its theological seminary, it simply took it for granted that the medium for instruction would be German. As late as the 1930s the bulk of the teaching at Wisconsin Lutheran Seminary was still being done in German, with English playing only a subordinate role for practical purposes.

Church services were in German. The people would not have had it any other way. With but few exceptions, they were Germans. Even when they were using English in their homes and on the streets, they still wanted to worship in church in German. In 1914 only a minority of the synod's congregations provided English services, and that was usually only on an infrequent and inconvenient, basis. That momentous year, 1914, incidentally, marked the first appearance of the synod's official magazine, the *Northwestern Lutheran*, but it would remain the *Gemeinde-Blatt*'s little sister another quarter century.

The original purpose and the long-time objective of the Wisconsin Synod had a distinctly German tinge. The founders and their successors viewed their assignment as providing pastoral service to the many German immigrants who were settling in Wisconsin in the second half of the previous century.

Since much of this settling was in rural areas, the synod's churches tended to be in the country or the little town that served as the center of the agricultural area. Larger city churches came into being as a matter of course, especially in Milwaukee, but this was more as by-product than by specific design.

The basically German and rural character of the Wisconsin Synod did much to shape its history. This will often be a factor to reckon with in the situations and decisions, successes and failures described in the pages ahead.

Specific Rhine Roots

Some of the Rhine roots have very definite locations, intimately related to the Wisconsin Synod's origin and early years. These are cities in the Rhine country where training schools of mission societies prepared many of the men who would found the Wisconsin Synod and serve it in its first decades.[3]

In the northwestern part of Switzerland, where the Rhine's Alpine waters turn north for the long trip to the sea, stands the city of Basel. In its environs were located two mission schools that sent pastors to the Wisconsin Synod, the one at Basel and the other at nearby St. Chrischona. Both schools owe their origin to the mission zeal of Christian Friedrich Spittler, born at Wimzheim in Wuerttemberg in 1782.

At Basel in 1815 a mission society had developed, growing out of its "Christian Society," founded in the previous century and serving as a sort of headquarters and clearing house for similar societies in various parts of Germany. Spittler was the driving force in the creation of the mission society and its training school.

In preparing its students for mission work among the heathen and eventually also among German emigrants in North and South America, the Basel institute concentrated on Bible study and practical courses. There were six semesters of study. It was not as ambitious a program as Halle had pursued with university students, but it was more thorough than others that put most stress on the student's own commitment and zeal and little on his educational advancement. In 1833 Basel, replying to an appeal from South German settlers in Michigan's Ann Arbor area, sent out to them one of their trainees, Friedrich Schmid. In his service there that stretched over a third of a century Schmid founded more than twenty congregations in the area and two synods, the short-lived "Mission Synod" in late 1842 or early 1843 and the enduring Michigan Synod in 1860. The latter eventually became the Michigan District of the Wisconsin Synod. Through Schmid's influence other Basel graduates came to Michigan, among them the synodical founders and stalwarts, Christoph Eberhardt and Stephan Klingmann.

Examples of Basel contributions to the original Wisconsin Synod are Gottlieb Reim and Wilhelm Streissguth, brothers-in-law and synodical presidents in the second decade. As vice-president, Reim served in place of President Bading in 1863 and 1864, while the latter was off on an extended European fund-raising trip to gather funds for the Watertown school. Reim was then elected president in 1864 but resigned in 1865. Vice-president Streissguth was acting president for a year and then was elected in his own right in 1866. He also resigned after a year. The two men played brief but important roles in the synodical presidency in the turbulent second decade of the synod.

Near Basel at St. Chrischona another mission school was established by Spittler. He was not breaking with the Basel society; he was finding a new outlet for his boundless mission zeal. For a long time he had been trying to train journeymen to do evangelizing at the same time that they were traveling to advance themselves in their trade. Such a journeyman was John Muehlhaeuser, a baker from Notzingen in Wuerttemberg who eventually became a Barmen emissary and the Wisconsin Synod's first president.

When it became obvious that the journeymen needed more training to be effective evangelists, Spittler determined to establish a school for them. After several false starts a St. Chrischona site was obtained. There the *Pilgermission* (Pilgrims' Mission) began operations in 1840 in a medieval chapel overlooking Basel.

Some St. Chrischona men served in the Wisconsin Synod, more in the Michigan and Minnesota Synods. The 1863 annual meeting of the Wisconsin Synod welcomed four such men. Unfortunately only two, L. Ebert and F. Hilpert, rendered useful service. Ebert soon joined the Minnesota Synod and other Chrischona men there, such as L. Emmel, F. W. Reitz, and A. Kuhn. The latter was the Minnesota Synod's president from 1876 to 1883 when he was followed by another Chrischona graduate, C. J. Albrecht.

In the Michigan Synod, St. Chrischona replaced Basel as the chief source of new pastors after Klingmann succeeded Schmid in the presidency and loosened the old ties to Basel. Among the first Chrischona men to come to Michigan were C. A. Lederer, a friend and classmate of C. J. Albrecht and fourth Michigan president, and W. Linsenmann, who headed Michigan Lutheran Seminary from 1892 to 1902.

Far down the Rhine from Basel in the Wuppertal area is a cluster of towns that merit mention. They are Elberfeld, Barmen, Koeln, and Wesel. They all had mission societies which in 1828 joined forces in the United Rhine Mission Society. A division of the larger group was the *Langenberger Verein*, officially "The Evangelical Society for North America." The mission school was located at Barmen. This is the society and the division and the school that contributed most heavily in missionaries and money to the cause of the Wisconsin Synod for almost twenty years from 1850 to 1868. The three ordained pastors who in 1850 established "The German Evangelical Ministerium of Wisconsin" were all Langenberg missionaries.

The Three Synodical Founders

When in 1837 the Langenberg division was formally organized and in a position to send missionaries to its designated field, the unchurched of North America, it selected as its first trainee for that work John Muehlhaeuser.[4] He has already been mentioned as the journeyman baker who was one of Spittler's evangelists.

The Wisconsin Synod's founder was born in 1803 at Notzingen in Wuerttemberg and seemed destined to spend his life as a baker in the Old World. He had already reached the rank of journeyman when religious interests caused him to seek to emulate an acquaintance, John Weitbrecht, another baker, who had entered the Basel school to prepare for foreign mission work. An exchange of letters ensued and brought Muehlhaeuser in 1829 to Basel and Spittler, and to enlistment as one of the latter's pilgrim missionaries.

His travels through Austria, Bohemia, and Hungary for the next four years brought him both difficulty and satisfaction. His evangelism efforts caused him to lose one job when employment was hard to find and even to suffer a long imprisonment in Bohemia. It was not, all in vain however. Two prisoners and two prison officials became converts during the prison term of the energetic evangelist.

This taste of missionary effort and success deepened Muehlhaeuser's desire to be a foreign missionary. In 1835 he entered the Barmen mission school with this goal in mind. He was not, however, sent to the kind of foreign field he had in mind, Africa or Asia. Director Richter and other school authorities decided that their student, already approaching the middle thirties, would have difficulty in learning native languages. Instead, they recommended that he be one of the first two missionaries the Langenberg society would send to North America. The other was the Erlangen graduate, Candidate Oertel, who had volunteered for such service. This was in 1837. The credentials are worth quoting:

> The deplorable spiritual condition of our Protestant German emigrants in North America has aroused the Christian sympathy of a number of friends here, and since the work of our mission society by its constitution is confined to non-Christian peoples it has been proposed to us that we designate from among our small number of seminarians a student who as a catechist and teacher will help the ordained theologian, likewise to be commissioned, to break the ground.
>
> Gladly are we acceding to this wish and rejoice that our brother Joh. Muehlhaeuser from Notzingen in Wuerttemberg is heartily willing to accept the proposal. This dear brother has spent about two years in our mission seminary, and we are fully confident that, constrained by the love of Christ, he will make conscientious use of the talents entrusted to him for the instruction in the truths of salvation, for the elementary teaching, and for the care of souls. It is a pleasant duty for us, therefore, to commend him most solicitously to all Christian brethren, asking that they render help to him for the achievement of his God-pleasing undertaking by word and deed, inasmuch as the friends here, who have offered the means for his passage, are confident that the brethren in North America and especially our wealthier countrymen over there will see to it that the man we have recommended will not suffer for want of the necessities of life, so he can devote himself entirely to his important calling.
>
> May our Lord Jesus then graciously approve of our dear Brother Muehlhaeuser, as well as of his colleague, Candidate Oertel, so that their service may redound to the eternal salvation of many souls.[5]

After landing in New York on October 3, 1837, and beginning his work, John Muehlhaeuser soon encountered difficulties in his teaching endeavors, as did Oertel in his preaching to the unchurched. Muehlhaeuser's main problem was his lack of ability in English. Many parents wanted their children instructed in the language of the land, and this Muehlhaeuser could not provide. When only meager contributions were forthcoming, he followed the advice of friends and went inland to Rochester.

The congregation there needed a pastor and, although hesitant because of his status as a catechist, Muehlhaeuser accepted the pastoral licensing of the New York Ministerium and took over the Rochester vacancy. He soon reunited a congregation that was badly split into Reformed and Lutheran factions. His pastoral work must have been viewed as satisfactory, for the next year he was ordained at the meeting of the New York Ministerium.

Muehlhaeuser proved himself to be a capable pastor during the ten years he served the Rochester people. A knowledgeable historian of the New York Ministerium, himself a Rochester pastor, describes those ten years in this fashion:

> At the end of March 1838 Candidate Johannes Muehlhaeuser presented himself to President Wacherhagen for assignment. Not too many weeks earlier he had landed at New York with Max Oertel, who fell away to the Roman papacy. Both were products of the Barmen Mission School.
>
> Muehlhaeuser hoped to find a place in New York but this did not materialize. The Mission Committee sent him to Rochester. The affairs of the Rochester congregation, which had run into financial problems in a church building project, were placed into the hands of a committee that made itself personally responsible for $663. During 1838 other congregations raised $213.25 for this purpose and $120 was collected in Rochester. The committee was responsible for the remainder. In 1839 Pastor Muehlhaeuser could report 140 communicants. Other congregations also in this year added $145.65 to the treasury. On December 14, 1839, the completed church could be dedicated. Debts were retired and the congregation prospered until in the spring of 1842 a licensed preacher, C. F. Soldan, who had been assigned Poughkeepsie as his field of labor, came to Rochester, won a following in Pastor Muehlhaeuser's congregation and erected an opposition altar. Later Soldan went over to the Unionists *[*Unierten* — the footnote, not reproduced here, refers to a similar disturbance at Syracuse].
>
> Because of the desertions the congregation grew only slowly the next few years. Yet Pastor Muehlhaeuser could report in 1847, not only that the church building had been enlarged, but that it was so crowded every Sunday that it would soon be necessary to add a gallery in order to provide place for all who wanted to attend the services. In May 1848, Pastor Muehlhaeuser re-

signed his post in order to enter the service of the American Tract Society and to work in Wisconsin. He, however, expressed the wish to maintain his ties to the Ministerium also in the future.[6]

Muehlhaeuser sums up the matter tersely in his history of the first ten years of the Synod as he simply says:

> I served the Evangelical Lutheran Church at Rochester ten years. Since the congregation was well established and capable of providing for a pastor adequately and I was still feeling healthy and strong, yes, especially prompted by Pastor Weinmann, I resolved to move with my family to Wisconsin so that I could still carry out mission work for some years.[7]

The Rochester service was terminated when two other Langenberg missionaries arrived in this country and all three eventually made their way to Wisconsin. The two, who came to New York in 1846, are John Weinmann and William Wrede.

John Weinmann of Bernhausen in Wuerttemberg enrolled at Barmen early in 1843. He showed his dedication by remaining at the school for additional Bible study after passing the examination that qualified him for assignment. Weinmann was the man who was sent to the Milwaukee area to answer an appeal for a pastor that Ehrenfried Seebach, a layman at Town Oakwood, had directed to the Rhine Mission Society. Weinmann was really the pioneer pastor of the Wisconsin Synod in Wisconsin. On his travels to his assignment Weinmann stopped at Ann Arbor to be ordained by Pastor Schmid.

To round out the story of this founding father, his work at Oakwood stretched southward and northward and involved stations at Caledonia, Greenfield, and New Berlin. Soon he was called to Racine. There he served until 1853, when he accepted a call to a Lutheran congregation in Baltimore. After five years he made a trip to Germany but never returned. On the way back his ship, the *Austria*, burned at sea.

The third of the trio of Wisconsin founders, William Wrede, came from the Magdeburg area. He applied to Barmen with imposing recommendations in the spring of 1845 but had to wait until fall for a commission as an American missionary. For reasons that can not be determined, he went to Osterburg in Pommerania to be ordained there and to serve briefly. The following spring he once again put himself at the service of Langenberg just in time to join Weinmann and a third companion for the overseas voyage.

This third companion deserves brief notice, even though he never served the Wisconsin Synod. This is Pastor Rauschenbusch, a Tuebingen graduate and already a pastor when he applied to Langenberg. He came from a long line of Lutheran pastors but in America switched to the Baptists. At Rochester his son Walter would pioneer in espousing the social gospel in the early years of this century. Except for the father's move from Lutheran to Baptist, the Wisconsin Synod might have become the cradle of the social gospel perversion of the gospel.

Muehlhaeuser met the boat that brought Weinmann, Wrede, and Rauschenbusch to New York. He took Weinmann with him to Rochester as the first leg of the trip to Wisconsin. Wrede took charge of the congregation at Callicoon in New York state. In 1849 he moved to Wisconsin to serve the congregation at Granville, near Milwaukee. In 1853 he came to Racine to fill the vacancy caused by Weinmann's move to Baltimore. After two years he returned to Germany.

In the meantime Muehlhaeuser had reacted to reports Weinmann had sent him about the many Germans in Wisconsin who had no pastors to serve them. The veteran missionary, already in his mid-forties, resigned his Rochester post to fill the need on the frontier. In order to have some livelihood, he applied to a tract society for licensing as a colporteur to sell their publications in his new area. He arrived in Milwaukee on June 27, 1848, in the year Wisconsin finally achieved statehood.

The rugged traveling involved in the colporteur's life proved too much for Muehlhaeuser's health. Friends advised him to found another congregation in Milwaukee. The venture began as an "evangelical" congregation, soon modified in a reorganization to "German Evangelical Lutheran Trinity Congregation." To avoid confusion with the Missouri Synod's Trinity Church, the name was quickly changed to Grace. Grace church is still in existence and is in fact looking to a downtown revitalization to asist in its own rejuvenation.

By the end of 1848 there were three Langenberg missionaries in the Milwaukee area: Muehlhaeuser at the Milwaukee church, Weinmann at Oakwood and Wrede at Granville. In addition Paul Meiss, a Barmen reject who had made his own way to the area, was at Slinger (*Schlesingerville*) after serving the Granville church for a brief time. The three, in a sense and also the fourth, all had roots that reached the Rhine country. Now they were ready for a new planting, the organization of the German Evangelical Ministerium of Wisconsin.

CHAPTER TWO

First the Stalk

There is a story behind the story of the founding of the Wisconsin Synod. It revolves around the *why* question. In a sense, it would not have been necessary for Muehlhaeuser, Weinmann, and Wrede to found a new Lutheran synod. In 1849 two German Lutheran synods already had holdings in the Milwaukee area. The Buffalo Synod, organized in Milwaukee in 1845, had its dual parish of Freistadt and Milwaukee, served originally by Pastor Krause. The Missouri Synod, organized in Chicago in 1847, had its Trinity Church in Milwaukee, served by Pastor Keyl. The Langenberg men deliberately refrained from affiliating with the existing synods and, by the same token, the existing synods would not have admitted them. It was a case of "Old Lutherans" versus "New Lutherans." A brief explanation is in order.

A "New Lutheran" Synod Founded

The conflict between "old" and "new" stemmed from the persistent efforts to effect a union between the Lutheran and Reformed denominations. Among many such efforts, that of the 1817 Prussian Union looms large in the background of this history. On the anniversary of the Reformation Prussia's Frederick William III instituted such a union and hoped many would follow the example he set. The idea was to bring Lutherans and Reformed into an apparent union, while allowing each group to retain its distinctive doctrines, such as actual or only spiritual presence of body and blood in the Lord's Supper. This undertaking became *the* issue in Prussia and other areas where similar programs were put into effect.

"Old Lutherans" were dead set against any such union. They resisted to the point of imprisonment. At best they succeeded in establishing "free" churches in areas where the state church espoused union. At worst they simply pulled out lock, stock, and barrel, taking their staunch Lutheranism to Australia or America. Such emigrants were the Prussians whom Pastor Grabau in 1839 led to Buffalo or sent on to Wisconsin. This is the origin of the Buffalo Synod. In Saxony there were similar difficulties. Also in 1839 "Old Lutherans" emigrated from there to St. Louis and Perry County in Missouri. This was a step in the organization of the Missouri Synod.

"New Lutherans," on the other hand, held the view that they could suffer the union situation if no doctrinal compromise were involved. They did not recognize that the union situation itself, in whatever form, was already such a compromise. In the Rhine country, where there had been "Evangelical" Lutheran-Reformed unions even earlier than 1817, it was easy to operate union mission societies and schools. The argument ran: "With so much to be done and so much support needed, why not join Lutheran and Reformed forces in the effort with each denomination retaining its integrity?"

The mission efforts and schools at Basel and Barmen and Berlin were such union undertakings. There could be differences in degree. A mission director at Barmen like John Wallmann might instill more Lutheran confessionalism in his students than Richter had in Muehlhaeuser and others earlier. But it was a difference of degree, not kind. Men trained under authentic Lutheran auspices by Loehe at Neuendettelsau or Harms at Hermannsburg had a different outlook than Basel or Barmen graduates had.[1] Both wanted to be Lutherans. Both wanted the brand name but they disagreed on how pure the ingredients of the product should be.

In a one-on-one confrontation with an "Old Lutheran" the "New Lutheran" comes off second best. It should be remembered, however, that he comes off better in other confrontations. He was more doctrinally concerned than the many Lutherans who were indifferent, who just did not care at all about "Old" or "New" Lutheranism. He was a much more confessional Lutheran than the liberal and rationalist who would simply have responded to any doctrinal concerns with the blasé reaction, "Why bother about Scripture's teaching? We can arrive at the solution without irrational aids." In such company the "New Lutheran" was not worst by any means.

On one occasion Muehlhaeuser himself made a specific case for his "New Lutheranism" when reproving an associate, Gottlieb Weitbrecht, for going over to the Methodists. Weitbrecht had questioned the validity of the "New Lutheran" stance and Muehlhaeuser replied by letter:

> Just because I am not strictly [Lutheran] or Old-Lutheran, I am in a position to offer every child of God and servant of Christ

the hand of fellowship over the ecclesiastical fence. Have quite often been together with English preachers of the various denominations in ministerial conference, and we respected and loved each other as brethren and deliberated on the general welfare of the church. So I am not, dear Methodist brother, withdrawing the hand of brotherhood from you if you are a Methodist in the spirit of the Methodist Church's founder. But I fear you will have to withdraw from me if you don't want to be looked at askance by your Methodist brethren . . . . However, as a non-theologian I am wondering how you a theologian, pledged to the confessional book, could take the step without a struggle. You won't expect me to believe that the teaching of the Methodist church, especially regarding the sacraments, yes, even pertaining to justification and sanctification, is Lutheran?[2]

The concern for Lutheran doctrine in such key points as sacraments and justification and sanctification was commendable. Weitbrecht, however, also had a point in his contention, which occasioned the Muehlhaeuser letter, that he could not join the Wisconsin Synod because "your practice is neither strictly Lutheran nor strictly Evangelical, and yet you aim to be both." In its early years the infant Wisconsin Synod would have to do much painful soul-searching as it struggled with the identity crisis involved in trying to be "neither strictly Lutheran nor strictly Evangelical." The problem would already surface in the organizational conventions.

The term *conventions* may well be on the pretentious side when used in connection with the two meetings that brought the Wisconsin Synod into existence. In December 1849 two old friends, Weinmann of Oakwood and Wrede of Granville, and a Langenberg reject, Paul Meiss, sat down with Muehlhaeuser in his church hall and discussed the founding of a new Lutheran synod. Next spring at Granville they were joined by Kaspar Pluess of Sheboygan, a Basel reject, and there put the plans into effect. Conventions or not, the two little meetings brought the Wisconsin Synod into being. "First the Stalk."

There is a brief protocol of the 1849 Milwaukee meeting available, and it is interesting and important enough to be reproduced in full:

Organization of
the Evangelical Lutheran Wisconsin Synod

On December 8, 1849, Pastors Muehlhaeuser, Wrede, Weinmann, and Meiss assembled in Milwaukee in the church hall of the Evangelical Lutheran Church in order mutually to consider and discuss the important matter of organizing a synod in Wisconsin. This assembly was opened with hymn and prayer and then the main agenda item was brought into consideration. After a wide-ranging discussion on the part of the pastors mentioned it was unanimously desired and deemed necessary at this time to organize a synod in Wisconsin. These resolutions were then passed:

1. That the synod to be formed should have and maintain the name, "The First German Evangelical Lutheran Synod of Wisconsin" and should be perpetuated for all time under that name and designation;

2. That the officers of said synod should on this occasion be elected for two-year terms.

In this election the following persons were chosen as officers: Pastor Muehlhaeuser as president, Pastor Weinmann as secretary, Pastor Wrede as treasurer.

President Muehlhaeuser was then directed to prepare as soon as possible a constitution for the synod which should correspond to its confessional stand. Finally it was resolved that the next year's synodical meeting take place on May 27, 1850 in Granville, Wis., to which the members are to bring their annual reports. Done on December 8, 1849, in Milwaukee.

John Weinmann[3]

On Trinity Sunday, May 26, 1850, the organization of the Wisconsin Synod was completed. Kaspar Pluess of Slinger joined the four men who had met the previous December in Milwaukee. The main agenda item was the constitution that President Muehlhaeuser had drafted. According to the minutes, the proposed constitution "was read and discussed section by section and after several changes was unanimously adopted."

Some of these changes must have occurred in those constitutional paragraphs "which should correspond to" the synod's confessional stand. Chief of these is the ninth paragraph of the fourth section, "Concerning Licensed Candidates," where this wording is found:

> When ordained each candidate will be pledged to the Unaltered Augsburg Confession and to the other Confessions of the Evangelical Lutheran Church and will be asked the following questions:
>
> 1. Do you believe that the fundamental teachings of the Holy Scripture are purely, essentially, and correctly contained in the doctrinal articles of the Unaltered Augsburg Confession and the other Evangelical Lutheran confessional writings?
>
> 2. Are you also definitely determined to make them the doctrinal standard in your important office and to teach according to them always?

The constitutional provisions for ordained pastors in the fifth section also requires in its third paragraph that all congregational arrangements must be "in harmony with the pure Word of the Bible and the Confessions of our Evangelical Lutheran Church."

These wordings in the manuscript of the original constitution were changed sometime later, and altogether unofficially. All references to confessional writings, except those in the questions for ordinands, were crossed out and replaced by such wordings as "pure Bible Christianity" and "pure Bible Word."

Given these between-the-lines insertions, one is forced, in the absence of any other explanation, to assume that the alterations were later additions and that the actual confessional commitments in the constitution came because of the stand Weinmann and Wrede took at Granville. Later Muehlhaeuser, in whose safekeeping the constitution manuscript no doubt rested, may have derived some small satisfaction in unofficially replacing wordings he was forced to accept at Granville with those he had originally written in Milwaukee.[4]

In May 1850 at Granville the infant synod was already engaging in its own version of the old struggle between "Old Lutherans" and "New Lutherans." The former were committed to the confessions; the latter could yield a point in the interests of expediency. No matter what President Muehlhaeuser's intentions may have been in 1850, his synod started off in the right direction at Granville. It would take almost two decades to reach the goal. But a good beginning had been made. "First the Stalk."

New Persons and Places

In the meantime the Wisconsin Synod experienced steady growth in numbers of pastors, congregations, and communicants. After a rather slow start during the first few years the growth rate accelerated considerably, as the following table indicates.

Year	Preachers	Among Them	Preaching Places	Among Them
1850	5	Muehlhaeuser	9	Sheboygan
1852	8	Goldammer	16	Racine
1854	10	Bading	—	Newtonburg
1856	11	Reim	—	Manitowoc
1858	17	Fachtmann	25	Watertown
1860	20	Gausewitz	59	Burr Oak
1862	32	Moldehnke	90	Platteville
1864	38	Hoenecke	104	Ahnapee
1866	52	Martin	125	New London

By 1867 the communicant strength had reached 12,741. The names of congregations and preaching stations spell out the early growth in geographical terms. Amid the transportation problems of the 1850s in Wisconsin, the Lake Michigan shore to the north and to the south would be a prime candidate for settlement and mission effort. A plank road stretched westward from Milwaukee to Watertown. Meanwhile the growth lines would also point in other directions, notably north and west to the stamping grounds of the Northwestern Conference.

The names of the synod's pastors on the list also point to heroic efforts in evangelism and home missions. Actually, all the pastors were pastors and missionaries. They would begin work at their assigned post but in short order would be establishing preaching stations in the surrounding area. Gottlieb Reim is one example among many. In February 1858 he moved from Ashford to Helenville. By the time of the next synodical convention in June he was reporting for four preaching places. Evangelism efforts did not begin in the Wisconsin Synod two decades or so ago. They built the Wisconsin Synod in its early years.

In those early outreach efforts, however, a few names stand out. At Manitowoc, Burlington, and Jefferson, Carl Goldammer, who joined the synod at its second convention and after Muehlhaeuser's death in 1867 became its senior pastor, was a missionary through and through. Gottlieb Fachtmann showed such ability at gathering unchurched people in the Lake Winnebago area in late 1857 and early 1858 that the next convention of that year made him the synod's first *Reiseprediger*, missionary-at-large. His journeys took him to La Crosse and points west and eventually into the newly founded Minnesota Synod as Father Heyer's successor in the congregation in St. Paul and as an acting synodical president during Heyer's semi-retirement.[5]

Edward Moldehnke was the next *Reiseprediger*, salaried by the Berlin and Rhine Mission Societies. A Halle graduate, he arrived in 1861 just in time to set out in the next year for mission explorations in the Mississippi Valley's woods while Indians were rising not too far away.[6] Through his efforts then and later numerous new preaching places were established. At the time of the 1863 convention he was already reporting for 22 stations. Unfortunately these efforts ended abruptly when Moldehnke's heroic attempt to be both *Reiseprediger* and lone theological teacher at the Watertown school resulted in efforts at relief that Moldehnke felt he could not live with. He left the synod in 1866.[7]

Founding the Watertown School

The mention of Moldehnke's added assignment as theological professor calls for an account of the beginning of the Wisconsin Synod's worker-training system. The mission zeal of men like Goldammer, Fachtmann, and Moldehnke enlarged the synod's number of parishes and its need for pastors. Make-do efforts to find a supply of pastors were simply not meeting the needs. Men came to the synod trained by the mission societies — Langenberg and Berlin and Basel and Hermannsburg — but these mission societies had to fill many other requests for their graduates. J. Henry Sieker's study at Gettysburg Seminary is an exception rather than an example. Apprentice-type training in the existing parsonages was attempted, but already busy pastors could scarcely find time for the extra tasks. Resort to fly-by-night, would-be pastors in time of desperate need too often proved to be the cure that was worse than the original bite.

For a brief time in the late 1850s the Wisconsin Synod was involved in discussions regarding the use of the Illinois State University for training its pastors. The plan was for Wisconsin to supply the German theological professor. There would also be an English and a Scandinavian section. Fortunately the 1860 synod convention rejected the proposal, resolving: "In view of the confessional sentiments in the two Illinois synods [Illinois and Northern Illinois] and at said university, further negotiations be abandoned."[8]

By 1863 questions involving the founding of a worker-training school had passed the *why* and *when* stage. At the convention it was really only a matter of *where.* A school would be built, even in a time of Civil War. Should the place be Milwaukee, Wisconsin's big city and the synod's birthplace? Or should it be Watertown, nearer the center and also the home of President Bading? There was strenuous debate over big city and small town advantages and disadvantages. Interestingly enough, the argumentation in many ways provides the original for a replay that this generation would hear a century later when the location of the teachers' college was briefly in question in the 1960s.[9]

Back in the 1860s the choice for location of the worker-training school was Watertown by a decisive vote of 45 to 19. Koehler in his history interprets the vote as a victory of the Bading forces over the Muehlhaeuser forces and consequently a blow for more confessionalism rather than less.[10] Whatever the case, the decisive step was taken. At Watertown a synodical school would be built.

Where would the money come from? The synod could not even provide salary for a *Reiseprediger* who had no parish to support him. Now a school was to be built and a teaching staff to be called. There was only one solution the fathers could envision, a resort to the resources of the richer Old World. The resolve to build a school at Watertown was followed almost immediately by the decisions to send President Bading on a fund-raising tour in Germany and also Russia.[11]

While that was going on, a beginning was made with theological training. In the fall of 1863 a seminary was opened in a rented house that also served as the dwelling of the one professor, Edward Moldehnke, who combined this assignment with those of traveling missionary and vacancy pastor for Bading. The one and only student at the beginning of the school year had to be dismissed before the end of October but another was enrolled in November to keep the seminary in operation. In the 1864-1865 year however, there were, eleven students.

By that time building operations for the Watertown school could begin. Bading's fund raising was so successful that the trip was extended by resolve of the 1864 convention. Over $10,000 was raised in the first effort, and that sum was available for the construction project. The extended collection in Prussia raised another $7500 but this amount was in the form of endowment funds that never actually served the synod because of subsequent developments in relations with the Prussian state church.[12] That, however, is another story—to be told later.

In the fall of 1865 the Watertown school building was dedicated. The total cost was very likely double the amount available through Bading's collection in Europe. The school began operations in a precarious financial situation. Heroic fund-raising efforts, including an ill-fated "perpetual scholarship" scheme, barely kept the wolf from the door.

Even worse for the school at this "stalk" stage was a most serious identity crisis. The first college president, Adam Martin, a Hartwick Seminary graduate, seems to have planned the school more on the lines of a "Harvard of the West" than as a worker-training school of a synod that sorely needed parish pastors. Considerable rethinking, eventually involving the replacement of Professor Martin and a successor with Professor Ernst, would have to take place before the Watertown school could advance beyond bare beginnings. "First the Stalk."

At the seminary level, changes also had to be made. When the 1866 convention insisted that a second man was needed because of Moldehnke's mission journeys, the latter insisted that he could not consent to such a lavish waste of manpower for such few students enrolled. There were no personal problems. Adolph Hoenecke, the synod's choice for the second post, was a Halle fellow student whom Moldehnke himself had recommended for a college teaching post.

Moldehnke, however, could not accept the suggested arrangement. He resigned and returned to Germany for a brief time before returning and becoming an outstanding member of the New York Ministerium. Adolph Hoenecke went on to become the synod's theological teacher. He filled that role at Watertown until the synod's seminary training was transferred to St. Louis in 1869 without him. When it returned to Wisconsin in 1878, he resumed the role for another thirty years, eventually training almost two whole generations of Wisconsin Synod pastors in theology, especially in its dogmatical and homiletical branches. By the time of his death in 1908 there were 250 pastors on the synodical roll. Over 200 were Hoenecke's students, and the synod's growth had advanced from "first the stalk" to "then the head."

CHAPTER THREE

Good Neighbors

While the Wisconsin Synod was struggling to cope with the many difficulties of its second decade, the most critical in its first century, its future partners in the 1872 federation and the 1917 merger were beginning to appear on the scene. Across Lake Michigan in December 1860 the Evangelical Lutheran Synod of Michigan and Other States was formed. Across the Mississippi River in July 1860 the German Evangelical Lutheran Synod of Minnesota came into being. And in nearby Nebraska in 1866 a group of pioneers, originally "Old Lutherans" from the Watertown-Lebanon-Ixonia, Wisconsin area, settled in their new home. Later, much later, they would become the Nebraska Synod. It is time to catch up with the story of these good neighbors.

Michigan Synod Beginnings

How Friedrich Schmid came to Michigan from Basel in 1833 has already been described. For almost a decade he carried on alone except for a co-worker or two whom Basel could send him. His tireless zeal, nevertheless, enabled him to establish a number of preaching places in the Ann Arbor area and beyond.[1] Then Schmid, with G. Cronenwett and G. W. Metzger, put together a synod, often referred to as the "Mission Synod" in view of its major objective which was to evangelize, also among the Indians.

By this time William Loehe at Neuendettelsau in Bavaria had been won for the work in the American midwest. The men he sent over — among them Fr. Craemer at Frankenmuth, Fr. Lochner at Toledo, Ph. Trautmann at Adrian and W. Hattstaedt at Monroe — joined Schmid's synod. But not for long. The familiar differences between "Old Lutherans" and "New Lutherans" asserted themselves. A test case developed when Schmid was willing to use Missionary

Dumser, who had rejected the Lutheran Confessions, in the Indian mission effort. When their protests went unheeded, the Loehe men withdrew in time to help found the Missouri Synod. When the remnant synod disbanded in 1848, most of the remaining pastors either joined the Ohio Synod or avoided new affiliation.[2]

Schmid struggled on in the vast field, aided by the few Basel men that trickled his way and by whatever others could be mustered for the labor. Then in 1860 two very able Basel men appeared on the scene: Christoph Eberhardt and Stephan Klingmann. This seemed the right time to carry through the idea of creating a new Michigan Synod that had been in the discussion stage for some time.

On December 10 and 11, 1860, eight pastors with their delegates met in the Detroit parsonage and brought that second Michigan Synod into being. A sound doctrinal basis was laid. The new church body pledged itself "to all the canonical books of Holy Scripture as the sole rule and norm of its faith and life; also to all the symbolical books of our Evangelical Lutheran Church as the true interpretation of Holy Scripture."[3] Of the eight founding pastors five soon disappeared from the synodical roster, returning to the Old Country or drifting into other church bodies. The three who remained to serve until their retirement or death were Friedrich Schmid, Christoph Eberhardt, and Stephan Klingmann.

Much has already been said about Schmid. In 1860 he was chosen president of the new synod and served as such until 1867. Then the leadership passed first to Klingmann (1867-1881) and later to Eberhardt (1881-1890). After being relieved of the presidency, Schmid continued his missionary endeavors another four years. Then what he termed "bodily weakness" called a halt to the long effort begun in 1833. He lived another twelve years, dying on August 30, 1883, fifty years after arriving in Michigan.

Despite the heroic mission efforts of Schmid and Eberhardt, who in his first Michigan years served as *Reiseprediger* and journeyed as far as the southwestern corner of the state and even to the Lake Superior region, the little synod did not really grow. In 1868 the communicant count was 3300. Ten years later in 1877 the number was 3350. The problem was a lack of faithful pastors.

There just never were enough pastors available to serve the many preaching places that Schmid and Eberhardt and others founded on their mission expeditions. Among the available pastors were a number who did not fall into the category of "faithful" pastors. By 1866 Michigan was looking away from Basel as a source of pastor supply "because it had lately undergone sad experiences with pastors who came from there."⁴ St. Chrischona was an improvement in the quality, if not always the quantity, of the supply. Membership in the General Council made available some ministerial candidates from the Council's Hermannsburg and Kropp connections. Even then when it came to supplying the vast field with pastors, it was always a matter of "too little, too late."

More heroic measures were needed. A worker-training school of the Michigan Synod by the Michigan Synod and for the Michigan Synod would have to be established. It would be, finally, in 1885. Before that story is told, a few words on the General Council membership, previously mentioned, should be inserted.

When those protesting the lax doctrine and practice of the General Synod in the 1860s were forced to withdraw and form their own new General Council, they won for the endeavor a number of unaligned midwestern synods, among them Wisconsin, Minnesota, and Michigan. Thus Michigan was one of the charter members of the General Council, meeting at Fort Wayne, Indiana, in November 1867 and creating a general body that pledged itself according to its "Fundamental Principles" to adhere to the Lutheran Confessions in doctrine and practice.

When that pledge was tested in the very first year by the "Four Points," questions regarding altar and pulpit fellowship, millennialism, and lodge membership, the infant church body could not muster the confessional will to match its practice to its pledge. It wanted to retain in its ranks both those that had brought old General Synod fellowship practices along into the General Council and those that were determined to reject such practices. An untenable situation developed.

The Ohio Synod never joined. The Iowa Synod would not become a full-fledged voting member. The Wisconsin Synod protested and withdrew in 1869. The Minnesota and Illinois Synods did the same in 1871. The Michigan Synod, however, lingered in the General Council until 1888. All that while it was playing a gadfly role, trying to serve as a sort of confessional conscience of the Council.

Matters came to a head in 1884. The Council's annual convention was held at Monroe in the congregation of the Michigan Synod. Two leaders of the Pittsburgh Synod, Dr. W. Passavant and Pastor G. Gerberding, followed the old practice of preaching on synod Sunday in a local pulpit, in this case of the Presbyterians. Members of Michigan's Zion congregation were upset. Protests were filed, to no avail. By 1887 Michigan was no longer sending delegates to the General Council convention. Formal severance of membership ties occurred in 1888.⁵

The Michigan Synod in its isolated position could now give attention to the possibility of new and better fellowship arrangements. A federation with the two other upper Great Lakes state synods was the most likely prospect. In just four years it would materialize.

To this federation the Michigan Synod brought a firm doctrinal stance, tried and purified in the recent struggles within the General Council. It brought a lively and energetic church body that had always been strong for mission outreach and that by 1892 had grown to 9552 communicants, 62 congregations and 37 pastors. It also brought a young worker-training school, opened in their anniversary year and just beginning to be of service to the synod in solving its old and enduring problem of pastor supply.

The 1884 Michigan Synod convention finally resolved in the matter of a worker-training school that "now is the time to begin to bring to a practical realization the concepts thus evoked" and that "we in our own midst maintain an institution in which young men may be trained for the office of the holy ministry."[6]

The year 1885 was the *now* time for several reasons. Pastor A. Lange, formerly a professor at the Buffalo Synod's school, had joined the synod and in that year had moved from Remus to Manchester. In Manchester a zealous layman, George Heimerdinger, made available to the synod a large house for school purposes on a two-year basis.

Michigan Lutheran Seminary could begin operations in August 1885 with six students and with Professor Lange doing the teaching. Because of the two-year limitation on the Manchester housing the synodical conventions had to busy themselves with the selection of a permanent site. In the 1886 convention Adrian was the clear choice. Hurriedly a special convention assembled the following January and reopened the site question. With President Eberhardt, donor of the Saginaw site and the Saginaw pastor, in the chair Saginaw won out over such other proposals as Ypsilanti and Saline. The Adrian members and pastor were not pleased at this sudden turn of events. In fact, they were so miffed that they actually withdrew temporarily from the synod by way of protest.[7]

Whatever the merits of the case, Michigan Lutheran Seminary moved from Manchester to Saginaw in 1887 and has remained there ever since. It would close its doors for three years from 1907 on and then re-open them in 1910, no longer as a full worker-training school, but as a preparatory school functioning on the high school level. As a theological school in the years 1885-1907 Michigan Lutheran Seminary trained forty men for the preaching ministry.[8]

Minnesota Synod Beginnings

Non-Scandinavian Lutheran pastors arrived in the Minnesota area during the 1850s. Among the earliest were Pastor Wier, who began to gather a Twin Cities congregation in 1855, and Pastor William Thompson who brought a riverboat load of English-speaking Lutherans from Ohio to Rice County in the same year. Scandinavian Lutheran pastors were already in the area. In 1849 Claus Clausen, a Danish Lutheran pastor in the country since 1843 and serving Norwegians at Muskego, Wisconsin, scouted the Twin Cities area. In 1854 Pastor Erland Carlsson from Chicago organized three Swedish Lutheran congregations in the Minnesota territory. In 1856 William Passavant came from Pennsylvania to Minnesota in the interest of an English-speaking mission in the Twin Cities.

This was the Lutheran scene that "Father" Heyer found when he arrived in Minnesota in 1857 to begin an English-speaking mission in the Twin Cities under the auspices of the East Pennsylvania Synod. Pastor J. C. F. Heyer had just returned to the United States from historic mission service in India. Heyer was the first U.S. Lutheran foreign missionary. Already in 1841 he had been sent out by the General Synod to Guntur in India under his terms that his field be a Lutheran, not a Protestant, endeavor. After almost forty years of rugged home and foreign mission service "Father" Heyer began a brand new venture in Minnesota Territory serving the English-speaking Lutherans in the Twin Cities and regathering the German-speaking ones that Pastor Wier had left high and dry when he moved to the Stillwater area.

Heyer had hardly arrived when his boundless enthusiasm prompted him to work for a Lutheran grouping in Minnesota. The first effort, planned in 1858, was to have been a union of German and Scandinavian and other congregations. When the Scandinavians formed their own Scandinavian Augustana Synod, Heyer had to settle for a German-English grouping. This was the Minnesota Synod organized in July 1860.[9]

The six founding pastors merit mention. Their leader was "Father" Heyer, who in two years would begin a semi-retirement that involved some service as the Minnesota Synod's president, home mission explorations in Minnesota, vacancy pastorates at Red Wing and St. Paul, another India mission stint, and a deanship at the General Council's seminary.[10]

William Wier, already mentioned, had been in the Buffalo Synod and held to its extreme views on church and ministry and promptly went his separate way. Pastor Brandt soon resigned because of eye trouble. Adam Blumer is praised as the "actual pioneer" in the golden anniversary history.[11] An Evangelical history, however, insists that Blumer, throughout his pastorates at Stillwater and Shakopee, "was under commission of the A.H.M.S. [American Home Missionary Society] and considered himself the pastor of a German Congregational Church."[12] There were also two English-speaking pastors in the group of six founders, Mallinson and Thompson, referred to as "American" in the records. They too withdrew from the synod after a short time.

In its first decade the Minnesota Synod had its share of problems, not the least of which was finding enough pastors for its many preaching stations. St. Chrischona served as the main source of supply in the early years, sending some sixteen men to Minnesota. In 1864 an informal arrangement was made with Wisconsin whereby Minnesota would use the Watertown school for worker training and President Heyer would gather funds for the school in his old Pennsylvania stamping grounds. First results were not encouraging but at least a pattern for a future partnership had been set.

Toward the end of the first Minnesota decade a division was caused by Gottlieb Fachtmann, Wisconsin's first traveling missionary. His La Crosse trip took him into Minnesota, where he developed an acquaintance with the pastors there. When Heyer resigned as pastor of Trinity in St. Paul in 1862, he hand-picked Fachtmann as his successor. When Fachtmann resumed a role of traveling missionary five years later, he seems to have attempted to found an opposition synod. By unanimous vote Minnesota's 1870 convention expelled him from its membership.[13]

Meanwhile, the Minnesota Synod was caught up in the identity crisis confronting United States Lutheranism in the 1860s. Heyer promptly took the young synod into the General Synod to which he belonged. This was in 1864. But in the 1866-1867 split that produced the General Council Heyer and Minnesota cast their lot with the Council. The 1867 Minnesota convention describes the action in this fashion:

> Membership of the Evangelical Lutheran Synod of Minnesota in the new Lutheran general synod was discussed. President Heyer declared that the old Lutheran General Synod called itself Lutheran without actually being that. The American preachers, Pastors Erline and Thompson, participated actively in the discussions in English. The latter stated his view that the new general synod was causing division and entered his protest against the synod's membership in the new general synod. Thereupon all the other members of the synod, pastors and delegates, expressed themselves as favoring membership in the new general

synod and with the exception of W. Thomson voted unanimously for the membership.[14]

The 1867 convention of the Minnesota Synod indicated in other ways that it was casting its lot with the more confessional Lutheranism that was emerging. Along with a move in that direction in federation membership, it expelled a pastor with lodge affiliations and also rejected a membership application from the New Ulm congregation because it was still calling itself a "Lutheran-Reformed" congregation. These were all steps that called for determination and conviction on the part of the young and small synod and a willingness to pay the price for its theological position.

That position was certainly solidified when J. Henry Sieker was installed later that year as pastor of St. Paul's Trinity congregation and was elected to the synodical presidency in 1869.[15]

Sieker was trained for the Wisconsin Synod's ministry at Gettysburg Seminary, where financial aid was generously extended in line with an old policy of the Pennsylvania Ministerium that willingly extended a helping hand to Muehlhaeuser's needy church body.[16] Sieker served at Granville and as a financial agent for the struggling Watertown school. The move to Minnesota and to a leadership position there enabled Sieker to play a key role in bringing about a Wisconsin-Minnesota partnership and a charter membership for Minnesota in the Synodical Conference in 1872. He would eventually accept a call to historic St. Matthew's in New York, a part of the oldest continuously existing Lutheran parish in this country, dating back to 1649. He succeeded in bringing the previously independent congregation into the ranks of the Synodical Conference.

The mention of Sieker's important contribution to cementing Wisconsin-Minnesota relations prompts an elaboration of this matter. These relations begin with Fachtmann's journeys into Minnesota and Minnesota's interest in the Watertown school. By 1869 the two neighboring synods were seemingly ready to work out a partnership, but the continuing membership of Minnesota in the General Council after Wisconsin had left proved a barrier. When Minnesota finally agreed in 1871 that the General Council was not taking a firm enough stand on the fellowship issues confronting it, the partnership could be achieved. It opened the doors of the Watertown school to Minnesota students under the provision that Minnesota would fund a professorship at the school with $500. It also made Minnesota a junior partner in Wisconsin's church paper, the *Gemeinde-Blatt*, with the right to share in the editorial staff and in the profits that the periodical in those days was regularly amassing.[17] In 1872 Minnesota became a charter member of the Synodical

Conference, along with the Missouri, Ohio, Norwegian, Wisconsin, and Illinois Synods.

The working arrangement between Minnesota and Wisconsin was disrupted in 1875 because of the "grasshopper plague." In 1873 and 1874 grasshoppers destroyed crops in Minnesota mission fields in the Renville County area. The impoverished congregations had to be given extra financial assistance. This added burden in a time of severe general depression brought the Minnesota Synod into financial difficulties. A treasury deficit of $700 developed.

In 1875 Minnesota asked to be relieved of its annual obligation of $500 for the Watertown professorship. It seems more Minnesota ministerial students were attending Missouri's theological institutions than the Watertown school at the time. The Wisconsin Synod was naturally disgruntled and consented to the Minnesota request most reluctantly. By 1879 improved conditions in the economy and in fraternal relations between the neighboring synods made it possible for Minnesota's new president, A. Kuhn, to propose mutually acceptable terms of agreement.

In 1883 the Minnesota Synod resolved to build its own worker-training school. It stipulated that $14,000 should be collected before any building was begun and that all congregations be granted an opportunity to offer site and funding proposals. President C. J. Albrecht and his New Ulm congregation were so enthusiastic that they chose to ignore the resolutions. The 1884 convention was faced by an accomplished fact, a building going up on the bluffs overlooking New Ulm. The school was dedicated on November 4 of that year.[18]

When the Michigan-Minnesota-Wisconsin federation began functioning in 1892, Doctor Martin Luther College at New Ulm terminated its theological department and became the teacher-training school for the federation. By 1892 the Minnesota Synod had grown to 16,594 communicants in 89 congregations and 18 preaching places served by 62 pastors; there were 54 schools and 14 called teachers.

Nebraska Synod Beginnings

The pioneers who trekked from the Lebanon-Ixonia area in Wisconsin to the Norfolk area in Nebraska in some fifty ox-drawn prairie schooners in 1866 did not make the long and hard trip to establish a Nebraska Synod. Quite the contrary! In fact, one of their motives was to escape from synods and synod strife.

These were "Old Lutherans" from Prussia who had had their fill of the bitter synodical and congregational battles that raged around them in their Wisconsin settlements. Buffalo and Missouri were contending bitterly regarding the church-ministry questions.

Congregations had a way of splitting and resplitting over these and other matters, such as Teacher Pankow's fiddling of danceable tunes on the instrument that led the congregational singing on Sunday morning.

In 1866 the Nebraska pioneers were putting all this behind them and seeking new and better frontiers. Their pastor, who joined them the next year, J. M. Hoeckendorf, shared and fostered the views of the flock. Already in 1847 Hoeckendorf had traveled with Pastor Geyer from Watertown to Chicago to oppose the formation of the Missouri Synod.[19] He had yielded to a certain extent but seems to have continued to harbor a deep-seated aversion to synods.

This largely self-trained pastor himself trained his son to be his successor. Entanglements with synods and synodical schools were being studiously avoided. God intervened. The son died suddenly and the father also. This was in 1877. Where would the Norfolk people find a pastor? They turned to President Ernst of Northwestern College at Watertown, who was known to be opposing a Synodical Conference "state-synod" plan.

Anyone opposing synods must be their kind of man, the Norfolk people reasoned. President Ernst did not bother to explain in detail that he was opposing a single specific instance while favoring the general concept. He proposed the calling of Michael Pankow, a recent graduate of Springfield Seminary and, more important, a son of Teacher-Preacher Erdmann Pankow.

Michael Pankow gradually eliminated the separatist thinking in his congregation and in its neighbors. Soon pastors were joining in conferences. By 1901 the formation of a Nebraska District of the Wisconsin Synod could be attempted. When the distance factor made such district operation unwieldy and inefficient, a Nebraska Synod was formed in 1904 and joined the Michigan-Minnesota-Wisconsin federation. In 1917 it participated in the merger and became one of the six charter districts of the Wisconsin Synod. In 1919 there were 2998 communicants in 25 congregations and 4 preaching places served by 21 pastors.[20]

CHAPTER FOUR

Turn to the Right

Almost from the time of its organization the Wisconsin Synod was a "house divided against itself." It wanted to be Lutheran but its early ties to a mission society that operated under Union auspices had a way of thwarting the intention. These auspices called for some accommodation with the Reformed. Conflict was inevitable, especially for an infant synod operating in a state barely out of the frontier stage.

A Wisconsin Synod pastor would bring the gospel to one of the many little settlements in the state and find there some Lutherans and some Reformed and some Roman Catholics and some others. The lines between Lutheran and Roman were clearly drawn. Those between Lutheran and Reformed had been blurred in the long effort to unite the two denominations and were all but obliterated in the Prussian Union situation. Time and again the little synod and its pastors had to face the question: Where are the boundaries between what is Lutheran and what is Reformed?

The "New Lutheran" answer that John Muehlhaeuser had brought with him from Basel and Barmen has been described.[1] This stance marked and marred the little synod's earliest years, even though its official and constitutional declaration called for a firm commitment to the Lutheran Confessions.[2] It was, however, "one thing to have the truly pure doctrine on paper and another thing to possess it in one's own clear understanding and one's own childlike faith," as President Bading reminded his brothers at the 1862 synodical convention.[3] Actual practice often fell far short of official declaration in those early years.

Consequently, the Wisconsin Synod was viewed by its Lutheran neighbors as very liberal and very unionistic. The Buffalo and Missouri Synods could not easily forget that it was in their own backyards that Muehlhaeuser had founded this "New Lutheran" synod. Soon their church papers, Buffalo's *Informatorium* and Missouri's *Lutheraner,* sounded warnings and leveled accusations.[4] In 1853 Pastor Deindoerfer from Michigan's Frankenhilf visited Milwaukee on his way to explore Iowa as a possible location for a new church body. What he found in Milwaukee was, in his words, "the unionistic Milwaukee Synod," which he then took to task for its indifference in his report to his German headquarters.[5]

What these early critics did not realize was that there was another side to the story. A more confessional view had begun to assert itself and to challenge the worst aspects of "New Lutheranism" almost from the beginning in 1850. Mistakes were still being made and old habits continued to assert themselves, but step by step the Wisconsin Synod was advancing in the right direction. *Was being led* would be a better term. The Lord of the church was doing the leading. He was sending the little church body men with sound training and firm convictions. He was helping these men react to the clashes that developed within the young church body, the criticisms of neighboring "Old Lutherans," and the challenges of the larger Lutheran scene that was marked by its own battles over confessionalism. The story of these struggles in a turning to the right during the first two decades makes up one of the more important chapters in the history of the Wisconsin Synod. The most significant episodes merit attention.

Long Search for Identity

Already at Granville in May 1850 there had been a reckoning of sorts, with Weinmann and Wrede pressing Muehlhaeuser for a stronger constitutional commitment to the Confessions than the latter had planned. On that occasion President Muehlhaeuser exhibited a commendable willingness to yield to the better opinion, even if it was not fully his own. Whatever his inclinations and reservations, he let his synod get started in the right direction, at least on paper.

In 1854 the synodical convention had to deal with the confessional issue because of a number of agenda points. One matter was a complaint from the Slinger congregation that their pastor, J. Sauer, was causing strife by introducing Lutheran ceremonies, such as chanting the Benediction. Obviously the congregation had a number of Reformed members, very likely a minority, since they would not let the question be settled at home by congregational vote. The synodical convention's reaction is strikingly illustrative of the problems and viewpoints relating to the confessional issue:

> Candidate Sauer explained that he was happy to abide by the synod's decision. Pastor J. Conrad, especially informed

about the circumstances, was requested to express his opinion on the issue. He explained in particular that the congregation had turned to the synod with the proviso that the latter would only send it such men as were known to be evangelical. He then pointed to the error that Sauer had begun his ministry in a way that demonstrated the opposite.

Moved and seconded that two delegates, namely Bading and Conrad, should be sent to the Slinger congregation and be instructed to suggest to the congregation that in communion distribution bread should be used and that the Lutheran party should omit the other ceremonies. Secondly, they should, if peace absolutely required it, make the congregation the proposal that wafers and bread be used in Holy Communion.

Pastor Goldammer protested the decision most emphatically. He explained that this duality in Holy Communion contradicted the very essence of Communion which is to demonstrate to the communicants the closest communion and unity . . . . But the matter received no further consideration.[6]

The synodical action and Goldammer's reaction strikingly illustrate a "duality" in the early Wisconsin Synod. Goldammer's point is well taken but the majority of his brethren were still caught up in the impossible dream of trying to serve the Reformed as they wanted to be served while remaining Lutheran. The custom of using bread and wafers, or only bread, in Communion distribution, incidentally, was not invented at Granville in 1854. It had surfaced already in the earliest years of the Prussian Union and became a popular and practical, though erroneous, way to proceed in the Union situation, also in this country. In our circles it unfortunately endured for decades. As late as 1882 Pastor C. J. Albrecht found it in existence in the New Ulm congregation he came to serve.

The practice ceased there immediately but not without a secession of some members and the erection of an opposition altar catercorner across the street.[7]

The 1854 *Proceedings* also close with the information that "a letter of Pastor J. Weinmann was read that gave occasion to many questions about our stand over against other confessions."[8] The Wisconsin Synod in 1854 still had more questions than it had answers in the large issue of confessionalism and fellowship. It was being tried and purified.

Sometimes hard-to-grasp conflicts of ideas and ideals can be crystallized and clarified when they boil down to a conflict between persons. That is the case in Wisconsin's "Turn to the Right." The two persons are President Muehlhaeuser, without whom there would not have been a Wisconsin Synod, and John Bading, who came into its circles in July 1853.[9]

John Bading was born in the Berlin area in 1824, baptized by Pastor Jaenicke, founder of the mission school out of which the Berlin Mission Society grew, and enrolled for mission training by Pastor Gossner, another mission society founder. Unrest in Berlin in the late 1840s caused Bading to apply for mission training at Hermannsburg, where Ludwig Harms had just opened his staunchly Lutheran mission school. Bading was a member of the school's first class but when that class was graduated in 1852 the society's record states: "After a four-year training there were left in the Mission House eight of the twelve enrolled. Two the Lord had taken away by death, two others became unfaithful."[10] Bading was one of the latter two. The problem, as Director Harms officially reports, was "because the earthly work became too much for them."[11]

The upshot of the matter was that Bading put himself at the disposal of the Langenberg Society and in May 1853 was declared ready for service in the church body that was Langenberg's special concern. This is how Bading came to Wisconsin instead of going to Africa and came to it with the more rigorously Lutheran training that Hermannsburg could provide but that was not available at Langenberg. That training would prove to be a very special boon for the synod and the man in the years ahead.

When the time came for Bading to be ordained at his Calumet post, President Muehlhaeuser did the ordaining. A clash developed between the ordinand, who insisted on being pledged totally to all the Lutheran Confessions, and the ordinant, who tried to put him off by referring to those Confessions as "paper fences."[12] The venerable synod father gave way, and the rookie pastor made his point even more emphatically by then preaching on the importance of the Lutheran Confessions.

The Muehlhaeuser-Bading duel at little Calumet typifies other differences that bear heavily on the history of the Wisconsin Synod. When President Muehlhaeuser in 1860 declined reelection to the post on the ground that the burdens of office were "becoming more pressing year by year," it was Bading who was elected in his place. Muehlhaeuser was granted the honorary title "Senior" with the privilege of sitting at the presiding officer's right.[13] From that vantage point the founding father could view his successor charting a pathway for the church body that was to the right of what was originally intended.

In his first two presidential addresses in 1861 at Watertown and in 1862 at Columbus Bading stressed the importance of confessional adherence in theory and practice. At Watertown he made a stirring plea that the brethren should be willing for the Confessions' sake to sacrifice "good and blood, life and limb and rather suffer all than depart one hair's breadth from the truth we have learned," and at Columbus he reminded them that he and they "were all pledged to the Confessions of our church and indeed not in so far as but because they agree with God's Word."[14]

In that 1862 convention the Wisconsin Synod had an opportunity to go on record as repudiating previous unionistic practices. We have already noted the 1854 synodical action in the case of Pastor Sauer and his Slinger congregation. It amounted to catering to the Reformed in the distribution of the Lord's Supper, either totally if possible by using bread instead of wafers or in part by using both bread and wafers. In 1862 the same pastor was censured *in absentia* for practicing what was synodically mandated in 1854. In one of his three congregations he was using a Reformed catechism in instruction and distributing the Lord's Supper in the Reformed fashion. This the 1862 convention condemned, allowing only a six-week period of grace for effecting a change and declaring to all concerned that "there is no room in our synod for unlutheran doctrine and practice."[15] A commendable turn-about, achieved in just eight years!

What human agency is to be credited with this abrupt "turn to the right"? With his Hermannsburg background John Bading was specially qualified to assume the leadership in the effort to make Wisconsin more and more confessional, especially in its practice. For seven years, from 1853 to 1860, he did what he could in a subordinate role. In 1860 he was elected synodical president and was able to provide effective leadership. He was by no means alone in the effort.

When Bading moved from Calumet to Theresa in 1855, he found in his new surroundings a number of like-minded pastors determined to make their church body a Lutheran synod in fact. At Ashford in Dodge County was Gottlieb Reim, who in 1861 would present the convention essay on confessionalism that marks on paper the turn to the right.[16] In the West Bend area was Philipp Koehler, the father of the great synodical historian, and a distinguished battler for the cause of true Lutheranism in his own right.[17] And in the Slinger area was Elias Sauer, whose synodical attendance may have been on the deplorable side but whose pastoral practice was better than that of many who censured him for his fault.

These four men made a team in the old Northwestern Conference that embraced in its name an honored term in the Wisconsin Synod. Today the church body has a Northwestern College in its ministerial training program, a Northwestern Preparatory School as one of that college's feeders. It has an energetic and recently re-planted Northwestern Publishing House that produces the WELS periodical, the *Northwestern Lutheran.* Until 1979 it supported a Northwestern Lutheran Academy at Mobridge, South Dakota. The overuse of the term tends to obscure the real significance of "Northwestern" in Wisconsin Synod history. Originally that term implied a deep commitment to a more confessional Lutheranism than was available elsewhere on the synodical scene.

The rest of the church body seems to have taken the cue. Frequently the Bading-Koehler-Reim-Sauer grouping was utilized as a source of theological training in the pre-seminary era. A candidate for Wisconsin Synod pastoral membership would be assigned to these men for additional teaching.[18] The result could be a well-trained pastor for the Wisconsin Synod. In 1856 the Northwestern Conference team was given the assignment to draft constitutional paragraphs on duties of member congregations to the synod and of the synod to member congregations.[19]

All these developments in the right direction needed struggles and crises to bring them to full flower. These the Lord provided in abundant measure. As the Wisconsin Synod began its second decade in 1860, it was confronted with a number of important and challenging opportunities.

Deeper Involvements

Just at the time that the young Wisconsin Synod was beginning to turn to the right, it was also unintentionally and unavoidably involving itself in more intimate and consequential ties with the Old World mission societies at Barmen and Berlin.

The involvement was not planned or desired by either Wisconsin or the societies. For their part, the societies in their dealings with the young synod were most generous and not at all demanding. They trained the missionaries and sent them to the foreign field at no cost to the synod being served thereby. As late as 1862 four Langenberg men came to Wisconsin, escorted by President Muehlhaeuser, who had gone back to Barmen to help the Langenberg Society celebrate the twenty-fifth anniversary of its organization in 1837. It was a silver anniversary for Muehlhaeuser also. In 1837 he had been sent out as one of the first two Langenberg missionaries to work in the United States. During the last half of that quarter century President Muehlhaeuser and his church body had benefited abundantly from the generosity of the Langenberg Society.

By 1862, however, the Wisconsin Synod was suffering growing pains. Ever-increasing demands were made upon it as it sought to gather the unchurched and supply them with pastors. The first larger enterprise to be undertaken was a synodical library, indispensable in the one-on-one parsonage training of candidates for the ministry. The resolve to enlist the support of the overseas mission societies in this undertaking was a part of the final resolutions of the 1859 convention. At the next convention President Muehlhaeuser could report: "The strenuous efforts of the two honorable societies and their personnel have had such results that the library already amounts to 500 classified volumes, which have been provided for us by friends and book-sellers in Germany."[20] This much needed and very useful acquisition, however, presented no great problems. For the most part it involved single and special donations.

It was another matter when, also in 1859, the Wisconsin Synod requested from the societies help in securing a permanent *Reiseprediger* [traveling missionary]. G. Fachtmann had rendered yeoman service previously but that was mostly on a short-term make-do basis. Now a regular salary would have to be provided, a major problem for a church body that in that year reported a gathering of $86.02 for home mission purposes and $46.17 for administration needs.[21] Obviously the mission societies would have to supply funding for the *Reiseprediger.*

They did. Both Berlin and Langenberg provided $200 for the salary of the man they sent, Edward Moldehnke. His energetic labors in finding prospective members and founding mission congregations resulted in one year in a report on twenty-two preaching places. But the regular funding of the traveling missionary inevitably led to a desire for tighter controls. Already at the 1862 synodical convention one could hear the well-intentioned but altogether unmistakable overtones in the committee report and convention resolve:

> Since a desire was expressed in the correspondence of the Berlin Society that our synod might enter into a closer association with that society through regular reporting so that also in this way the efforts of the society might be actively maintained and the synod on the one hand deemed it a duty of responsive love and gratitude and on the other hand as useful and beneficial that this desire receive a response, therefore be it
>
> Resolved that every existing conference in the synod yearly submit to the president a report for the Langenberg and Berlin Societies but with the proviso that the synodical president retains the right to make corrections that he deems necessary.[22]

The handwriting was on the wall. Instead of the previous informal individual reports by the missionaries to the society that sent them out, more formal reporting was desired by both parties. The unionistic society that was providing annual funding for a missionary wanted a "closer association." The synod that was becoming more confessionally minded wanted some control over its sometimes maverick members in their "closer association."

An annual outlay of $400 was causing concern. When the numbers moved into four-figure and even five-figure rubrics, the pressures and tensions could not but increase. The bigger sums came into the picture when President Bading went overseas in 1863-1864 to gather funds in Germany and Russia for the proposed Watertown ministerial training school. That school's origin has been related previously.[23] We are now concerned with the repercussions in fellowship relations that resulted.

Especially involved were funds gathered in Prussia. The church authorities there consented to a collection only after some delay and with considerable reluctance. They were concerned that Wisconsin's growing confessionalism might bring it to a clash with the Prussian state church. The $7500 that was gathered in Prussia was not immediately released. Instead, it was placed into an endowment fund to be used for scholarships or perhaps for a preparatory school in Germany. When the clash did come, the money was frozen and never benefited the Wisconsin Synod.

Crucial Conventions in 1867 and 1868

The big issue of the Wisconsin Synod's theological identity came to a head in the 1867 synodical convention and was finally settled a year later. Castigated by the mission societies for being too strict and by the Missouri Synod for being too lax and challenged also by similar conflicts on the larger Lutheran scene in the land that brought about the creation of the General Council, the Wisconsin Synod was led to a showdown on the confessional and fellowship issue. A top agenda item in 1867 at St. John in Milwaukee was the Synod's position on the Union.

The committee that was assigned the convention's hot potato was headed by Professor Adolph Hoenecke, one of that large and illustrious group of new additions at the 1863 convention. There are fourteen names in that category, including such men as A. Lange, eventual founding professor of Michigan Lutheran Seminary in 1885, and longtime pastors A. Denninger, C. G. Reim, Phil. Brenner, and J. Brockmann. In that year of great growth for the Wisconsin Synod eleven congregations were also added to the synodical roster, among them Fountain City, Forest, and Lomira.

Adolph Hoenecke, trained at Halle, came to the Wisconsin Synod under the arrangement that service in this mission field for some five or six years would count as seniority points on the placement roster of the state church back in Germany. By the time those years had run their course Hoenecke was completely won for the Wisconsin enterprise and also for its theological position. He first served at Farmington near Watertown and was a logical choice for supply work in Watertown during Bading's absence for overseas collection. When a second teacher at the synodical school at Watertown was called, Hoenecke again was the logical choice. He went on to become the Wisconsin Synod theological instructor. Already in 1867 he was regarded as reliable and knowledgeable when it came to sticky technical issues. As synodical secretary he had already handled complicated correspondence with the mission societies that questioned Wisconsin's handling of cases involving dealings with the Reformed.[24]

Hoenecke's eight-man committee at the 1867 convention brought in a divided report.[25] The majority report signed by six men first of all pointed out that it was making history in that this was the first time that the church body was declaring itself publicly and officially on the union issue. The report went on to a clear definition of the term, distinguishing first between a God-created unity and a man-made union. The latter was then subdivided into doctrinal union and organizational union. The latter kind, typified by the Prussian Union, was described as "a misuse of the power of the state over the church" whereby "consciences were enslaved and the church was robbed of its possessions." The report concludes: "Therefore not only a manufactured doctrinal union, but also an enforced organizational union are to be categorized as definitely worthy of condemnation."

Dr. Theodore Meumann, a university-trained pastor who joined the synod in 1861, submitted the minority report that was accepted after some revision. This minority report minced no words in denouncing man-made doctrinal union but then attempted to justify having fellowship with the mission societies of the Prussian Union and accepting their gifts and trained workers. The argument was that there were good Lutherans trapped in the Union against their will and over their protest. "As long as there are Lutherans to be found in the state churches under consideration," the minority report states, "among whom the gospel is purely proclaimed and the sacraments are rightly administered, and as long as these protest against a union forced on them as an accomplished and continuing injustice to the Lutheran Church, we can accept only thankfully the loving services of the Union societies."

After considerable debate the convention accepted the amended minority report. It then resolved, however, to print both reports and a summary of the debate on them, "in order to let the synod's stand on the Union in all respects come to full expression."

Even the minority report proved to be too much for the mission societies. They protested and demanded that the Wisconsin Synod renounce the stronger stand it had taken at the 1867 convention or else its gifts and workers would no longer be forthcoming. The 1868 convention granted that the societies had a right to take such action and once again thanked them for past favors but it stood firm.[26] The long associations with the Langenberg society and also those with the Berlin society were broken off so that biblical fellowship principles could prevail.

Actually, this issue received little attention at the 1868 convention. What loomed much larger was the same fellowship issue in another form, the debate over altar and pulpit fellowship that arose because of Wisconsin's membership in the newly formed General Council. That matter, along with other interchurch relations, will now receive attention.

CHAPTER FIVE

Early Interchurch Relations

The Wisconsin Synod's connection with the German mission societies is the prime instance of the relations the chapter title promises to treat. It has, however, been given considerable coverage in the previous chapters. The story of this connection could be rounded off with brief references to its demise and to a recognition of a temporary effort at replacement.

The Berlin society confronted the Wisconsin Synod, as President Bading reported to the 1869 Helenville convention, with the declaration that it would not release the Prussian collection or send any more workers to Wisconsin if the anti-Union position persisted. The convention resolved "that the synod make no claims to the collection gathered for it in the Prussian State Church."[1] Synodical legend has it that decades later Bading was still dreaming and scheming about unfreezing the frozen fund. One could understand the motives of a hard-working collector of charitable gifts and his attachment to gifts and givers. Whatever the case, Bading was in the chair when the disclaimer resolution was passed.

He was also instrumental in seeking and finding new mission society ties. It was natural for him to turn to Hermannsburg, his alma mater of sorts and a definitely Lutheran undertaking. To the Helenville convention Bading could announce:

> Favorable outcomes can be reported about the ties being established with Pastor Harms in Hermannsburg. After he expressed his joy over the definitely Lutheran character of the synod . . . he gave the assurance in several letters that he would gladly join forces with us and send candidates to us from his mission school in return for which we would have to direct our mission offerings to the Hermannsburg Society. This was promised him on our part, since already for years most of our mission offerings by agreement have been going to this mission.[2]

THE WISCONSIN SYNOD LUTHERANS

Very soon seven Hermannsburg candidates came to Wisconsin and ten students were sent to Watertown. The last reports about this overseas connection are not as rosy as this first one. In the 1880s Wisconsin was forced to turn from Hermannsburg as an outlet for its mission offerings and seek an orthodox mission society to which it could conscientiously channel its offerings. The search did not yield any promising replacement. The good outcome was that the synod was forced to venture out independently. The result was the Apache mission of the 1892 federated body. But this is getting far ahead of the story. It is time to return to the subject at hand.

Early Interchurch Relations in the East

The first two decades of Wisconsin's history afford abundant evidence of a lively and diverse interchurch relationship on its part. It was definitely not an era of rigid isolationism.

Muehlhaeuser's friendly ties with Lutherans in the East were not broken when he went west in 1848. It will be recalled that he wanted his associations in the New York Ministerium to continue. He seems also to have established some Pennsylvania connections, for from the start of its existence the Wisconsin Synod was the beneficiary of the Pennsylvania Ministerium's largess.

This was a time when Pennsylvania was in the process of re-entering the General Synod, from which it had withdrawn in 1823 because it feared that this earliest of Lutheran federations might crimp its association with Reformed congregations. Thirty years later, however, the Pennsylvania Ministerium had been so influenced by the general revival of Lutheran confessionalism that it would rejoin the lax General Synod only under the famed "escape clause" that required its delegates to the General Synod conventions to withdraw from the sessions if violence was done to the cause of true Lutheranism. A decade later this stipulation would make and remake Lutheran church history in this land.

Among the benefits that regularly came to Wisconsin from Pennsylvania was an annual grant of several hundred dollars that President Muehlhaeuser could then distribute to the neediest in his small and struggling synod. No strings were attached to the generous gift; all that Pennsylvania wanted was an accounting of the distribution of funds. If details were available, one could no doubt point to special instances where a sorely tried and sorely needed pastor or congregation was enabled to persevere and eventually prosper. In the absence of the details one can only suggest that the best chapters of church history remain to be read in an entirely new setting.

When Wisconsin finally found one of its own sons willing to prepare for the ministry, John Henry Sieker, he was able to attend the Gettysburg schools through the courtesy and generosity of the Pennsylvania Ministerium. Professor C. F. Schaeffer arranged that the usual charges would be waived and that financial aid would be provided. Sieker finished his training at Gettysburg in 1861 and immediately began to serve the Granville congregation. He was called by Trinity of St. Paul in 1868 and in the next year became the Minnesota Synod's president.

Mention of Gettysburg calls to mind another example of the close, even if informal, ties that existed between Wisconsin and Pennsylvania. This involved the German chair at Gettysburg endowed by the Pennsylvania Ministerium. In the late 1860s a number of men were being called to that chair who would play large roles in the history of the Wisconsin Synod and especially of Northwestern College.

The first of such men called to fill the vacant Gettysburg post was August F. Ernst, who declined because he could not leave his congregation in New York state at that time. When he eventually accepted a teaching call it was to Northwestern College. He soon became the school's president and served in that capacity well into this century. In the 1868-1869 school year Dr. Friedrich Notz, longtime Hebrew instructor at Northwestern, filled the Gettysburg German post before moving on to Muhlenberg College, from where he was called to Northwestern. The vacant Gettysburg post was then filled permanently by Adam Martin, Northwestern's first president, who served as such until the spring of 1869.

Other Eastern associations can be mentioned. When William Passavant of the Pittsburgh Synod came to Milwaukee to establish Milwaukee Hospital, he received much help in the fund raising from Muehlhaeuser. In fact, some feared that so much good Lutheran money had been donated for this purpose that they thought the Wisconsin Synod's school should be located in little Watertown with its untapped resources.[3] A number of men came to Wisconsin from New York. Two of the early Northwestern College presidents, A. Martin and A. Ernst, were among them. Another was Pastor R. Adelberg, who recommended Ernst to Wisconsin and then followed him there quite promptly. From 1897 to 1901 he taught at Wisconsin Lutheran Seminary on an auxiliary basis while still serving his Milwaukee congregation. The main purpose of this arrangement was that someone with some ability in English should aid seminarians in that aspect of their future calling. Pastor Adelberg may have been the best English-teaching talent available, but he soon turned off his students in lectures on the Psalms by pronouncing the title word phonetically.

With all these bonds and associations with eastern Lutheranism the question suggests itself: Why didn't the Wisconsin Synod join the General Synod to which Pennsylvania, New York, and Pittsburgh all belonged? That question was actually asked by the German mission societies in 1862. When the synod's praesidium pressed for a definite answer, the convention merely resolved that "the officials are to answer the question as knowledgeably and conscientiously as they can."[4] Since President Bading would be doing the answering, one can surmise the content, even though no copy of the letter exists. The overseas reaction indicates some displeasure with Wisconsin's aloof attitude to the General Synod because of weakness in its confessional position.

Somewhat earlier, in 1856, Wisconsin had an opportunity to voice an opinion about the least confessional elements in the General Synod. The year before, their Definite Platform calling for an American revision of the Augsburg Confession had been issued. The 1856 Wisconsin Convention took a clear stand, declaring: "The newly fabricated so-called Definite Platform is definitely rejected by us, the Evangelical Lutheran Wisconsin Synod, because it recognizes (1) that the Unaltered Augsburg Confession is grounded in God's Word, (2) that accepting the so-called Platform amounts to nothing less than a definite suicide of the Lutheran Church."

Actually, Wisconsin's resolution was no heroic stand for confessionalism. Only a very few area synods supported the Definite Platform. But its proponents continued to advance their brand of vague Lutheranism and to resist the rising tide of confessionalism in Lutheran circles. A clash was inevitable. It came a decade later when the more confessional wing of the General Synod, represented by majorities in such large synods as Pennsylvania, New York, and Pittsburgh and in such small synods as East Ohio and Minnesota, withdrew to form a new body, the General Council. They invited other like-minded independent synods to join the venture, among them Wisconsin, Michigan, and Minnesota. This led to the Wisconsin Synod's brief membership in the General Council.

Short-Lived General Council Membership

Wisconsin was alert to these developments on the larger Lutheran scene and reacted to them promptly. President Streissguth reported to the 1866 convention in this fashion:

> The latest happenings in the circles of the Lutheran General Synod justify the expectation that very shortly the withdrawal

of several synods from that body will result in one that is more firmly founded on the Lutheran Confessions and on Lutheran practice and our respected synod should be urgently requested to review and perhaps to renew its resolution of two years ago [found on page 11 of the 1864 *Proceedings*]: "that should indeed the attempt be made to form a new larger association of Lutheran synods on a more solid confessional basis, a delegation of our synod should be sent to the meeting that prepares the way for such an association."[5]

President Streissguth and President Martin of Northwestern were the synod's delegates to the preliminary meeting at Reading, Pennsylvania, in the fall of 1866 that determined to form the General Council. They brought back with them for synodical approval the document, "Fundamental Principles of Faith and Church," prepared by Dr. Charles P. Krauth, the Pennsylvania Ministerium's ranking theologian, as a doctrinal platform for the new general Lutheran body.

This statement and the proposed constitution looked good to the 1867 Wisconsin convention.[6] After a thorough discussion that extended over a number of sessions the doctrinal basis and constitution were approved, with only a few clarification questions that were to be raised at the 1867 Council convention. Wisconsin's communicant count of 12,741, second highest among the General Council's synods and surpassed only by the Pennsylvania Ministerium's 50,000, entitled it to three pastors and three lay delegates. Those chosen as pastor delegates were President Bading, Senior Muehlhaeuser, and Professor Martin. The laymen selected, H. Inbusch, D. Kusel, and N. Schoof, did not attend the General Council sessions.

One of the pastor delegates, it should be noted, could not carry out his assignment. Professor A. Hoenecke had to replace Muehlhaeuser, who died on September 15, 1867. By that time the synod he had founded and fashioned could no longer by any stretch of the imagination be called the "Muehlhaeuser Synod," as had been done in the early years. Wisconsin had shed its "New Lutheran" image and by 1867 was ready to stand in the front ranks of those struggling for a firm confessional Lutheranism committed to all the Confessions and determined to match its practice with that commitment.

The time for standing had come in 1867. The place for it was Fort Wayne, where the General Council's constituent convention was held in late fall. The issue was the famed "Four Points." Two interested synods, Ohio and Iowa, instead of joining the General

Council immediately, had put a series of questions to the body that revolved mainly around fellowship practices. The two sets of questions were put together into a set of four points that asked what the Council's position would be on:

1) Millennialism — false views about a 1000-year reign of Christ;
2) Pulpit fellowship — sharing Lutheran pulpits with pastors who were not Lutheran;
3) Altar fellowship — admitting to Holy Communion those who were not Lutheran;
4) Lodge membership — allowing Lutheran members to join antichristian societies.

Iowa and Ohio and others feared that bad habits acquired in General Synod membership would be retained in the new association. It was known that strong millennial views were held by Joseph Seiss, prominent Philadelphia and Pennsylvania Ministerium pastor, and also by many in the Iowa Synod and other bodies. Lodge membership was a major problem that the Wisconsin Synod had to address in its 1867 convention.

In its reply to Ohio the General Council simply referred to its constitution and its "Fundamental Principles." This was also the first reply to Iowa, but subsequently an amplification appeared which begged for time as it stated "that the General Council is not prepared to endorse the declaration of the Synod of Iowa . . . and that we refer the matter to the District Synods, until such time as by the blessing of God's Holy Spirit and the leadings of his providence, we shall be enabled, throughout the whole General Council and all its churches, to see eye to eye in all the details of practice and usage."[7]

As a protest to what they regarded as temporizing and evasion on the key fellowship issue, the Wisconsin delegation, Bading, Hoenecke, and Martin, augmented by Heyer of Minnesota and Welden of Pennsylvania, had negative votes recorded. Ohio declined Council membership. Iowa refrained from a voting membership. President Bading declared that he would have to report the situation to the next Wisconsin convention so that it could reach its decision.

That 1868 Racine convention, one of the most important of the first two decades, reached a number of key decisions in the matter of its fellowship relations. As has been related, it broke with the overseas mission societies. As will be soon related, it sought an entente with Missouri that quickly resulted in fellowship declarations and school cooperation. Thirdly, it threshed out its own stand while carrying out the General Council's action at Fort Wayne the previous November, which referred the "Four Points" to area synods.

The discussion that ensued ranged widely and touched vital issues.[8] The time had come, figuratively and literally, for the Wisconsin men to stand up and be counted. In his farewell to them Pastor Vorberg, highly regarded by the brethren, pointed out that since he joined the synod just four years previously it was not he but the synod that had changed and that it was now requiring more Lutheranism than it had then. Vorberg was right in that contention. But he was on the wrong side in the voting; he left the synod and his Milwaukee congregation to join the New York Ministerium. Pastor Kittel of La Crosse, not willing to give up the practice of communing the Reformed, also resigned his pastorate and synodical membership. President Martin of Northwestern insisted that the day Wisconsin broke with the General Council he would break with the Wisconsin Synod. By the next Easter the break between him and the synod had come to pass. Pastor Lukas of Reedsburg first voted against the majority but changed his stand in a subsequent session. Two lay delegates voted against it on the technical grounds that they had no instructions from their congregations in a matter of such far-reaching consequence.

Except for this handful of men, the forty-seven pastors and thirty-one lay delegates present favored the resolution that the synod "with the whole orthodox Lutheran Church rejects each and every altar and pulpit fellowship with those that believe falsely or otherwise as contradictory to the doctrine and practice of the Lutheran Church." The die was cast.

A number of the majority's arguments are worth quoting, even though more than a century has passed since that Racine convention. "The question of altar and pulpit fellowship is the ABCs of the ecclesiastical practice of a Lutheran synod." "As to the earlier stand of the synod, one ought to thank God that it has been overthrown and the synod has come to greater clarity." "Not persons but the principle must be regarded." "There might possibly be circumstances in which one could preach in pulpits of those not united in the faith without doing violence to the principle but these could not come into consideration in the establishment of the principle."

Special attention has been given to an old convention debate and resolution that many others might dismiss as a mere tempest in a teapot. Actually, what transpired at Racine in 1868 was the crucial event in the first two decades of the synod's history. It was also a harbinger of things to come. The fellowship principle would repeatedly be a consideration and determinant of Wisconsin Synod history, also in the future.

What about Wisconsin's General Council membership? It came to an end promptly. President Bading informed the General Council of Wisconsin's resolve: "Unless resolutions are passed at the next convention of the General Council that are satisfactory to us and accord with our resolution concerning altar and pulpit fellowship, we will no longer consider ourselves members of that church body."[9] The General Council at its convention in late 1868 at Pittsburgh passed resolutions on the "Four Points" that were better than those of the previous year but still left much to be desired. Even though President Bading, Pastor Eberhardt of the Michigan Synod, and Pastor Adelberg of the New York Ministerium withdrew their minority report, they felt constrained to offer a declaration that sought to pinpoint and buttress weaknesses in the majority report accepted by the convention.[10]

Their declaration rejected all millennialism, not just the "Jewish opinions" condemned by the Augsburg Confession. It mentioned specific names such as Free Masons and Odd Fellows when discussing any fellowship with "those not Lutheran" instead of only with him "of whom there is grave doubt that he will preach the pure truth" and "heretics and fundamental errorists," as the Council resolution put it. The interest was that a clear stand be taken by the General Council. It was not.

When President Bading reported the matter at the 1869 convention at Helenville, the convention simply resolved to put its 1868 resolution into effect. The action may seem simple but a step with far-reaching implications was being taken. An old association was broken but a new fellowship was thereby made possible. The General Council subsequently charged Wisconsin with "hasty withdrawal" and "uncharitable assault" on grounds "obscure and dubious."[11]

The Wisconsin Synod did not then nor does it now apologize for having been the first to withdraw from the General Council after a membership of less than two years. Wisconsin had just finished its own internal struggle over the fellowship issue and had broken with its European benefactors. It was not going to allow that gain to be jeopardized by another prolonged debate on the issue or by an unsatisfactory alliance.

The historical record confirms the judgment of Wisconsin's men in their 1869 General Council decision. The Minnesota Synod subsequently pressed for a definition of "heretics and fundamental errorists" and found that it did not necessarily include members of sectarian churches. Minnesota withdrew in 1871. Preaching in sectarian pulpits, as has been previously recounted, led to the

Michigan withdrawal in 1888. This practice was, in fact, endorsed by being reported in the Council's Proceedings in 1869 and thereafter. When the General Council reunited with the General Synod a half century later, the "Four Points" were no longer in the picture.

The 1868 Wisconsin convention broke two fellowship ties but they were promptly replaced by others. In the very next year President Bading could report that agreements had been reached with the Hermannsburg mission society.[12] In just four years the General Council membership would be replaced by one in the Synodical Conference. How that came about will be recounted in the next section and the next chapter.

Early Interchurch Relations in the Midwest

Several such relations have previously been mentioned in passing. There were contacts with the Illinois and the Northern Illinois Synods when it was proposed that Wisconsin use and help staff Illinois State University at Springfield for ministerial training. The proposal died a quick death in 1860, and Wisconsin went on to open its own seminary in 1863 in Watertown.

There were some interchanges with the Ohio Synod in the late 1850s when both synods had agenda and hymn book projects in the works. In 1857 Wisconsin voted to "endorse the resolution of the Ohio Synod, according to which it would request the honored Pennsylvania Synod at the time of the next edition of the agenda to make provision for a thorough revision."[13] Apart from these casual and workaday contacts there is little to report in Ohio-Wisconsin relations until 1870 when Ohio circulated the momentous proposal that led to the founding of the Synodical Conference.

With Iowa there were closer contacts. An Iowa historian states: "For a time a friendly relationship existed between the Iowa and Wisconsin Synods. And Iowa's influence had more than a little to do with the fact that a more determined stance developed."[14] Iowa may have had problems with millennialism and an "open question" approach to certain doctrines, but it knew what proper Lutheran practice was when dealing with the Reformed. It joined Buffalo and Missouri in rebuking Wisconsin's early "New Lutheranism."

Synodical pathways touched at Platteville, where Iowa founded a congregation later served by Pastor Starck of the Wisconsin Synod. Some consideration was also given to using the Iowa seminary, but in 1862 Wisconsin declared that it was unwilling to use either the Missouri or Iowa seminaries because it did not approve of their "exclusive tendency."[15]

In 1867 an imposing group of ten Iowa men, including President Grossmann, Professors S. and G. Fritschel, and Pastor G. Schieferdecker, attended the Wisconsin Synod convention in an effort to win adherents to its historical approach to the Confessions. Wisconsin devoted a morning session to hearing the Fritschels endorse "open questions" and mild millennialism but the synod was evidently unconvinced.[16] That evening Professor S. Fritschel preached a convention sermon on election as described in Ephesians 1:3-7.

This close relationship between Wisconsin and Iowa cooled considerably later that year when the Iowa-Missouri colloquy in Milwaukee provided a closer look at Iowa's doctrinal position. Professor S. Fritschel was still visiting Wisconsin conventions in 1868 and 1869, bringing Pastor Vogel with him in 1868. Relations that had peaked in the spring of 1867 soon dwindled to almost nothing as Wisconsin turned more and more in the direction of Missouri, Iowa's oldest and bitterest theological opponent.

Wisconsin's relations with the Minnesota Synod, founded by Father Heyer in 1860, had an unpromising beginning. The very first mention of its western neighbor in Wisconsin minutes is unflattering, to say the least. The 1862 Proceedings report: "The Evangelical Lutheran Synod of Minnesota consists of only eight pastors, of which only two or three are in full-time service. The others are farmers from Pennsylvania who on special request hold services in homes in the English language."[17] This information is presented as another argument for starting a seminary. The thought is that the Minnesota Synod is in no position to take care of its many German immigrants and will need a great deal of help from its eastern neighbor.

In 1863 President Heyer visited the Wisconsin convention and requested the establishment of closer relations between the two synods. The next Wisconsin convention released G. Fachtmann to the Minnesota Synod and reacted favorably to Minnesota's request that President Heyer collect for the Watertown school in the East in exchange for the privilege of sending its students to Watertown.[18]

These friendly and neighborly gestures soon led to the desire for closer fraternal ties. In 1868 Pastor J. H. Sieker, who had just moved from Granville to St. Paul, came to the Wisconsin convention bearing his new synod's wish to join with Wisconsin in forming one church body. Wisconsin reacted with pleasure and voiced the intention of doing all in its power to bring the proposal to reality.[19]

When President Bading and Professor Hoenecke attended the 1869 Minnesota convention, they offered for discussion a proposal for federation of the two synods and when requested to put their suggestion in writing, Bading and Hoenecke drew up a basic five-point plan. Without hesitation the Minnesota convention adopted as the necessary first step the fifth point which called for a meeting of doctrinal commissions to achieve mutual certainty of unity in the faith.

The meeting, held that fall at La Crosse, was attended by Presidents Bading and Sieker, Professor Hoenecke, and Pastors Emmel, Kuhn, and Reitz of Minnesota. Both delegations declared that doctrinal unity existed and reported the same to the next conventions of the synods.

A problem developed at the 1870 Wisconsin meeting. The convention endorsed all the between-conventions actions of President Bading, including his part in the outcome of the La Crosse colloquy with Minnesota representation. Yet it rejected Minnesota's request for closer fellowship and even refrained from passing any resolution acknowledging Minnesota's orthodoxy.

Three reasons for the rebuff are stated in the Wisconsin minutes: lack of time to consider all ramifications of the proposed closer ties, the necessity of obtaining congregational consent, and the desirability of becoming better acquainted before establishing closer ties. President Sieker, who was present, reported to his synod that the underlying reason for the failure of the proposal was the concern of three Wisconsin men who feared that any connection with the continuing Minnesota membership in the General Council would blunt and contradict the testimony given by the Wisconsin withdrawal.[20] Wisconsin risked the rebuff to its neighbor so that it could stand firmly and unequivocally on the fellowship principles it had only recently and after much struggle achieved.

Several circumstances contributed to the prolongation of Minnesota's General Council membership. Because of a transfer of the presidency from Heyer to Friedrich Hoffmann the synod was not represented at the 1868 Council meeting that influenced Wisconsin to withdraw. At the 1869 Council meeting President Sieker, representing Minnesota under instructions to test the Council's stand on fellowship issues, encountered parliamentary difficulties when his test questions were ignored as being only private and not official.[21]

President Sieker went to the 1870 Council convention with "official" questions that he regarded as being at least adequately answered by Chairman Krauth's verbal dictum: "Lutheran altars are only for Lutheran Christians and Lutheran pulpits only for Lutheran preachers." When, however, the events of a few months revealed how liberally the dictum was being interpreted, Sieker in 1871 urged the Minnesota Synod to withdraw from the General Council. It did and the way was paved for a formal establishment of Wisconsin-Minnesota cooperation.

In their 1871 conventions the Wisconsin and Minnesota Synods recognized one another's orthodoxy. They would cooperate in ministerial training, with Wisconsin opening the door of its Watertown school to Minnesota students and Minnesota paying the salary of one professor. There would also be a partnership in Wisconsin's periodical, the *Gemeinde-Blatt.* Minnesota would use its columns for official notices, supply an editorial staff member, and share in the annual profits.[22]

One other facet of Wisconsin's "Interchurch Relations in the West," in certain aspects the most significant of all, remains to be described. This is the establishment of brotherly relations with the Missouri Synod. That subject, however, is such an integral part of the Synodical Conference story that it will be treated in the next chapter.

CHAPTER SIX

In the Synodical Conference

In the 1860s the Lutherans in this country began to take positions that would remain for a half century. The conflict over slavery and secession brought about the creation of a southern grouping, known after 1886 as the United Synod of the South. In 1866 the old General Synod came apart at the seams. Those determined to carry on its lax and liberal position continued, however diminished, as the General Synod. Those who urged more confessionalism formed the General Council in 1867. When it became apparent in the "Four Points" issue that the Council was not ready to match its theological practice to its confessional declaration, those who wanted a firmer stance either remained aloof from the beginning or soon withdrew.

Thus a number of unaligned synods found themselves standing to the right of the General Council as the 1860s drew to a close and the 1870s began. These were the Ohio, the Missouri, and the Norwegian Synods, which had never joined the Council, and the Wisconsin Synod, which withdrew in 1869, and the Minnesota and Illinois Synods, which did the same two years later. It would be quite natural for them to think about a grouping of their own in an era when new groupings seemed to be the order of the day.

The Ohio Synod took the initiative, having just come to a fellowship agreement with Missouri in a series of doctrinal discussions. The 1870 Ohio convention approved President Loy's recommendation that "steps be taken towards effecting a proper understanding between the synods of Missouri, of Wisconsin, of Illinois, and our own synod, which all occupy substantially the same position, and arranging a plan of co-operation in the work of the Lord."[1] To that end Ohio established a correspondence committee, and already in early 1871 the first of several conferences that paved the way for the formation of the Synodical Conference in July 1872 took place there.

Wisconsin could participate and become a charter Synodical Conference member because in 1868 it had finally reached an understanding with Missouri, its foe and critic of long standing. This important development in Wisconsin Synod history merits special attention.

Pathways to the Synodical Conference

The development came with surprising suddenness. For almost two decades Missouri had resented the establishment of a "New Lutheran" enclave in an area where it had holdings. Criticisms and rebukes of Wisconsin's theological practice soon surfaced in the Missouri periodicals, *Der Lutheraner* and *Lehre und Wehre.* There was some justification for the Missouri charges but there were also instances where the case was overstated.[2] After 1865, editors of Wisconsin's *Gemeinde-Blatt* could offer a rebuttal in the latter instances. Although the Wisconsin Synod was well on the way to improving its position by the mid 1860s, Missouri took little notice. Right up to 1868 it continued its charges that by that time were anachronistic, to say the least.

In the course of almost two decades it was inevitable that two unsympathetic synods working in the same state would cross paths and establish opposition congregations. These clashes on the parish level added to the Wisconsin-Missouri differences. The worst trouble spots were Milwaukee, Racine, Watertown and vicinity, Oshkosh, and Burlington. Each battleground had its own local history, too lengthy to be recounted here, but they all shared the common characteristic of contributing to the strife between Missouri and Wisconsin.

It was not all strife, to be sure. Bading himself could and did testify to a better side in Missouri-Wisconsin relations. As he related the incident to J. P. Koehler and the latter recorded it in his *History of the Wisconsin Synod,* Bading in his first years in the Wisconsin Synod became extremely discouraged about prospects in his Calumet congregation and in the church body he had just joined.[3] He approached President Ottomar Fuerbringer of Missouri's Northern District with the purpose of joining the more confessional Missouri Synod. President Fuerbringer, demonstrating the ideal in interchurch relations, urged Bading to stick it out in Wisconsin, where his confessional concerns were needed more than in Missouri. There is no record that Fuerbringer ever regretted the advice he gave, even when later he and Bading stood over against one another as synodical representatives in parish disputes at Watertown and elsewhere.

In 1868 Bading, as Wisconsin's president, directed to the attention of Fuerbringer, as president of Missouri's Northern District, a resolution of the Wisconsin Synod's Racine convention that requested a discussion of parish problems in the interest of establishing brotherly relations. In his presidential report at Racine Bading could refer to "opportune private discussions with pastors of the Missouri Synod, who desire peace as earnestly with us as we with them," and the "hope that our relations to that church body also will become more and more friendly and brotherly."[4] These informal "discussions" had been taking place in Watertown and vicinity, with Philipp Koehler meeting with Pastor Multanowski of Missouri's Town Hubbard, congregation, and with Pastor Strassen and other Missouri men conferring with Professors Hoenecke and Meumann and President Bading.

The Racine convention reacted to this suggestion of its president by first of all declaring that it knew of no "church divisive differences" keeping Wisconsin and Missouri apart and that conflicts involved "practical questions, aggressions of individual members of both synods and articles in public periodicals, which often expressed more the tone of strife and scorn than sincere regret over such evils and loving correction."[5]

Both Professor Hoenecke and Pastor Lange formally protested the wording, "church-divisive differences," which was actually a floor substitution for the committee's original "differences in doctrine." The protesters were making the point that all "differences in doctrine" were "church divisive" and that there were not some "open questions" in doctrines that were not "church divisive." While Hoenecke and Lange correctly protested the faulty wording, they had no quarrel with the thrust of the resolution, which was that there was a proper and biblical basis for brotherly relations, namely, unity in doctrine.

On that basis the convention then instructed President Bading to take the "proper steps to bring about peace so that there might be mutual recognition as Lutheran synods and brotherly relations between members of both synods in the spirit of truth on the basis of pure doctrine." President Bading acted promptly. Through President Fuerbringer he placed the two Wisconsin resolutions before Missouri's Northern District meeting at Milwaukee on the day the Racine convention closed.

The Northern District was disturbed because the Wisconsin overture implied that there had been parish aggression from both sides. It was concerned that discussion should center on doctrine and that there should be a clear disavowal of unionistic practices of the past. It modified a previous charge made about communion celebration in congregations of the Wisconsin Synod. There was, however, general agreement that the overture should be favorably received and that discussions should be held. President Walther of the Missouri Synod, who was present, urged that the committee the Northern District would elect should represent, not just the district, but the whole Missouri Synod.[6]

The Missouri-Wisconsin colloquy took place in Milwaukee on October 21 and 22. President Bading, who headed the Wisconsin delegation, consisting also of Professor Hoenecke and Pastors Damann, Gausewitz, and Koehler, yielded to the Missouri demand that doctrinal issues receive prime attention, even though he had been officially instructed to concentrate on parish problems and felt that Wisconsin's orthodoxy had been sufficiently demonstrated. Discussion of "open questions" and other burning doctrinal issues of the day revealed that there was full unity of faith. President Walther, previously the stern critic, was overjoyed. He included in his November 1 *Lutheraner* report the declaration, "All our reservations about . . . Wisconsin . . . have been put to shame."

The following May the worker-training agreement between the two synods was developed. It stipulated that Wisconsin should transfer its seminary operation to St. Louis and supply one of the theological teachers there, while Missouri should provide one professor for the Watertown school that would now open its doors to Missouri students.[7] This agreement and the mutual recognition of orthodoxy that went with it were ratified by 1869 synodical conventions, Missouri's at Fort Wayne and Wisconsin's at Helenville. A brotherly association had been brought about that would endure for ninety-two years. This key event in Wisconsin Synod history in its own right also was the main factor in enabling both synods to enjoy joint membership in the Synodical Conference that came into being three years later.

Before that event is described, some notice should be taken of the establishment of fraternal relations between the Missouri and Minnesota Synods. Across the Mississippi a situation similar to that found in Wisconsin prevailed in Missouri relations before 1872. Missouri pastors felt constrained to speak out against practices of pastors belonging to a synod they regarded as much too lax to be considered orthodox.

An especially thorny problem presented itself in the Twin Cities. There was parish strife between Missouri's Zion, founded in the early 1860s by disgruntled former members of Trinity, and Trinity, pioneer congregation of the Minnesota Synod, served by Heyer and Fachtmann. The Zion founders objected to the unionistic practice of both men.[8] Early in 1871 efforts on the congregational level were made to improve the situation. Joint meetings for members of Trinity and Zion were set up, but the neighboring congregations were not able to compose all their differences.

In January 1872, however, both the *Gemeinde-Blatt* and the *Lutheraner* carried this announcement:

> At the request of the pastors of the Minnesota Synod and the honorable Missouri Synod a mixed conference will be held in St. Paul, Minn., in the congregation of Pastor J. H. Sieker, beginning on Jan. 10, 1872, to which hereby all concerned are invited. . . . The main subject under discussion will be the question: How should congregations and pastors of two confessionally faithful synods in one and the same field of labor deal with one another according to God's Word?[9]

The *Gemeinde-Blatt* report of that conference, submitted by "S," obviously Sieker, mentions the attendance of several pastors of the Norwegian Synod that was also taking part in the efforts to establish the Synodical Conference. The report also stresses the unity that prevailed when Pastor Herzer's theses on the theme question were discussed.[10]

These eight theses were introduced by three presuppositions: the duty of orthodox Lutheran bodies to recognize orthodox brethren and to work toward unity with them, the awareness that such unity will lead to joint work when the brethren are in the same area, and the special implications of these truths for pastors. The theses themselves might be summarized as follows:

1. Fellowship of faith will lead to altar and pulpit fellowship, especially at pastoral conferences and synod meetings;
2. Pastors are not to serve members of a brother's congregation or those excommunicated by it, unless the brother consents;
3. If possible, congregational boundaries should be located and then respected; if no such boundaries exist, then membership rolls and even communion guest lists should be respected;
4. New congregations should not be established in the field that a sister congregation is working;
5. A sister congregation's discipline and excommunication are to be respected;
6. Proper releases should be issued and respected;
7. No call should be accepted to a congregation that has without just cause deposed its pastor;
8. When one brother observes another brother's official or personal error, he should take this up with the erring brother privately; the matter should be taken to the synodical level only if it cannot be disposed of in brother-to-brother confrontation.[11]

These eight theses were to play an even larger role in the story of the formation of the Synodical Convention. When the Missouri Synod's colloquy team, headed by Pastors Bauer and Fick, arrived at Mankato to attend the 1872 Minnesota Synod convention after a slow boat trip upriver which provided ample time for a perusal of Minnesota convention proceedings, the Missouri representatives stated that what they had so far learned made them willing to regard an acceptance of the eight theses as full and final proof of Minnesota orthodoxy. They would even dispense with a formal doctrinal colloquy.[12] After devoting four morning sessions to a thorough discussion of the eight theses in somewhat different arrangement but with the original content intact, the Minnesota Synod accepted them without reservation.[13]

Meanwhile, brotherly and neighborly conferences of Minnesota, Missouri, and Norwegian pastors had served the purpose of cementing fraternal relations. The unity that prevailed there served as a stepping stone to the unity that brought the Synodical Conference into existence.

Before the actual founding of that federation two preliminary meetings were held. In January 1871 representatives of the Missouri, Ohio, Norwegian, and Wisconsin Synods met in Chicago. Minnesota and Illinois had not yet fully disentangled themselves from the General Council and could not be officially represented, although President Knoll of the Illinois Synod attended as a guest. The Wisconsin delegation consisted of President Bading, Professor Ernst, and Pastors Adelberg, Thiele, and Hoenecke. The latter had not accompanied the seminary in its move to St. Louis and was serving St. Matthew in Milwaukee. The main assignment of the Chicago meeting was to work out a proposed Synodical Conference constitution and to discuss the possibility of joint efforts in worker training, especially in a joint theological seminary.

The second meeting, held at Fort Wayne in November, was only semi-official and allowed any interested person to attend. Minnesota, however, was officially represented by President Sieker and Illinois by President Erdmann and Pastor Wollbrecht, and the two synods were welcomed as participants in the consultations. A few minor changes in the proposed constitution that synods had requested were included in a revision. Not all synods had had an opportunity to declare themselves in general conventions, but reports indicated that in all of the six a strong sentiment for Synodical Conference membership prevailed.

The main task of the Fort Wayne gathering was the consideration and ratification of the *Denkschrift* written by F. A. Schmidt of the Norwegian Synod.[14] This document was a declaration of the reasons why a fourth general Lutheran body was being called into existence. In brief, the reasons stated were that the General Synod, the General Council, and the Southern Synod did not fully commit themselves in doctrine and practice to confessional Lutheranism. Stated positively, the Synodical Conference was declaring a full commitment to the Holy Scriptures and to all the doctrines of the Lutheran Confessions and to a practice that was in harmony with the doctrinal stand.

In July 1872 the constituent convention of the Synodical Conference was held in President Bading's St. John's Church in Milwaukee. In the opening sermon Professor Walther exulted, "*O gesegneter, seliger Tag*" [O blessed and blissful day]! Forty years later, bidding the Synodical Conference farewell as its president for the last thirty of those years, Bading vividly recalled Walther's words. He wrote: "This declaration echoed joyfully at that time in the hearts of all of us who had worked together in the founding of the Synodical Conference. To these co-workers the writer of these lines belonged, and he can certainly say he belonged to them with joy."[15]

In 1872 Wisconsin was not an aloof, isolationist synod. With great enthusiasm it entered a Lutheran federation that stood for the kind of confessionalism toward which the Lord had led it during its early decades. It participated energetically in such Synodical Conference undertakings as the publication of English day school readers. Most of all, it shared in the Conference's outreach to Blacks, begun in 1877, the very year when Reconstruction officially ended and most of the North was turning its back on those it had fought to free.

In its first decade the Synodical Conference encountered two major threats to its unity. The one was the great controversy over election and conversion that seriously diminished the numerical strength of the body. The other was the effort to create state synods, in which Wisconsin became heavily involved.

State Synod Squabble

The state synod effort, simply defined, sought to effect a breakdown of existing synodical bodies in the Synodical Conference and substitute for them units that would conform geographically to state lines. A common language, German, was assumed. Those using Norwegian or English were not included in the planning. In the ensuing strife the state and the synod of Wisconsin became a sort of storm center. The Wisconsin Synod's role in the conflict has been

55

frequently misunderstood and misdescribed and will therefore be detailed in full.

It should be recognized at the outset that the state synod development was not some ill-conceived brainstorm that caught Wisconsin off guard. On the contrary, the idea was part and parcel of the Conference's founding, a congenital and constitutional commitment from the beginning. In the Synodical Conference's constitution the all-important Section III on purpose lists: "elimination of potential or threatening disturbances thereof [of the unity]; an endeavor to fix the limits of the synods according to territorial boundaries, provided that language does not separate them; the consolidation of all Lutheran synods of America into a single, faithful, devout American Lutheran Church."[16] Of this Wisconsin was well aware from the outset.

It should likewise be recognized that the motivation behind the state synod plan was not necessarily sordid aggrandizement on the part of Missouri, but rather an honorable desire on the part of Walther and others to keep interparish conflicts to a minimum and to settle them as promptly as possible.[17] When feuding parishes belonged to different synods, the effort at peace-making could be a difficult and drawn-out and frequently futile process. Walther was as much concerned about unity and peace in the parish life of the Synodical Conference as he was about its doctrinal unity. A joint theological seminary would help preserve the doctrinal unity; a system of state synods would promote peace in the parishes. Both became pet projects of Doctor Walther and his synod.

With Wisconsin and the Norwegians already using Concordia Seminary at St. Louis for theological training and Ohio being asked to do the same, the joint seminary was already taking shape. The 1876 Synodical Conference convention unanimously endorsed a state-synod plan by passing the resolution "that we advise all our synods without delay to take steps to bring state synods into being, if not everywhere immediately, then certainly there where it can be done without difficulty, detriment and disadvantage."[18] The convention then passed, again unanimously, a worker-training plan with these stipulations:

1. Joint seminary and teachers' college under the Conference's control;
2. Feeder schools under the control of the state synods;
3. An English and possibly also a Norwegian division attached to the joint seminary;
4. The joint seminary should be promptly established even if the creation of state synods cannot be as speedily effected.

These were the resolutions that the Wisconsin convention of 1877 was to consider. By May of that year that consideration was influenced by a fact that had become apparent and by a fear that had asserted itself.

It was a fact that there was much agitation for a Wisconsin state synod, but not very much in other areas. Seemingly forgotten was the caution that the creation of state synods should take place "if not immediately everywhere, then certainly there where it can be done without difficulty, detriment and disadvantage." There were such places, Missouri for example, but Wisconsin was not one of them. Three of the Synodical Conference synods, including the Norwegian Synod, had strong holdings in Wisconsin. To bring the congregations of the German synods into one state synod would not by any means be easy. But that is just what was being urged, urged in fact by a contingent of Missouri men at the 1877 Wisconsin convention at Watertown.[19]

The fear concerned the status of a state synod that was created before the Synodical Conference's synods dissolved. It was assumed that such a synod would for the time being attach itself as a district to an existing synod. If a state synod were formed in Wisconsin, the whole Wisconsin Synod would be involved and absorbed. The resultant attachment to an existing synod, very likely Missouri, would mean an end to the independent existence of the Wisconsin Synod, at least for the interim and for longer than that if for some reason the full plan was not carried through.

In view of all this, the 1877 Wisconsin convention passed five interrelated resolutions. The first three resolutions reacted to the state synod plan (the first two were passed unanimously and the third by a strong majority):

1. The Synod endorses and approves heartily the original plan to unite all orthodox Lutherans within the Synodical Conference into individual, independent state synods;
2. The Synod asserts that it is ready for such an amalgamation into a state synod of Wisconsin, as soon as the possibility is precluded that this state synod might as a district attach itself to an existing synod and thereby lose its separate identity and independence;
3. The Synod asserts that it cannot view any such attachment to an existing general synod either as commanded in God's Word or as essentially necessary for true unity and profitable and advantageous for our congregations.[20]

Two other resolutions reacted to the Synodical Conference's school plan, in which it was already participating in fact, if not in theory, by declaring first of all in a standing vote of sixty-four to thirty-four: "We do not view the establishment of a large, general theological seminary, in so far as we are concerned, as good and beneficial and cannot therefore participate therein." The next resolve called for the establishment of a Wisconsin seminary by next September, subject to congregational approval.

The result was the return of Wisconsin Lutheran Seminary from St. Louis to Milwaukee and the re-engagement of Pastor Hoenecke as a Wisconsin theological teacher, a post that would last thirty years until his death in 1908. Not all the Wisconsin students were willing to move. August Pieper repulsed the school recruitment efforts of President Bading by insisting: "For two years I have studied under Walther and his colleagues, Schaller, Guenther, Lange, Brohm, each one a model in his particular field, and now my brother Franz. I should trade all this for a few teachers and leaders of whom I know nothing? You cannot ask this of me."[21] It should also be noted that August Pieper repulsed the indirect synodical recruitment efforts of Doctor Walther, carried out through the agency of the brother, Francis Pieper, a year later, as he himself related: "I let him know that in the past God through my mother had led me into the Wisconsin Synod. I therefore felt an obligation to show my gratitude to this synod to serve it."

From 1877 on and into the present Wisconsin has been accused of sabotaging a well-intentioned unity endeavor of the Synodical Conference by a regrettable tendency to rugged individualism and extreme isolationism. Walther himself castigated the second of the resolutions quoted above as *widergoettlich* [antigodly] in the Missouri convention of the next year and as infringing on Christian liberty and the province of the Holy Spirit.[22] This reaction and so many that have followed its pattern tend to overlook Wisconsin's unanimous approval of state synods, if only some guarantee of synodical integrity during the developing stage would be supplied. If Wisconsin flouted anything, it was not the Holy Spirit and his work of unifying the brethren but rather an overstress on one kind of synodical structure by a synod that would in time become the strongest advocate of local congregation supremacy over any synodical structure.

Whatever the case, other events soon rendered the strife over state synods superfluous. A much more important and divisive issue disturbed and dismembered the Synodical Conference. While some last-ditch efforts were being made to keep the state synod plan alive in altered form, the election controversy heated up. It would take two synods out of the Synodical Conference but also cement the unity and brotherhood of those that remained.

Election Controversy

The big and bitter election-conversion controversy began to surface in the early 1870s, when controversial articles on the subject began to appear in religious periodicals.[23] Soon, however, a debate about the universal aspect of justification pre-empted attention, achieving a major place on the agenda of the very first Synodical Conference convention. But the election debate could not be submerged for long. It resurfaced in 1877 and became a cause for strife within and between Lutheran synods.

The election issue, stated as simply as possible, revolved and revolves around the question: Why does God elect those who finally get to heaven? The Bible supplies a twin answer: because of his mercy and because of Christ's merits. Many, however, including some of the outstanding Lutheran dogmaticians, wanted to inject a third element into the answer of the *why* question, either as a cause or a condition. They spoke about an election *in view of faith.* At best, the phrasing could be stretched to suggest the thought that God's electing in eternity presupposed that all the elect would be brought to heaven on the pathway of faith. At worst, an election *in view of faith* could be thought of as being caused by the person's faith that God foresaw in eternity. This reading, which unfortunately many favored, could not but inject some human merit into a matter that the Bible presents as pure divine grace.

When Professor Walther in 1877 in an essay on the subject for Missouri's Western District suggested that the scrapping of *in view of faith* in the Lutheran teaching of the doctrine of election was long overdue, the controversy that had temporarily subsided broke out anew. It was at first a Missouri conflict, with Walther being challenged by men in his own synod, such as Professor F. Stellhorn and Pastor H. Allwardt. Soon, however, the Synodical Conference and the Wisconsin Synod and also other synods not in fellowship became involved.

The Wisconsin Synod had, in fact, been brushed by the controversy in its preliminary stage in the early 1870s. Professor Stellhorn, the man Missouri sent to Watertown as its part of the 1869 worker-training arrangement, was already then rejecting any total exclusion of man's role in the election and conversion process. The subject surfaced at Missouri pastoral conferences in the Watertown area, and on one occasion the Missouri pastors let Pastor Hoenecke be their spokesman. A colorful eyewitness description of the verbal duel between Hoenecke and Stellhorn has been preserved.[24] The color is intensified when one recalls that this set-to in a little conference in the Watertown area would be replayed three decades later on the larger stage of the Free Conferences held on the subject from 1903-1906 by midwestern Lutheran synods. Then Doctor Hoenecke was a major spokesman for the Synodical Conference stand, and Doctor Stellhorn, then in the Ohio Synod, often voiced the opposition.

By 1880 the controversy had reached far beyond the borders of the Missouri Synod. In that year Professor Schmidt of the Norwegian Synod began to attack the Missouri position openly in the periodical, *Altes und Neues.* Missouri reaffirmed its position, first in a special pastoral conference in 1880 and then officially in the regular synodical convention the next year. The 1881 Ohio Synod convention declared for an election *in view of faith* and thereby for a break with Missouri and the Synodical Conference.

The Wisconsin Synod, under the guidance of Professors Hoenecke and A. Graebner and President Bading, consistently stood with Professor Walther and Missouri, its recent opponents in the state synod issue. This was no blind following where Missouri led but a deep-seated conviction that the Missouri position was the scriptural position. Wisconsin's 1879 pastoral conference, in fact, raised objections to certain extreme statements in Missouri writings and eventually received an explanation.[25]

The crucial year for the Wisconsin and Minnesota involvement in the controversy was 1882. Synodical conventions were held simultaneously at LaCrosse, June 8-15, and the two synods joined their sessions when doctrinal discussions were on the agenda. Professor A. Graebner was the essayist and his subject was "Theses on Conversion." The second of these dealt with the cause of conversion, and this brought election into the discussion. By mutual consent Professor Hoenecke supplied a brief but thorough presentation of the Bible's teaching on election, ascribing it alone to God's mercy and Christ's merits without any human contribution, be it a foreseen faith or anything else. A Minnesota spokesman in a brief review seconded the presentation.[26]

In the subsequent joint session that afternoon the Wisconsin and Minnesota men stood up to be counted on the issue. Those objecting to the previous doctrinal presentation on the Wisconsin side were Pastor J. Klindworth, of Galena, Illinois, a recent acquisition from the Iowa Synod; Pastor C. Althoff of Winchester, Teacher J. Gruber of Oshkosh, and the Galena lay delegate. Pastor Kleinlein abstained temporarily but remained in the synod. Pastors J. Siegrist of Stillwater, J. Vollmar of New Auburn, and G. Kittel of Armstrong were the members of the Minnesota Synod that held to election *in view of faith.*

There were naturally also some parish problems and losses, although not as many as might have been expected. In Stillwater a majority of the congregation left the synod but a minority established one of their own. The Springfield church left as a body. The Wisconsin congregational losses were Galena, Winchester, and Beloit. There were also three congregations that split: Green Bay, Nikimi, and Oshkosh.

The Oshkosh developments deserve special mention because they became a main basis for a Wisconsin protest against the seating of Professor Schmidt at the 1882 Synodical Conference convention.[27] There was a faction in the Oshkosh congregation, led no doubt by Teacher Gruber, that upheld *in view of faith* election. When Pastor Dowidat returned from the LaCrosse synodical meeting he found himself almost without a congregation. His efforts to win back the erring at a tumultuous congregational gathering were unsuccessful. Professor Schmidt and Pastor Allwardt were on the grounds to advise the faction opposing Pastor Dowidat. Those siding with Dowidat founded Grace Church.

The Synodical Conference, with no Ohio Synod delegates on hand, refused to seat Professor Schmidt. The next year the Norwegian Synod withdrew from official membership in the Synodical Conference but not from its fellowship. It hoped that this step would make a settlement of differences with Professor Schmidt and his followers easier. It did not work out that way.

There were costs and losses for the Wisconsin Synod in this phase of the election controversy. But the gains outweighed the losses. A precious Bible truth was more deeply appreciated than ever before. Brotherly ties with Missouri and Minnesota were more firmly established. And in another phase of the controversy a Norwegian Synod remnant, the present Evangelical Lutheran Synod, would rejoin the Synodical Conference in 1920.

CHAPTER SEVEN

Silver Anniversary Perspective

The twenty-fifth annual convention of the Wisconsin Synod was the first not held near the time of the Trinity festival. The previous winter during Christmas vacation, the empty dormitory at the Watertown school had been destroyed by fire. It was agreed that rebuilding should not occur without full synodical blessing. The Northwestern board pressed for and gained a specially summoned early convention. It met April 15-20, 1875 at Pastor Adelberg's St. Peter Church in Milwaukee.

Jubilee Convention

Not even a belated winter's last hurrah, a storm that put snow on the streets and frost on the church windows, could dampen the anniversary enthusiasm of the sixty-eight pastors, twenty teachers, thirty-nine lay representatives of the synod's six-score congregations, and numerous guests.[1] They saw on the arch of the altar alcove in green-gold design *1850-1875* surmounted by crown and cross. It was fitting that President Bading, a veteran of over twenty years of synod service and third in seniority behind Goldammer and Conrad, should preach the festival sermon.

Bading briefly recalled the three founders, Muehlhaeuser, Weinmann, and Wrede, the first two dead and the third returned to Germany, and then he called on the delegates joyfully and gratefully to praise God who had exalted his name and his Word in their midst. The sermon summarized the key points in the quarter century of Wisconsin history; after pointing to sectarian defamings of God's name and Word, Bading went on:

> And we will want to admit that such thinking also pervaded our flesh. Aren't there years in our past history that testify to this to a greater or lesser degree? Didn't we, pastors and mem-

bers, bring to a great extent this kind of spirit with us from the old homeland? Wasn't our practice possibly the kind that gave others the impression: Wisconsin permits a very different meaning to be contained in an expression of God's Word, permits love to be placed above faith, permits such tendencies as do not harmonize with the truth to have their place next to the truth? Even the previously mentioned romanizing tendency was no stranger in our midst. But God be praised, all that belongs to the past history of our synodical life. We can exult and give praise: the old has gone, the new has come.

And how has the new come? Not through our merit but through God's goodness and faithfulness. It is the Lord whom we are to thank. Through trying inner conflicts, he forced and he pressured us until the erroneous spirit in us was destroyed, the false chains were broken and the true unity in the Spirit was produced, that unity, namely, that stands on the true Word and the true Confession, as the Lutheran Church possesses it and for which our fathers shed tears and blood.

It was fitting that the jubilee convention's doctrinal discussions should be led by Pastor Adolph Hoenecke, Wisconsin's ranking theologian, who in three years would resume his main work of training seminarians. At St. Peter, Milwaukee he presented theses on the theme "The Glory of the Church." Like Bading's sermon, Hoenecke's first thesis, "The Glory of the Church Consists in the Glory of Its Members Before God and in the Glory of the Gifts Given It," was launched by a reference to David's words in Psalm 138: "I will bow down toward your holy temple and will praise your name for your love and your faithfulness, for you have exalted above all things your name and your word."

It was fitting in 1875 that a thankful synod should conduct its business in a way that demonstrated gratitude for the grace of the past and determination to press on in the future. The convention was ready to rebuild at Watertown and, in fact, insisted that the projected one-story part of the structure should be so built that a second story could be added when more dormitory space was required. It was announced that $100 had been donated for the project anonymously, a princely sum in those hard dollar and depression days.

In accepting four congregations into membership—Mishicot, Elkhorn, Slinger, and Waterloo—the convention took special notice of the latter's constitution, which called for an annually stipulated pastoral salary. This old American device for turning shepherds into hirelings, dating back to early Colonial days, was disavowed and a committee of Pastors Brockmann, Dowidat, and Ungrodt was appointed to develop a new model constitution for synodical congregations. A previously mandated annual fee of $5.00 from all pastors to provide for widows and their children was rescinded in view of the development of a support system on a voluntary basis. A standing agenda committee was augmented and ordered to produce in time for the next convention.

The 1875 statistical report lists 64 pastors and professors and 119 congregations. Large Milwaukee congregations could add to the membership count such yearly baptism and confirmation statistics as:

St. John's -	306 and 81
St. Peter's -	174 and 52
St. Matthew's -	136 and 41
Grace -	132 and 52

In the Northern District, Oshkosh could list 103 baptisms and 38 confirmations, while the Western District's Watertown congregation could total figures of 69 and 55. Obviously the synod was growing, naturally and internally by leaps and bounds.

Serious efforts were being made to retain the young. Seven of every ten congregations operated some kind of school. They may have varied widely in number of school days per year and in the length of the school day. Much of the teaching was done by very busy pastors. Every congregational school, however, represented a real commitment to Christian education that harked back to the resolve of the first convention in 1850 that "every pastor in our church body is to be especially concerned about the youth and should conduct day schools, Bible hours, mission studies, and the like."

Resumé of Synodical Administration to 1875

Four men served as synodical presidents in the first twenty-five years. Two had lengthy tenures: Muehlhaeuser, 1850-1860, and Bading, 1860-1863 and from 1867 on. In the intervening years, 1863-1867, two men had brief but important presidential terms, Gottlieb Reim and William Streissguth.

In those early years the president was elected for a two-year term in the even years. The original constitution actually limited the president to two consecutive two-year terms, but since Muehlhaeuser proved himself to be the "indispensable man," that provision was simply ignored in 1856 and 1858. Having learned its lesson, the church body dropped the limitation in the constitutional revision that occupied synodical conventions, conferences, and committees off and on until final adoption in 1880.

Because of the confused situation that prevailed in the presidency during the 1860s a chart of the first presidents and their terms is supplied.²

President	Acting	Elected
John Muehlhaeuser		1850-1860
John Bading		1860-1864
Gottlieb Reim	1863-1864	1864-1866
William Streissguth	1865-1866	1866-1868
John Bading	1867-1868	1868-1889

When Bading was sent overseas to gather funds for the Watertown school in 1863, the synodical convention of that year established the office of vice-president and chose Gottlieb Reim of Helenville to fill the post. He acted as president in Bading's absence from September 1863 on, and when the European collection was extended, Reim was elected to the presidency at the 1864 convention.

Gottlieb Reim's twenty months of synodical leadership were much more than a stand-pat interim operation. The thin ranks of active pastors, still numbering less than fifty, were augmented by six newcomers to the 1864 convention and eight to that of 1865. Among them were G. Vorberg, already mentioned as an 1868 dissenter; G. Thiele, one of the six seminary professors of the nineteenth century; J. Brockmann, longtime Watertown pastor; and Th. Jaekel, who eventually succeeded Muehlhaeuser at Grace Church and was for many years synodical treasurer and a member of the Bading-Hoenecke-Jaekel Saturday morning coffee club. During those twenty months the growing synod was officially incorporated.

More significant than this legal development was the beginning of the synod's worker-training enterprise. While Reim was discharging presidential obligations, the seminary opened its doors in Watertown, and planning for the full-fledged school got underway. Reim could include in his June 1865 presidential report this good news: "A beginning has been made in the matter of the synodical school which has progressed so far that in a few weeks the building, the construction of which was undertaken in the previous year, can be occupied."³ No more significant worker-training report ever was made to a synodical convention, either before 1865 or afterward up to the time of this writing.

In Reim's 1865 presidential report this school subject is the last to be treated. It is followed by the explanatory note that Vice-President William Streissguth provides:

> On June 4 I received from the honored President G. Reim the written notice that he was resigning the presidency and

according to the constitution was transmitting it to me as the vice-president.

On June 9 Pastor G. Reim sent to me a written request for a temporary release from synodical membership, which I granted him on June 10.

W. Streissguth, President p.t.

One's first surmise about the reason for Reim's resignation might include the assumption that the tension built up in a church body headed for a doctrinal and fellowship crisis was just too much for him. This was not the case nor the cause that the record presents.[4] A problem in Reim's Helenville parish was the actual *bete noire* of this surprising development. A woman in the congregation slandered Reim to some of the church's day school children. The disciplinary case that ensued resulted in the exoneration of Reim by the Helenville church council and congregation. There were, however, lingering problems. The 1865 synodical convention itself referred to the happening as a "clouded matter" and utilized a Scotch verdict when it stated that it "could not convince itself of the guilt of Pastor Reim, instead left it to the omniscient God to bring light to this clouded matter."[5]

Reim moved from Helenville to Beaver Dam, serving there five years without rejoining the Wisconsin Synod, and then to New Ulm, where his pastoral services were ended by a fatal buggy accident on a pastoral call in 1882. A best construction, the right construction, offers the conclusion that the heart of the issue was Reim's concern that the "ministry might not be discredited" according to St. Paul's injunction in 2 Corinthians 6:3, a fitting example for his first synod, also and especially in this century.[6]

Vice-President William Streissguth filled out the final year of Reim's term. He was Reim's brother-in-law, both having married sisters of the prominent Milwaukee publisher George Brumder.[7] Upon the death of his first wife, Streissguth had, in fact, married a younger sister. His election as president in 1866, occurring after the second marriage, indicates that the young Wisconsin synod had no scruples about marriage with a sister-in-law or brother-in-law.

Streissguth's two-year leadership, brief as it was, was also studded with major synodical decisions and developments. The school building at Watertown was dedicated on August 31, 1865. The original synodical periodical, *Das Gemeinde-Blatt*, was launched the next month. At the next convention Streissguth pressed for and obtained the resolution that "the periodical by and large represents the confessional position of the synod, but that the synod does not subscribe to every single expression."[8] Streissguth was instrumental in bringing the Wisconsin Synod into the ranks of the General Council and himself served on its German hymnal committee.

Streissguth's main administrative concern seems to have been the advocacy of a strong praesidium functioning with growing cooperation from the field. In his final presidential report in 1867 — almost a century before the proposal was realized — Streissguth urged the synod to establish a president-visitor office without congregational responsibility.[9] The sometimes maverick group of pastors did not take too kindly to such thinking and planning, and Streissguth was aware of such opposition. In his last presidential report in 1867 under the subhead, "Our Worker-Training Schools," he tells us that he delayed plans to investigate the possibility of starting a preparatory school in Germany in part "because the project especially encountered from its inception great and, for me, painful, misinterpretation in synodical circles already at a time when the first outline of the plan had hardly been developed."[10]

Whatever the concerns Streissguth might have had about image and other pastors may have had about dictatorial power grabs, the stated reason for his sudden resignation, with one year of the presidential term still to be served, was undermined health in a difficult situation.

This was in 1867. Streissguth served another score of years and lived until 1915, by then the synod's senior pastor. Before being tempted, however, to dismiss the sickness excuse as hypocrisy or hypochondria, one should take the whole medical record into account.

Streissguth seems to have been prone to stress-induced migraines. In his pastoral service at Newton, Liberty, Milwaukee, Fond du Lac, St. Paul, and Kenosha there was a recurring pattern. Streissguth functioned capably when the assignment was not too pressing. He was, however, too good an evangelist to keep any assignment in a populous area from becoming pressing in short order. His congregations had a way of growing by leaps and bounds. When presidential responsibilities were added to those at the burgeoning St. John in Milwaukee, Streissguth resigned the presidency after two years of service to avoid what he termed "the greatest disadvantage for my health, my family, my congregation, and the synod."[11]

The official obituary in the 1915 *Northwestern Lutheran* did not even mention his synodical presidency, but that presidency, as well as that of his brother-in-law Gottlieb Reim, should not be forgotten. Both served well in the turbulent years between Bading's first and second stints. When Vice-President Bading picked up the presidential reins in 1867 to hold them another twenty-two years, he could do so with a modicum of stress and strife. The interim officiants had capably minded the store.

More than a century after the fact it might even be in place to suggest that the main concerns prompting the resignations make them much less deplorable and much more memorable. Reim resigned out of considerations that "the ministry might not be discredited." Streissguth resigned in the interest of a smoothly functioning synodical administration that his impaired health could not supply. Both motivations merit mention in a day when they are often in short supply.

When Vice-President Bading took over the leadership from the resigning Streissguth in 1867, he began a long term of service that lasted until he insisted on bowing out in 1889. The press of the St. John's church building project was the resignation reason that prevailed. Bading's main tasks in the 1867-1875 years involved such intersynodical developments as General Council membership, Missouri accord, and Synodical Conference founding. These have already been described in some detail. Further attention to the Bading administration may well be deferred to the post-1875 era.

The other president, Muehlhaeuser, loomed large in the early years of the synod and the first chapters of this book. Here may be the place for a summary and a final farewell. It is provided by Bading's 1868 presidential address, the first section of which is entitled "The Blessed Departure of Our Senior Muehlhaeuser." The first two presidents had not always seen eye-to-eye, especially on confessional and fellowship issues, but they both respected the other's synodical service.

Bading's formal tribute to the departed Muehlhaeuser at the Racine convention is worth quoting in full:

> John Muehlhaeuser, born in the Wuerttemberg area in 1803, was trained in the mission school at Barmen for church service among the German immigrants to America. After he had found and for years served Lutheran congregations in Rochester and other eastern cities as a member of the Lutheran Synod of New York, he came to Wisconsin in 1848 in order to further gather the scattered people of our homeland and our faith into congregations in the service of his Lord. Amid indescribable difficulties, great self-denial, and personal sacrifice he was able to make a firm planting in Milwaukee and found Grace church, the oldest in our synod. In 1850 he joined with several other members of the Lutheran Church in a closer association and established the Wisconsin Synod, whose leader and president he

was for ten years. Most of us know with what love and patience he nurtured the synod and how faithfully he labored and prayed for it. After he was granted in 1862 the joy of celebrating his silver anniversary, of traveling to the fatherland, and of seeing his mother who was almost ninety, his strength speedily declined except for a few remissions. At the time of our last synodical convention illness in the chest organs had noticeably sapped his strength, although he was still able at times to preach and participate energetically in the convention discussions. But his last hour was fast approaching. On September 15 of the previous year he fell asleep peacefully and blessedly in his Lord. On September 18, on the day of his silver wedding anniversary, his mortal remains were interred with a great number of members of city congregations and of the synod and town citizens participating. May the Lord grant those remains a peaceful sleep to the day of the great resurrection.[12]

Pioneer Pastors and Parishes

The 1867 synodical *Proceedings* contain a "Register of Congregations That Belong to the German Ev. Lutheran Synod of Wisconsin and Other States Together with an Indication of the Year They Were Admitted to the Synod."[13] That portion of the listing which covers the first twenty-eight congregations still in membership at that time and the first ten conventions is being reproduced to give the pioneer congregations some of the recognition they deserve. Rural congregations are located by town and county. Some congregations were admitted before they had chosen names for themselves or have changed their names since.

Convention	Congregation
1850	Milwaukee - Grace
1852	Racine - First German
	Granville - Salem (left 1858 - readmitted 1862)
1853	Greenfield - St. John
	Town Hermann (Dodge) - Grace
1854	Town Hermann - Immanuel
	Newtonburg - St. John
1856	Manitowoc - First German
	Town Wayne (Washington) - St. Paul
	Port Washington - Peace (left but readmitted 1864)
1857	Milwaukee - St. John
	Oak Creek - St. John
	Caledonia - Trinity
1858	Theresa - Immanuel
1859	Fond du Lac - St. Peter
	Maple Grove - St. John and James

1859   LaCrosse - Peace
Lomira - St. Paul
Caledonia - Immanuel
Columbus - Ev. Lutheran
Burr Oak - Ev. Lutheran
Kenosha - Peace
Town Addison (Washington) - St. Peter
Town Trenton (Washington) - Immanuel
West Bend - St. John
Burlington - St. John
Helenville - St. Peter
Town Lebanon (Dodge) - St. Matthew

The pioneer pastors, the first twenty-six of them to have been full-fledged and ordained synod members in the first decade, are also listed with their year of admittance, place of training, the time and reason of the termination of that membership, and their fields of labor:

Pastor	Training/ Background	Left	Reason	Parishes Served
1850				
J. Muehlhaeuser	Langenberg	1867	death	Milwaukee (Grace)
J. Weinmann	Langenberg	1858	death at sea	Oak Creek, Racine, Baltimore
Wm. Wrede	Langenberg	1855	return to Germany	Granville, Racine
1851				
C. Goldammer	Langenberg	1895	resigned	Newton, Manitowoc, Barington, Jefferson, Green Bay, Wheatland
C. Pluess	Basel (inc.)	1852	expelled	Sheboygan
1852				
C. Koester	Langenberg	1864	death	Oak Creek
1853				
W. Buehren	Methodist pastor by Wrede	1857	withdrew	New Berlin, Granville
J. Conrad		1890	death	Theresa, Racine, Theresa, Racine, Theresa
1854				
J. Bading	Hermannsburg Langenberg	1913	death	Calumet, Theresa, Watertown, Milwaukee (St. John)
D. Huber	Roman priest	1870	withdrew	Kenosha, New Berlin, Prospect Hill, New Berlin, Germany
G. Weitbrecht	Basel - Tuebingen	ca. 1855 to Michigan		Sheboygan, Port Washington

Pastor	Training/Background	Left	Reason	Parishes Served
1855				
Ph. Koehler	Langenberg	1895	death	Town Addison, Manitowoc, Hustisford
J. J. E. Sauer	Teacher	1887	released	Calumet, Slinger, Town Hermann, Theresa, Iron Ridge, Wheatland, Leeds, Bloomfield, Montello (Hammond, MN-died 1899)
1856				
G. Reim	Basel	1865	withdrew	Ashford, Helenville, Beaver Dam, (New Ulm)
Ch. Starck	Basel (inc.)	1870	released	Port Washington, Kenosha, Platteville, LaCrosse, Oshkosh
Wm. Streissguth	Basel	1915	death	Newton, Milwaukee - St. John, Fond du Lac, Minneapolis - St. John, Kenosha, retired 1886
1857				
C. Diehlmann	Basel	1859	released	Montello, MO
F. Hennicke	by Pastor Sumser	1860	released	Slinger, Niles, IL, Marshall, MI
Ph. Sprengling	Langenberg	1882	death	Newton, Town Mosel, Sheboygan, Beaver Dam, Center, Fort Atkinson
1858				
G. Fachtmann	University	1864	released	Richfield, Reisepredigt, Fond du Lac, LaCrosse, (St. Paul - Trinity, Reisepredigt, Henderson)
J. Roell	New Jersey pastor	1863	expelled	Port Washington, West Bend
1859				
C. Braun	Berlin	1868	death	Town Addison, Columbus, Reedsville, Two Rivers
H. Duborg	Norwegian	1860	released	Columbus, (Norwegian congregations)
Jul. Hoffman	Berlin Society	1868	expelled	Town Polk, Kenosha, Racine

THE WISCONSIN SYNOD LUTHERANS

Pastor	Training/ Background	Left	Reason	Parishes Served
A. Rueter	Ohio Synod	1860	expelled	Columbus, Maple Grove
Fr. Woldt	St. Chrischona	1887	resigned	Winchester-Menasha, Oshkosh, Eldorado, Neenah, Racine

In the "Parishes Served" column, it should be noted, the place mentioned is seldom the only place served by the pastor. Rather, it usually represents the pastor's residence from which he served any number of smaller congregations and preaching places. Today it is hard to imagine Columbus and Beaver Dam as part of one parish, but that situation was suggested as workable back in 1858.

The pioneer congregations were characterized by smallness and this made multiple parishes the rule, not the exception. Although there were large Milwaukee congregations that kept one pastor busy, the average Wisconsin Synod pastor toward the close of the first quarter century was serving 2.8 congregations or preaching places. All pastors were not just parish pastors but also evangelists and home missionaries.

In the first quarter century no foreign missionary was sent out. But a synod whose pastors in the main had been trained by societies interested in foreign missions could hardly be expected to be unconcerned about this item of top priority. As one might surmise, even though the synod was poor and small and overextended at home, it sought outlets for its mission zeal. The popular device was the joint mission festival.

One presentation serves as an example of numerous others that appear in the early *Gemeinde-Blatt* in the fall months. This one is to be found in the August 1, 1872 issue under the heading "Mission Festival" and is reproduced here, in translation of course. It was written by Pastor Ungrodt of Jefferson, an eleven-year veteran of Barmen Mission service in South Africa.

> On the seventh Sunday after Trinity the four Lutheran congregations at Farmington, Jefferson, Fort Atkinson, and Helenville celebrated their joint mission festival in a grove located near the last-named church. Pastor Schneider of the Missouri Synod at Concord with most of his congregation had also joined the festival in response to a friendly invitation. Already by 8:00 A.M. there appeared, coming from all directions, an almost unbroken procession of buggies, carriages, and wagons, enveloped in thick dust clouds and crowded with festival participants dripping sweat in the almost tropical heat, yearning for the inviting

shade of the festival grove and then seating themselves on the prepared benches.

At 9:30 the festival service began with the singing of "All Glory Be to God on High." After the liturgical service, led by the pastor of the host congregation, Pastor Schneider mounted the pulpit and read the glorious mission prophecy that the Lord proclaims in the first part of the Prophet Isaiah's chapter 60 and showed, following the passage point for point, how all men are by nature blind and dead in trespasses and sins; how God, however, has let the glory of his grace in Christ Jesus come over them, first the Jews and then the Gentiles, through the gospel; and how he intends further to glorify himself by gathering the Gentiles into his kingdom of grace until the end of the world and the last of the days.

The undersigned was to present the historical address. On the basis of Genesis 40:14, he — by referring to slavery, the humiliation and dishonor of the female sex, the social and religious customs of the African tribes in so far as they are known — sought to depict their deep misery, from which the cry for help reaches out to the hearts of Christians: "When all goes well with you, remember me and show me kindness." Then he pointed out how, just as the chief cupbearer had forgotten the imprisoned Joseph for a time but then, aware of his sin, sought to make good the neglect, so most Christians for a long time forgot the miserable, enslaved heathen and it is now time to acknowledge the sin, regret it in sincere repentance and by heartfelt intercession and faithful labor try to make up in some way for the neglect so that the imprisonment of the heathen can be ended.

Since time for the noon meal had come, a two-hour break occurred during which the present guests were refreshed bountifully with food and drink by the Helenville congregation and pastor. For this I herewith express friendly thanks in the name of all the guests.

Shortly after 2:00 P.M. the afternoon service began. After the singing of a mission hymn, Pastor Opitz preached on the Lord's command, "Go into all the world," recorded in Mark 16:15,16 . . . .

Finally, Pastor Brockmann showed in a down-to-earth and moving way on the basis of the Judges 7 story of Gideon's conflicts and conquests how mission work, both within one's own church and without among heathen nations, is just such a story of conflicts and conquests in which the Lord through paltry and unpretentious means and weapons accomplishes what is great and glorious. This was also applied to our synodical school at Watertown and they were recommended to the caring love of the festival gathering.

Between the festival sermons several edifying chorales were sung by the Jefferson choir that added their part in enhancing the festival joy.

This edifying mission festival closed with prayer, a brief final word by Pastor Gensicke, in which he in his own impressive way made the festival collection a special concern of the celebrants, and the the Lord's blessing. . . .

The collection at the festival service was about $90.00. This sum was raised to $115.00 by late offerings from members of the Helenville congregation who were not able to attend the festival.

The Lord be praised for everything!

B. Ungrodt

This chapter section, "Pioneer Pastors and Parishes," might well conclude by quoting verbatim a pioneer pastor's letter to his fiancee about a pioneer congregation and parsonage. The letter from Pastor J. Meyer to Meta Behnken in Germany tells it like it was in pioneer days.

Winchester, February 6, 1871

Jesus Christ, the same yesterday, today, and forever.

My Beloved Meta!

You perhaps are becoming impatient and dissatisfied about my long silence. If you are, I cannot blame you, for a whole month has passed since I wrote my last letter. But if it is truly bad of me that I made you wait so long, I must heartily beg your pardon. You no doubt have also experienced it that there always is so much to do when one arrives at a new place. The last letter I wrote at brother Haak's. I stayed there almost three weeks.

There I wrote to you that I would go to Neenah and brother Hagedorn to Winchester. But while we were at brother Haak's there were some changes so that the two of us made an exchange and now brother Hagedorn is going to Neenah and I here to Winchester. I am very happy that it turned out that way because I would much rather live in the country than in the city.

Winchester lies in the woods so that I rightly call myself a bush preacher. The houses here are fairly far apart, for here in the woods in America each one buys himself a place and builds his house on it so that he has his land close around his house. But you will make big eyes when you see the castle of an American Bauer (or farmer as he is called here). In some houses there is only one room; hall, kitchen, sitting room, and bedroom are all in one. Large trees are chopped down and laid on one another until the wall is high enough; then a small roof is placed on it and the house is finished. But when they have been here for a longer time and have earned more, then also beautiful houses are built.

My house is also such a log house, built of large blocks of wood; but there are nevertheless several rooms in it (but you should not picture it to yourself as a stately parsonage like in

Germany). When I go from the road through the door I step immediately into the living room. The door into the house and into the room are one and the same door. To the right in the room there is first of all a bedroom and then beyond that another little room which now is my study, and in which I am now sitting and writing these lines. It is very small, about ten to eleven feet long and seven to eight feet wide, but I am very comfortable in it. If you go straight through the large living room you get to the kitchen and to the right of the kitchen there is another small room. That is all the room downstairs. Then upstairs there is a small room and a room to store all kinds of things. There you see, that is our house; to be sure not large and beautiful, but I believe that we can [word missing?] if we only have something.

Besides the house I also have a barn in which there is a place also for a cow and horse and a woodshed [?]. Then I have a garden of six acres (an acre is a little more than a *Morgen* in Germany).

The church is close to the house, but it looks deplorable, just like a sheep barn over there, but I will soon get a better one, for next summer something new is to be built. Besides this congregation I have three others and may get a fourth on top of it, so that I will have five churches where I must preach.

Here it is just the opposite from Germany. While there in some congregations two to three pastors serve, here one pastor has several congregations. Now you must not imagine that a congregation in the woods is as large as the congregations in Germany are. For example, this congregation in Winchester has about thirteen or fourteen families. But that is also the smallest. The others I have are considerably larger. My predecessor here was Pastor Wiese, who also had studied in Hermannsburg at the mission house, and then went to Africa. There he worked for a number of years as missionary but about three years ago came to America.

Last spring toward Pentecost he died. Since then there has been no preacher here, but occasionally another pastor preached here. The wife of the deceased Pastor Wiese still lives in this house and also looks after all my needs so that I don't have to worry about anything but to carry out my ministry. Oh, the poor woman has gone through a hard year; the faithful Lord severely afflicted her. Her husband and two children the Lord took from her through the pox, and she herself had them so that she was near death. She still is far from being better, her face still looks terrible; it can take till summer before everything is properly healed. Nevertheless, she is very cheerful and patient in her severe suffering, so that I often marveled at it. For it certainly isn't easy to lose husband and children and then many months to lie alone without any human help or encouragement because everyone is afraid of being infected. She still has one child, a boy of four, and a servant girl who has to do the work. I also believe she will stay here until you come, which I am glad about. If she would not be here I wouldn't know what to do. I would have to board with other people and it would be much more inconvenient for me.

I do not have time to keep house as a bachelor. Therefore, I beg you, hurry as much as possible to come here. But I would like to ask one more thing: how is your sewing skill? When you are here, you will have to make everything yourself, your clothes and also my pants and vests [?] for those things are too expensive here. If one wants to have pants or vest [?] made, it costs about two dollars for labor and that much a bush pastor does not earn here. So learn as much as possible about sewing.

You don't have to bring too many things along, only a featherbed, for it is very cold here in winter, still colder than in Germany, and feathers are expensive here, but don't bring along cotton things. Cotton goods are as cheap here as over there. But it is different with silk and things of that kind; that is much more expensive here. Then Mrs. Pastor Wiese said I should write to you to bring along good knives. Here you don't get any knives that are sharp.

How large my salary here will be I don't know as yet, but I believe it will be enough that we can get along well. I think when you come I will already have a horse and wagon. At present the people still come and get me. Every Sunday I have to preach twice. In the morning [I am] at one church and when it is over I quickly eat and go up to five miles to other congregations. There I have to preach in the afternoon. The most distant congregation is ten to eleven miles from here. If I should also get the fifth congregation, that one is supposed to be fifteen miles from here, three to four German miles. So you see here in America one has to travel about and besides has to be everything, pastor, schoolteacher, and janitor. That is why you must excuse me if it takes longer for me to get at writing.

Today I started confirmation instructions, which I expect to have the first three days of each week. The children here are so very stupid, so that they don't know anything at all. Many can't even read properly as yet. On the twentieth of January I arrived here and on Sunday, January 22, I preached my trial sermon here and in St. Peter's congregation, and on the next Sunday in Zion and St. John's congregations. Last Sunday, February 5, I was installed here by Pastor Spehr. Brother Hagedorn was installed, I believe, a Sunday earlier. We are eighteen English miles apart.

Now, dear Meta, I must close. Only hurry to come here. I think you will like it here. Our garden is also waiting for you.

You will not have to be afraid that there will be a lack of work. So far everything is still going well with me and I hope the same is true of you.

Farewell until we meet again. Greet all those who ask about me. Soon I hope to get a letter from you.

With warm greetings I remain your ever loving, J. Meyer

My address is: Rev. J. Meyer, Winchester, Winnebago Co., Wisconsin, North-America

Meta assented to the request that she "hurry as much as possible to come here." On February 27, 1873, there was born in that humble parsonage Johannes Meyer, who became a prominent leader in the Wisconsin Synod and was still teaching at Wisconsin Lutheran Seminary in 1964. But that is another story in another century.

CHAPTER EIGHT

Fifteen Good Years: 1876-1891

From the silver jubilee to the forming of the federation with Minnesota and Michigan in 1892 the Wisconsin Synod enjoyed an era of relative peace and progress, so far as internal affairs were concerned. On the interchurch scene, as has been related, there were controversies over state synods and election but these did not severely hamper the synod's growth. In fact, those intersynodical conflicts in the late 1870s and early 1880s helped unite more firmly a synod that had passed through its own identity crisis just a few years before.

The Wisconsin Synod could begin the second quarter of its history with its mind made up about its theological stance. It had committed itself to the confessional position of the Synodical Conference that in doctrine and practice sought to espouse all the Lutheran Confessions. Opponents liked and still like to call this position "the extreme right." Wisconsin and the other synods of the Synodical Conference had no quarrel with the last part of the designation. They could even tolerate being called "*extreme*," if that was understood as meaning concern about all of the Word and every doctrine of the Confessions.

Sure of itself in its doctrinal position, the Wisconsin Synod could reach out all the more vigorously in seeking souls and gathering members. The fifteen years 1876-1891 were years of *good growth*.

Good Growth

Numbers tell the story. The 64 pastors in 1875 had by 1891 become 150; a good share of them were the synod's own sons. They graduated from the seminary, which had returned to Milwaukee from St. Louis in 1878. The number of congregations served by these pastors had increased from 119 to 252. In 1875 there were 28,345 guests at the Lord's Supper; in 1891 that number had grown to 74,754. The continuing immigration into the country and the state certainly was a major factor in producing these growth figures, but the outreach in evangelism and home missions was definitely another.

Another kind of outreach began to demonstrate itself in the very first of the "fifteen good years." Meeting in 1876 just a week before Custer and Crazy Horse met at the Little Big Horn, the Wisconsin Synod embarked on its first foreign mission venture. The effort died aborning within a year and has been all but forgotten in the meantime, but it is an important "first" in this history and merits attention.

In his 1876 presidential report to the Watertown convention Bading drew the synod's attention to a Pastor Dreves, a former mission inspector and theological teacher at Hermannsburg, who had volunteered his services as a *Reiseprediger* and Indian missionary.[1] Bading, not willing to let a mission opportunity be wasted, had even invited to the meeting as an expert witness Pastor Matter of Des Moines, a four-year veteran of Indian missions for the Iowa Synod.

Pastor Matter, pointing to the continuing Sioux Wars and to many other problems that had caused the Iowa Synod to close down its Indian mission, painted a most discouraging picture. It seemed to say, almost as if he had prophetic foreknowledge of what would happen to Custer and his men within days, "This is the worst of times to begin an Indian mission."

The delegates, however, were not dismayed. Arguing that many of the problems had been created, not by those of red color, but by those of white and confessing that it was high time to make a beginning of doing their part, the convention delegates voted an Indian mission venture on the spot, not subject to any later funding delay or veto.[2]

What was resolved was a *Reisepredigt* combined with a sort of railroading Indian mission along the tracks of the recently built Union Pacific. Contemporaries often fault their Wisconsin fathers for being shortsighted in outreach efforts. They should ponder this mission thrust in "the worst of times," utilizing a very up-to-date transportation achievement of the day. The fathers were both innovative and daring in their first foreign mission effort in 1876.

Unfortunately, President Bading had to report to the very next convention that the project had floundered so badly that it ought to be officially terminated.³ Pastor Dreves had followed the Union Pacific all the way to California, bypassing the restive Indians on the way and concentrating on immigrant German Lutherans. It would be some seventy-five years before Wisconsin could become interested in a California home mission venture. Back in 1877 it simply wrote off the well-intentioned Indian mission effort as a human failure. As far as Pastor Dreves and his California mission are concerned, the next year's Synodical Conference convention rebuffed his appeal for support on the grounds that the Conference concerned itself exclusively about foreign missions and left home missions in the domain of the member synods.⁴

While it was embracing the Synodical Conference mission to the Blacks, begun in 1877, the Wisconsin Synod's mission conscience would not let it forget the Red heathen of the country. Six years later the convention celebrated the four-hundredth birthyear of Martin Luther by reviving interest in Indian missions through the establishment of a permanent committee that was to seek out a mission society that was both orthodox and zealous in its outreach and to channel the synodical foreign mission offerings into its coffers.⁵ Those with even a nodding acquaintance of synodical personnel will realize that this was serious business, with such men as Ph. Brenner, J. Brockmann, W. Dammann, Ch. Dowidat, and Koehler, sen., being appointed to the committee.⁶

However prestigious the committee, it could not perform miracles. A year later it had to report it could not carry out its assignment, because no such mission society could be found.⁷ At its suggestion, however, the church body resolved to begin to train suitable young men for foreign mission work, especially among Indians, utilizing mission offerings for this purpose. The final committee suggestion and convention resolution merits quotation in full: "The committee has the firm trust in God that he will graciously accept this our puny effort and will in the future show us ways and supply us means whereby we can help further his cause." The committee's and the synod's trust was not misplaced, neither in the long-range nor the short-range view.

Way back then the beginning was made by enlisting for such mission training at Northwestern J. Plocher and G. Adascheck from the Old World and P. Mayerhoff, a junior at the school. A century later the fruits of this first foreign mission venture are marvelous to contemplate. The immediate development of that 1884 resolution will be described in the next chapter, since it involves the efforts of the federated Wisconsin Synod, organized in 1892.

What may have been the most significant outreach effort in the "good years" was a minor matter on the 1891 convention agenda.

It resulted in permission that funds be gathered in synod circles for a St. Paul, Minnesota, English mission.[8] Possible causes of this somewhat surprising development can be listed: an aftermath of the Bennett Law conflict to be described subsequently, the synodical presidency in the hands of a man residing in Winona who could preach in English, or simply a dawning of the idea that English was the outreach language of the future. Whatever the case and whatever the causes, English was beginning to figure in synodical thinking, if not as yet in its actual planning.

Meanwhile there were also "good years" for the Wisconsin Synod in its educational endeavors.

Educational Endeavors

In this category there are numerous positive items to record from 1876 to 1891 on the various educational levels from day school to seminary and in various areas from Wisconsin to Minnesota and Michigan. The single most important development, nearly all would agree, was the retransfer of theological seminary training from St. Louis to Wisconsin. The reasons have already been described in the Synodical Conference chapter's section on the state synod, joint seminary strife. What remains to be supplied are the details involved in the move.

When the 1877 synodical convention turned thumbs down on the joint seminary plan and opted instead for a seminary of its own, it determined that a pastoral conference in August of that year should thresh out details, guided by the congregational opinions that should in the meantime be ascertained.[9] The Oshkosh pastoral conference recommended that in the fall of 1878 a synodical seminary be relocated from St. Louis to Milwaukee. The following regular synodical convention endorsed the decision and specified two seminary teachers, A. Hoenecke and E. Notz, and a location in rented quarters in Milwaukee.[10]

For financial reasons it was deemed necessary to cut the Watertown staff by one to help enable the calling of two new synodical teachers to the seminary. Actually, the Lord of the church impelled the placement of three men at that seminary. During the calling process Adolph Hoenecke became so ill that it was deemed necessary to extend a call also to Professor A. Graebner of Northwestern. A blessed recovery made possible the installation of Professors A. Hoenecke, E. Notz, and A. Graebner at the beginning of the 1878-1879 seminary school year. Six students were enrolled in that year, three St. Louis transfers and three recruits. One wonders if any seminary ever enjoyed for a whole school year such a favorable 2-1 student-teacher relationship. In this respect the Milwaukee seminary got off to a most favorable start.

The seminary's low enrollment of only six in its first Milwaukee year should not be thought of as the start of a pattern. The speedy pace of the novel development, coupled with an understandable reluctance of St. Louis seminary students to transfer from the known to the unknown and the greater to the lesser with no doctrinal issues at stake, predetermined a low beginning enrollment. Before the next school year, however, the seminary board was already pointing to the need for quarters that were owned instead of rented and large instead of cramped.

The result was the purchase of Eimermann's Park, at a Thirteenth and Vine location, with buildings that could be converted to school purposes. This was the seminary's Milwaukee location until the move to the Wauwatosa site at 60th and Lloyd in 1893. During the fifteen years, 1876-1891, over one hundred of the seminary's students were graduated for pastoral service in the Wisconsin Synod.

There was only one change in the faculty during those years. The move of Professor Graebner to the St. Louis Concordia Seminary in 1887 necessitated the calling of G. Thiele, an old Halle University schoolmate of both early seminary presidents, E. Moldehnke and A. Hoenecke.

One other adjustment needs to be mentioned. The strain of doing double duty as seminary professor-president and pastor of the large St. Matthew congregation forced Hoenecke to submit to the seminary board a resignation from the former post. The board reacted by calling the Wisconsin Synod's ablest theologian to full-time service in theological teaching and administration. The loss to St. Matthew was a gain for the Wisconsin Synod and remained so for another eighteen years until 1908, the year of Hoenecke's death.

In the last of the fifteen good years, 1891, the synodical convention set up a seminary building committee. The facility at Thirteenth and Vine needed extensive repair and remodeling, and it was deemed prudent to erect a new building.

Two sites were available as donations: the as yet undeveloped Downer College part of the University of Wisconsin - Milwaukee campus, offered by the leather manufacturers, Pfister and Vogel, and some three acres of the Pabst farm in Wauwatosa, offered by the owner with the stipulations that a $30,000 building be erected and a division of the proceeds between the Pabst estate and the synod occur, should there be a sale and a conversion to non-educational use. The latter site was chosen by majority vote in a congregational referendum held before the next convention. That is how a Wauwatosa Seminary came into being that would through J. P. Koehler, A. Pieper, and J. Schaller foster the "Wauwatosa Theology."

For the Wisconsin Synod's other training school, Northwestern at Watertown, the years 1876-1891 were also good. Progress was made under President Ernst's leadership in the attempt to provide preparatory and college training for those who would become synod's pastors. The *university* designation was still in use but was being recognized more and more as a misnomer. Efforts were made to bring into the faculty men who would dedicate themselves to the endeavor to achieve the school's aim.

This made for some sifting and considerable coming and going. On the small staff of some eight men from 1876-1891 there were fifteen who came and ten who left during these years. These constant changes contrast with the stability the seminary experienced in those years.

There is another and brighter side of the picture. Of the fifteen who came, six came to stay. Among them were men who would shape the history of the college and the synod. Doctor Notz came in 1872 and taught until 1911. For fifteen long years he served as dormitory dean and in the process supplied material for the best legends in the unwritten synodical history.[11] The man who supplied us with the written history, J. P. Koehler, began his synodical teaching career at Watertown in 1888 with the special responsibility of dormitory supervisor that Doctor Notz relinquished in 1887. In 1900 Koehler accepted a call to the Wauwatosa seminary.

In 1885 J. Henry Ott was graduated by Northwestern in what a classmate, G. E. Bergemann, liked to refer to as the "model class." He was immediately called by his alma mater, interrupted his teaching in the early 1890s for doctoral studies in Europe, and then taught English and served as librarian until 1939. One who knew him well says of him, "Of no one who ever served on the Northwestern's faculty can it be said more truthfully that he gave of himself completely and ungrudgingly to the school that had called him into its service."[12] A classmate of Doctor Ott, William Weimar, also began to teach at Northwestern upon graduation and continued for eighteen years to 1903.

The Watertown enrollment had jumped as a result of the Wisconsin-Missouri school agreement of 1869, more than doubling from the 64 students in the spring of 1870 to 132 that fall. President William Sihler of Missouri's Fort Wayne school was in fact concerned that too much Missouri support was bypassing Fort Wayne and ending up at Watertown.[13] The matter is mentioned to underscore Missouri's sincerity and effort in its relations with Wisconsin. It waited patiently while unsuccessful efforts were being made to send Hoenecke to St. Louis as the promised Wisconsin exchange professor, at a time when Professor Stellhorn was its man at Watertown. It allowed William Notz, called as potential exchange professor, to go to Watertown and serve the greater needs there.

When a belated effort to move Professor Brohm from Watertown to Springfield did not succeed, the school agreement was terminated in 1874 by mutual consent. Professor Stellhorn and numerous Missouri students left Watertown for work at Fort Wayne. How one can think of a separate Wisconsin theological seminary in St. Louis from 1874 to 1878 is difficult in the extreme. The effort, however, must be made, for those years are officially included when seminary years are counted. In 1988 a pipe organ dedication highlighted an anniversary of a century and a quarter of teaching at a school begun in 1863. Even the hard facts of history must sometimes bend and even break to the force of established traditions.

The Missouri exodus from Watertown after 1874 caused a temporary decline in enrollment but by 1891 the loss had been offset by gains. The 1874-75 total enrollment was 180 while that of 1890-91 was 185. More importantly, the actual college enrollments for those years were 22 and 48, an increase that is in line with synodical growth during the 1876-1891 years. In spite of some downs and ups these were also good years for the synod's Watertown school.

A reminder, highlighting some startling similarities, is in place here about synodical schools in the Minnesota and Michigan Synods. The reminder harks back to the content of an earlier chapter, "Good Neighbors." The similarities involve time of establishment and site selection.

In 1884 the Minnesota Synod dedicated its all-purpose worker-training school at New Ulm. A year later the Michigan Synod began a similar school at Manchester, MI, and moved it to Saginaw two years later.

There were irregularities in the determination of both present day locations. The birth of the New Ulm school was premature, defying synodical regulations that might well have placed Doctor Martin Luther College in Shakopee. After the two-year temporary establishment at Manchester, Michigan Lutheran Seminary was slated to move to Adrian. A specially called synodical convention scrubbed Adrian and substituted Saginaw as the eventual site.

In both instances energetic synodical presidents had their way and sway, putting up the schools in their own place of residence. President Albrecht in Minnesota simply confronted his synod with an established fact, a school under construction on the New Ulm bluffs. President Eberhardt in Michigan himself set up the special convention that accepted his generous and personal offer of a Saginaw site at Court-Bay-Hardin streets.

The point is not to fault the presidents for such irregularities. The writer himself has lived and labored at both Saginaw and New Ulm amid the best of neighbors and at flourishing schools. The point is simply to set down the historical record.

"Educational enterprise" dare not ignore such efforts in local congregations on the grade-school, pre-confirmation level. The 1876 *Proceedings* lists 82 schools for the 138 congregations. By 1891 the congregations had not quite doubled to 253 but the schools had increased more than that to 179. The original 1850 intent that all pastors should exert themselves in the matter of training the young was not forgotten. There were "good years" also for Christian day schools in the 1876-1891 years.

Ample evidence attests to the fact. Already in 1872 a synodical teachers' conference was established and in 1876 a *Schulzeitung* [School Gazette], forerunner of today's *Lutheran Educator,* began to appear. In school statistics of those days, however, it must be remembered that almost any kind of congregational education endeavor, be it a short winter or summer program or a Saturday morning schedule or something else, had a way of falling into the rubric of "Congregational School." This presents a problem for today's researcher and also presented one for yesterday's state school authorities. Way back then the question developed: Are all church schools really filling the bill in training tomorrow's citizens, especially when all that training goes on in a language that is not the language of the land?

We are getting into one of the most interesting episodes in the history of the Wisconsin Synod's educational efforts, the fight about Wisconsin's Bennett Law that raged just before and after 1890. In his 1889 gubernatorial message to the state legislature William Dempster Hoard had stated as his second aim, behind only the first that declared war on oleomargarine, that it should be made the "duty of county and city superintendents of schools to inspect all schools for the purpose and with the authority only to require that reading and writing in English be daily taught therein."[14] The legislation that eventually developed was the Bennett Law, passed on April 16, 1889, under the sponsorship of Michael Bennett, a combination farmer-schoolteacher in Iowa County, who was a Catholic in good standing. His legislation called for school attendance of at least twelve weeks, outlawed child labor under thirteen, defined truancy and, most important of all, declared in a brief Section Five, "No school shall be regarded as a school, under this act, unless there shall be taught therein, as part of the elementary education of children, reading, writing, arithmetic, and United States history in the English language."

No matter how feeble the twelve-week term requirement or how innocuous the English stipulation may seem to us today, the Bennett Law of 1889 generated the first real political battle the Wisconsin Synod felt called upon to wage. In some of its church schools there could have been problems about the length of the school year and, in many more, about the teaching of basic subjects, including English, in the English language. The fathers mounted a full-scale legislative battle with allies found in the Roman camp.

The opponents were not all anti-German atheists. Their leader, Governor Hoard, should be allowed a chance to make a point or two. He wrote in his autobiography, describing a meeting in his Madison office:

> I was waited upon by five of the leading Lutheran clergymen of this state who urged me to turn my back on the Bennett Law, to refuse to execute it, and [they] accompanied their request with a very thinly veiled threat that unless I did so, I would be defeated by the united action of the Catholics and Lutherans who had entered into a compact, under the leadership of Archbishop Katzer to fight the Republican Party and to demand and service the repeal of the law.
>
> I looked at these clergymen somewhat with astonishment and then said to them, "Do I understand you gentlemen to be ministers of the Gospel of Jesus Christ?"
>
> "Most certainly," they said. "Why do you ask that question?"
>
> I further said, "Do I understand that you believe in the Bible and the sanctity of an oath taken upon that Bible?"
>
> "Most assuredly," they answered me. "We cannot understand why you ask such questions."
>
> "Well," I replied, "I had begun to have most serious misgivings. I took my oath upon your Bible that as governor of this state, I would maintain and support the constitution of the State of Wisconsin and of the United States, and all laws made in pursuance thereof, so help me God, and you come here, professing to be ministers of the Gospel of Jesus Christ and believers in the Bible and the sanctity of the oath, and urge your governor to commit perjury, to rightly make himself subject to impeachment.
>
> "Do you see, gentlemen, where your ecclesiasticism has taken you? . . . As you intimate, you may very likely defeat the Republican Party and myself, but that's a small matter, particularly so

far as I am concerned. But I wish to warn you here and now, as representatives of a great denomination, that if you take your church into the political arena and make of it a football to be kicked from one side of that arena to the other by contending politicians, you will rue the day you did it.

"Further, if you plant your church across the pathway of human enlightenment, thus preventing the young people of your denomination from receiving as good and thorough an American education as other more favored children, you will lose the respect of the young men of your church when the selfishness of that action has become apparent to them, and in my opinion, you will be heard in less than five years, saying in your synods, 'Men and brethren, what shall we do to keep our young men in the church?' "[15]

Some of Governor Hoard's surmises did prove true. He and his party were soundly defeated in the 1890 state elections. Democrats captured fifteen of seventeen contested state senate seats. In the other chamber Democrats changed a 71-29 minority into a majority of 66-33. While all this in part reflected results in the national elections, in which the Republicans lost the House of Representatives, there is general agreement that in Wisconsin the key election issue was the Bennett Law and that church opposition from both Catholics and Lutherans contributed heavily to the Republican defeat and the quick repeal of the Bennett Law.

The Wisconsin Synod involvement, which was considerable, began with President Bading's presidential address to the 1889 Milwaukee convention, meeting just two months after the Bennett Law was passed.[16] The theme of the address was religious freedom and separation of church and state, with Pilgrims, Salzburgers, and Russians providing specific instances. Two great dangers, Bading insisted, threaten the Christian's freedom. "One is the growing power of the Pope's church. . . . The other dangerous and threatening power is making itself felt in the legislative bodies of this land. These have, especially in these times, taken schools under their wings, but they have done it in a way to press all life and breath out of parochial schools, if they succeed in entwining their purposes and thoughts around our necks in the form of laws."

The convention reaction was vigorous. A pre-convention committee had prepared an extensive analysis of the bill, bearing down especially on the admittedly ill-conceived requirement that parents must send their children to a school in the city, town, or district of their residence. In all there were twelve points in the committee's bill of particulars against the Bennett Law. A second section of the report dealt with what was now to be done. Several important principles were set forth: "We are not enemies of public schools, rather regard and declare them to be necessary institutions" . . . . "We oppose any granting of public school funds to private schools." After declaring the Bennett Law "tyrannical and unjust," the report demanded "repeal or amendment of the law" and declared, "We are determined to give expression to our desires according to circumstances in judicial actions or at the ballot box."

The convention set up a committee to examine English textbooks and another to coordinate school curricula and statistics, useful services if the Bennett Law would be enforced. The main concern, however, was to prevent such an outcome, and to this end the convention established a standing committee, consisting of Professors Ernst and W. Notz, Pastors Aug. Pieper and Chrs. Sauer, Teacher H. Graebner and Attorney Chrs. Koerner. This committee was to inform itself about school legislation in Wisconsin and other states where similar battles were being waged and was especially to head the effort to overthrow the Bennett Law by "educating the public through the public press." President Ernst was especially active in the campaign. George Brumder's *Germania* and the *Milwaukee Journal* provided such "public press" space.

By the end of the year the Wisconsin and Missouri school committees joined forces with counterparts in other denominations. This meant, in the main, some cooperation with the Roman Catholic forces headed by Archbishop Katzer. The first great danger in Bading's presidential address was being looked to as an ally in the fight against the other threat.

The 1890 Watertown convention in the doctrinal sessions discussed the first four of six theses on parochial schools Reinhold Pieper had developed. Thesis One, as an example, read: "Christian parochial schools are such educational institutions in which children are instructed in the pure doctrine of God's Word, in which temporal subjects are taught in the spirit of Holy Scripture and in which the Word of God serves as the tool for training."[17] In other sessions it heard reports from two of its three school committees.[18] The curriculum and statistics committee reported that it had ready a school plan for one-room schools but not much else.

The standing committee reported on its activities at length. There was the good news that local school board elections were going well and that no parochial schools had as yet suffered any great harm. There was encouragement to press on in the all-important fall statewide elections. Press on the anti-Bennett Law forces did. This ballot victory has already been described. By the time of the 1891 convention the objectionable legislation had been wiped off the books.

What about Governor Hoard's other predictions voiced to the Lutheran clergy delegation that called on him to urge non-enforcement? Was there a wholesale loss of the church's youth after some five years? There are no statistics to bear this out. By the same token, no statistics report how many of the youth were lost because of the insistence on German in church and school until World War I days and even after.

Did the Bennett Law opposition turn the synod into some sort of social action football to be kicked hither and yon by special interest groups? Today few Lutheran or other denominations surpass the Wisconsin Synod in a commitment to preach the gospel and not the social gospel. The synod has, however, been extremely sensitive about church-state educational issues since 1890. Many will recall the anguish and conflict about accepting government gifts of milk and hot lunches in the Depression and of bus transportation somewhat later.

The sensitivity could even have the effect of overreach beyond the wall of separation. As late as 1963 the synodical convention accepted as its own a statement of the Conference of Presidents on "Federal Aid to Church-Related Schools" that flatly declared that "such assistance also violates the constitutional principle of Church and State, using tax monies gathered from all citizens for the promulgation of a specific religion or faith."[19] Church bodies should be very concerned about their schools and their youth, but they also do well to refrain from judicial decision-making in matters that give even the United States Supreme Court pause and then often result in five-four decisions.

In the Area of Administration

The synodical administration may well have become too political in the Bennett Law battles, as Professor Koehler surmises in his discussion of the issue.[20] Yet by and large there was a wholesome reluctance to rush to off-the-cuff verdicts in burning social issues of the day. Bading, for example, closed his 1887 report to the synod with the reminder that the previous convention had neglected to determine a doctrinal topic for the 1887 gathering.[21] The president then reported that for a time he toyed with the idea of making the topic what he called "the raging malady of the times, the all-encompassing creation of labor unions." This was, of course, the aftermath of the Haymarket Riot in nearby Chicago and the temporary hiding-out of Edward Parsons on the Hoan farm on the outskirts of Waukesha.

Bading then declared that after discussion with numerous fellow pastors it was decided to divert this issue to pastoral conferences. The synod convention was assigned the much less here-and-now topic of "The End Time," with Professor Hoenecke as essayist.

Mention of pastoral conferences calls to mind the administrative decision in 1890 to create a "Milwaukee Conference" in line with the facts of synodical growth in its original outpost.[22] The growth continued until eventually Metro-North and Metro-South Conferences were created. Even at that both are by now much too large to provide opportunity for the pastoral study that ought to be the main business of pastoral conferences.

The last synodical convention in the period under discussion made the important decision to put the synod in the publishing business. There had previously been a synodical book-selling operation that had, in 1891, provided from the profits $1200 for the synodical treasury. George Brumder was still doing most of the publishing and still returning to the synod five cents for every hymnal, large or small, that was sold. After much debate and divided opinion the 1891 convention allowed the establishment of a synodical publishing company.[23] The result was the founding of the Northwestern Publishing House on October 8, 1891. In the next two decades it would issue the dogmatical and homiletical writings of Adolph Hoenecke and then the volumes produced by the Wauwatosa theologians, J. P. Koehler, August Pieper, and John Schaller.

While these rich blessings to the church were still in the offing stage, a momentous development in synodical administration took place. In 1889 President Bading was replaced by President Ph. v. Rohr. Did this change make 1889 a good or a bad year in synodical history?

It was a "good" year for Milwaukee's St. John congregation. Without presidential responsibilities Bading could concentrate on the chore that he presented as the main reason for refusing re-election in 1889, the erection of a new St. John church building. The building still stands and should somehow be preserved, even though membership has dwindled below the century mark and the congregation has ceased celebrating baptisms. The building represents all that was best about the second-generation churches built in Wisconsin Synod circles.

It was a "good" year for Bading himself. Reaching the age when there should be some conserving of energies and when retirement is often mandatory today, he bowed out of synodical presidential chores. He was still able to serve on the influential Watertown-Wauwatosa board that called into synodical teaching service any number of key men. He could still serve St. John as pastor until 1908 and then for another five years in limited service. As late as 1912 he was still president of the Synodical Conference, then the largest federation of Lutherans in the land.

When Bading died in 1913, he was a synod veteran of sixty years. When he arrived in Wisconsin in 1853 there were seven pastors in the Wisconsin Synod. When he died there were 298. His history is the early history of the synod. His theological stance is also that of the synod.

Let Bading himself supply an evaluation of his presidency. Declining re-election in 1889, he declared, "My efforts during my long tenure in office, as is well known, were extended in one direction to ward off all so-called union endeavors against the ecclesiastical independence of our synod." The reference is obviously to the state synod battle that raged ten years earlier and in which Bading ably counteracted the efforts of Doctor Walther and others. In that final address to the 1889 convention Bading then continued, "In the other direction, however, [I endeavored] also to foster and maintain fellowship with those who are one with us in doctrine and faith."[24]

Not a bad resumé for a tenure in the synodical presidency that was as long as any since! The twin goals of a century ago still loom large: synodical independence and integrity and the ongoing search for those united in the faith. In the years ahead there may well be occasions for looking back to the lessons of the Bading synodical presidency, 1860-1864 (1863) and 1867-1889. There is no more influential presidential service on the record.

Does this signify a large let-down in administration when Philipp von Rohr assumed the post?[25] Not necessarily. The fact that a graduate of the seminary of the Buffalo Synod, a Wisconsin Synod member of only a dozen years, should be elected to replace Bading in the synodical presidency and then be re-elected another score of years until death speaks eloquently of the abilities of Philipp von Rohr and the esteem in which he was held by the brethren.

In the course of the 1866 split in the Buffalo Synod, during which only a few pastors remained with President Grabau and eleven joined Missouri, another small group headed by the von Rohrs remained independent. After the father, Captain Heinrich, died in 1874, the son Philipp dissolved the body. In 1877 he and his large Winona parish joined the Wisconsin Synod.

His death came after a 1906 trip to Europe to seek medical help for a continuing health problem. The diagnosis was cancer and the warning was issued that there was little time left. Later that year, however, an emergency operation was performed by Rochester's Will Mayo on the dining room table in the Winona parsonage. Philipp von Rohr was granted an additional two years and more to serve as St. Martin's pastor and Wisconsin Synod president.

The two assignments are placed in that order deliberately. President von Rohr was above all a pastor. As synod president he functioned more as a pastor of pastors than as an executive and administrator. With his great ability he could, of course, do what had to be done in synodical administration and do it very capably, but the work he loved was the pastor's work.

During his presidential years from 1889 to 1908 there is one development that stands out above all others, the forming of the federation of Wisconsin and Minnesota and Michigan in 1892. That is the concern of the next chapter.

CHAPTER NINE

The Federation Years: 1892-1917

At the very outset the reader should be cautioned, in the manner of the old Lutheran dogmaticians, that "a distinction must be made." The terminology can be confusing. When the Wisconsin, Michigan, and Minnesota Synods federated in 1892, they named their creation the *Allgemeine Evangelisch-lutherische Synode von Wisconsin, Minnesota, Michigan und andern Staaten*, often shorthanded to *Allgemeine Wisconsin Synode* or, what is worse, *Wisconsin Synode*.

All through the federation years the Wisconsin Synod had its own existence, as did Minnesota, Michigan and, after 1904, the federation's "other state," Nebraska. When the federation became a merged synod with districts in 1917, the first name used was the *Allgemeine Synode von Wisconsin, Minnesota, Michigan und andern Staaten.* This compounds the problem of designation.

In this writing an attempt will be made to keep confusion to a minimum by referring to the grouping of Wisconsin and its neighbors before 1917 as the "Federation" or the "Federated Wisconsin Synod" and speaking of its replacement as the "Merger" or "Merged Wisconsin Synod." After 1917 the problem begins to solve itself because the old Wisconsin Synod by then has become three districts in the new Wisconsin Synod with their own separate names.

Another aid to clarity during the federation years might be a listing of the presidents of both the federation and its members.

Federation	Wisconsin	Minnesota
A. Ernst, 1892-1900	von Rohr 1889-1908	C. J. Albrecht, 1883-1894
C. Gausewitz, 1900-1907	G. Bergemann, 1908-1933	C. Gausewitz, 1894-1906
H. Soll, 1907-1913		A. Schroedel, 1906-1909
C. Gausewitz, 1913-1917		A. Zich, 1909-1910
		E. Pankow, 1910-1912
		J. Naumann, 1912-1917

Michigan	Michigan District	Nebraska
(not in membership 1896-1910)	*(after 1895)*	*(after 1904)*
C. A. Lederer, 1890-1894	J. Klingmann, 1895-1901	T. Braeuer, 1904-1919
C. Boehner, 1894-1898	C. A. Lederer, 1901-1910	
W. Bodamer, 1898-1904	F. Krauss, 1918-1926	
J. Westendorf, 1904-1905		
F. Krauss, 1905-1917		

Organizing the Federation

The Wisconsin Synod which gave its name to the federation and was in size its big brother, strangely enough, had little to do with the original impetus to federate. This was basically a Michigan-Minnesota thrust.

The story begins with a mission exploration of a Michigan team of President Lederer and Seminary Director Huber in Minnesota in the summer of 1891. Lederer took the opportunity to call on an old St. Chrischona classmate, C. J. Albrecht, New Ulm pastor and Minnesota Synod head. Minnesota was enjoying good results from its working relationship with Wisconsin during the previous decade. Michigan had finally terminated its restive General Council membership in 1888 and was understandably lonely. How natural that the two old friends would develop plans for an association that would involve Wisconsin, Minnesota's partner, and the neighbor of both.[1]

Events moved forward rapidly, perhaps too rapidly.[2] That August a preliminary planning meeting was held in Watertown, attended by a Michigan delegation of President Lederer, Pastors Mayer and P. Kionka, and Director Huber of the Saginaw seminary, by Minnesota's President Albrecht and by President Ernst of Northwestern, representing Wisconsin's President von Rohr. The latter, no doubt estimating that the key factor in the development of a federation was the articulation of the worker-training schools, wanted his brother-in-law, President Ernst, to be involved in the planning from the very outset.

The preliminary planning done at Watertown was then presented to fall pastoral conferences of the three synods. All three meetings expressed general approval. The next spring synodical representatives put the proposals into final form for presentation to the 1892 conventions. These conventions adopted them and empowered the presidents to set the date for a constituent convention. That meeting was held October 11-13 at Milwaukee's St. John Church, where the Synodical Conference had been called into being twenty years before. That, however, had been old St. John Church. On July 13, 1890, the new building was dedicated at the new site.

At the opening service Professor O. Hoyer preached on, "So whether you eat or drink or whatever you do, do it all for the glory of God."[3] His first and third sermon sections treated the positive points of Christian freedom and doing all to God's glory. In between the preacher stressed that what was being done at the constituent convention of the federation of Wisconsin, Minnesota, and Michigan could in no way be an offense to anyone, neither inside the circle of those joining together nor in the larger circle of their brethren in the Synodical Conference. Unfortunately it did not work out that way. More on that later.

Another significant service was held on the convention's closing day, October 13, 1892. This was the cornerstone laying for the new Wisconsin seminary in Wauwatosa.[4] President Philipp von Rohr preached on Isaiah 41:27: "I was the first to tell Zion, 'Look, here they are!' I gave to Jerusalem a messenger of good tidings" and encouraged those worshiping to joyful thanksgiving, hallowed resolve, and believing petition. The cornerstone laying came in the nick of time. Wisconsin's earlier resolve to build and relocate made possible the use of the seminary at Wauwatosa as the top worker-training school of all three synods.

At the federation's constituent convention there was strong representation. The roll call revealed this attendance:

	Pastors	**Teachers**	**Lay Delegates**
Wisconsin	112	22	43
Minnesota	18	1	4
Michigan	22	1	6

For future conventions to be held every two years an attendance of 120 voting delegates was resolved. Half were to be lay delegates. Wisconsin was allotted half of the 120, Minnesota a third, and Michigan a sixth. Minnesota delegates made an effort at the next convention to get equal synodical representation but cheerfully yielded the point when those with half the votes did not see it their way.[5]

In the all-important matter of purpose, the 1891-1892 agreement stipulated three general areas of cooperation.[6] The first of these was publication. The federation was to put out "a common church periodical, a theological journal, a school journal, and an annual." It took until 1904 to get the second item under way. Only then did the *Theologische Quartalschrift*, forerunner of today's *Wisconsin Lutheran Quarterly*, appear. The very first January 1904 issue came out two months late. Although other issues have been late since, none has ever failed to appear. The veteran *Gemeinde-Blatt* and the somewhat younger *Schulzeitung* could simply be continued by the federation as its church periodical and school journal.

The second field of cooperation was missions. The point as it appears in the 1892 *Wisconsin Synod Proceedings* states: "Home missions is at the present to be the assignment of the district synods but is to be under the supervision of the federation, which will allocate men and monies available for this purpose."[7] The 1892 constitution stipulated: "All missions are under the direction and supervision of the federation, which is to elect for this purpose a superintendent and which is to allocate men and monies available for this purpose. Home missions is at the present the assignment of the district synods. World missions on the other hand should be the province of the federation."

The 1893 federation convention added some fine-tuning in the matter of the election of a mission board but more importantly resolved to adopt as its own the Indian mission that Wisconsin was ready to launch. This effort receives more attention in this chapter's second section.

The third cooperative endeavor was worker training. A conflict, also to be treated in a subsequent chapter section, developed in this matter, and that is an additional reason why it merits special attention. The main reason is that the federation's educational planning set the basic pattern for today's worker-training effort. Except for the 1979 move of the New Ulm preparatory school to Prairie du Chien, what was desired in 1892 is what prevails a century later.

The educational proposals adopted in 1892 stipulated: "The federation should have control over the present and future schools. These schools should be: a) a theological seminary in Wisconsin, b) a general gymnasium and common teachers' college, c) in both Michigan and Minnesota a gymnasium and pre-seminary."[8] Translated into today's terms, that meant all theological seminary work at the new Wauwatosa school. It meant a college and preparatory school at Watertown. It meant a preparatory school and teachers' college at New Ulm to provide teacher training for the federation. The theological department was discontinued. It meant a prep school at Saginaw.[9]

In the conventions in odd-numbered years after 1892 the federation would for the most part occupy itself with this troika of tasks: missions, worker-training, and publication. In 1905 it welcomed to its ranks the sons and some grandsons of the Nebraska pioneers, but in the main the proceedings devote most of their space to mission and educational efforts. These will be given a measure of detailed treatment.

The Indian Mission

Leaving all other considerations out of the picture, the Apache mission effort has to be regarded as a major theme in Wisconsin's history. For over fifty years it signified to two generations of synod members what we today call world missions.[10] The Poland effort, begun in 1924, was an overseas mission but it was not a foreign mission in the sense of an outreach in another language. In Poland the first concern was service to the Germans who were inside that country because of the shift in boundaries when the Curzon Line was drawn after World War I.

From 1893 on, the Apache field in Arizona was the object of the Wisconsin Federation's mission concern and zeal. It was, at the same time, the object lesson by which such concern and zeal were inculcated. In that sense the field gave as much as, and perhaps more than, it received. The Apache work became the theme of the mission festivals. Ladies' Aid societies practiced doing mission work as the members sewed blankets and clothes to be sent to Arizona.

The young in the church learned also. Every year shortly before Christmas there was a gathering of toys and games for the young Indians. The instructions were, "Don't bring a used-up, broken-down toy. Bring one of your favorites." This led to some agonizing decision-making on the part of youngsters up in the Great Lakes states, but it also provided an invaluable and unforgettable learning experience.

The first mention of this practice in the official record occurs in the 1897 Proceedings of the Federation. The mission board's spokesman states: "At the time of the Christmas festival we tried to bring some joy to the Indian children being instructed by our brothers through little presents. Dear friends of the mission cause and also many school children have made this possible for us through their gifts of love; we hope that a repetition will be possible for us next Christmas."[11] In another century the practice might have been discarded as outmoded or demeaning. If so, one hopes an adequate substitute in mission instruction has been developed.

The fifth section of the 1893 Proceedings of the Federation's second convention supplies both the background and the beginning of the Indian mission under the heading, "World Missions." The section reads:

> World missions is to be conducted by the Federation. The previously existing mission committee of the Wisconsin Synod for some time had centered its attention on a mission field among the Apache and Navaho Indians in Arizona and had determined to send them three ministerial candidates who had been trained for the purpose of world missions.
>
> The Federation deliberated this matter earnestly and resolved to make this proposed mission among the designated Indians its own and to establish immediately a commission for world missions. The members of the committee are the following:
>
> Pastor Th. Hartwig   Pastor Ph. Brenner
> Pastor A. Mousa six years   Mr. O. Griebling four years
> Teacher W. H. Amling
> Pastor C. Dowidat
> Pastor O. Koch two years
>
> The Federation empowered this commission to proceed in carrying out the resolutions pertaining to world missions in a most knowledgeable and conscientious manner. Since the preparations for this undertaking will take some time, it was resolved to place the three mission candidates for the time being under the superintendent of home missions. Pastor C. Dowidat was elected treasurer of the commission for world missions.[12]

Some commentary is in place to flesh out the bare bones of the report. In the fall of 1892 the Wisconsin Federation sent out two scouts to find a virgin Indian mission field, Th. Hartwig of Helenville and O. Koch of Columbus. They crossed paths with a veteran Arizona missionary, Pastor Cook, operating for the Presbyterians on the Pima reservation. He was really Pastor Koch, born a Lutheran in Germany, who had done independent mission work until the Presbyterian alliance developed.[13] Missionary Cook directed the attention of the Wisconsin spiritual scouts to the just barely pacified Apache Indians.

The three students trained for the work were: G. Adascheck, who requested recall after a year because of language difficulties in English as well as in Apache; J. Plocher, who served until 1899 when the illness of his wife forced a return to a pastorate in Minnesota; Paul Mayerhoff, who was sent as a tardy replacement for

Adascheck in 1896 and because of language facility could serve ably until 1903.

The special training these men received was not all that special. The only difference between the prospective missionaries and other students at the synodical schools seems to have been that the former did not have to pay the customary fees.

When Adascheck and Plocher arrived in Arizona territory in October 1893, they established themselves at Peridot on a tract of land near the San Carlos River obtained from the national government through the offices of Chief Casadora. Soon the tents that had to shelter them at the outset were replaced by a house and a small school.

The last word in the previous paragraph is the key in getting a grasp on the work in this pioneer mission outpost at the beginning. Children were to be instructed in Bible history and in the catechism. There were two avenues of approach, the school that the mission would set up for some twenty children, as was done from the first at Peridot, and the government agency school at San Carlos, where a type of released-time arrangement enabled Plocher to reach and teach as many as a hundred children twice a week.

There was an ongoing effort to reach beyond the children to the adults in their camps. The early records speak eloquently of the tremendous difficulties encountered: the distance and time factors involved, the Indian's natural reserve, the ingrained opposition to Whites and their ways, and the old, old opposition of natural man to the gospel.

The early records speak even more eloquently of the first gospel victories. Here is one notable account, the first of its kind, of blessed results from the work in the agency school: "This instruction the faithful God has blessed in that four of the girl students were thereby converted and expressed a desire for Holy Baptism. After adequate preparation they were baptized in that school on April 2 of this year, that is on the first blessed Easter day, in the name of the triune God after they had confessed their faith."[14] The next report, 1901, adds the poignant postscript: "Of the four girls, who had been baptized by Brother Plocher, one died, one married and moved away, the other two are being cared for by Brother Guenther and he is trying to prepare them for confirmation."[15] Subsequently that report indicates that eleven more baptisms occurred, among them the first male youth and the first husband of a baptized wife. The mission undertaking was enjoying the first fruits of its labor.

The mention of "Brother Guenther" in the previous quotation calls to mind the changing personnel on the Arizona mission field.

Carl Guenther, of the theological seminary's class of 1900 left school early to take Plocher's place at Peridot. To give him more time for camp work among adults, Teacher Rudolph Jens was called to help with the teaching in both the mission and the agency schools. A runaway accident cut short his very useful service after only three years. His replacement, Teacher Kutz, could not acclimatize himself and left after a year. By that time a new government school had cut into the mission school's enrollment, and it was closed.

On the Fort Apache reservation at East Fork, the second mission station, a seminary graduate, Henry Haase, replaced Paul Mayerhoff when the latter requested a release from his mission post to assume a parish pastorate. Meanwhile, as at San Carlos, a teacher had been placed. This was Otto Schoenberg. When the Fort Apache school closed because of dwindling enrollment, Schoenberg used the available time to prepare for a colloquy to become a pastor and missionary. This goal was achieved in 1905, and from that time on Schoenberg served as a missionary pastor until he entered government work in 1914. Schoenberg seems to have been adept in the Apache language.

The year 1905 brought to the Apache scene an almost legendary figure in synodical annals, Gustav Harders, who up to that time had distinguished himself as a talented and zealous pastor at Milwaukee's Jerusalem congregation. He was a founder of the original Milwaukee Lutheran High School in 1903. The next year his health deteriorated, and the leave of absence in 1905 was spent in the empty schoolhouse at Peridot where Harders found some satisfaction for his restless zeal to win lost souls for Christ in the limited assistance that he could give to Missionary Guenther.

After an attempt to resume the Jerusalem pastorate Harders moved permanently to Arizona. He was called to serve the Globe field and to act as overseer of the whole mission effort in Apacheland. Globe was not on the Fort Apache Reservation but was a bordering mining town in which many Apaches, driven by river floods from their Reservation farms, sought a livelihood. In his earlier furlough Harders had helped Carl Guenther serve these Globe Apaches. Now he would serve them again, along with those of his own race and Chinese miners and others.

Harders, if he could, would probably bridle at the term *race*. The only White and Red and Black colors Harder's missionary eye could distinguish were the black that colored souls lost in sin, the red that Christ's blood provided for cleansing, and the white that indicated forgiveness and oneness with God in time and eternity. Somehow this busy mission superintendent managed trips all over the territory scouting for promising locations for future missions. Synodical lore has it that on one train trip he encountered a Missouri mission executive looking for the same thing and worked out then and there a "gentlemen's agreement" that Missouri would work in California, not in Arizona, and Wisconsin would work in Arizona, not in California.[16] However unofficial the arrangement, Arizona was the last of the forty-eight states to have a Missouri mission. This was in 1938. Wisconsin did not send a missionary into California until 1950.

During the twelve Arizona years, Harders wrote three novels with Indian settings: *Jaalahn, La Paloma,* and *Dohaschtida.* They attest to his empathy for those in his spiritual care and were widely read throughout the synod. In fact, seventy years after the author's death the latter two, in English translations by Henry and Alma Nitz, still had a listing in the catalog of Northwestern Publishing House.

With Harder's death in 1917 the pioneer period of the mission in Apacheland can be thought of as ending. By that time there were men in the field who would make this work their life's calling and carry it forward for a half century. Also in 1917 the mission field acquired a new sponsor, the merged Wisconsin Synod. A break in the story seems in place at this point.

One remaining point, however, merits some attention. It revolves around the question of the mission morale of the Wisconsin Federation. Unfortunately, not all its pastors were as enthusiastic about this one foreign outreach of the church body as one might expect. The pastors trained in the mission schools of Europe for work in Africa or Asia, such as Bading and Goldammer, we can be sure were heartily in favor of the Apache work. One hesitates to say that anyone heartily opposed it, but certain misgivings surfaced.

Maybe the blame can be put on the Pietists of an earlier age, in line with a blaming process very prevalent and very popular in Wisconsin circles. Around 1700 the Halle Pietists under August Herman Francke mounted the first great Lutheran outreach effort that stretched to India and America and points in between. In their commendable endeavor the Pietists sometimes tended to elevate mission zeal to the status of an actual *mark* of the church at the expense of pure doctrine and right sacramental administration, which Article Seven of the Augsburg Confession stipulates as the true marks of the church.

When in the late 1880s and early 1890s a foreign mission outreach was under discussion in Wisconsin circles, some felt constrained to issue a caution against such overreach. Other motivations no doubt played a part. In any event there developed under the leadership of Professor Hoenecke, himself an emissary of the Berlin Mission Society but one trained at a reborn Halle, certain caveats about world mission work.[17]

These viewpoints can be summarized and simplified in the declaration, "World missions is not an essential work of a church body." Or, "Matthew 28:19—'Go and make disciples of all nations' —has been fulfilled. Now we wait for very special indications from the Lord to undertake such work in any definite place." Or, "A church body may have a certain assignment of its own that makes world missions, not a both-and, but an either-or matter."[18]

The divergence in viewpoint was not large enough to thwart completely the Apacheland thrust, but it may well have hobbled support at critical junctures. Worst of all, the cautious approach to the Matthew 28:19 assignment gained ground and was a formidable factor a half century later when at the end of World War II mission doors opened for the Wisconsin Synod. But that is another story in another time.

This section should not close on a downbeat note. Whatever the obstacles and the opposition, the Wisconsin Federation undertook a soul-saving world mission effort in the second year of its existence. The positive note should sound out loud and clear because the negative tone will prevail in the next main section of the Federation's story, the Michigan separation.

The Michigan Separation

The Federation's second convention at Milwaukee's St. Matthew in 1893 had before it, among many other items, the following resolution of that year's Michigan Synod convention: "Resolved that we put before the Federation the most humble plea that because of still prevailing circumstances in our midst it permit us to re-introduce for an indeterminate period of time the former arrangements at our seminary."[19]

To what seemed a justifiable plea of the Michigan brethren the Federation responded with a reluctant but brotherly resolution: "It would be very difficult to achieve the desired theological training in the manner requested by the honored Michigan Synod in its school at Saginaw. We, however, because of the conditions prevailing there, will have to let the provisional regulation of the matter in the hands of the honored Michigan Synod itself."[20]

In Michigan the all-purpose school had been turned into a preparatory school in 1892 according to the stipulations of the federation plan. Soon, however, a save-the-seminary campaign got under way. These were "the prevailing circumstances" that obtained in 1893. It wasn't just a matter of stubborn synodical pride or misplaced school spirit, although a good share of that developed later.

The Michigan Synod, only four years out of the General Council, was having some difficulties adjusting to the new brotherhood. Added to these were concerns about seminary training and pastor supply. The latter issue had plagued the synod for all of its first quarter century. Field after promising field had to be surrendered because no pastor could be sent.

The Saginaw school began to fill these needs. From 1888 to 1892 twelve men were graduated into the clergy ranks, among them such future leaders as W. Bodamer, F. Krauss, G. Wacker, and J. H. Westendorf. Second thoughts about the termination of the theological department suggested themselves. There were concerns that high school graduates might not be willing to cross the lake for college and seminary study or, if they were, that they might prefer Wisconsin and its parishes to a return to Michigan.

This was the thinking behind the 1893 request. Hindsight suggests that the better way to deal with the development would have been for the Wisconsin Federation to decline the request politely but firmly. By granting the Saginaw theological department a new lease on life temporarily in 1893, it succeeded only in prolonging the agony and setting the stage for strife. Soon pro-seminary and anti-seminary developed in Michigan and points west. The pro-seminary forces elected their man as Michigan president in 1894. This was C. F. Boehner whose name appears in the Wisconsin records already in 1856 as the Basel-trained pastor at Fond du Lac, where he had been serving since the previous September. After a stormy Beaver Dam tour of duty he served as a China missionary for the Episcopalians. His return to the states brought him to Michigan and a Marshall pastorate and in 1894 to the Michigan presidency as a strong pro-seminary man.

His erratic, shoot-from-the-hip leadership tactics were no doubt a major cause for the Michigan turmoil. It was not, however, the single cause. No one would want to cast all Michigan Synod men into the role of blind followers of the blind. These men honestly thought they had a case and a cause, the theological wing of the Saginaw school. This had become the divisive issue. In 1895 matters came to a boil.

A peace conference had suggested the compromise of another three or four years of lame-duck existence for theological training at Saginaw. The Michigan Synod demanded enough time to graduate all presently enrolled students. This could have insured Saginaw's theological department a life into the new century. At the Michigan convention in 1895 a minority of some ten men protested the resolutions to continue theological training at Saginaw and carried their case to the Federation's meeting later that year in St. Paul.

The Federation sided with the minority and passed this resolution:

> Since we have after careful and thorough investigation come to the conviction that the lack of confidence in the seminary's administration is not without reason, because what should according to God's Word be accomplished is not being accomplished there, therefore we see ourselves for conscience' sake compelled not to grant the request of the Michigan Synod regarding the continuation of the seminary in Saginaw and, since the lack of trust in the synodical administration also has good grounds, steps ought necessarily be taken here in this matter, as well as in the previous one.[21]

In Michigan serious conflict arose. The minority withheld monies from Saginaw and was suspended. It promptly organized as the Michigan District of the Wisconsin Synod with the blessing of the larger body. Protests against the Michigan Synod were carried to the 1896 convention of the Synodical Conference. Its investigating committee could barely get a hearing at the delayed Michigan Synod convention at Sturgis. That convention voted without any discussion to break with both the Wisconsin Federation and the Synodical Conference.

From 1897 to 1900 the Michigan Synod formed an alliance with the midwestern Augsburg Synod that had no theological seminary and was happy to cooperate in the Saginaw school. Differences in doctrine and practice, however, soon surfaced. The key issue seems to have been an Oregon mission that went into the hands of the General Council.[22] The short-lived union was terminated in 1900 at the instigation of the Augsburg Synod but with the hearty concurrence of the Michigan Synod.[23]

All was not well at the Saginaw school, the original bone of contention in the Michigan division. When Director Beer replaced Linsenmann as school head, an enrollment decline set in. By 1907 with only one student enrolled the school was officially closed.

There is a happy ending to this story of the Michigan problem. By 1907 serious efforts to reunite the Michigan Synod and Michigan District were already under way. In 1905 a referendum of Michigan Synod congregations on the question of reunion had resulted in a tie vote but soon, especially after the Saginaw school closing, reunion sentiment increased.

The reunion was in effect in 1910. Both sides had had some repenting to do: the synod for its unbrotherly dealing with the district, the federation, and the Synodical Conference; the district for its rash charges that the synod was guilty of false doctrine and had forfeited its Lutheran orthodoxy.[24]

On September 12, 1910, the Saginaw school officially reopened its doors, but now as a federation preparatory school. Five students were on hand. The school head and only instructor was Otto Hoenecke, a son of Doctor Adolph Hoenecke and previously pastor of Milwaukee's Bethel church. He came somewhat reluctantly but stayed to serve over fifty years, forty of them as school head.

CHAPTER TEN

Doctrinal Concerns at the Turn of the Century

The year 1900 was the time for the golden anniversary of the Wisconsin Synod. The convention met at August Pieper's St. Mark Church in Milwaukee, June 20-26. On Synod Sunday the special service was held at Milwaukee's exposition hall with sermons by President Philipp von Rohr of the Wisconsin Synod and President August Ernst of the Wisconsin Federation and an address by President Franz Pieper of the Missouri Synod. No Synodical Conference church in Milwaukee could have accommodated the throng of some 6000 worshipers.[1]

By 1900 the little stalk, barely visible at Granville fifty years before, had grown considerably. The three ordained Granville founders had become 214 pastors and 84 teachers. The one member congregation, Milwaukee's Grace, had become 329 with 49 additional preaching places. The lonely trio that met at Granville to form a little fellowship had grown into a synod that held membership in both the Wisconsin Federation and the Synodical Conference. "First the stalk, then the head, then the full kernel in the head." And, as always, the growth was God's.

As the Wisconsin Synod entered the new century and its own second half-century, there were administrative concerns. A nagging debt, occasioned by annual deficits that had almost become a way of life for the synod, was pushing toward the $50,000 mark in a synod with an annual budget of about $33,000. The jubilee convention could hear the first report of an "agitation" or debt-retirement committee established the year before at the request and actual instigation of laymen.[2] The debt had been more than halved in the first year of collections that netted $18,600 in only about one third of the congregations. The other two thirds, incidentally, did not do as well. In 1902 current deficits were matching debt retirement efforts. By 1904 the debt was back up to $27,000.

The major concerns of the Wisconsin Synod and Federation, however, as it entered the first decade of the 1900s, were not the mundane and practical but rather the doctrinal. Studies made and stands taken in those years have had a way of reaching into the history of subsequent decades, including the one during which this book is being written. One can surmise that the same will pertain in the future, and one is minded to insist that this is a most important subject area for both reader and writer.

The doctrinal concerns confronting Wisconsin in the first decade of the 1900s take one into the heartland of Bible doctrine. They include such basic teachings as church and ministry, election and conversion, and church and prayer fellowship. The issues would bring to the fore the theological teachers at the new seminary and their Wauwatosa theology set forth in the publication begun in 1904, *Theologische Quartalschrift.*

Church and Ministry Concerns

The 1904 Wisconsin Synod convention accepted this report of a special committee:

> The committee instructed by the synod to consider the membership application of Trinity Church at Cincinnati, Ohio, as well as those of its Pastors A. and E. von Schlichten, respectfully reports that after careful consideration it has come to the conviction that the membership application in question cannot at this time be given consideration because dealings going on between this congregation and the two pastors on the one side and the honored Missouri Synod on the other have not yet been concluded.[3]

Because the Missouri Synod would not meet for two months, the synodical committee and the synod convention were able to avoid taking a stand on what had been and would be a hotly contested synodical problem, the Cincinnati case. As one of so many, this case *per se* would barely rate a footnote mention in a book on Wisconsin history. It merits attention, however, because it raised and crystallized issues in an ongoing discussion of the Bible's teaching regarding church and ministry and thus served as an agent in the clarification of the synodical stand in these doctrinal areas.

What was the Cincinnati case?[4] A member of the Missouri Synod's congregation in that city was excommunicated because he had withdrawn his son from the Christian day school so that the young lad approaching confirmation age could beef up his grade school education in the public school, especially in English. This was in the fall of 1899, but from the start there was unclarity in the excommunication procedure, with the record stating two reasons: the disregard for congregational regulations regarding day school attendance and confirmation, and an Eighth Commandment breach in subsequent efforts of the layman to justify his actions.

When the Missouri district and eventually the synod took up the layman's appeal, they had to disavow the excommunication as unbiblical if the first reason were to count and as improperly conducted if the second reason was the basic issue. The congregation and pastors stood on their case and also refused to deal in an attempt to regularize relations with an English Synod congregation that was their thorn in the flesh of long standing. In the meantime, to complicate the whole situation, a second English congregation, this one a prospective Missouri Synod member, was emerging.

The upshot was that the district president temporarily suspended the two pastors in 1903 and that this suspension was made permanent by the August district convention. Meanwhile the congregation resigned from the synod and applied in June for Wisconsin Synod membership, as did the two pastors. Obviously the Wisconsin convention was correct when it refrained from taking sides before even the district of the sister synod had acted.

The Cincinnati case would be a synodical problem until 1911. By then one of the Cincinnati pastors had died and the other had been deposed, along with the church council, by the congregation. In 1911 the congregation lifted the excommunication of the layman in an action that President Pfotenhauer of Missouri, present at the meeting, declared involved only a *de facto*, but not a *de jure*, excommunication.

Meanwhile the Wisconsin Synod could not avoid the problem, even had there been a unanimous desire to do so. The membership application had to be dealt with, and there was a group in the synod that favored acceptance. In some instances the reasoning ran along the line that congregational action in excommunication action is supreme and inviolable or that in this instance the action had been proper. How much expansionism and synodical rivalry contributed to the motivation is difficult to ascertain at this late date.[5]

In any event, the 1906 convention put off action on membership applications of two Trinity, Cincinnati, teachers.[6] The 1907 convention set up a special committee to deal with the whole issue and the new material supplied by the sister synod. Those with any acquaintance with synodical history will recognize the names of committee members and will realize that the Cincinnati case was regarded as an issue of major importance. The high-powered committee consisted of Ph. v. Rohr, C. Gausewitz, Fr. Soll, G. E. Bergemann, E. G. Dornfeld, and J. Klingmann.[7] The committee was instructed to consult with the Wauwatosa faculty, if it found that necessary or expedient.

The committee's report to the 1908 convention had to be withheld because the Missouri Synod wanted to try a new approach in the case.[8] At the convention in 1909 the action, or rather inaction, again points to the touchiness of the issue. The resolution states: "Since a judgment of our committee's action necessitates a judgment of the action of officials of the Missouri Synod, we deem it advisable to refrain from any judgment, but express the hope that the Missouri Synod, before whom the whole case by its origin belongs, will still find ways and means to bring the matter to a God-pleasing conclusion."[9] The report, however, continues, "But protests in the protocol were registered against this resolve by numerous synodical delegates." No doubt committee members and their supporters were irked that their support of the original excommunication of the Cincinnati layman had been shunted and shelved.

The next convention in 1910 actually expunged the 1909 resolution and thanked the special committee.[10] Even the report of the final outcome in the September 1, 1911, *Gemeinde-Blatt* engendered protest. Professor Koehler in writing objected to a wording of the report that implied the correctness of the original excommunication. In this connection he set down in the record a strong view regarding judgment that would be involved in disputes of much larger proportions. Koehler closed his protest letter to the publication's editorial committee by pleading, "Do help to stem the judgment upon our church that just through the accumulation of such unadjusted matters is in the making."[11]

The letter writer was obviously much less concerned about parliamentary and organizational matters in the involved Cincinnati case, than he was in its doctrinal issues. That is the key point and the only justification for what may have been to many a boring set of paragraphs. What happened in Cincinnati in 1899 and in various points west thereafter made the Wisconsin Synod think hard about basic points of Bible doctrine, as congregational disciplinary action came into conflict with its synodical counterpart.

The question suggested itself: Which body is supreme, the congregation or the synod? The generally held view was that the local congregation is the one grouping of believers that was instituted and commanded by God. A related question, previously debated especially at conferences of teachers, was: Which is the divinely instituted form of the ministry?[12] Again, the generally held view was that the office of pastor of the local congregation is the one divinely instituted form of the ministry.

In the discussion of these issues — first at pastoral conferences, then in pamphlets and periodicals, and finally with Missouri theologians—the Wauwatosa Seminary teachers, J. P. Koehler, August Pieper and after 1908 John Schaller, guided their church body in a clarification of its position on church and ministry. Koehler did the exegetical pioneering and Pieper did the bulk of the writing, speaking of the result later on in his classroom as *meine Amtslehre* (my teaching of the ministry), a term that Koehler does not gainsay.

Setting aside traditional thinking and dogmatical formulations for the time being, the three men took a fresh look at what the Scriptures say about church and ministry. They found that there was not as much said about local congregations and the pastoral office as was frequently assumed. What was said in the Scriptures, they found, was that the Lord had indeed instituted and commanded a gathering of believers and an office of the gospel ministry but that he had never specified a single form or type of either, above all other forms or types.

The three Wauwatosa teachers had not set themselves an easy task in this effort to change traditional thinking. It took many one-on-one discussions, many conference papers and debates, and many articles in the *Quartalschrift* before their position became a generally held position.[13] Some never agreed. Professor Ernst is a notable example.

The strongest and longest opposition came from the Synodical Conference brethren in the Missouri Synod. Professor Franz Pieper was the chief spokesman for the view that the local congregation and its pastor are the one and only divinely instituted forms of church and ministry. The difference in thinking remained despite serious efforts to reach an understanding. An outstanding instance was the drafting of "The Thiensville Theses" in 1932, to be described in a subsequent chapter of this book. Also to be treated later are the Synodical Conference's attempts to settle the difference when it was itself heading for dissolution over other issues.

Overseas Lutherans who disagree with Wisconsin in its stand regarding church and ministry like to refer to this as Wisconsin's *Sonderlehre* (distinctive doctrine). They may do so if that means that Wisconsin is thereby set apart from a position that will not even allow a local congregation to hold title to its property or one that limits both church and ministry forms without scriptural warrant. There will be dissent if the meaning is that in this matter Wisconsin has separated itself from Bible truth.

Another Election Debate and Its Important By-Products

Just twenty years after the 1882-1883 first rending of the Synodical Conference over the doctrines of election and conversion, as described in a previous chapter, a replay of the controversy was enacted in a series of free conferences in which men of the Wisconsin Synod and Federation were very much involved. A new generation of theologians was on the scene, wondering whether their efforts at agreement could succeed. Enough of the original battlers—Franz Pieper, George Stoeckhardt, and Adolph Hoenecke on the one side and Friedrich Schmidt, F. W. Stellhorn, and Henry Allwardt on the other — were still active enough to make such an outcome most unlikely. That is the way it turned out eventually.

Nevertheless, at the outset there were some good prospects. The original 1902 Beloit free conference, it is true, fizzled. Poor attendance could be attributed to too little, too late publicity. The main mover in the Beloit fiasco, however, persevered. This was Pastor M. Bunge, an Iowa Synod transfer in 1902 to the Wisconsin Synod. He chaired the committee that was to plan future conferences.

The result was a series of five intersynodical free conferences on election and conversion: at Watertown in the spring of 1903, Milwaukee in the fall, Detroit in 1904, and Fort Wayne in 1905 and 1906. At the first two meetings there were more Wisconsin men in attendance than those from any other synod. Total attendance peaked at 700 in Milwaukee and dwindled considerably at subsequent meetings.

At Watertown Franz Pieper's paper set down the Synodical Conference stand on election, limiting causes to two and only two: God's mercy and Christ's merits. It left no room for any "in view of faith" theorizing. Ohio and Iowa theologians challenged the presentation on the grounds that it clashed with John 3:16 and a so-called "analogy of faith," which they viewed as a sort of harmony of Bible truth in which all doctrines would have to fit neatly and logically. They wanted no part of any election that was not "in view of faith."

The Synodical Conference men insisted that an "analogy of faith" could only be the sum of all Bible passages that spoke on the doctrine under study. What Scripture teaches about election should be found in those passages that treat election specifically, Ephesians 1:4 as an example, but not John 3:16. For the clarification of this key point J. P. Koehler supplied a major, seventy-page study in the first *Quartalschrift* volume, 1904, under the heading, *Die Analogie des Glaubens.*

The "analogy" difference carried over from Watertown to the 1903 free conference in Milwaukee and from there to Detroit in 1904.[14] Not even the efforts of a program committee chaired by Dr. Hoenecke that met between the Milwaukee and Detroit conferences to clarify issues and set up an agenda could minimize the differences. The committee's report simply suggested additional discussion on two questions: What is the "analogy of faith"? and how is it to be used?

When the 1904 Detroit free conferences revealed a deep difference between the Synodical Conference and the Ohio and Iowa Synods on the election issue in general and the "analogy of faith" in particular, an Ohio Synod member in attendance injected a new controversial point. He insisted that there had been so little progress toward unity because the sessions of the free conferences had not been opened by joint worship and prayer. In the facts of his case the Ohio man was correct. Doctor Ernst had opened the 1903 Watertown meeting by setting aside a time for silent prayer. This practice seems to have been followed at subsequent free conferences.

The cause-effect reasoning and the proposal for procedure change, however, were sharply challenged by Synodical Conference men. Dr. Hoenecke remarked that he had prayed for the conference's unity on his train trip from Milwaukee to Detroit. That gave a lot of time for praying, even using today's rail transportation as the measure. The main point he and others made was that praying springs from faith and that praying together assumes a common faith. The discussions at Detroit and subsequent writings on the subject demonstrate clearly that the Synodical Conference position then left no room for any later distinction between a full prayer fellowship of those united in the faith and a "joint prayer" association suitable for certain other occasions.[15] The issue will not be treated fully at this point but is mentioned as a background to the disagreement that would eventually split the Synodical Conference sixty years later.

Free conferences at Fort Wayne discussed election in 1905 and conversion in 1906. They demonstrated that interest was decreasing as much as disunity was increasing. Actually the Synodical Conference men had already agreed before the 1906 meeting to make that the finale. Within a decade, however, one more effort at finding unity in the doctrines of election and conversion would be mounted, originally in Minnesota. The story peaks in the 1920s, and its telling will be deferred.

In the first decade of the century the doctrine of objective or universal justification also became a point of controversy between the Synodical Conference and other Lutheran groupings. How closely this was related to the sharp election-conversion debate is not easy to determine, but it is striking that the same theological camp that could not bear an election without faith at the same time raised objections to a justification without faith.

The point at issue has nothing to do with any demeaning of the importance of faith. Faith is the one and only pathway on which the elect are led to the eternal goal, and faith is the one and only means by which God's justification becomes the personal possession of the believing sinner. The point at issue is the truth the gospel presents to the believer as the object of his faith. That is in the one case an election of grace because of God's mercy and Christ's merits and in the other a universal justification of sinners achieved when Christ died and signaled when he rose. These are gospel truths that precede faith. They are presented that they might be believed and those believing be saved.

These are issues that August Pieper raised in a 1906 *Quartalschrift* article with the title, *Ohio's neuer Angriff auf die Lehre von der Rechtfertigung* ("Ohio's New Attack on the Doctrine of Justification"). Pieper concluded by flatly declaring: "One cannot oppose any doctrine of God's Word with impunity. . . . But whoever molests the doctrine of justification stabs the gospel in the heart and is on the way of losing entirely Christian doctrine and personal faith and of falling into the arms of heathenism, even if he ever so much emphasizes justification through faith."[16] It is interesting to note that the statement would be quoted thirty-four years later in John Meyer's "Objective Justification" and thirty-five years after that in a synodical essay for the 125th anniversary.[17] The heart doctrine of the Scripture has always been a heart concern of the Wisconsin Synod from generation to generation.

Wauwatosa Theology and Theologians

This may be the place to highlight the men who guided the Wisconsin Synod in its doctrinal concerns in the first years of the new century. Adolph Hoenecke's efforts reached back thirty-five years into the previous century and were by 1900 beginning to wind down. This is not to gainsay his influential role in training Wisconsin pastors that ended in 1908 but that would be a force in synodical history for another half century through the students that learned their dogmatics and homiletics from him. Nor is it to gainsay his influential role in the calling of other seminary professors.

He could, for example, insist that G. Thiele, his old schoolmate, be called to replace August Graebner and in 1900 insist that Thiele give way to the calling of a replacement, J. P. Koehler.

The subject, however, centers on the new breed of the new century: J. P. Koehler, called in 1900 to the seminary and in service there to 1929; August Pieper, called in 1902 and active until 1941; and John Schaller, called in 1908 as Hoenecke's successor and deceased in 1920. These are the three men who espoused the Wauwatosa theology in their books and in their *Quartalschrift* articles. A brief *vita* of each will be supplied, beginning with the first to leave the seminary scene.

John Schaller was born on December 10, 1859, the son of Loehe's own "Timothy" sent over to head the Saginaw enterprise.[18] Because the father, Gottlieb, was won for the Missouri cause in the dispute with Loehe over church and ministry, the son was reared in St. Louis. From 1874 to 1878 he was a student at Northwestern in Watertown and a schoolmate of older students, August Pieper and John Koehler. In 1881 he finished the St. Louis theological course and subsequently filled pastoral posts at Little Rock (1881-1885) and Cape Girardeau (1885-1889). He was then called to the New Ulm school and in 1893 became president of the teachers' college established in a reorganization of that year. In 1908 he was called to succeed Adolph Hoenecke as professor of dogmatics and school head.

His theological writings are slim but strong. There is the *Book of Books*, a basic isagogics that many synod pastors and teachers used in their student days. It was updated and published anew in 1990. There is the *Pastorale Praxis*, which the *Northwestern Lutheran* obituary calls "the first book of the kind stating the principles of pastoral theology in a form applicable to the peculiar conditions obtaining in the Lutheran Church of our country." *Biblical Christology*, originally appearing in 1918, has recently undergone a revision and republication under the editorship of a grandson, Loren Schaller.

As the titles in the previous paragraph indicate, John Schaller operated equally well in both German and English. He was one of the synodical pioneers in this respect. Koehler and Pieper, for instance, could work in both languages, but the writings show that German was the preferred, the mother tongue. In Schaller the leaning to German is much less in evidence.

Another often overlooked contribution of John Schaller is his administrative ability as seminary school head. This gift does not appear black-on-white in the synodical records, but the historical developments before and after 1920, the year of Schaller's death, testify to his contributions. A team effort was in operation at Wauwatosa before 1920. After that, division set in.

In any history of the Wisconsin Synod J. P. Koehler deserves special attention. He was its premier historian, commissioned to provide golden and diamond anniversary writings and supplying finally *The History of the Wisconsin Synod,* published by the Protes'tant Conference in 1970.[19] All writings on early Wisconsin Synod history must rely heavily on Koehler's contributions. If they do not, they will err in most major issues.

J. P. Koehler's father, as has been previously mentioned, was a pioneer Wisconsin pastor, joining the synod in 1855. The son was born at Manitowoc in 1859, also Schaller's birth year. He studied at Northwestern College and the St. Louis Seminary. After stints as aide to Adolph Hoenecke and his father, Koehler was pastor at Two Rivers from 1882 to 1888. Then he accepted a call to Northwestern as dean of students.[20] In 1894 on the advice of his physician he resigned that post but continued as classroom instructor until the move to Wauwatosa in 1900.

At the seminary Koehler took over the chair that Gottlieb Thiele had filled. The main teaching areas were church history and New Testament studies. Natural talents in art and music were also put to use. Slide lectures on church art and architecture were developed, and a seminary chorus was trained in singing the best of Lutheran church music.

When John Schaller died in 1920, Koehler became school head, serving until 1929 when a year's leave of absence was followed by the troubled termination of his Wauwatosa tenure. This is a matter that will receive attention in later chapters. To round off the *vita* here, Koehler lived another two decades with his son Karl at Neillsville. He died there at the age of 92 on September 30, 1951.

Koehler left a large legacy of writings in addition to the synodical history previously mentioned. In 1917 his church history compendium, *Lehrbuch der Kirchengeschichte,* appeared.[21] It supplied in book form the content of Koehler's classroom lectures in one of his major teaching assignments. The other, New Testament studies, gave rise to another publication. This is the 1910 *Der Brief Pauli an die Galater* (Paul's Letter to the Galatians). In 1957 E.E. Sauer provided an English translation.[22]

Naturally Koehler supplied his share, and more than his share, of articles for the theological journal of the seminary and synod. In addition, reference should be made to his numerous conference and convention essays. As late as 1959 one of these, *Gesetzlich Wesen*

115

unter uns ("Legalism in Our Midst"), was read in translation to the synodical convention by Waldemar Gieschen.[23]

In 1902 August Pieper began a seminary teaching assignment that would not end until 1941. He was already then a veteran of twenty-three years of service as a Wisconsin Synod pastor at Kewaunee (1879-1885), Menomonie (1885-1890) and after a health leave Milwaukee-St. Mark (1891-1902). As has been related, Pieper studied at Northwestern and then at St. Louis under Doctor Walther.[24]

At the Wisconsin seminary August Pieper filled the post vacated by Eugene Notz. Old Testament studies was the major assignment. After almost two decades of teaching in this field Pieper wrote his *Jesaias II* (*Isaiah II*). The Roman numeral should not lead anyone to assume that the author held to any theory of multiple authorship. Pieper was writing under the assumption that his good friend and relative, George Stoeckhardt, the great St. Louis exegete, would be supplying an "Isaiah I" as a companion volume. The latter never got beyond the first dozen chapters, and by now the team aspect of the project has been all but forgotten and the title, *Isaiah II*, is sometimes misunderstood.

A book of daily devotions, *Biblische Hausandachten*, was put out by Pieper in 1912. He delivered many convention essays and wrote extensively for the theological journal. A fall and hip injury when he was well over eighty ended his classroom teaching. He died in 1946.

The quarter century that began in 1904 with the first volume of the *Theologische Quartalschrift* and ended in 1929, the year Koehler's seminary teaching was terminated, looms in synod annals as a golden age of theological writing and teaching. In the first half of those years that fall into the time slot of these chapters four men were active at Wauwatosa: Adolph Hoenecke until 1908, J. P. Koehler, August Pieper, and John Schaller. Almost any listing of the five premier theologians of the Wisconsin Synod would include all four men.

They were able and influential teachers. They were also able and influential in their writing so that their theological leadership did not have to cease when their teaching did. Their books have been, for the most part, mentioned. In this connection one might call attention to another vehicle for their proficient and prolific pens.

In 1904 the *Theologische Quartalschrift* began to appear, just in time to include material on the current intersynodical free conferences in the form of Koehler's *Analogie des Glaubens* and of blow-by-blow accounts of the Fort Wayne debates.

These free conferences should not be viewed as a cause for the origin of the *Quartalschrift*. It will be recalled that back in 1892 in the publication goals of the Wisconsin Federation one of the items envisioned was a theological journal. For one reason or another this project was delayed for a dozen years. Finally in 1904 it could be realized.

The early volumes of the *Quartalschrift* contain a wealth of theological thinking and writing, so much so that the impression is of a back-up pushing the dam to the bursting point. Koehler's *Analogie des Glaubens* has already been mentioned. Soon the church-ministry articles, also previously mentioned, were appearing. John Schaller's best contribution is a lengthy treatise, *Das Reich Gottes* (The Kingdom of God) in the 1918 volume. Students having trouble with lessons on the Second Article and Second Petition are still referred to this writing for the needed clarification. Language problems prevent many from applying the suggested remedy.

This difficulty calls to mind the on-going but as yet unrealized desire of producing an anthology of the best of the early *Quartalschrift* writing in translation. There is much merit in the proposed project, but if it is delayed too much longer, the desire could very easily diminish to dream and then pipe dream for want of able translators. Some sporadic translation has been done but so far it is, if not too late, much too little.

A term has been coined to designate the theological teaching and writing under discussion. It is either "Wauwatosa Theology" or "Wauwatosa Gospel" and is supposed to describe what went on there for the quarter century, 1904-1929. As with any such intangible term, there will be about as many definitions of this one as there are definers. The writer will offer one of his own.

Let the church-ministry clarification serve as one example. What happened was that the Wauwatosa theologians simply looked beyond the current viewpoint and the ready dogmatical explanation and the deposit of an ecclesiastical situation of the past to what Scripture actually said about church and ministry.[25] This and nothing else was determinative for them in their doctrinal formulations and should be for us in ours.

What this amounts to is employing the historical-grammatical approach to Scripture. This contrasts with a historical-critical approach, so much in vogue at this time, that sets itself as judge over Scripture. It contrasts also with a deficient dogmatical approach, divorced from the foundation of exegesis, that ignores Scripture. The goal in Bible interpretation remains what Eli told Samuel to say to God long ago, "Speak, for your servant is listening."

That was the goal of those who espoused the Wauwatosa gospel and theology. It remains the goal today, despite relocation from Wauwatosa to Mequon.

CHAPTER ELEVEN

From Federation to Merger

The year 1917 was a good year for Lutheran union in the United States. In June 1917 three Norwegian Lutheran church bodies, the Norwegian Synod, the Hauge Synod, and the United Norwegian Lutheran Church, merged into what would become known as the Evangelical Lutheran Church and would be involved in the 1960 creation of The American Lutheran Church. Later that year final conventions of the General Synod, the General Council, and the United Synod of the Evangelical Lutheran Church in the South set in motion the 1918 creation of the United Lutheran Church in America. In between those epochal events in the history of United States Lutheranism the Wisconsin Federation in August 1917 turned itself into the merged Wisconsin Synod, known today in the acronym as WELS (Wisconsin Evangelical Lutheran Synod).

This Wisconsin move from federation to merger involves a basket-upset in the arrangements and designations in this history. The old 1850 synod that Muehlhaeuser had founded with Weinmann and Wrede was divided into three districts of the new body, the Northern, Southeastern, and Western Wisconsin Districts. Three other districts were formed out of synods, two venerable bodies created in 1860 in Minnesota and Michigan and a third, the newcomer in Nebraska. These six districts made up the new Wisconsin Synod of 1917.

There were some notable differences in the Wisconsin merger, when compared to the two other 1917 union developments. The Wisconsin merger was much smaller. More important, it was a union created without any tensions in the doctrinal area. The Norwegian merger could only be accomplished by granting equal validity to both contending viewpoints in the conversion-election debates. The United Lutheran Church in America union represented a

General Council gain on paper in that the General Synod had officially enlarged its commitment to the Lutheran Confessions. In actuality, however, the old General Synod position on the confessions, or rather lack of position, would not only survive but definitely augment itself.

In the 1917 Wisconsin merger, however, doctrinal discussions or compromises are notable only by their absence. Wisconsin, Minnesota, Michigan, and Nebraska were one in doctrine and practice when they federated. The federation experience underscored that unity. The merger came as naturally as the leaves on a tree.

As natural as that may have been, a pause at the 1917 threshold is in place to look back on and recount any important developments in the final years of the single synods and their federation that may have been overlooked in previous chapters. The actual moves to merger, predictable as they might be, should also be given brief mention.

Last Years of the Synods

The Nebraska story is unique and may be given first attention. In 1903 the third convention of the Nebraska District of the Wisconsin Synod took the steps that converted a district into an independent synod and nailed down a claim to the "other States" designation in the Federated Synod of Wisconsin, Minnesota, Michigan, and Other States. It seems the distance difficulties involved in a district status were the predominant motivations for this step, which both the mother synod and the young daughter district favored. When the step was taken, the Nebraska group consisted of fourteen pastors: E. Berg, T. Braeuer, G. F. Gruber, R. Gruber, Ph. Hoelzel, M. Lehninger, E. Monhardt, G. Press, E. Redlin, C. W. Siegler, E. Strube, J. Witt, E. Zaremba, and H. Zimmermann.[1]

By 1918, the first year of the second Nebraska District, the fourteen pastors had increased to twenty-two. The sparsely settled state was being diligently served, even though mission stations tended to be small at the start and remained so for extended periods of time. The result was a unique synodical parsonage building program not to be found in other federated synods. Such ventures were undertaken at Merna and at Colome in South Dakota, into which state the energetic mission efforts of the Nebraska Synod had reached.

These specially owned synod parsonages caused some problems when the move from federation to merger neared its goal. In 1916 the Nebraska Synod, acting on the proposed merger, felt compelled to pass the resolution: "The trustees of the area Synod of Nebraska and Other States are ordered and empowered to turn over, if required, all property of the area synod, consisting of two parsonages in the mission field, to the merging body, but with the proviso that any actual proceeds from the possible sale of these parsonages should flow into the treasury of the area synod."[2]

The old anti-synod feelings were not necessarily asserting themselves in this resolution. What should rather be read between the lines is a manifestation of real brotherly concern and mission zeal and an honest stewardship of hard-to-come-by mission offerings.

That the old antipathy to larger organization had not outlived the century of its origin is abundantly manifested by the Nebraska reaction to the proposed intersynodical discussions on conversion and election, emanating from St. Paul. In 1917 the Nebraska Synod adopted a resolution that is quoted in full because of its significance for the Nebraska story:

> We rejoice that the heartfelt longing of all devout Christians for the unity of the sundered Lutheran Church is manifesting itself in so-called intersynodical conferences in various parts of our country.
> We now recommend, in order to give our heartfelt opinion in this matter expression, that we as a synod establish a committee empowered to represent us in meetings with other synods.
> We encourage all definitely to obtain and with a prayer for enlightenment to study documents that have appeared and will appear in the interest of this unity endeavor.
> We implore the God of all grace to grant his blessing so that there may be achieved a unity in the truth on the basis of God's Word and the Lutheran Confessions that is pleasing to him.[3]

Committee members signing the adopted report include Pastors M. Lehninger, Ph. Martin, J. Witt, Teacher G. Hofius, and Delegates John Kothe and John Heins.

In the Minnesota Synod's last dozen years five men served as its president. The first was Carl Gausewitz, whose main endeavor was to put the synodical fiscal house in order. The Minnesota golden anniversary history reports:

> Only in the year 1894, when Pastor C. Gausewitz was elected president, did the synod find the right way to rid itself of its debt. It was resolved that the congregations should themselves gather their offerings. Thus salaried collectors were rendered superfluous and the synod was spared a yearly expense of about $1000. Carrying out the resolution may have left much to be desired, but at least we could again breathe a sigh of relief and the

threat of bankruptcy was averted. The debt has been decreased year by year and with but a slight effort will soon be liquidated.⁴

In 1906 Gausewitz was called to fill the prestigious pulpit of Grace Church, Milwaukee, as the third pastor after J. Muehlhaeuser and T. Jaekel. At the time of the 1917 merger Gausewitz was serving as president of the Wisconsin Federation and of the Synodical Conference. He held the latter post until his death in 1927.

After Gausewitz moved from Minnesota to Wisconsin in 1906, he was followed in the presidency in rapid succession by four men. President A. Schroedel, pastor of historic Trinity, St. Paul, served from 1906 until his death in 1909. August Zich served briefly from 1909 to 1910, when he left Sleepy Eye for Green Bay, Wisconsin. He subsequently was president of the Northern Wisconsin District, 1928-1931, and professor at Wisconsin Lutheran Seminary from 1931-1939.

From 1910 to 1912 Pastor E. A. Pankow of St. Paul Church at St. James filled the presidential post. He was succeeded by Pastor Justus Naumann of Wood Lake until 1913, the Goodhue area until 1915, and St. Paul until his death in 1917. During the Wood Lake pastorate a son, Oscar, was born who would in 1953 become the Wisconsin Synod president. Vice-President J. R. Baumann led the synod until it became a district and the district after that for the first three years.

Referring to the years after the Gausewitz debt-retirement efforts up to the time of its publications in 1910, the golden anniversary history says: "Regarding the development of the synod since the founding of the Wisconsin Federation, there is little more of significance to report. There is a slow outward growth. There is faithful labor in the fields allotted with the powers God has given, and the Lord is acknowledging the efforts."⁵ If this writing says little about Minnesota Synod history at the turn of the century, it is because there is little to be said.

After 1910 a notable development took place in Minnesota. This is the 1915 establishment of a full-time synodical president without any parish responsibilities. This is a first in Wisconsin Synod circles and harks back to a proposal President Streissguth made to the Wisconsin Synod back in 1867.⁶ In 1867 this was an idea whose time had not yet come in Wisconsin and would not come even in 1915. In Minnesota, however, with its large vistas and far-flung Dakota missions, such a step seemed sensible.

It was the laymen who took the lead. They caucused at the 1915 New Ulm convention and then reported this resolution to the body: "The delegates held a meeting and resolved that we should salary our president, so that he will have no congregation and can devote his whole activity to the nurture of the synod. There were 23 negative and 35 positive votes."[7] The convention in a ballot vote then favored the proposal eighty-eight to fifty-four.

The result was that President Justus Naumann resigned his Goodhue parish and set up a synodical headquarters in St. Paul. His death less than two years later cut short his service there. By 1917 merger developments definitely suggested that the successor, J. Baumann, remain at his Red Wing parish. History sometimes repeats itself, at least in part. Almost a half century later the Wisconsin Synod in its 1959 convention made its president a full-time official and thus President Oscar Naumann, the son of Justus, followed in the father's footsteps.[8] This time, however, the move to set up synodical headquarters was, not to, but from St. Paul.

After the 1910 reunion of the Michigan Synod and District there was a quick return to a normal situation, demonstrating that this first Lutheran union in a century that would see so many others was a true unity endeavor. In fact, in not too many years a striking synodical and district *esprit de corps* was manifesting itself.

Naturally much concern centered on the Saginaw school, reopened in 1910 with only a preparatory department that developed year by year as additional classes were added. The early enrollments were small, actually disappointing, and would remain so until World War II years. Accommodation to the new feeder-school role, however, came with dispatch and with determination. In 1915 the second graduating class had four members. All four enrolled in Northwestern's ministerial program and became pastors in the Wisconsin Synod.

The four were Gerald Hoenecke, long-time New Testament professor at Wisconsin Lutheran Seminary; Karl Krauss, Lansing pastor and district, synod, and Synodical Conference official; Arthur Wacker, spearhead of the belated foreign mission endeavor of his synod; and Bernhard Westendorf, Flint pastor whose outstanding efforts in evangelism and education were a boon to his district and synod.

In the first two post-reunion conventions in 1911 at Jenera, Ohio, and 1912 at Lansing the doctrinal essay concerned itself with a burning social question of the day, prohibition.[9] One might conjecture that the program committee considered prohibition a safe topic on which the previously divided district and synod forces could unite.

123

Whatever the case, the essayist was Director O. J. Hoenecke, suffering the fate of many a newcomer in our circles who barely gets his books unpacked in time to carry out an essay assignment. The theme was: "Prohibition in the Light of the Holy Scripture." The first thesis, covered in the 1911 convention, read: "Correctly considered, prohibition is basically nothing else but a renewed onslaught on the glorious liberty of the Christian, in that thereby the attempt is made to impose a yoke, similar to the old one from which he has been freed, once again on his neck and thereby put him in danger of losing entirely his freedom."

Since the forty-three pages required to present this first thesis filled the agenda time allotted for the essay, the two remaining theses were discussed the next year. The first of these declared: "Since we dare not in any way let the precious blessing of Christian freedom be curtailed for us, we therefore dare not and cannot make common cause with the advocates of prohibition, must rather all the more oppose their dangerous error with the weapon of the Word in the areas assigned to us by God." The final thesis stated: "When the state, however, pressured by prohibition agitation, passes laws forbidding the use, sale, etc., of potable spirits, then we for the sake of God conduct ourselves as obedient Christians also in this matter in all things that do not conflict with God's Word, but at the same time continue our testimony against prohibition in so far as it presents itself as a moral demand."[10]

The essay and its declarations are not recalled after all this time because they were unique. Quite the contrary! They represented, by and large, most of the synodical thinking and speaking and writing on the subject during the decades of enactment and enforcement of prohibition. It is understandable that the Michigan Synod, in a state where Reformed influence predominated, should be in the vanguard of those concerned about the religious impact of the prohibition movement. In Wisconsin, where huge Lutheran and Roman Catholic populations offset the Reformed approach, there was less concern about threats to Christian liberty while the campaign for prohibition was being waged. After 1920, however, voices could frequently be heard expressing the same viewpoints that the 1911-1912 Michigan Synod essay expounded.

The subject matter has turned to the Wisconsin Synod, and this is the natural place to recall some of the more important items in its history not previously discussed. At the head of the list one could very well place the beginnings of the Milwaukee Lutheran High School in 1903. At the outset the caution is in place that this is much less a synodical or intersynodical venture than an educational enterprise of certain concerned pastors, teachers, and laymen. Operating on the maxim, currently in disfavor, that the best way to start a school is to start teaching, the first Synodical Conference high school, using the term in its commonly accepted sense, was launched by Wisconsin and Missouri pastors, teachers, and laypeople. A Missouri congregation provided space, energetic laymen provided and gathered necessary funds, and volunteer teachers manned the classrooms, among them Professors Koehler and Pieper of the Wauwatosa seminary.

Another significant educational effort of those days was the development of synodical catechisms in both German and English. The project spanned the years 1907 to 1917. The result was the frequently revised but still-used "Gausewitz" catechism that the bulk of the church's adults of today know firsthand. At the outset a prestigious committee was entrusted with the work, consisting of Professor Ernst, Professor Schaller, President Soll, and Pastor Gausewitz.

After six years and the addition of Teacher R. Albrecht to the committee, however, little had been accomplished, perhaps because the committee was too prestigious. The 1913 synodical convention expressed regrets about the lack of results and resolved that "the present committee be discharged and the production of the catechism be entrusted to one man."[11] The one man selected was Carl Gausewitz, pastor at Grace, Milwaukee. The selector, President Bergemann, was fond of recalling this in later years as a prime instance of the superiority of one good man over the best of committees.[12] In 1917 the finished product appeared in both languages, a catechism in which "the gospel appears, not only as one of the matters that are also treated, but as the precious bond that runs through the whole Catechism, ties all of its sentences tightly together and alone makes possible the biblically correct understanding."[13]

In his pastorates at East Farmington, Wisconsin; St. Paul, and Milwaukee, and in his presidencies in the Minnesota Synod, the Wisconsin Federation, and the Synodical Conference Carl Gausewitz rendered yeoman service. His greatest service, however, was the catechetical endeavor.

In 1908 the Wisconsin Synod suffered a series of losses which make that year memorable in that respect. In 1908 Pastor Bading resigned the pastorate at St. John's, Milwaukee, and was succeeded by John Brenner, who in 1933 would follow his predecessor into the synodical presidency. Bading would carry on in a limited way as an assistant pastor, a synodical official, and the Synodical Conference president for a few more years. He died in 1913 and with him died one of the longest and strongest links to the synod's founding years and its early confessional battles.

In 1908 Adolph Hoenecke died, to be succeeded as school head by John Schaller, up to then filling a similar role at Doctor Martin Luther College. Hoenecke's synodical connection began in 1863, his theological teaching in 1866. That teaching, interrupted briefly in the 1870s while the seminary training was transferred to St. Louis, shaped the doctrinal convictions and the homiletical contributions of two generations of Wisconsin Synod pastors. It can safely be said that the Lord of the church poured out more benefits on the Wisconsin Synod through Adolph Hoenecke than through any other of its leaders. The benefits may be the intangible kind but they are very real, for they involve the preservation and proclamation of the biblical truth that saves sinners.

When it was time to call a successor to Adolph Hoenecke, the electing board had to travel to Winona to carry out the assignment. by then President von Rohr was too sick to do any traveling. Before the year was out he too had died. Another link to the formative years of the previous century was broken. Another notable career was ended. In 1908 the Wisconsin synod suffered great losses, as great as those of any other year in its history.

The year also brought its blessing. The Lord of the church transfers, retires, and buries his workers but the work goes on. In the presidential office the names of Bading and von Rohr are replaced by those of G. E. Bergemann, who had the stamina for the rugged task of supervising the transfer from federated to merged synod, and John Brenner, who would not yield a jot or tittle of the doctrinal position of the Synodical Conference Bading had helped found. Even before the torch of true theological teaching had been taken out of Adolph Hoenecke's hand, it was already being held high by J. P. Koehler and August Pieper, soon to be joined by John Schaller. The work goes on as losses and blessings blur and blend under the Lord's guiding hand. This also holds true in the consideration of the *last years of the Wisconsin Federation.*

Last Years of the Wisconsin Federation

On October 1, 1900, Professor Ernst of Northwestern abruptly resigned the Federation presidency which he had held since the 1892 organization. The reason for this action in the middle of a two-year term was, according to the record, "the increase in the work assigned to him as president of the school at Watertown."[14] Northwestern was experiencing difficulties at the turn of the century, especially in the work of the dean or inspector. Ernst had to assume some of the responsibilities. His assistant soon resigned. In 1902 even John Meyer resigned the deanship before his first year in the post was completed "because of nervousness."[15]

Vice-President Carl Gausewitz, president of the Minnesota Synod, took over the presidency of the Wisconsin Federation in 1900 and was elected and re-elected in 1901, 1903, and 1905. He was not especially happy with this second presidential responsibility, arguing before the 1903, 1905, and 1907 conventions that the office should be filled by a man from the largest federation member synod. His pleas that he not be re-elected went unheeded until 1907, when he was already in that largest member synod. The Wisconsin delegation could understand the difficulties of working into the Grace, Milwaukee, pastorate and were willing to elect Pastor Soll in his place. After a six-year period of grace the Wisconsin Federation again summoned Gausewitz to the presidency, even though by this time he was also Bading's successor as president of the Synodical Conference.

One Wisconsin Federation concern that Gausewitz was especially equipped to take to heart was the Belle Plaine, Minnesota haven for orphans and the aged. This began as a Minnesota Synod undertaking when Gausewitz was its president. Mrs. Sophia Boessling had offered Minnesota her entire estate, valued at almost $6000, for the establishment of an orphanage at Belle Plaine. In 1895 the Minnesota Synod promptly turned the gift over to the Wisconsin Federation. Its committee, on which Gausewitz served, persuaded Mrs. Boessling to allow the aged to be served in addition to orphans.

After some additional $3000 from a special offering in the involved synods and also Missouri had been added to the original bequest, a suitable building could be erected. It was dedicated on November 8, 1898. In an age when homes for the elderly have become commonplace, this pioneer effort in our church body's circles should not be overlooked. It has been an inspiration and guide for later ventures.

Perhaps the happiest chapter in the whole story came almost at the beginning. The first death in the Belle Plaine facility occurred two days after its dedication. The person deceased at the age of eighty-three was Sophia Boessling. The Lord had granted her the joy of seeing her dream and her offering come to fruition before granting her even greater joy. The story of this heroine of the faith has been written in the historical record.[16] One wishes that would be true also of many other heroines and heroes of the faith who remain unknown and unsung but who by their services and sacrifices, by their prayers and concerns have enabled and ennobled the continuing existence of their church body.

Along with its mission in Apacheland, described in an earlier chapter, the Wisconsin Federation briefly conducted another "foreign" mission of sorts. This was the Lithuanian mission that had become a part of its outreach efforts at the turn of the century when Pastor Keturakat turned over to the Wisconsin federation his Lithuanian congregation in Chicago upon his move to Collinsville in the same state.

The background can be supplied by quoting President Ernst's report to the 1899 convention:

> Up to the present we have not been doing any home mission work as a Federation. Nor was this necessary since missions in their own territory were naturally the concern of the individual synods. But already at the foundation such work drew the attention of the founders and was designated in the constitution as something that could be carried out jointly. They were especially thinking of such fields that did not lie within the boundaries of any individual synod, but rather outside of them. Now an opportunity is presenting itself.
>
> The commission for home missions of the Wisconsin Synod will be asking the Federation to take over the mission among the Lithuanians. This is a necessary and promising undertaking. The Protestants among the Lithuanians are a devout and solidly Lutheran people and up to now no Lutherans have worked in their midst. Presently a missionary is serving them. But since they are so widely scattered, additional help is needed. Some of them live in New England. Others are in Philadelphia and have there a congregation of their own. Also others are to be found in western Pennsylvania, in southern Illinois, and in South Dakota. In time at least four pastors should be gained for this huge field. . . . The Federation will have to reach a decision in the matter.[17]

For seven years the Lithuanian mission was part of the Wisconsin Federation's concerns. The missionary mentioned in the 1899 presidential report was Pastor W. Herrmann at Chicago. When the Chicago congregation was disintegrating, he was called first to the Missouri high school in Chicago and eventually to Northwestern, serving there from 1926-1938. For a time William Notz, son of the long-time Northwestern professor, served the Philadelphia Lithuanians while a student at the University of Pennsylvania. The long-term worker in this field was, however, Pastor M. Keturakat, who joined the synod in 1898 and did dedicated service for the cause of his people in wanderings from Chicago to Collinsville to

Philadelphia to Eitzen, Minnesota, and again to Collinsville, wanderings that incidentally cost him his life's savings.

The far-flung Lithuanian field actually extended far beyond the normal reach of the midwestern Wisconsin Federation. Discretion replaced the original valor. In 1905 the Federation heard the report that the Synodical Conference would be taking over the Lithuanian mission.[18] From that time on this endeavor would be carried on jointly with the Missouri Synod, as was the continuing mission to the Blacks.

The on-going Wisconsin Federation's worker-training concerns up to 1917 should also be highlighted where they have not been previously described. Little remains to be said about the Saginaw school. Its temporary demise and 1910 reopening as a preparatory school have been adequately noted. In the Wauwatosa seminary story one perplexing development merits some additional attention. It is the 1900 dismissal of Professor G. Thiele.

Thiele was a Halle schoolmate of both Edward Mohldehnke and Adolph Hoenecke in the 1850s. At the latter's insistence he was called to the seminary in 1887 to replace August Graebner, who had moved on to St. Louis, where in 1892 he would publish his history of the Lutheran Church in America.[19] A dozen years later Thiele had become *persona non grata* at Wauwatosa. Perhaps it was the scholar's overattention to minutiae that bogged down the church history courses far from their goal. In any event, Hoenecke pressed for and gained the dismissal of his old schoolmate. The 1901 Wisconsin Pastoral Conference protested the procedure on conscience' grounds.[20] The protest went unheeded, but the nominal pension payments to Thiele would continue throughout the Federation's existence.

At New Ulm and at Watertown the Federation's colleges continued to pursue the worker-training goals that had been established for them. Northwestern's enrollment was just over 200 in the 1916-1917 school year. Doctor Martin Luther College's had slipped back to just below 100. The main developments at both schools were in the calling of men who for decades to come would help shape the work of the colleges and the synod.

At New Ulm, Professor G. Burk, a veteran whose DMLC years matched those of the school, was joined in the music work in 1908 by F. A. Reuter, who ranks with the synod's very best musicians and hymn composers. In that same year Professor E. Bliefernicht began a tenure that would stretch over four decades and would include service in the presidency from 1920 to 1936.

Professor A. Ackermann, who had been called already in 1894, was president from 1908 to 1918. His forced resignation in World

War I years will be given special attention in the next chapter. In the Federation's last years two other men began long tenures at New Ulm: M. Wagner in 1916 as dean and R. Albrecht in 1917.

At Northwestern, Watertown, in the Federation years of the twentieth century five men were called into professorships they would fill for at least a quarter century. They were C. Bolle (1902-1945); W. Huth (1911-1936); E. E. Kowalke (1913-1969 and 1919-1959 school head); E. Wendland (1913-1959); and G. Westerhaus (1916-1966).

Mention might well be made of the able service of Professor Martin Eickmann as dean from 1903-1915. After his sudden death in June 1915 a new dormitory supervision system was developed. Suggested by Professor J. P. Koehler, dean from 1888-1894, and favored by a committee of representatives of all worker-training schools, the plan called for so-called "tutors," dormitory assistants recruited from the most recent seminary graduates for a term of two years and serving under the school head. By and large the system is still in operation, except for the fact that in the 1930s a dean was called to oversee the work of the tutors. Among the first tutors was Carl Schweppe, who helped President Ernst draw up the set of regulations according to which the system was to operate.[21]

Steps to the Merger

It is not necessary to probe deeply or to write extensively when reasons for the 1917 Wisconsin move from federation to merger are to be set down. This was basically a realization that the limited joint efforts in publication, worker-training, and missions were proving so beneficial that they ought to be enlarged. That the realization coincided with a major Reformation anniversary stressing Lutheran roots and togetherness was simply in the nature of a catalytic agent. It determined the timetable of an event that would have happened sooner or later.

Back in 1903 an overture signed by nineteen pastors raised the issue of merging the independent synods of the Wisconsin Federation. The Federation reacted by appointing a study committee of twelve.[22] In 1905 this committee's report favoring more federation cooperation but not an outright merger was for all practical purposes tabled.[23] In 1907 an overture of the Eastern Conference of the Wisconsin Synod asking for merger was sent back to its source with the request that the matter be resubmitted after more study.[24] There was, however, no action to report in 1909.

In 1911 lay delegates to the Mankato convention of the Wisconsin Federation renewed the effort in an overture that the convention endorsed to the extent of urging that the subject be studied first by committees of the individual synods and then by a federation committee that these synodical committees would constitute.[25] This resolution broke through parliamentary problems and paved the way for positive proposals.

The federation committee recommended a four-point plan that the convention accepted: creation of a merged body; division into districts without consideration for previous synodical boundaries; transfer of properties to the merged body; and retention of debts by the individual synod that incurred them.[26] Nebraska removed its last concerns, and the whole project seemed to be headed for successful completion.

At this point a threatening roadblock emerged. It was not a matter of opposition to merger but rather a desire to enlarge the merger by bringing the whole Synodical Conference into the picture. Laymen of both the Wisconsin and Missouri Synods sought to revive the old dream of Synodical Conference state synods under a larger general grouping.[27] Some favorable sentiment manifested itself in Minnesota and in other Synodical Conference circles.

This belated drive for a bigger merger lost its steam when the proposal for the smaller merger made headway. In 1915 a constitution based on the 1913 proposal was adopted. It became operative in 1917. Final ratification occurred in 1919 after the last legal hurdles were surmounted and the last property transfers were effected.

In 1920 the Synodical Conference received this formal notification:

> The undersigned take this opportunity to give notice that the merger of the Synods of Wisconsin, Minnesota, Michigan, and Nebraska into a corporate body, which for many years had been cultivated, was in the course of time realized and the result that has transpired is that there now exists a Joint Evangelical Lutheran Synod of Wisconsin and Other States embracing within itself . . . eight districts . . . .
> In the name and at the instruction of the Joint Synod,
> Most respectfully,
> G. E. Bergemann, President
> G. Hinnenthal, Secretary
>
> Goodhue, Minnesota
> August 17, 1920[28]

The special role of that undersigned president, G. E. Bergemann, in the whole proceedings — will be deferred to the next section. Also to be deferred is the explanation of why in 1920 there are eight districts instead of the six involved in the 1917 merger.

CHAPTER TWELVE

Merger Beginnings in War Years

The First World War marks the midpoint of Wisconsin Synod history. From 1850 to 1918 is sixty-eight years. From 1918 to the time of this writing is about the same length of time. The first half of the Wisconsin Synod story has been completed.

In another sense, one could begin the Wisconsin Synod story in 1917-1918. That is when the church body we today know as the WELS actually began to take its present shape. Allowance must, of course, be given to growth factors over two thirds of a century. Aside from these, however, today's church body is exactly what was developed in 1917: a synod created by a merger of parts that remained its districts. There may be twice as many districts today and they may lie far beyond the old midwestern stamping grounds, but the synodical structure is basically the same.

Making the Merger Work

The merger picture will be more sharply focused if there is a numbers breakdown. The best available statistics are to be found in the 1919 synodical report.

The listing of stations adds preaching places to organized congregations. There were ninety-three preaching places in the *stations* total. The *schools* listing may well include part-time agencies. In the teaching force were also many pastors conducting school. The Northern Wisconsin District lists fifty-four and Michigan thirty-four. Obviously pastors were manning the two Pacific Northwest schools. That district will be more fully described in a subsequent section of this chapter.[1]

1919 Statistics for the Merged Wisconsin Synod

	Stations	Pastors	Commun.	Schools	Teachers M	F	Pupils
Wis. North. Dist.	167	84		69	23	30	
Wis. SE Dist.	96	97		68	42	26	3,505
Wis. West. Dist	140	81	31,132	79	66	32	3,508
Wisc. Totals	403	262	ca 90,000	216	131	88	ca 10,000
Minn. Dist.	178	103	21,791	57	16	13	2,303
Mich. Dist.	76	45	11,791	34	12	6	1,162
Neb. Dist.	29	21	2,998	16	4	2	354
Pacific NW Dist.	12	7	503	2	0	0	113
Synod Totals	698	438	ca 127,083	325	163	109	ca 13,952

Perhaps the most striking item in the extensive statistical reports being summarized is an addendum to the Pacific Northwest report. In a listing one of its congregation reports: "We have Woman Suffrage. Our committee [sic] list is our membership list." There were obvious but unreported dealings in this matter. The 1920 statistics still list for the involved congregation 164 communicants and 164 voting members.[2] By 1921, however, the record shows 169 communicants and 125 voting members.

The 1919 general synodical convention at New Ulm, the first at which the merged body could flex its newly found muscles, may well have been as busy and productive as any since. World War tasks had to be wound down while postwar problems had to be faced in Poland and elsewhere. As the silver anniversary of the teachers college was being observed in the host location, the looming threats to Christian day schools had to be addressed and the move into Christian education in the high school years had to be considered. In the worker-training area of concern, low enrollments were viewed with alarm and building needs and seminary relocation were presented as challenges.

The best news of all was that the fiscal officers could report for the biennium income of $562,570.56 and disbursements of $546,717.55. After its first two years of operation the merged synod could report $15,853.01 cash on hand, in contrast to $2467.31 on hand July 1, 1917.

The 1919 synodical convention was certainly better prepared for its important decision making than any of its predecessors. In those days, when easy and instantaneous document reproduction was not yet known, the synodical president reports as an innovation that he made available all incoming synodical reports and memorials "to every professor, every pastor and every teacher and every delegate."³ That procedure may have made the convention's tremendous work load bearable and manageable. The 1917 *Proceedings* embrace 101 pages. The 1921 *Proceedings* have 205. The 1919 *Proceedings* contain 287 pages.

This may be the place to center attention on the synodical leader, President G. E. Bergemann, who succeeded President von Rohr as Wisconsin Synod head in 1908 and then went on to lead the merged body until 1933. In that year he was unseated, although still willing to serve, in the only instance of that kind in the long history of both Wisconsin Synods, the one begun in 1850 and the other organized in 1917. A discussion of the causes for this unique turn of events really belongs in subsequent chapters.

This is the place to highlight the administrative abilities and accomplishments of G. E. Bergemann. Muehlhaeuser founded the Wisconsin Synod. Bading shaped its confessional stance. Bergemann gave it its organizational form. Bergemann made the merger and then made it work.

He himself describes these efforts in his report to the 1919 convention:

> The work at times increased tremendously, especially in the first year of the biennium. In that period of time I was able to have only eight full weeks in my congregation uninterrupted by necessary travel. In the past two years I logged over 20,000 railroad miles and carried on an extensive correspondence. Because of lack of time and energy it was not possible for me to carry out an important part of my assignment, the visitation of the worker-training schools.⁴

A quarter century later President Bergemann could still vividly recall and recount those 20,000 miles without benefit of planes or perks and then conclude, "It just had to be done to make the merger work." The 1933 unseating because of dissatisfaction over Depression debts and internal synodical strife has tended to cast President Bergemann in a less than favorable light. He deserves better.

Gustav Ernst Bergemann was born on a Hustisford farm, August 9, 1862. He was instructed and confirmed by Philipp Koehler.⁵ His high school and college training was at Northwestern, where he graduated in 1885 as a member of what he liked to call "the model Northwestern class." His seminary studies at Milwaukee were ended prematurely when he was sent out in 1887 to fill a vacancy at Bay City, Michigan. Sixty years later he could still inveigh bitterly against such early terminations of seminary training as unfair to both seminarians and congregations.

The Bay City pastorate lasted until 1892 and was followed by seven years of service at Tomah. In 1899 Bergemann moved to Fond du Lac, where he would remain until his death in 1954. He had retired from the ministry seven years before on the sixtieth anniversary of his ordination.

After service on the synodical board of trustees and the board of Northwestern College and on the Federation's boards for the theological seminary and teachers' college and the Indian and Lithuanian missions, Bergemann was in 1907 elected the synod's first vice-president as successor to John Bading. Because of President von Rohr's illness and death in 1908 this vice-presidency was no sinecure. In 1909 he was elected president in his own right and then served the original Wisconsin Synod as such until the merger and then the merged synod, as previously indicated, until 1933.

In the area of administration Bergemann introduced a number of practices that were sorely needed and served well in the infant years of the merged synod. The 1919 effort to place convention reports in the hands of delegates for advance study before the actual meeting blossomed in 1923 into the first BORAM (*Book of Reports and Memorials*). Offsprings of this prototype are still appearing in the spring of every convention year. In those first years of the merger Bergemann also oversaw the development of a "Synodical Council" consisting of representatives of the various mission and educational and administrative boards and meeting at least annually. Improved communication and more centralization have made it possible to streamline and de-emphasize the "Synodical Council," but back in the twenties it rendered yeoman service in actually merging what had been four independent synods.

As the chapter title indicates, the first years of the Wisconsin merger were the years of World War I. That complicated further what was in itself a difficult enough development for the merged synod and its president. Special problems had to be faced in serving men in the armed forces and in dealing with the anti-German feeling directed against a predominantly German church body.

Over Here and Over There

The order is deliberate. In the World War, as "the war to end all wars" was naively named in its own time, the Wisconsin Synod as a church body was not deeply involved "over there." There may have been some 2000 synod members "over there," if the ratio of synod and country population holds true in this instance. Actual statistics are not available. What is on the record is that there was no Wisconsin Synod chaplain "over there." In its final report the synodical

135

board for the spiritual care of men in the armed forces reported: "What under the prevailing circumstances could be done for our brothers has been done. That we could not send any camp pastors to them in Europe is not the fault of the board."[6]

"Over here" the involvement in serving the spiritual needs of the men in the armed forces was much more extensive. In the comparatively unstructured military chaplaincy of that time there was also a limited participation in its programs. The whole scope of the church body's effort to serve men in the military can best be seen by a first-hand account. At the first Michigan District convention at Scio, June 17-24, while American doughboys were getting their first full test of combat readiness and passing it successfully, the district secretary set down a report quoted verbatim. It should be noted that President Bergemann is not reporting on Wisconsin Synod work alone but on the joint Synodical Conference activity in which Wisconsin followed where the Missouri Synod led.

> The synodical president, Pastor G. E. Bergemann reported to the convention on the work of the "Army and Navy Board." The merged synod at its St. Paul convention [1917] resolved to make the honored Missouri Synod's established committee its own. Since a committee had also already been named by the Wisconsin Synod, it was to be placed at the side of the Synodical Conference committee in an advisory capacity.
>
> Up to now we have assigned 37 chaplains [camp pastors] who are devoting their full efforts to the military; 12 more are presently being urgently requested. It is very difficult to find suitable men for this work. The government has appointed 7 men from our circles, one of whom is in France. In addition to their own parishes, 75 pastors are serving our boys in army camps. Although this is a considerable number, we cannot be satisfied with it for the future. We have to supply more workers. In order to acquaint our people more fully with our work in the camps and to interest them in it, the committee issues a little monthly periodical called *Lutheran Soldiers and Sailors Bulletin*. This pamphlet ought to find wide circulation and many readers in our circles.
>
> Experience has taught us that it is better for us to erect our own barracks in the camps, because our church services in those of the YMCA are given an atmosphere that in our opinion does not harmonize with the spirit of the gospel. Recently we have found out that we can achieve the right to erect our own buildings without having to work together with other Lutheran bodies in this land.
>
> The "Lutheran Brotherhood," incorporated in the state of Iowa, has as its goal to erect barracks in the camps in which

church services can be held. Another society, the "Lutheran Federation," has as its goal to achieve the certification of our chaplains by the government. These people told us that if we Lutherans wanted to achieve these two things then we would have to stand before the government as a united Lutheran church, not as Missouri or Ohio, or Wisconsin or General Council, since the government will not concern itself with separate synods. Thus it appeared at the outset that we would be compelled to work outwardly with the others, while at the same also faithfully adhering to our doctrinal position. Very soon, however, it became apparent that it was not possible to maintain this separation of externals and doctrinal matters in joint practical work. For those people have a definite purpose in mind in this joint work. They want to erase the previously maintained boundaries and differences in doctrinal matters; they want to employ the prevailing circumstances to force a general union. But with the passage of time we found that we could also as Synodical Conference have the previously mentioned matters carried through with the consent of the government.

A chaplain costs us monthly about $200, not because their salaries are so exceptionally high, but because of the costly extras. Because of the great distances involved we had to buy Fords for several chaplains. We also have to supply our boys gratis such things as books, writing materials and church periodicals. Next year we will need $400,000, of which a fifth is the responsibility of our synod. What has previously been collected and submitted by our congregations has sufficed for the needs up to this time but more will be needed in the future. For the gathering of these monies preparatory plans have been made. Consequently a special finance committee has been placed at the side of the Army and Navy Board which has undertaken the drafting of a plan for collecting the funds.

Experience in this work has taught us that we should have in Washington, D.C., a standing committee that furthers our cause there. This committee, which represents the whole Synodical Conference, should consist of three members. Through such a committee many a difficulty could be ameliorated in advance and many a threatening danger could be nipped in the bud.

As a last point it was resolved [by the district] to endorse the requests of the federation president and to make them our own. It was also resolved to approve the work of the Army and Navy Board and to encourage those involved to continue their endeavors and to assure them of our support.[7]

It is to be noted in the report that in World War I days the Wisconsin Synod energetically strove to do all it could to care for the spiritual needs of servicemen but at the same time was concerned about doing this in a way that would not violate cherished doctrinal and confessional and fellowship principles. It should also be noted that in World War I the military chaplaincy was less rigidly structured than it would become in World War II days and that a Synodical Conference identity could be maintained. It would be well also to note that the man President Bergemann appointed to head the synod's committee for this cause was John Brenner, Bading's successor at St. John, Milwaukee. He learned to know the military chaplaincy operation first hand. He reacted with experience when World War II chaplaincy problems arose during his synodical presidency. In a letter to the Chief of Chaplains dated March 31, 1943, he expressed his World War I experiences when he wrote, "In our estimation the 'civilian camp pastor' of the First World War came much closer to meeting our requirements."[8]

The deepest synodical involvement in wartime problems in 1917-1918 was at the New Ulm college. The school head, President Alfred Ackermann, had to resign by official request. The "official" refers to both state and church governing bodies. What was involved was a spirited attack on the World War I draft on the grounds that there had not been any invasion to be repelled, as the United States Constitution stipulates when granting the right to "provide for calling forth the militia." This is a point Ackermann made in speeches at anti-draft meetings in New Ulm and elsewhere.[9]

It may sound like a very technical and legal point and in a way it was. It merited the attention of the United States Supreme Court in its 1918 *Selective Draft Law Cases* but produced a ruling adverse to draft objectors. The anti-draft argument never had much chance of winning friends and influencing people in peace time. In time of war, with not a little anti-German war hysteria loose on the land, the argument simply could not prevail.

The Minnesota Commission of Public Safety might not have proceeded so rigorously against Ackermann had he stayed home. New Ulm may well have seemed to the Minnesota authorities a troublesome German enclave to be controlled and contained, since it could not be converted. Ackermann, however, determined to take his protest on the road. He spoke to a rally of 2000 at nearby Gibbon and in a number of other area towns. This seemed intolerable to the authorities. They demanded that the synodical authorities take action; the school's governing body requested Ackermann's resignation and received it on January 29, 1918. Tendering what was demanded, Ackermann declared, "What is right remains right."[10] Ackermann went on to become president of the Minnesota District and served as such from 1936 to 1948.

The World War I superpatriotism that could even object to a term like *Sauerkraut* and replace it with *liberty cabbage* caused the church body some problems in the language field during and immediately after the war. In the long run, however, and in the good governance of the Lord of the church, the temporary problems were turned into enduring blessings.

There were difficulties when states passed official legislation forbidding the use of German in public gatherings and when communities and citizens unofficially objected to German church services and school lessons. Our sister church body, the Evangelical Lutheran Synod, with a Norwegian language problem of its own, had to organize in 1918 by straddling the Minnesota-Iowa border to circumvent one state's laws directed against foreign language use in a public meeting.[11] The incident itself, however, indicates that it was possible to make do in spite of the difficulties.

The long-range benefit was that the long-overdue transition from German to English was speeded up in World War I. The war was not the cause of the transition, but it certainly acted as a catalyst. The synod's periodical for all its members, our *Northwestern Lutheran*, is a case in point. It began publication in 1914 before any Sarajevo assassination or war declarations but the war certainly helped in gaining sorely needed subscribers in the trying infant years. In the 1920s official proceedings began to appear also in English.

The reader might want to know the precise year when English moved from a minority to a majority status for the church body. This is impossible. Those making the transition never were conscious of the fact that they were making history in the process. They were simply reacting to a necessary and inevitable change and gradually buried the language problem.

Efforts at dating the turn from German to English might scrutinize *Gemeinde-Blatt* and *Northwestern Lutheran* subscriber totals and spot 1939 as the year when the latter first outnumbered the former. Such a reading of the record overlooks the fact that the *Gemeinde-Blatt* had over the years gained a very loyal following out of all proportion to German's numerical strength in the church body. Counting congregations with services in both languages or one or the other will not tell the full story either. Those who had founded those congregations in years past and had been its pillars for so many years were naturally indulged when language preferences had to be evaluated and voted on in a congregational meeting. If pressed for a specific date for the transition, the writer would suggest the years 1929-1930. It was then, he estimates, that the Wisconsin Synod ceased being a German and became an English synod.[12]

The subject of the language transition should not be concluded without a tribute to a whole generation of Wisconsin Synod pastors who conducted a bilingual ministry as a matter of course and without any idea that they were rendering a special service. In their parishes were some members whose church language was German and others whose was English. The pastors served both groups in the public services and the private devotions. There were only a few exceptional veterans who could not adjust to the new situation. Almost to a man the newcomers mastered a language foreign to them because they wanted to serve the flock entrusted to them.

In those transition decades leaders in the church frequently pointed to dangers involved in the change inevitably taking place. This was almost always a concern about theological consequence when pastors no longer could understand Luther and read instead the vast Reformed literature available in English. The leaders wanted the gospel to be preached and taught and communicated one-on-one in the language of the land.[13] They also wanted the pastors doing the preaching and teaching and communicating to have their theology rooted in the languages of both Bible and Reformation. A half century ago it was clearly demonstrated that pastors could without too much sweat or strain serve people in both German and English and at the same time study theology in German and other languages. The lesson should not be forgotten just because some fifty or sixty years have passed.

New Districts for the New Church Body

The merged structure of the church body made it possible for two rather thinly populated and quite remote areas to become districts. An independent synodical existence for them seemed unthinkable; a district status within a synod was a live option. The two areas were the long-established home mission field of the Minnesota Synod in the Dakotas and Montana and the Pacific Northwest, which had a number of congregations that had joined the Wisconsin Synod. In 1918 the Pacific Northwest District of the Wisconsin Synod came into being. In 1920 the Dakota-Montana District was formed.

This sudden jump from six to eight districts in the Wisconsin Synod is worthy of note. In the next half century only one other instance of the creation of a district would be noted. This was the birth of the Arizona-California District in 1954. It would take until 1973 before there would be a tenth Wisconsin Synod district.

The birthplace of the Pacific Northwest District was Tacoma. There in 1898 a Lutheran congregation which had been organized back in 1894 under the leadership of Pastor F. A. Wolf, formerly of the General Synod, sought and gained membership in the Wisconsin Synod. It was only a matter of time before there would be neighboring congregations. In 1910 the pioneer pastors, R. Ave-Lallemant, Wolf's successor once removed, L. C. Krug, M. Raasch, and F. E. Stern, were holding pastoral conferences. Two years later Pastor F. H. K. Soll, who later served as the district's first president, came to Yakima when L. C. Krug was granted a health leave.[14] In the same year a pastoral conference was formally organized. By 1918 there were eight pastors in the area serving ten congregations and sixteen preaching places.

During July in 1918, the Pacific Northwest District was formally organized. Synod President G. E. Bergemann was present at the occasion. The constituent convention was held in Yakima. Travel was a major concern. Let the *Northwestern Lutheran* report tell the story:

> Because of the great distance the expense account of travel to the synod is a considerable item in this district. To lighten the burden one pastor and his delegate had come a distance of over 200 miles by automobile; two other pastors with delegates came by automobile over the mountain passes where they found occasion to prove their general fitness by helping the motor mount the steeper grades through the exertion of personal push. Overnight they camped in the open; in the morning, refreshed by cold mountain water, they moved onward.[15]

The "personal push" needed to get delegates across mountain passes on the way to conventions also had to be exerted to get reluctant prospects into the mission congregations of the Pacific Northwest District. The growth would be slow in the years ahead. Too many who went west left behind their earlier religious persuasions and previous congregational memberships before they crossed those mountain passes.

On this side of the passes a Dakota-Montana District of the Wisconsin Synod came into being in 1920. The roots go back to outreach efforts of Minnesota Synod missionaries in the late 1870s, among them C. Boettcher, E. L. Luebbert, G. Lahme, and Z. Johl. The work went on whether the Dakota prairies were experiencing the alternating boom and bonanza or bust and dust years.

Among those gathered into the small and struggling Dakota congregations were the German Lutheran immigrants from Russia, especially the pietistically inclined among them who were known as *Betbrueder* or "praying brothers." An inexperienced pastor could summarily be, if not unfrocked, at least unflocked if he committed what the *Betbrueder* regarded as the unpardonable sin of substituting a reading for an *ex corde* prayer.[16]

By 1919 the Dakotas and Montana were definitely among the "other states" included in the merged body's official title, The Evangelical Lutheran Joint Synod of Wisconsin, Minnesota, Michigan, and Other States. In the 1917 proposed constitution for the merged body Dakota, Montana, and "Pacific" districts have already been mentioned.[17] In the process of district formation three major reasons were advanced:

1. Much travel time and money would be saved when it came to attending district meetings;
2. The area would have district officials of its own living in the actual field of labor;
3. A more stable ministry could be envisioned, since pastors tend to remain in their districts.[18]

While the third reason may have turned out to be more of a devout desire than a hard fact of Dakota-Montana District history, the new district was created with the best of hopes for the future on the part of those who would be its members and with the parental blessing of the releasing Minnesota District.

In the course of the Minnesota District's 1920 convention at Mankato twenty-three pastors and six congregational delegates organized the new district. The date was June 25, 1920. Pastor William F. Sauer of Watertown, South Dakota, soon to be called to the pastorate of Grace, Milwaukee, was the first president. The key post of home missions superintendent in the far-flung district was assigned to Pastor Carl Schweppe of Bowdle, South Dakota. He would leave the district before the year was out, accepting a call to Doctor Martin Luther College, which he would hold both as instructor and president until his retirement in 1966.

The exodus of pastors from the Dakota-Montana area may not have been arrested during the first decades of the district's history. In the mid-century years this comparatively small district would often claim the lion's share of the graduates of the theological seminary. The district learned to live with this problem and survive, even during the Depression. A great source of district *esprit de corps* in those years was the synodical preparatory school at Mobridge, established in 1927. That story, however, belongs in the next chapter.

CHAPTER THIRTEEN

Focus on Education

World War I may not have been the longest or broadest or costliest of our country's armed conflicts, but the impact and influence it exerted on American life was profound, even traumatic. America in the twenties was poles apart from the America of the first two decades of the twentieth century. Not the least of the postwar transformations occurred in the field of education.

There were feverish efforts to upgrade the old three-R curriculum in the little red school houses of the land and to turn the buildings themselves into something less small and less red. Sometimes the efforts became so intense that they could even tread on the toes of private and religious schools with new curricular or building or attendance requirements.

But the biggest educational boom in the twenties was on the high school level. There the rather limited pre-college program of the previous era began to give way to all-inclusive practical courses that offered something for everybody. Attendance swelled as more and more teenagers received the high school diploma that had previously been attainable for only an elitist few. In the decade the total of high school graduates more than doubled from some 300,000 in 1920 to two thirds of a million in 1930.

It is not surprising that such an upswing in educational endeavors on the national scene should be reflected on a much smaller scale in the Wisconsin Synod. It too saw advancement and growth on both the elementary and secondary educational levels during the decade of the twenties. The first of the levels receives first attention.

Christian Day Schools

A resume of pertinent items that were given random treatment in previous chapters may well be in place to provide the setting.

THE WISCONSIN SYNOD LUTHERANS

From its very beginning in 1850 the Wisconsin Synod expressed a firm commitment to Christian education for the youth of the church. In the earliest years the pastors were the teachers, and the length of the school term and day depended on the time they could devote to the task.

Gradually the congregations began to call teachers. By 1858 the pioneer congregation, Grace in Milwaukee, had two teachers. In 1872 nineteen male teachers met at St. Peter, Milwaukee to form the General Teachers Conference of the Wisconsin Synod that lives on in today's Wisconsin State Teachers Conference. At the time of the silver anniversary of the synod there were eighty-five schools.

In that same year the records show that the wife of Teacher Voss in Watertown was joining her husband in his work on a part-time basis. Five years later Winona also secured a woman to assist Teacher Walz when his pupil count passed 110.[1]

Large pupil count in a schoolroom, strange as it may seem to us, was the order of the day in synod schools before 1900. In 1880 a classroom at St. Jacobi, Milwaukee even passed the 120 mark. If this sounds unbelievable, one should recall that these were the days of large families and sturdy discipline in home and school.

By 1882 the teaching force had grown to forty-seven male teachers, thirty-two pastors serving in the classroom and twelve women teachers. They were teaching some five thousand students in eighty-five schools. There was one teacher for fifty-five pupils.

In the course of the battle over the Bennett Law, previously described, a synodical school secretary was appointed as part of the upgrading that quite naturally resulted from the fight to save German parochial schools. This was Northwestern's Doctor F. Notz, whose statistical reports seem to be much more accurate than their earlier counterparts cited in previous paragraphs. In the 1893 report, the second for the Wisconsin Federation, Dr. Notz offered these figures:

Synod	Congregations	Schools	Teachers	Pupils
Wisconsin	278	141	119	8621
Minnesota	106	57	14	2238
Michigan	53	35	4	1088
Federation	437	233	137	11947[2]

Readers will recall that 1893 was a memorable year in the educational history of the Wisconsin Synod. It was then that Doctor Martin Luther College began to play its assigned role in the Federation's worker-training arrangements. This was to serve as the one school for preparing parish teachers for the three synods in the federated church body. To the time of this writing DMLC has endeavored to fill that assignment.

What happened at the New Ulm school in 1893 had its effect on the school at Watertown—Northwestern. What had begun there in the 1860s as an all-purpose worker-training school had yielded the theological department first to St. Louis in 1869 and then to Milwaukee in 1878. In 1893 the teacher-training department ceased to function, in deference to the New Ulm development. A brief obituary of this little-known educational venture is in order.[3]

For some dozen years before 1893 Northwestern had offered a course to train Wisconsin Synod teachers. Those enrolled were included in a non-ministerial department that consisted also of general academic students. In the last year of its normal training Northwestern graduated six such students, including daughters of Professors Ernst and Notz. In 1890 there were also six normal graduates.

Normal departments at Watertown and New Ulm in those years should not be thought of as providing four-year college programs. While some comparison of oranges and apples is involved, the program could be described as a stiff high school course with one additional year. In the Northwestern program, as it has been described in the records, students "were excused in the two upper classes of the academy from mathematics and science courses and received instead special training in religion, music, and educational psychology and methodology."[4]

If a one-year college training for teachers strikes us as woefully inadequate, we should remind ourselves that such a program compared favorably with the course of a typical county normal school in the public school system of that era. If a scrapping of advanced science and mathematics in a teacher-training program seems to us to be unwise, we might recall that this was a half century before the advent of *sputnik*. It was an era when the three-Rs still predominated and the third R stood for rudimentary arithmetic.

When the Wisconsin Synod's teacher training moved to New Ulm in 1893, so did the *Lutherische Schulzeitung* (*Lutheran School Periodical*). In the interest of professional advancement Wisconsin teachers had launched this monthly magazine in 1876. Doctor Notz was the first editor and already in 1879 persuaded the synodical convention to make the *Schulzeitung* an official publication of the church body. Under the aegis of Doctor Martin Luther College and Editor John Schaller the *Schulzeitung* ceased publication after a dozen years because of a dwindling subscriber list. In this connection one might recall that in earlier days a Minnesota Synod school journal had been forced to break off publication.

The cause of the Christian schools in the congregations of the Wisconsin Synod received a big boost when a major worker-training study, to be described more fully in the next section of this chapter, gained for the teacher-training course a sixth year of study, two on the college and four on the high school level. At the same time a synodical "school visitor" was appointed. Claus Gieschen was the first to fill the post. Before the end of the twenties New Ulm college freshmen would begin a three-year study program. The years after World War I were a time for special concerns for the parish schools and for their pupils.

Out in Nebraska these concerns were intensified when in 1919 the state legislature passed two laws that threatened the future of the Christian day schools in the state. One law required that all instruction in the grades be in English and the other set up a program of mandatory teacher certification.[5]

The language law was tested in the courts with Teacher Meyer of the Missouri Synod offering himself for the role of violator. The case went all the way to the United States Supreme Court, and there in 1923 in *Meyer v. Nebraska* the Nebraska statute was voided as an infringement of parental rights guaranteed by the Fourteenth Amendment.

In the certification problem the Nebraska District reluctantly complied to avoid any closing of the schools while a long court battle dragged on. None of the teachers or pastors teaching in the Nebraska District's schools held any certificate to start with, but a hastily arranged summer program of eleven weeks at Fremont College provided all concerned with such a certificate by the time of the fall school term.

A modern-day researcher might conclude from listings of the number of schools in the synod that the grade schools suffered tremendous setbacks after World War I. The figures, in a sense, lie. There may be reports of some 350 schools in the synod around 1910, while the 1923 figure is 146 schools. The facts in the case are that the general improvement in educational endeavors also dictated a new definition of a school. The 146 schools in 1923 include no summer or Saturday schools; they are all full-term operations.

Upgrading Worker Training

There has been previous reference to a 1919 synodical convention education report.[6] The report is significant enough to merit more than passing mention. By a synodical resolution of 1917 a special educational survey committee was authorized and President Bergemann appointed to it the following: August Pieper, chairman, Doctor

Ernst, Director O. J. Hoenecke, Professors Bliefernicht, H. Frank, W. Henkel, and R. Albrecht, Pastors W. Bodamer, J. Brenner, J. Witt, District President Baumann, and Teacher Eggebrecht. Later, Director J. Meyer replaced Professor Bliefernicht as the Doctor Martin Luther College representative and Professor E. Sauer replaced H. Frank. The committee met for fifteen plenary sessions between March 1918 and July 1919 and presented the synod with a condensed report of twenty-seven pages with no less than twenty-seven proposals.[7]

The more important of these that the convention adopted are:

1b) That Watertown and Saginaw should have four-year high school programs;
2) That the proposed high school curriculum be approved;
5) That a parallel German course be offered in the high school years to novices in the language;
8) That New Ulm add a sixth year to its program and call two additional professors;
11) That high school and college laboratories be provided;
12) That adequate funds for library purchases be made available;
21) That salaries be raised to meet rising living costs;
23) That Director Meyer's curriculum for summer and Sunday schools be disseminated;
24) That a school visitor be appointed to work under the direction of a committee consisting of President Bergemann, Director J. Schaller, and Professor Henkel.

Even the committee's suggestions that the convention saw fit to reject or defer for further study are interesting enough to cite as examples of the kind of educational thinking and planning that was surfacing in the post-World War I era. The more important of these tabled or rejected items are:

1a) That the Watertown college course comprise four years;
4) That the previous German-English training be maintained;
6) That physical education be required of all students but that a so-called "sports mania" (*Sportgeist*) be energetically resisted;
7) That the college years of Doctor Martin Luther College be transferred from New Ulm to Watertown;
13) That summer courses for pastors and teachers be established;
14) That there be regular and competent visitation at all synodical schools;
15) That suitable text books be published for use at our colleges and seminary;
20) That provisions be made for advanced study by synod's professors.

Such forward-looking educational planning would obviously include also concerns for the physical plants at the synodical schools. Proposal 16 in the report mentioned previously in fact insisted: "That the boards of the various schools be instructed to keep the properties of the schools in good condition. We especially point to conditions at Wauwatosa."

The seminary at Wauwatosa, although only some twenty-five years old, was badly overcrowded. In 1918-1919 the enrollment swelled to fifty-eight and the next year reached sixty-one. Since there had always been legal strings attached to the donation of the Wauwatosa site, it was decided at the outset that a new property should be acquired for the new seminary which the synod resolved in 1921 to build.[8]

There was a long search for that property. In its first stages a Bues Farm in the vicinity of Oconomowoc received consideration. Then a Van Dyke property in Wauwatosa was purchased but later resold on the grounds that a $100,000 site was simply too rich for the synodical bloodstream. Eventually an 80 acre farm bordering on the village of Thiensville was acquired for about $25,000.[9] It is still the seminary location, even though the post office address is now Mequon.

By 1928 building operations could begin. In the planning of the building the school head, Professor J. P. Koehler, played a very active role that occupied so much of his time in the spring of 1927 that he occasionally had to skimp and stint on other assignments. One such occasion would have disastrous consequences that will be recounted in the next section. In any event, very satisfactory blueprints were drawn and a very attractive building was erected. Dedication day was August 18, 1929, the Sunday of that year's synodical convention. The cost of the building and the four professors' residences was a little over $350,000.

Since a huge synodical debt loomed large in synodical history in the years of the Depression, some special attention to building expenditures in the twenties is in place. It should be noted at the very outset that all due prudence was exercised from the time of the first resolution to build to the completion of the venture. Building at Thiensville was no reckless boom venture that failed to count the cost. That first resolution of 1921 to build a new seminary carried the stringent rider that "no building operation be begun until at least two thirds of the necessary sum has been collected or at least pledged" and "that the total cost should not exceed $500,000."[10] In 1923, at the urging of Chairman J. Brenner's seminary building committee, the convention upgraded the 1921 resolution to the effect that no building operation be begun "until the whole present debt has been paid and also the whole sum for the seminary building is on hand."[11]

The story of the Thiensville building operation repeats itself at New Ulm, at least in part. There the year added to the student program and the high hopes for an upsurge in parochial education had pointed promptly and directly to the need for an upgraded classroom building. This was granted by the 1927 convention with the provisions that "costs should not exceed the sum of $327,000," and since $52,000 was already on hand through the diamond jubilee offering, the trustees "were empowered to borrow up to $275,000."[12] The "pay-as-you-build" policy had become something else under the press of needs that would not and could not be ignored or postponed. The 1929 financial report credits the New Ulm building fund with one third of the $275,000.[13]

In the late years of the decade under discussion Northwestern College began to call attention to library needs. The calling was too late, if not too little. Two decades, embracing the Depression and World War II, would pass before there were tangible results.

Ventures on the High School Level

The 1919 educational survey committee also suggested a transfer of the college work at New Ulm to Watertown. The reasoning was that combining the college work in ministerial and teacher training would make possible more effective teaching. While the plan never gained synodical favor, it did generate some thinking about schooling on the high school level. After college training was concentrated at Watertown, the committee suggested, "The already existing synodical schools in the districts could become fully established high schools with a four-year program. In addition other high schools should be established immediately in Nebraska and Dakota."[14] High school training, also for general students, was beginning to claim its share of attention.

In 1920 Friedens Congregation in Kenosha resolved to add a ninth grade to its large parochial school and to add a grade each subsequent year until there would be a full high school for the youth of the congregation.[15] That a single congregation would determine to develop its own high school certainly demonstrates exemplary zeal for Christian education. This is a unique accomplishment in the annals of our church body.

Unfortunately there is a sad ending to the story. In 1930 Friedens felt compelled to close its high school. The Depression was leaving its mark by then and the heroic congregational effort could not be sustained. It would take until 1934 before Friedens reopened its ninth grade.

The scene shifts to Fond du Lac where another high school in Wisconsin Synod circles began to see the light of day in 1925. The long-time pastor there, Synod President G. E. Bergemann, always insisted that all credit for getting Winnebago Lutheran Academy started should go to an eighth grade graduate of the St. Peter day school. His story was that at the graduation service this young girl broke off from her prepared address to beg the congregation, "Please give us at least one more grade at our school."

With what happened after that Pastor Bergemann became very much involved. If he cannot be accused of overt coaching—he denied this emphatically—he was quick to react to the graduation speaker's cue. The congregation supplied a classroom in its new school building and a teacher, Mr. E. C. Jacobs, who was assisted in Latin instruction by the head pastor, Hans Kollar Moussa, who had accepted the St. Peter call the year before.

In the summer of 1926 a Winnebago Lutheran Association of interested members of St. Peter and of neighboring congregations was formed to foster Christian education for another three high school years. There were trying times ahead. A resolution to postpone for a year the addition of the next grade in the sequence because of financial problems was overturned when the St. Peter pastors went on a last-ditch fund raising effort. In just three days, Pastor Bergemann would fondly recall, he gathered $2300—in times when dollars were still hard. Winnebago Lutheran Academy remained alive and remains alive to the time of this writing.

More important than any fiscal trials and triumphs is the original aim of this school. Let its own little history explain: "The aim of Winnebago Academy was to align the course of training with that of the Synod on the one hand, and on the other offer a broad general education for those who planned to enter some secular calling."[16] Previously synodical schools had stressed the "one hand," worker training, and ventures in Milwaukee and Kenosha had stressed the "other." At its founding Winnebago resolved to stress both. If pressed for a single top priority, it would have used the order that appears in the quotation from its history and opted for worker training.

This kind of aim or aims for a Lutheran high school would also be emphasized in a special synodical educational report that appeared in the years Winnebago Lutheran Academy was developing. This is the so-called "Moussa Report" that occupied the attention of the 1927 synodical convention at St. Lucas in Milwaukee.[17] The Moussa of the report is of course the Fond du Lac pastor who helped found Winnebago Lutheran Academy. He died prematurely in 1928 but promptly enough so that he did not have to see much of his educational planning bite the dust, the dust of the Depression's Dust Bowl.

Moussa was secretary of the educational survey committee ordered by the 1925 convention. Serving with him were Chairman A. Ackermann, Pastor Plocher, and two laymen, Herman Aufderheide of New Ulm and Fred Wolff of Jefferson. The main concern of the committee was overcrowding at the synod's colleges, chiefly because of preparatory department enrollment. The committee's reaction to the problem had such far-reaching implications that it was ordered by the Synodical Council to print the report and send it to all pastors and teachers and others for discussion and study prior to the 1927 convention. The report and its introductory letter went out over the signature, "H. Kollar Moussa, Secretary." Hence the shorthanded title, "The Moussa Report."

The report offered five recommendations:

I. Every parish in our Synod should have a day school with the aim of providing eight years of instruction.
II. Our college at Watertown and our Teachers' Seminary at New Ulm should not continue as preparatory schools.
III. The Synod should authorize and subsidize the establishment of preparatory schools, or academies, in many different parts of its territory, preferably according to conferences.
IV. The Teachers' Seminary should extend and vary its normal course to meet the needs of our day.
V. Northwestern College, which now has reached the full standard of the American college, should likewise, as prudence dictates, offer college courses that would serve others than those who intend to prepare for the ministry. If the commercial department is retained, it should be open to those only who have finished a satisfactory preparatory course.

The committee's supporting argumentation indicates a strong emphasis on lay education. Worker-training concerns are not being shortchanged but a plus is being urged: Christian training on both high school and college levels for those who will be laymen and laywomen in the congregations. Various plans for organizing the area academies are proposed, involving either associations of congregations or individuals. The report looked far into the future as it urged the church body in its teacher training to "extend the course for all men to three years" and "provide at some time in the future a fourth year for normal students."

Sound as the thinking and proposing was, it was a bit too much for one synod convention. The first recommendation caused no difficulty. It was after all nothing more than an update of a decision of the founding convention of the Wisconsin Synod in 1850.[18] The other proposals caused so much controversy that a floor committee was created to find a *modus vivendi*. Pleading that the synod lacked practical experience in the matter of the controversial academies, the floor committee offered four stopgap measures:

1. Make the proposed Dakota-Montana academy a synodical school subsidized and controlled exclusively by the synod.
2. Subsidize the Fond du Lac academy with $1200 per year, contingent on synodical supervision.
3. Refer the "Report" to the Synodical Committee,
4. Instruct the Synodical Committee to create a visiting team to deal with other academies in the matter of synodical supervision and support.

With the exception of Point 2 which was tabled for two years and then tabled once more, the committee's proposals were adopted.

The important result was the creation of Northwestern Lutheran Academy at Mobridge, South Dakota. It opened its doors in the fall of 1928 with one grade and one teacher, Professor K. G. Sievert. In the next three years grades and instructors were added. The school persevered through five decades in spite of minimal facilities, Depression setbacks, and low enrollments, providing the synod with worker training on its level and the district's youth with Christian high school training. The school's doors were shut in 1979 when Martin Luther Academy moved from New Ulm to Prairie du Chien and the Mobridge students joined them there.

Eventually the Moussa Plan's suggestion that the synod colleges operate without an attached preparatory school was adopted. What was done at New Ulm has just been indicated. At Watertown the preparatory department shares the campus with the college but has become a separate school with its own administration, faculty, and dormitory.

The dream of area high schools serving all of the synod's worker-training needs on the high school level and all sections of the synod in the Christian education of its teenagers, however, did not materialize. It died aborning. Before the synod could adjust to the novel plan, the Depression dampened and deterred educational expansion.

When the era of high school building came after World War II, the schools that surfaced at Appleton and Manitowoc and elsewhere never were quite the kind the "Moussa Report" had envisioned. Worker-training tracks were provided but the emphasis definitely lay on serving the area's needs in Christian high school education. This is not to blame the areas and their high schools. They labored zealously for the goals that lay before them. It was the synod itself that turned thumbs down on the "Moussa Report" because it felt that it could not put the future well-being of its preparatory schools in any jeopardy.

At the time of this writing the whole proposal of sixty years ago still looms large as an intriguing attempt to cope with the church's ever-increasing educational needs. In that area the "Moussa Report" remains as the great might-have-been.

The 1920s were heady days for those with a heart for the educational work of the church on the synodical and parish level. It was not, however, all sweetness and light. In that decade two of the synodical schools were rocked to the foundations by a bitter conflict known as the Protes'tant Controversy. That is the subject of the next chapter.

CHAPTER FOURTEEN

Protes'tant Controversy

The 1986 statistics of the Lutheran Council in the USA for Lutheran church bodies in this country include these totals for the Protes'tant Conference: seven pastors and congregations with 979 souls. The figures may not seem particularly impressive, with seven active pastors serving souls that taken together would make up one good-sized congregation in other church bodies.

Figures can lie and deceive. This set of numbers, far from suggesting the insignificant and forgettable, represents the up-to-date accounting of the most turbulent and tragic episode in Wisconsin Synod history begun over three score years ago and still running its course and causing its controversies.

The name of the church body under discussion suggests the broad outlines of the whole episode. The group protested and protests certain developments in the parent church body, the Wisconsin Synod. The protesters view themselves less as a distinct organization on the Lutheran scene and more as a temporarily disengaged part of their original synod, waiting for the day when the protests are finally heeded. That is at least what "Protes'tant Conference" seems to say.

Even after the passage of some sixty years it remains difficult to get agreement on what the real causes and issues in the conflict were and are. If anything has become completely clear, it is the inability of any single cause or issue to serve as the sole key that clarifies the whole complicated controversy. A number of factors come into play in any consideration of the *origins of the controversy*.

Origins of the Controversy

The beginnings of the Protes'tant Controversy played themselves out on the backdrop of revolt against established moral practices and religious creeds that dominated the nation's social and religious scene in the 1920s. In mainline denominations new views about the Bible and about the origin of this world gained the upper hand. Embattled conservatives, calling themselves Fundamentalists and fighting for the old beliefs and ethics, seemed unable to stem the tide. It was a time of anti-establishment and the establishment was on the defensive, if not on the run.

This is not to say that the protesters that challenged Wisconsin district and synod establishments in the 1920s espoused liberal theology, evolution, or the "new" morality of that day. Quite the contrary! What was often called for in the protests was a stiffer morality and theology. That the protests were aimed at the establishment, the officialdom in the synodical structure, however, is beyond dispute. In the early literature of the controversy, attacks on this officialdom, *Beamtentum,* so abound that they cannot be missed.

In the interest of historical presentation it should be stressed that the 1917 shift to a merger of four synods was by then only a few years old. That shift had of necessity created an abundance of new officialdom, new synodical machinery that could not but irk the rugged individuals that abounded then and abound now in the Wisconsin Synod.

It is no secret that some of that new synodical machinery had a way of creaking and grinding and sometimes breaking down completely. This was not so much the case in the "other states" of the Wisconsin merger. In Michigan and Minnesota and even Nebraska there was experienced leadership that simply and easily could transform itself from a synodical to a district variety. In Wisconsin the old synodical leadership had for the most part moved up to serve the merged Wisconsin Synod. The three Wisconsin districts had no source of supply to look to for experienced leadership, and it was in these districts that the bitterest conflicts developed and were often mismanaged.

Among many post-merger adjustments that had to be made, one that caused special difficulty was the assignment of discipline in doctrine and practice to the districts. The matter seems simple enough in theory, especially to those who have learned to live with the arrangement in the course of a half century and more. Back in the 1920s the lesson was still being learned and sometimes forgotten. There could be indecision in decision-making and also disregard of decisions made.

In the thinking and the theology of the protesters a viewpoint that loomed large was the judgment of God that hovers threateningly over his wayward children and church bodies. J. P. Koehler sounded the theme, as has already been noted.¹ His son discussed that issue especially in dealings with the Synodical Council in 1924.² Professor Ruediger emphasized the point in lectures in his seminary classroom. Pastor Beitz underscored it in the conference paper that became a rallying point for protesters.³

It is a vital and undeniable truth of Scripture that God's judgment looms for sin and sinner both when the single person is concerned and also when he is linked with others in a church body. The Bible supplies abundant examples of even the repented and forgiven sin resulting in dire consequences. Even more than the individual sinner, the church body with its longer life and larger temptations can make itself ripe and ready for the judgment. A warning along those lines is always in place.

When the warning verges into a precise identification of the who and the when and the where, however, the outcome can be less than salutary. An unsatisfactory development can seem to signify the knell of judgment's doom. For some predetermined hour of judgment there must be heralds and harbingers that have to be identified. The result is the fixed determination and the final declaration, "Ichabod," that is, "Where is the glory?"

After a half century the Protes'tants were still debating among themselves just what kind of judgment they were proclaiming on the Wisconsin Synod. In 1973 one in their fellowship protested the unclarity and withdrew from the brotherhood.⁴ Among the underlying causes of the Protes'tant Controversy this issue of judgment and obduracy must rank as one of special significance.

More overt developments occurred on the banks of the Rock River and its tributaries that flow through towns of the Western Wisconsin District—Watertown, Fort Atkinson, and Beaver Dam. At Watertown's Northwestern College in the midst of a spring snowstorm during the weekend of March 28-30, 1924, wholesale thieving on the part of some two dozen students was uncovered.⁵ On the following Monday a special faculty meeting, held in place of the scheduled classes, put the culprits into three equally divided groups, expelling one group, suspending another, and campusing the third who seemed to be least guilty.

The college board, after extensive meetings with and without the faculty, determined to set aside this disciplinary action of the faculty. The main rationale of the board was that a deadletter school statute vested expulsion power in the board. It is surprising that only two of the teachers, whose educational abilities had been publicly disavowed by their calling board, resigned their positions. Those resigning were Karl Koehler, son of Professor J. P. Koehler then on leave to research synodical roots at Barmen, Basel, and Berlin, and Herbert Parisius, soon to become a high-ranking official in F. D. Roosevelt's Department of Agriculture.[6]

Naturally a district and even synod-wide dispute resulted. A 1924 commencement gathering at Northwestern College, billed as an informational meeting, presented in the main only the protest side of the story.[7] Synodical committees to sort out the facts and set down the principles in the case endeavored to smooth the troubled waters. Difficulties and disagreements, however, remained and rankled.

At the Watertown school objectors were thwarted at every turn by a college board that maintained control. It filled posts vacated by protesters and resigners in spite of protests challenging such action. The frustrated protesters sought and found a new avenue of approach.

Twenty miles down the Rock River at Fort Atkinson a bitter conflict had developed between Pastor A. F. Nicolaus and the church council on the one side and two parochial school teachers, Elizabeth Reuter and Gerda Koch, on the other. The serious-minded teachers, upset by the changes the 1920s were producing in the world and the church, waged a vigorous rear-guard campaign against what they saw as sins of the times but what others, including Pastor Nicolaus, viewed as matters lying in the field of adiaphora.

When the mild-mannered Pastor Nicolaus did not back the teachers in their endeavors, they turned on him and went so far as to call him a false prophet. These are fighting words for even an easy-going pastor. A showdown developed. The two teachers, strangely enough, under fire and without a release were recommended to and called by the Marshfield church. The Fort Atkinson congregation was incensed enough to withdraw temporarily from the synod.

The complicated Fort Atkinson case dragged on, with a number of committees unable to arrive at a satisfactory conclusion. Without necessarily agreeing with all the ideas and tactics of the two teachers, a number of disgruntled synod members took up their cause when they saw what they viewed as blunders of the establishment in handling the case, especially when a suspension notice regarding the teachers was published officially in May 1926.

The Western Wisconsin District, meeting a month later at Beaver Dam, ratified the suspension by a majority vote. Seventeen, however, refused to go along. They entered a written protest against the procedure, adding to their specifics a reference to a "bigger problem" that needed airing.[8] This formal *protest* at Beaver Dam soon provided a name for the controversy and for the group that formed.

The "bigger problem" received an airing before the year was out. It came in the form of a paper read by Pastor William Beitz to the Wisconsin-Chippewa Valley Conference at Schofield, near Wausau, in September 1926. Actually the paper had been assigned by the area mixed conference of Wisconsin and Missouri pastors. Beitz read it first to Wisconsin pastors and then three weeks later to the joint group. At both and also subsequent readings the paper engendered more than a fair share of discussion and disagreement.

The paper had the title, "God's Message to Us in Galatians: The Just Shall Live by Faith." Using the great Reformation passage in Habakkuk and Galatians as a starting point, Beitz put the spiritual life of his church body under scrutiny or, as he put it, tested harps "to see whether they be in tune with God's."[9] The test result, according to Beitz, showed a reprehensible failure in the spiritual life of congregations, in preaching, in seminary training, in pre-confirmation instruction, in just about every aspect of what to "live by faith" should mean.

At the first readings of the Beitz paper there were those who questioned its sweeping denunciations. Others rallied round, claiming the paper contained the right diagnosis and the sure cure for the synodical malaise. As the clashes over the paper and over other issues worsened, Western Wisconsin District officials decided to obtain an official verdict, a *Gutachten*, on the paper from the Wauwatosa seminary faculty. This called forth a second divisive document in the controversy. Before considering it, however, a backtracking is in order to catch up with the *formation of the Protes'tant Conference.*

Formation of the Protes'tant Conference

At the Beaver Dam meeting in the spring of 1926 the Western Wisconsin District had empowered its officials to deal conclusively with protesters.[10] That action and the furor that the Beitz paper engendered seem to have motivated protesters to act in concert. The first get-together took place in November 1926 at Wilton. Early in the following February the group again assembled, this time to the accompaniment of "church service and Lord's Supper."[11] A fellowship was forming well in advance of any issuance of a seminary *Gutachten*.

Almost simultaneously with that issuance the first suspensions of Beaver Dam protesters occurred. They were those of William Motzkus and Oswald Hensel. The former had been called to the Globe congregation and had been installed there by the latter in spite of protests. In July 1927 William Beitz was suspended when meetings and correspondence failed to accomplish any kind of agreement. About that time Pastor H. W. Koch had lost his congregation at Friesland and had been suspended. The fifth suspension was that of Pastor W. K. Bodamer at Prairie du Chien. The congregation there was lost to the Wisconsin Synod at that time. Wisconsin would not re-enter Prairie du Chien until it established Martin Luther Preparatory School there in 1979.

More and more the original issue of officialdom, in which protesters clashed with the establishment, was giving way as *cause celebre* to a pamphlet war that pitted the Beitz paper against the Wauwatosa *Gutachten*. Even then officialdom remained as an issue, however, because it ranked itself quite solidly on the side of the *Gutachten*. That *Gutachten* merits a word of explanation.

As has been mentioned, the beleaguered Western Wisconsin District officials appealed to the Wauwatosa Seminary for a theological opinion on the Beitz paper that was causing so much conflict in their bailiwick. The appeal was made and acknowledged, even though the care and cure of doctrine and practice should have been a district concern. Under the direction of J. P. Koehler the Wauwatosa faculty went to work producing an evaluation of the controversial Beitz paper that was dividing the church body.

The men at Wauwatosa realized the seriousness of the synodical situation and of their own assignment. Here is how one of the participants describes the procedure:

> In order to be as correct and careful as possible, it was determined in this important matter affecting the peace and unity of the synod that each of the four of us should make a written appraisal without prior consultation with the others, that then the four appraisals should be jointly evaluated and then brought together by one of us. The amalgamation should then be again reviewed and after that put into final form.[12]

When the time came for the evaluation of the four appraisals only three were on hand, those of W. Henkel, J. Meyer, and A. Pieper. President J. P. Koehler begged off on the grounds that he had been busy working on blueprints for the new seminary building. That blueprint work may have helped produce what others have called the most attractive layout of all Lutheran seminaries in the land, but at the moment it engendered large repercussions. At Koehler's insistence August Pieper's writing, with some slight modifications, became the official *Gutachten*.[13]

This *Gutachten* rejected the Beitz paper sharply on three counts: (1) it confused justification and sanctification by using "the just shall live by faith" as a text, or rather pretext, for a paper evaluating the sanctification level in the church body; (2) it demeaned the role of the law in the doctrine of repentance; (3) it issued wholesale judgments of what was going on in heads and hearts. Koehler signed the evaluation but with the stipulation that it be withheld until he could have a face-to-face meeting with Beitz on the matter. His colleagues had no objections but pointed out that disciplinary dealings were being conducted by Western District officials and that therefore they should be apprised of any approaches to Beitz.[14]

This understanding of theirs may explain why the *Gutachten* was sent to President Thurow in spite of the proviso to Koehler's signature. The assumption may have been that Koehler would inform Thurow of his intentions and that Thurow would act accordingly. Whatever the case, the *Gutachten* was already in the hands of Beitz when Koehler arrived for the face-to-face discussion. Understandably, the meeting was fruitless. Blaming the early release of the *Gutachten* for the fiasco, Koehler withdrew his signature and became a foe of the *Gutachten*, eventually producing such opposition writings as *Ertrag* and *Beleuchtung.*

The fat was in the fire. The synodical turmoil now became the Wauwatosa Seminary's strife. It had already begun to be that when Professor Ruediger, energetic in the June 1924 Watertown meeting in the defense of the Fort Atkinson teachers and in pointing to the judgment in his classroom, lost his teaching post. Even a forced confession was judged to be inadequate for restoring in the church body confidence that had been lost. There were those who protested the ouster.

That was bad enough. Now the two veteran teachers at Wauwatosa were clashing openly over interpretations of two documents that were dividing the Wisconsin Synod—the Beitz paper and the seminary's *Gutachten.* The clash was bitter. Professional interpreters did not see eye-to-eye in interpreting the documents. These were human writings, to be sure, and one might wish that they had not been elevated to the stature of shibboleths that set party against party. But that is just what the writings had become. In his June 7, 1930, farewell to the church body he had served for 50 years, a three-part writing titled "Witness, Analysis, and Reply," Koehler asserts, "The *Gutachten* was and is and had to be the issue alone that had to be considered."[15]

In a special meeting at Watertown, November 15-18, 1927, the Western Wisconsin District made the *Gutachten* its own and declared that all who continued to uphold the Beitz paper were to be regarded as such who had broken the brotherhood. There were of course negative votes and abstentions, which the body resolved to deal with.[16] All this naturally heated up the protest movement.

In the following December the so-called Protes'tants met at Marshfield. Although they did defeat a resolution to break off all relations with the Wisconsin Synod, they established a treasury, a board, a La Crosse mission, and an editorial committee. Most important, they adopted the "Elroy Declaration," so named because it was mailed from there by the secretary. The writing expressed the group's reaction to the recent district resolutions by declaring flatly: "We shall be ready to deal only if the resolutions of Beaver Dam and Watertown are rescinded, all cases are reopened as new cases and the Synod thereby shows a new attitude which might give hope of profitable dealings."[17] This statement obviously would make any subsequent olive-branch overtures difficult in the extreme.

One more early meeting of Protes'tants should be mentioned to round off this section on the development of the Protes'tant Conference. It took place at Wilton in January 1928 and resolved to start publishing *Faith-Life*. It began on Easter of that year as a bimonthly and is now in its sixty-fourth volume, appearing every two months. By contrast the 1929 synodical convention resolved: "the Synod earnestly desires that in the future no additional writings concerning the synodical strife be published, neither by the synod nor by those who are serving the synod."[18]

Subsequent Developments

In 1929-1930 the most regrettable of these developments occurred. J. P. Koehler's synodical and seminary service was terminated. After long discussions about the Beitz paper with others on the faculty and with school and synodical officials, Koehler brought to the attention of the 1929 synodical convention his *Beleuchtung*, his own *Gutachten* of the Beitz paper and the seminary's own *Gutachten* of it. His point, in the main, was that the *Gutachten* had not put the best construction on the Beitz paper and that Beitz could in most instances be correctly understood.

The other two seminary instructors (Ruediger had been deposed and Henkel had died), August Pieper and John Meyer, hastily replied in an *Antwort* dated August 9, 1929, just a week and a day after the *Beleuchtung*'s issuance. The synodical convention was at a crossroads. It cast its lot with the *Antwort*, although it did amend a seminary board resolution to terminate Koehler's call by mandating a year's leave of absence from the classrooms and presidential office for research of synodical history and further dealings in the controversy.

As far as the first purpose is concerned, some good result must have been achieved. Eventually Koehler's *History of the Wisconsin Synod* would be published by the Protes'tant Conference. In the matter of the more pressing issue of the moment, nothing was accomplished. In line with the earlier "Elroy Declaration," Koehler set a fresh start as the price for discussions. When this was not forthcoming and the year ran out, Koehler's seminary call was terminated. He moved to Neillsville where his son Karl lived and worked. The father's main task at Neillsville was to finish work on his synodical history and to produce conference papers and *Faith-Life* writings. In 1933 his fellowship ties with the synod were declared broken. The Wisconsin Synod's premier church historian died on September 30, 1951, at Neillsville.

The synodical convention took little official action before 1929. It appointed committees and heard their reports. In 1927 it called for an arbitration committee but in the main viewed the controversy as still a Western Wisconsin District matter. Along with the actions already mentioned, the 1929 convention called for the establishment of the "Peace Committee." This committee's reports in 1931 and 1933 were hotly debated, but in each instance the problem was referred back to the district level. Meanwhile the controversy was spreading beyond the Wisconsin borders. The Minnesota District was concerned already in 1924. In 1928 that district's convention deplored the events and then set down this reminder and rebuke for its sister district, "Christ has given instruction for church discipline not for the purpose of condemnation but the salvation of souls."[19]

In 1930 in a lengthy discussion of the issue the Minnesota District made the point that misunderstandings regarding the two contested documents, the Beitz paper and the *Gutachten*, must be clarified if peace and harmony were to be restored.[20] When the district committee was subsequently rebuffed by Beitz, Minnesota efforts at reconciliation cooled. The 1932 report on the controversy is brusque and orders correspondence on the subject to be filed as matters "not within the judgment or control of the district."[21]

In the late 1950s and early 1960s a striking conciliatory move was made. At the synodical convention's urging, the Western Wisconsin District rescinded the original suspension resolution on the grounds of unclarity and lack of unanimity. The demands of the "Elroy Declaration," at least in part, seemed to have been met. There were, however, no tangible results. Unfortunately a new Protes'tant suspension was being enacted at that time. The reactions of the Protes'tant Conference members agreed that the conciliation effort offered too little and came too late.

More recently in the early 1980s congregations at Fremont and Green Bay, Wisconsin, were disturbed by the Protes'tant controversy. At Fremont a pastor, making common cause with the Protes'tant Conference, had his call terminated by the congregation. In Green Bay, St. Paul Lutheran Church was split when the pastor declared his fellowship with the Protes'tants. Thus the controversy lives on. Since the Green Bay strife there are no official efforts at reconciliation to report.

CHAPTER FIFTEEN

Missions Old and Missions New

Church history has its sad chapters. Some of the saddest can be those that deal with controversies that divide the flock and bewilder the believers. Church history has its happy chapters, and the happiest are those that deal with mission endeavors.

In the era between World War I and World War II the mission enterprises of the Wisconsin Synod—both the old and the new, both the overseas and the home variety—stepped up the pace. It isn't so much that the Wisconsin Synod planned it that way. In fact, given its own inclinations and programming, it might well have opted for the opposites in Poland and Nigeria and in home mission developments. The Lord of the world at war and the church in mission overruled man's propositions to his glory and the salvation of souls.

The Polish Venture

The setting was Poland, to be sure, but the mission venture had the old German stamp. When the peacemakers of World War I gathered at Paris in 1918-1919, they drew a Curzon Line and recreated a Poland on Europe's map. Behind that line were numerous Germans, lured there either by earlier Polish agricultural entrepreneurs or by later Prussian aggrandizements. Among them were Lutherans with long-standing guarantees of religious and language integrity.

The physical hardships during and after World War I were bad enough. Relief efforts were mounted in Wisconsin Synod circles by pastors and lay people who had come from the area and left relatives behind. Pastor Otto Engel of Randolph, Wisconsin, was especially active in this work, even going overseas to supervise distribution of supplies personally.

Even worse were the spiritual trials. The new Republic of Poland recognized the Roman Church as the majority religion of the land but offered religious guarantees to others. In the state-church tradition that predominated in Europe, however, such guarantees were seldom ironclad. The Lutheran Church of Poland, called the Augsburg Church, lost some of its old rights to the aggressive new regime. In turn, the Augsburg Church came down hard on those who objected to its easy-going Lutheranism and wanted to break away to form free churches.

In the city of Lodz such objections had been energetically mounted by Pastor Angerstein. In the interest of confessional Lutheranism he urged young men in the area who wanted to study theology to attend Synodical Conference seminaries, also ours at Wauwatosa. Through Pastor Angerstein's efforts there were in Lodz after World War I a sizable number of Lutherans who saw the need of breaking with the Augsburg Church if they wanted to retain their Lutheran heritage in doctrine and practice.

One of these young men merits special mention. This is Gustav Maliszewski who began as a school teacher but soon became an energetic evangelist in Lodz and then sought to prepare himself as a pastor of faithful Lutherans. After training at the seminary of the Saxon Free Church in the Berlin-Zehlendorf area, Maliszewski returned to Lodz to carry on the work of gathering those who wanted to be faithful Lutherans.

The work prospered. In 1923 the convention of the Wisconsin Synod had before it calls for Wisconsin Synod pastors from two congregations, one in Lodz and the other in nearby Andrespol. Without knowing that only Polish citizens could serve Polish congregations under the Polish constitution, the Wisconsin Synod at Bethesda Church in Milwaukee in 1923 took the historic step of committing itself to an overseas mission venture. It was finally ready to repay in a small measure the overseas mission impulse from the other direction that had generated its founding seventy-three years before.

The record is worth quoting. After the mission board and Pastor O. Engel had reported, the minutes say: "The result was that the synod after lengthy deliberation resolved that our General Board for Missions should undertake the mission in Poland with all energy."[1] It may not have been a truly heathen mission and it may have had language and ethnic limitations, but that resolution put the Wisconsin Synod squarely into the work outlined so clearly in

Mark 16:15, "Go into all the world and preach the good news to all creation."

Regrettably, this was one of many instances where a convention mission resolution was not matched by synodical performance in the subsequent biennium. Reporting to the 1925 convention, the chairman for the executive commission for the mission venture, John Gauss, had to state: "We are aware of the fact that we have not pursued the work with the dedication and the zeal that might have been expected from the resolution. We ask, 'Why not?' Because we lacked men and money. . . . According to the treasurer's books $5,297.42 of the intended $10,000 has been up to now received. For the next biennium the commission requests $15,000."[2]

On the brighter side of the ledger that same report could emphatically state, "We can and must here state that through our efforts the Lutheran Free Church in Poland has been established." These efforts merit recounting.

After Pastor O. Theobald of Grace Church in Oshkosh felt compelled to decline the call to go to Poland and head the synod mission venture there, the previously mentioned Pastor Engel was sent. He knew the area and was requested by the people there. His place of residence was Lodz, and almost immediately he pushed for a second worker. The request was granted and in 1924 at Lodz Candidate Gustav Maliszewski was ordained and installed by Pastor Engel. At the ordination service Professor J. P. Koehler and his son Kurt served as assistants. Thereby hangs a tale or two.

Professor Koehler was on a short sabbatical from Easter to Christmas in 1924 to search out the synod's historical roots at Basel, Barmen, and Berlin. That research provided the basis for his writings on Wisconsin Synod history and also for the earlier portions of this book.

It was quite natural that the commission for the mission in Poland should ask Professor Koehler to investigate their enterprise on the spot and report his findings to them. Here was a seasoned leader of the church within miles of the area of concern. There were those who no doubt recalled that on another earlier and incidental brush with a synodical mission venture, Professor Koehler had provided useful insights on the then infant Apache undertaking.[3] That is why J. P. Koehler was able to assist in the Lodz ordination in 1924.

What is more important, on his return Koehler reported: "Poland presents a great and ripe mission field and it ought to be worked by a Lutheran church body."[4] The point is that there is no need to cast Professor Koehler in a sort of anti-mission role, as has been done on occasion. To be sure, he could theoretically expound on the overriding importance of inner growth and educational advancement for his church body.[5] After all, this was his own field of endeavor. When he, however, encountered mission endeavors face-to-face, as he did in Apacheland on an illness sabbatical in 1901-1902 and in Poland on a research sabbatical in 1924, he came down hard on the side of missions. Perhaps the ultimate point to be made is that, whatever the other considerations might be, no believer can turn his back on and his heart from mission work.

The 1925 synodical convention, meeting in the diamond jubilee year at the first member congregation, Milwaukee's Grace Church, reacted to the reports presented to it on Poland in this fashion: "After a rather lengthy deliberation the commission was encouraged and ordered to carry on the mission in Poland. For this mission $15,000 was authorized."[6] The raise in the fiscal allotment from $10,000 to $15,000 indicates that the church body was becoming serious about the overseas mission venture. It has been customary to set the beginning of this mission venture at the time of the Lodz ordination of Gustav Maliszewski. That first step, however, was energetically followed by a second step at Grace, Milwaukee in 1925. The Wisconsin Synod then and there committed itself to overseas missions and has not rescinded the commitment since.

In Poland the years before and after 1925 were marked by severe trials, often in the form of church-state battles. The Augsburg Church was not reluctant to use its favored position to throw legal roadblocks in the way of the emerging mission. Sparing the irksome details, a very useful and thought-provoking quotation can be supplied: "One can only wonder what our people in America would do if they were subjected to the persecutions, the sneers, and the ridicule which have been the lot of these brethren, both in Poland and later in Germany."[7]

The mission persevered and prospered in spite of the hardships. When Pastor Engel returned to the states, Pastor A. Dasler of Kingston, Wisconsin was sent overseas in his place on a temporary basis. The temporary basis stretched from a year to two and then into a third and a vacancy. Finally, in 1929 William Bodamer went to Lodz to head the mission operation.

The next decade saw the work progressing. Men trained at Berlin-Zehlendorf manned the pastorates of the young congregations. Among them were such stalwart evangelists as A. and H. Schlender, A. Wagner, and L. Zielke.[8] Eventually a dozen such congregations were organized.

Since Bodamer viewed his assignment of mission director as including a personal report to the sponsoring synod's conventions, he was stateside in the summer of 1939. The *Blitzkrieg* and its aftermath prevented his return to Poland. The Russian advance in the last phase of World War II put to flight all Germans in Poland. The telling of these sad developments properly belongs in a subsequent chapter.

Into Africa

In the meantime the Wisconsin Synod had begun to share in the Synodical Conference African mission outreach in Nigeria. If the full story of that venture belongs in the history of the Synodical Conference, at least those aspects that involve our church body more directly deserve highlighting here.[9] This is especially so because this Nigerian effort, closed to us in 1964 after the Synodical Conference split, opened doors for us into other African fields and harvests.

One impetus for the move into Nigeria had its origin in the stateside Black mission of the Synodical Conference. Members in the mission congregations exercised their own stewardship by gathering funds for chapels in India and China. Quite naturally they soon asked, "Why not Africa?"

Meanwhile a Nigerian tribe became dissatisfied with its interdenominational mission society over such issues as infant baptism and worker training. They decided to send their outstanding evangelist, Jonathan Ekong, to the United States for additional training. If epics were still being written, the story of his travels and studies would supply material for a modern rival of the Odyssey.

After long delays in getting to the United States and false starts at Howard and Livingston, he finally learned that the Synodical Conference had in 1930 resolved to explore mission outreach in Africa. As a result he enrolled at the worker-training school at Greensboro and was eventually graduated and ordained in the spring of 1938, eleven years after he had set out from Nigeria.

Before that the African commitment of the Synodical Conference in 1930 had resulted in a change of name for the overseas church body from Ibesikpo United Church to Ibesikpo Lutheran Church. In 1934 the Conference ordered an on-the-spot survey by a three-man team of O. C. Bocler of the Missouri Synod, I. Albrecht of Wisconsin, and H. Nau, the Greensboro school head.[10] After a seven-weeks survey of the field in early 1935, during which a translation of Luther's Catechism was supplied, reports could be made to conventions of all but one of the members of the Synodical Conference, which itself would not meet until 1936.

The Norwegian Synod had met prior to the reporting of the three-man survey team and its leaders could offer only personal interest and support. The other members of the Synodical Conference, the Missouri, Slovak, and Wisconsin Synods, reacted favorably. Missouri, meeting in convention earlier than the Wisconsin Synod, voted to begin the work on a temporary basis until the Synodical Conference could act in 1936 with as many other Synodical Conference members as were willing to join them. They invited the other synods to share in the work but most of all wanted no delays.[11] The Slovak Synod reacted favorably.

The Wisconsin resolution at its August 1935 convention made these points:

1. Work in Nigeria should begin at once on a temporary basis until the Synodical Conference could act in 1936;
2. The Nigerian mission should be a joint venture of the Synodical Conference;
3. An appropriation of $1600 for the work should be made.[12]

While Dr. Nau was laying the foundation in Nigeria on a temporary basis, the Synodical Conference in its 1936 convention adopted the terse, but historic, recommendation, "That the Synodical Conference take over the African Mission."[13] In that mission endeavor Wisconsin would share for a quarter century and more.

The first permanent worker called from the United States into the Nigerian field was William Schweppe of the Wisconsin Synod. From that time on until his death in an automobile accident in 1968, Missionary Schweppe worked in Africa. He served as superintendent of the Nigerian field and taught at its pastoral seminary. He extended the work into Ghana. In 1960 he was granted a leave of absence to assist in the Northern Rhodesia (Zambia) mission that our synod had begun in the previous decade, and in the following year he accepted a call into that field. He was a born missionary and he died one.

The other five Wisconsin Synod pastors, the four teachers, and the two lay workers who served in the Nigerian field merit mention. Norbert Reim arrived in 1946 and remained until 1960, serving especially in the seminary and helping train Black pastors in New Testament Greek. Pastor George Baer was in the field from 1946 to 1949 and Pastor Edgar Greve from 1950 to 1958. In 1952 Pastor William Winter began a long service that reached beyond 1961. Pastor Alvin Werre's service was from 1958-1960.

The teachers were Edmund Baer (1949-1956), Aileen Krueger (1950-1956), Raymond Spangenberg (1951-1958), and Robert Meyer (1954-). Two lay workers, Kenneth Mundstock (1954-1956) and Agnes Winter (1958-) complete the roster of Wisconsin Synod workers in Nigeria.

As has been mentioned, the Nigerian field went with the Missouri Synod when the Synodical Conference divided in 1961-1963. By that time our Northern Rhodesia (Zambia) effort was well underway. Subsequently a Nigerian remnant would seek our aid. These are all developments, however, that are properly treated in chapters on the Wisconsin Synod's mission history after World War II.

Efforts in the Homeland

Out in Apacheland there were plenty of problems in the twenties and thirties. There was the dislocation of many Apaches during and after World War I as the war jobs disappeared as quickly as they had appeared. The old San Carlos station had to be abandoned in 1929 when the waters rose behind Coolidge Dam. Then came the Depression and the closing of mines at Globe and elsewhere. Add such difficulties to the always difficult endeavor to win the Apaches for Christ and one has the makings of what could be a very bleak chapter in the story. That a very different kind of chapter actually emerges can be accounted for by a very special gift the Lord granted the field in those and following decades: a number of men who were enabled to make the work their lifetime careers and who are buried there.

Over the years they were aided in their efforts by many other missionaries and teachers who in their brief tenures rendered valuable service. That service is not being minimized as special attention turns to E. Edgar Guenther, Henry Rosin, and Francis and Alfred Uplegger.[14]

Edgar Guenther arrived in Apacheland already in 1911, fresh from the Wauwatosa seminary. After he had put in a year of work at the Ft. Apache station, the mission board reported to the 1912 Wisconsin Convention: "Missionary Guenther was able to make a good beginning in the mission school. . . . And the children came to school eager and regularly. He writes about himself and his dear wife, who is also his faithful helper in the school work, 'We both find our joy in our school.'"[15]

That was the beginning of a work that would go on for decades to come. The wife, Minnie, became a legend in her own right and in her own time, both to Apaches and whites, both to those who served in the field and those who awarded her the title of "Mother of the Year." In 1918 Edgar Guenther succeeded Harders as superintendent of the field and held the post until his silver anniversary in the field, 1936. He worked in Apacheland until his death in 1961, completing a half century of work there.

In 1917 two classmates at the Wauwatosa seminary renewed their long association in synodical training schools out in Arizona as helpers to Superintendent Harders at Globe. Within a year both were assigned posts of service on the Apache reservations. Both remained in the work until retirement. They learned the difficult language. They built chapels. They watched over Apache children in school during the day and at dusk visited their parents in camps. They were all things to all Apaches.

The brothers in the work became brothers-in-law when Henry Rosin married Alfred Uplegger's sister Johanna, who came to the field when Alfred's father, Francis, accepted a call to San Carlos in 1920. A family mission enterprise, a latter-day version of the Mayhews on Martha's Vineyard, was in the making.

To Francis Uplegger, gifted in semantics, fell the task of revitalizing and systematizing the study of the Apache tongue. He gave it a written form that eased the work when missionaries tried to learn the difficult language and when they in turn tried to put gospel truths in the native tongue of Apache hearers and learners. In his lifetime Francis Uplegger became the authority on the language of the Apache.

He also became superintendent of the field, succeeding Edgar Guenther in 1936. He served in that post for over a quarter century until 1963. During the twenties and thirties and beyond, the growing stability in the Apacheland mission force could aid in producing some reportable advances. In 1923 the *Apache Scout* began publication. It is still being published as the *Apache Lutheran* to further the cause of the Wisconsin Synod's oldest mission. In the previous year the East Fork orphanage was established in a concern for Apache babies that were abandoned by parents. Over the years the orphanage grew into the East Fork Lutheran High School.

This jump into the years ahead may allow a further leap. Let this tribute to veteran missionaries in Apacheland conclude with an event of February 1984. Edgar Hoenecke writes: "We laid Alfred Uplegger's tired body to rest up on Peridot Mesa in the tiny cemetery where his dear Irma, his father, Dr. Francis, his son Karl, his sister Johanna, and her husband Henry Rosin, Al's lifelong friend and co-worker on the San Carlos Reservation, and a number of other colleagues all lie awaiting the sound of the last trumpet and their resurrection to life everlasting."[16] Together the Uppleggers, father and son, and the brother-in-law had accumulated more than eight score years of mission effort in Apacheland.

In the thirties there were concerned but misguided efforts to cut back or close down the costly mission in Apacheland. In subsequent decades there would be pleas to divert some Apache mission money to more energetic evangelism in the cities. It was the dedicated efforts of the veteran Apache missionaries that squelched opposition from within and without. The veteran mission of the Wisconsin Synod would not and could not and did not die.

This is not to say that the time for more evangelism in the cities had not come for the Wisconsin Synod. The era after World War I profoundly altered its outreaching or, more specifically, its ingathering efforts.[17] The old pattern of serving German Lutheran immigrants had ended when the open door to immigration was closed and the Lady of Liberty became more symbol than fact of life.

As this occurred in the twenties, another far-reaching change was in evidence on the American scene. It was the shift from rural to urban residence. The official statistics for this revolution are included in the 1920 national census. In the rural midwest of America, the Wisconsin Synod's abiding home ground, the shift may have been delayed for a few years. The handwriting, however, was on the wall.

The brethren in Michigan were the first to sound the clarion. In 1929 they presented to their fellow synodicals in convention a significant memorial, perhaps the most significant of the dozens of Michigan memorials that would dot and clot synodical proceedings in the years ahead. This 1929 memorial states:

> The church's main assignment Jesus himself has set down in the words: "Go into all the world and preach the good news to all creation." This assignment we seek to fulfill first of all in that we carry on home or traveling mission efforts. It goes without saying, however, that our home or traveling missions are today very different from what they were 75, 50, or 25 years ago. Then they were for the most part a matter of locating the inhabited areas, searching out there those German Lutherans that could be found, serving them with Word and sacrament and gathering these for the most part immigrants into congregations.
>
> In those days this was a traveling mission. The term describes the work at this time only in individual instances. Added to that is the fact that America in the last decades has developed from an agricultural to an industrial nation, that this development is gaining momentum from year to year, that the occupation of tillable acreage has all but ended, and that immigration is almost entirely occurring in the cities.
>
> The development and flowering of industry has led to an immense growth in city population and at the same time to a relative decline in the population of the farm lands. Another result is that the metropolitan areas sprout like mushrooms out of the earth and that their population increase is almost unbelievable. Along with this many rural inhabitants, and most especially the youth of the farm lands, are attracted and absorbed by the cities.

In our state of Michigan this lies before the very eyes in the almost unprecedented growth of the cities of Detroit, Flint, Pontiac, the suburbs of Detroit and to a lesser degree of Lansing, Jackson, Kalamazoo, Grand Rapids, Muskegon, and others.

It is obvious that through this growth of the cities many opportunities for establishing mission stations present themselves and what is at stake is mission in the true sense of the term. In the cities all kinds of people live together and close by one another: Christians and unbelievers, Lutherans and those from the sects. We therefore prefer to speak of mission assignments that the cities present to the orthodox church, rather than mission opportunities. It is not only a matter of finding in the cities the members of our church that have moved there and serving them spiritually, but also to approach with the gospel the unchurched masses. Never has the devil had more and more attractive temples, more and more tricky snares, more and more dangerous pitfalls, and more and more diligent missionaries than in the cities.

Never have temptations been greater, the lust of the world and the flesh more luring and misleading, sins more attractive and dangers for souls more looming than in the cities.

That is why the church must make every effort in the battle for Christ and against the devil and his troops in the cities. And that is why we would like to say that in the cities we have not only mission opportunities and that the cities not only afford us mission assignments, but that the cities present us with a mission need.

Is our church, that is our synod, aware of this? And if it is aware, what is it doing?

Since in our synod the work of missions is, not a district matter, but one of the merged body, our district's duty can and must be to alert the merged body, that is its general mission committee, to the mission opportunities, the mission assignments, and the mission need and to do all in our power to alert the church body to the situation and to encourage it to come to grips with it.

What is required is that our district mission board be encouraged to take note of these opportunities and that it be allocated necessary money from the mission funds; that, further, the church extension fund be employed; for only if the church extension fund supplies generous support will it be possible in any way to begin missions in the cities.

>On behalf of the Michigan District,
>Oscar J. Peters, secretary of the committee for finalizing the memorial. Wayne, May 15, 1929.[18]

The memorial, which was quite naturally referred to the general mission board of the synod, should be read with the reminder that this was Michigan in 1929. These were brethren who had "before the very eyes" the example of Detroit that swelled beyond belief after the 1914 lure of a minimum $5.00 a day wage. That made them somewhat more aware of the American scene in the twenties than their brothers to the west. They may have still betrayed that old fallacy of those times that original sin is less powerful and homely virtue more abundant on the farm than in the city. But they were trying desperately to alert their church body to a change in the country's vistas and to the need for a change in mission modes.

The memorial's date, however, tells a story of its own. Less than a half year after May 1929 the Depression set in. It had its beginnings in bank failures in Detroit and ravaged that bellwether city of urbanization in the Midwest in the twenties as few other cities. The sorely needed evangelism in the cities received setbacks in the thirties and early forties as the church body had to cope with Depression and war problems.

That, however, is subject matter to be treated later. Before that is done, the very significant intersynodical scene of the twenties and thirties calls for attention.

CHAPTER SIXTEEN

Significant Intersynodical Developments

Church bodies, like individual Christians, are to live up to the dictum of the law's second table, "Love your neighbor as yourself." A church body's intersynodical relations may tell more about it than many another report or statistic can. This chapter directs attention to such concerns and emphasizes their importance in the history of our church body.

Election-Conversion Discussions Renewed

When the intersynodical discussions of the doctrines of election and conversion in the early years of the century broke off amid even greater doctrinal disagreement than at the outset, the cause of Lutheran unity seemed hopelessly at dead end. No one could have surmised that within a decade a new effort along the same lines would be mounted. But that is just what happened. The upcoming quadricentennial of the Reformation worked the magic. This is how it began.[1]

In the spring of 1915 out in Minnesota's Sibley County a mixed conference of Wisconsin and Missouri pastors pondered what they could do to enhance the area's observance of 1917, especially in the matter of bringing together in doctrinal unity those who shared the Lutheran heritage and name. The conference's senior, August Hertwig, Missouri's pastor at Gaylord, set up a July 12 meeting for the mixed conference and the Ohio Synod men in the area. At that meeting poor attendance but good support prevailed.

A second Gaylord meeting on July 28 attracted seventeen pastors, eight from the Ohio, six from the Missouri, and three from the

Minnesota Synod. A third gathering at Winthrop on August 25 saw an enlarged group begin a critique of the "Madison Settlement" that was being used to bring about a union of Norwegian Lutheran synods by granting right to both contending positions in the doctrines of election and conversion. At Arlington on September 15 "Sibley County Theses" were subscribed to by twelve of the thirteen in attendance and subsequently by five others. It was a breakthrough, at least for Sibley County, Minnesota.

Let a participant describe the happening:

> After this discussion and correction of the Opgjor [Madison Settlement] the Ohio men present declared that they no longer dared view us as Calvinists and we on our part responded that we could no longer view them as synergists. We felt ourselves to be so united in the faith that we closed the session with the hymn, "Now Thank We All Our God," and a joint Lord's Prayer. In subsequent meetings this was not repeated; but not because we were afraid of becoming guilty of religious syncretism but in order not to give offense to those who did not sufficiently understand the circumstances.[2]

Those were good days and good men. When the writer had occasion some years back to travel every fortnight from New Ulm to Arlington through Winthrop and Gaylord, he never did so without paying a silent tribute to the dozen or so pastors willing to meet in the hot Minnesota summer in the cause of Lutheran unity. They did what they could. They pushed the venture beyond the little towns in their rural county to a statewide and even Midwest movement. It was no fault of theirs that the effort finally failed in 1929. They put their hearts and heads and hands into the cause and at the same time respected the consciences of brethren less involved and informed.

Soon the "Sibley County Theses" were transformed into the "St. Paul Theses" after being broadcast statewide and then studied at a series of Twin Cities meetings. On November 9 and 10, 1915, over a hundred pastors of the various synods began to discuss the "Sibley County Theses." At a subsequent January 5-6, 1916, meeting the discussions were completed and the amended theses were subscribed to by seventy-four pastors: seven from the Iowa, nineteen from the Minnesota, thirty-one from the Missouri, and seventeen from the Ohio Synod. Copies were distributed for consideration of the post-Easter area conferences. On May 3-4 these reactions were reviewed, and then the "St. Paul Theses" in final form were sent out to pastors of those synods that had shown interest in the proceedings.

Within a month, precisely by June 7, 1916, 555 Lutheran pastors had subscribed to the "St. Paul Theses." This is the synodical breakdown: Iowa, 170; Michigan, 17; Minnesota, 80; Missouri, 165; Nebraska, 3; Ohio, 70; Wisconsin, 50. The response paved the way from unofficial to official action. The Wisconsin, Minnesota, Missouri, Iowa, and Ohio Synods all appointed representatives to an intersynodical committee, with the Buffalo Synod joining them later.

A typical reaction took place at the 1917 convention of the Minnesota Synod. President Baumann included the matter in his official report, stating:

> The four hundredth Reformation anniversary, occurring this year, brought in its wake the beginning of an effort to unite various unaligned Lutheran synods. . . . Since the objective was, not a mere outward union, but a unity in the spirit (in doctrine and faith) on the basis of Scripture, the doctrinal discussions resulted in a draft of certain theses which form the basis of the rapprochement. The energetic conduct of these intersynodical conferences attracted great attention with the result that the theses became a fact of history and are now known in church history as the "St. Paul Theses." The esteemed synod will simply have to give attention to this development in church circles.[3]

The Synod passed these resolutions:

1. To thank God heartily for the good results achieved up to this time and to welcome this development with joy;
2. To pledge itself with its pastors, teachers, and congregational members to the theses and explanation of the conferences contained in "Toward Unity - Nos. 1 and 2."
3. To appoint suitable people to a committee that in the future is to meet with the committees of other synods.

On the Minnesota committee were Pastors H. Boettcher, Wm. Bauer, Im. Albrecht, and J. Pieper; Teachers F. Blauert and F. Kannenberg; Laymen J. Schlacht and F. Christgau. The members of the Wisconsin Synod committee, incidentally, were Professors J. Schaller and H. Meyer and Pastors A. C. Haase, M. Lehninger, and Wm. Bodamer. Soon Professors J. P. Koehler and J. Meyer had to step in as replacements.

Before turning from the statewide to the broadened efforts, one more aspect of the St. Paul gatherings should be mentioned. Invitations were not sent out to professors at the Twin City and New Ulm synodical schools. When some attended nevertheless, they were granted the privilege of seating but not of debating. The reasoning seems to have been that professors had dominated at the unsuccessful discussions in the 1870-1880s and in the 1900-1910s.

Now the pastors were to be given their chance at trying to settle the knotty election-conversion doctrinal division.

The representatives of the synods involved, forming an "Intersynodical Committee," went to work with a will. After a two-day meeting in St. Paul in February 1918 they assembled for three-day meetings on two occasions in 1918 and three in 1919. By the time of the 1919 synodical conventions the committee could present a statement on conversion that gave all credit to God when someone is saved and all blame to the person when someone is lost. The Wisconsin Synod accepted the report of these happenings at its 1919 New Ulm convention.[4]

In the next years the "Intersynodical Committee" worked diligently to produce a statement on election and then on other doctrines that had been in dispute among Lutheran synods. This enlarged assignment prolonged the work to 1928. During the latter years of its work the committee regularly met in Chicago. That is why the final results are known in our circles as the "Chicago Theses." Most other Lutheran bodies, who as a result of their World War I joint endeavors set up in Chicago in 1920 "Chicago Theses" of their own, prefer to use the term, "Intersynodical Theses."[5]

Whatever the name, the theses in final form were presented to the synods involved in 1928. The crucial election section specifically rejected an "in view of faith" theory. In the discussions on that doctrine representatives of synods that had advocated the theory themselves described the doctrine as "the gospel in the superlative" and "the quintessence of the gospel."[6] Unfortunately representatives of those synods, while personally disavowing "in view of faith," felt compelled to allow this in the preaching and teaching and believing of others.[7]

At its River Forest convention in 1929 the Missouri Synod summarily rejected the "Chicago Theses." It held them inadequate in actually settling previous doctrinal differences.[8] There were good reasons for that action. The footnote that tolerated "in view of faith" was certainly one. Another was "the ambiguities that nevertheless had crept into the phraseology."[9]

Worst of all was a hard and unpleasant fact of ecclesiastical developments. Iowa and Ohio representatives, who seemingly could agree with the Synodical Conference representatives on conversion and election, had also been able to agree in Minneapolis in 1925 with Norwegians of what would be known as the Evangelical Lutheran Church.[10] But that Norwegian church body was at loggerheads over the same doctrines of conversion and election with the Synodical Conference member, the "little" Norwegians known today

SIGNIFICANT INTERSYNODICAL DEVELOPMENTS

as the Evangelical Lutheran Synod. It was becoming obvious that it was no longer a matter of removing but of minimizing and compromising the differences.

The Wisconsin Synod, meeting after Missouri's 1929 convention, could do no more than pass resolutions that expressed a willingness to continue discussion with other synods and an eagerness that the documents produced should receive more conference study. The sentiment obviously was that not all should be lost.[11] As a final solution of old doctrinal disagreements the "Chicago Theses" were admittedly inadequate. As a first step in the right direction they merited a second that never really could be taken. Before the end of the next year Buffalo, Iowa, and Ohio were joined in the first American Lutheran Church.

It may seem that too much space has been given to nothing more than a will-of-the-wisp on the intersynodical scene of Lutheranism a half century ago. Important points, however, have been made in the discussion. For one thing, the Wisconsin Synod in its past history certainly demonstrated a lively concern for Lutheran unity on the larger scale. To view it as always and only introverted and isolationist is to misread history.

For another, the "Chicago Theses" endeavor must be reckoned as the last viable effort to enlarge the sway of the Synodical Conference's theological stance. In intersynodical discussions thereafter that body was not adequately represented by the Missouri Synod. That is, however, a large subject for later chapters.

Most important of all, this failed effort at Lutheran unity revealed a new approach, a "different spirit" in intersynodical dealings. Union was becoming more important than unity. A way had to be found to agree in the doctrines of conversion and election with both the one side and the other in the debate. Matters would get even worse as Lutheran bodies in the 1930s continued their dialogs with the Wisconsin Synod on the sidelines. That is what the next chapter section emphasizes.

An Invitation with RSVP and the Response

With the Synodical Conference firmly entrenched on the right and a so-called "middle" position developing around the American Lutheran Church and the American Lutheran Conference it formed with Scandinavian church bodies, the United Lutheran Church in American (ULCA) saw fit to stake out clearly its own theological stance. This it achieved in a series of position papers: the Washington Declaration issued already in 1920, the Savannah Declaration of 1934, and the Baltimore Declaration of 1938.[12]

179

The ULCA called for a distinction between Scripture and Word and for a "catholic spirit" in the church. What is most important here, however, is the statement on fellowship with other Lutheran bodies, spelled out especially in the 1934 Savannah Declaration. Because of the far-reaching implications of the ULCA position, a substantial quotation is supplied:

> We recognize as Evangelical Lutheran all Christian groups which accept the Holy Scriptures as the only rule and standard for faith and life, by which all doctrines are to be judged, and who sincerely receive the historic Confessions of the Lutheran Church (especially the Unaltered Augsburg Confession and Luther's Small Catechism) "as a witness of the truth and a presentation of the correct understanding of our predecessors" . . . and we set up no other standards or tests of Lutheranism apart from them or alongside of them.
>
> We believe that these Confessions are to be interpreted in their historical context, not as a law or a system of theology, but as "a witness and declaration of faith as to how the Holy Scriptures were understood and explained on the matters in controversy within the Church of God by those who then lived . . . ."
>
> Inasmuch as our now separated Lutheran Church bodies all subscribe these same Confessions, it is our sincere belief that we already possess a firm basis on which to unite in one Lutheran Church in America and that there is no doctrinal reason why such a union should not come to pass. . . .
>
> We direct the President of the United Lutheran Church to bring these resolutions to the official attention of the other Lutheran Church bodies in America and to invite them to confer with us with a view to the establishment of closer relations between them and ourselves.[13]

As a result of the convention order in the final paragraph of the quotation, an invitation to discuss "closer relations" from ULCA President F. H. Knubel reached President John Brenner early in 1935. President Brenner was then in his first term of office but reacted to the situation with all the poise of a seasoned veteran. He recognized the importance of the development both for Lutheran bodies in general and for his own church body in particular.

Nowadays a matter of this sort would routinely be handled by the Commission on Interchurch Relations. In 1935 there was no such commission. When intersynodical matters called for attention, they were taken care of by the praesidium or an ad hoc committee. When the ULCA "friendly invitation" arrived in January 1935, President Brenner after consultation with the Conference of Presidents appointed such an ad hoc committee with orders to report to the 1935 convention.

On that committee were Pastors E. C. Reim, J. Schultz, and H. Kleinhans, all in the Lake Winnebago area. In addition, President Brenner requested Pastor Reim to read to the upcoming convention an essay prepared earlier for the Northern Wisconsin District but not yet delivered there. The title was "Church Fellowship and Its Implications."[14] For the synodical convention Reim added a section with the subtitle, "With Additional Notes on the Possibilities of Lutheran Union."

The dual assignment in 1935 pushed Reim into a center-stage position in the church body's intersynodical dealings. He played a major role in that area for over twenty years as Wisconsin Lutheran Seminary professor and president, member of and spokesman for the emerging church union committee and writer of the series of articles, "Where Do We Stand?" that sought to alert synod members to fellowship problems in the Synodical Conference.[15] By 1955 he was disagreeing with his own synod on the subject and in 1957 he severed his membership. The details of that event will be supplied in a later chapter.

To get back to 1935, the synodical convention under the guidance of the presiding officer and the essayist, the ad hoc and the floor committees passed unanimously one of the most important resolutions to appear in Wisconsin Synod proceedings, both in those that preceded and those that followed.[16] A good share of attention to detail is in order.

To the ULCA claim in the invitation that subscription to the Lutheran Confessions is a sufficient testimony to orthodoxy and a basis for fellowship, the convention reacted with "two facts":

1) That doctrinal issues may arise which did not exist and were not even foreseen at the time these confessions came into being.
2) That confessional writings, even as Scripture itself, may meet with varying and often contrary interpretations.

Obvious examples for both points readily come to mind. Among controversial matters that have arisen since 1577, when the Formula of Concord was written to complete the Lutheran *Book of Concord*, one could mention inerrancy of Scripture, origin of species, ordination of women, denial of the Antichrist doctrine, and many others. In the second category of differing interpretations of the Confessions one can mention such classic examples of claiming to find an "in view of faith" election in Formula of Concord XI or limiting the gospel in Augsburg Confession VII to the Good Friday atonement and the Easter proclamation.

The Wisconsin convention resolution then pointed to three "practical considerations which preclude any" ULCA-WELS approach:

    a) Tolerance of doctrinal statements not in agreement with Scripture and the Lutheran Confessions.
    b) Lodge practice inconsistent with the "Washington Declarations."
    c) Tendency to unionism, demonstrated by increasing pulpit fellowship with non-Lutherans.

Admitting that some of these questions were less doctrinal and more practical, the convention report went on to state: "We hold that it is dangerous thus to segregate practice from doctrine. On the contrary, the practice followed by a church in such matters is the clearest manifestation of the doctrine which it holds. Tolerance here becomes synonymous with liberalism, indifference, and denial. "A little leaven leaveneth the whole lump."

In its R of the RSVP of the ULCA's invitation the convention resolution closed with a paragraph that sought to forestall misunderstandings of its position that might occur and actually did and do occur. It pleaded: "We ask that this statement be taken not as captious criticism or willful faultfinding on our part, but as offered in a sincere spirit of good will and out of earnest concern that fellowship between Lutheran bodies of our land, if and when it comes about, may be based upon a true unity of the Spirit and thus be a God-pleasing union."

The historical narrative has been cluttered by an overly generous review and reproduction of the record because of the abiding significance of that record. Both what the ULCA and what Wisconsin did in the year 1935 chartered and charted pathways for the future.

The ULCA adhered consistently and persistently to its minimum demands for Lutheran fellowship: subscription to the Lutheran Confessions, if only in a "historical" sense. Over the years that position would win more and more advocates. A half century later that position would be the basis of a large United States grouping of Lutherans, two-thirds of those in the land. Give the advocates high marks for consistency and persistency in a cause that reaches back far beyond 1918 when the ULCA was founded! The cause is the cause of the old General Synod of 1820 and of its founders even earlier.

Give the Wisconsin Synod the same good marks for consistency and persistency. What it did in 1935 was another step that followed the A of its 1867 and 1868 and 1869 conventions: fellowship rests on agreement in the Scriptures and Confessions and on a concomitant practice. It would follow that pathway in subsequent decades, eschewing dialogs that assumed doctrinal differences did not really matter, disavowing documents that claimed to but did not actually remove disagreements in doctrine, even breaking cherished fellowships when that had to be done.

When the United Lutheran Church in America assembled in Savannah in 1934 and when the Wisconsin Synod met in New Ulm in 1935, the representatives and also those they represented may not have been fully aware of what was happening, but a momentous episode in church history, in Lutheran church history, in Wisconsin Synod church history was being enacted. Wisconsinites represented and representing at New Ulm may well have been more concerned about intersynodical matters closer to home.

Missouri Causes Concern

In the early 1930s a major effort was made to come to grips with the church-ministry difference within the Synodical Conference. The upshot was a meeting at the site of the new Wisconsin Lutheran Seminary in 1932 at Thiensville (now Mequon) which produced a set of four "Thiensville Theses." The outcome was far from satisfactory from the perspective of full agreement. Representatives of Missouri and Wisconsin could agree on these four statements:

1. It is God's will and order, as we learn from the Scriptures, that Christians who live together also enter into outward associations, to perform jointly the duties of their spiritual priesthood.
2. Again, it is God's will and order, as we learn from the Scriptures, that such Christian local congregations have shepherds and teachers to discharge the common task of the office of the Word in their midst.
3. It is also God's will and order, as we learn from the Scriptures, that Christian local congregations manifest their fellowship of faith with other congregations and jointly with them perform the work of the Kingdom outside of their own circle too as that is done among us in the optional form of the synod.
4. Inasmuch as every Christian has title to the keys of the kingdom of heaven, judgment rendered in accordance with the Word of God by an individual Christian, or several too, in whatever grouping, is honored in heaven. However, as we learn from the Scriptures, God's will and order is that proceedings against an erring brother are not to be considered conclusive until his local congregation has taken action. The discipline of a local congregation and the discipline of a

> synod cannot properly come into conflict with each other because the local congregation expels from the local congregation, not from the synod, and the synod from the synod, not from the local congregation. Note: The expulsion performed by the local congregation is what we, according to ecclesiastical usage, call excommunication.[17]

The reader who recalls the description of the church-ministry difference in a previous chapter will immediately recognize that an agreement on four theses has been achieved by substituting for the real bone of contention—the *divine institution* of special forms of church and ministry, namely, the local congregation and its pastor —the more general phrasing of God's *will and order.*[18] Does this make the "Thiensville Theses" a compromise document unworthy of member synods of the Synodical Conference? Not necessarily.

If the four theses were assumed to be the final word on the subject, the charge of compromise would be in order. If they, on the other hand, represent the maximum agreement attainable on the issue at the 1932 meeting and leave the unresolved issues for subsequent discussions then a more charitable judgment is in order.

There is good reason to opt for the latter viewpoint. Brethren spiritually united in the faith were discussing a difference and seeking agreement. The difference transcended synodical boundaries with Missourians, often parochial school teachers, siding with Wisconsin and Wisconsinites, President Ernst as a notable example, never agreeing with the Wisconsin position. The difference often seemed more practical than doctrinal because the well-oiled synodical machinery of Missouri could be viewed as an exhibit for the Wisconsin position. Contrariwise, the overabundance of "rugged individualism" in the Wisconsin parishes and pastorates seemed to endorse Missouri views. It is not surprising, therefore, that issues did not come to a head at Thiensville in 1932.

It is true that no immediate follow-up meetings were held. The time was, it should be remembered, the thirties and meetings then did not come a dime a dozen in the economy of the decade. The discussions would eventually be resumed over a decade later when a new order of problems plagued the Synodical Conference. That is, however, another and subsequent story. Most important of all, soon after the Thiensville meeting Missouri became involved in discussions with other Lutheran church bodies. After stating its doctrinal case in its *Brief Statement,* it first met with ULCA representatives in response to President Knubel's invitation. Almost immediately the wide difference regarding the Scriptures became apparent and discussions were broken off.

More important for this history were meetings between representatives of the Missouri Synod and of the recently founded American Lutheran Church. The meetings began in 1935 and by 1938 the Missouri convention had before it "union resolutions" that touched off the long battle within the Synodical Conference that finally led to a break in fellowship and the dissolution of the Conference. Those outcomes would not occur until the 1960s. Before they can be discussed fully, attention will have to be given to the problems the intervening years brought the church and the country in the form of the Great Depression and World War II.

CHAPTER SEVENTEEN

In The Great Depression and World War II

The church may well have been at its best in zeal for the truth of the gospel and for its spread when its spokesman, the Apostle Peter, declared, "Silver or gold I do not have." What is true for the infant and quite unorganized church, however, may not apply to a church body pushing the century mark in age and maintaining a worker-training venture and a mission outreach effort of some size. Financial concerns loomed larger for the Wisconsin Synod in the 1930s when the Great Depression was having its effects.

These effects varied. In a huge industrial metropolitan area the unemployed could equal in number those still hanging on to a job; in the small town that served as a trading center for an agricultural area there was work, even if at low pay. Farmers in the Dust Bowl saw their holdings blow away and took to the highways in search of food and a new livelihood. On farms in the Great Lakes states few went hungry.

With so much of its membership concentrated in the rural Midwest, the Wisconsin Synod was in a position to escape the worst Depression ravages. Even so, there were inescapable effects.

Not all of them were altogether bad. In the country at large during the 1930s the ratio of church and charity contributions to gross national product climbed to new highs. In the Wisconsin Synod, members joined in a gallant effort to pay off debts incurred earlier and at the same time to maintain the ongoing work, even if on a reduced scale. The Depression signs, however, were plain to see: stand-still mission programs, synodical salary slashes that cut thirty-six cents out of the dollar and, worst of all, long lines of idle candidates for the preaching and teaching ministry who could not be called and sent.

By the time of the 1933 synodical convention such hard facts of Depression life had to be faced. Two years before that the church body, much like the country, tried hard to believe that prosperity was "just around the corner." The 1933 convention was more hard-headed in dealing with the mounting problems. First of all, it called for new leadership.

Brenner Takes Charge

As has been previously mentioned in chapter 12, only one Wisconsin Synod president has been voted out of office by either the original or the merged body while still willing to serve. Neither before nor after 1933 has there been any similar occasion, but in that year President G. E. Bergemann was replaced by John Brenner. A presidential tenure equaling that of John Bading and Oscar Naumann and stretching for more than a quarter century was abruptly ended.

There were mainly two reasons why the Wisconsin delegates felt they should retire Bergemann from the presidential office. One was, of course, the huge debt that had been allowed to accumulate and that was now stifling any forward-looking effort in mission expansion. Brenner, it was felt, with the experience he had gained in heading the seminary building and the synodical debt retirement committee, might prove to be a better steward of whatever synodical treasuries were still at hand.

The other reason was President Bergemann's inability to settle the Protes'tant problems that came to a head in the synodical bailiwick in 1933. The convention struggled hard to cope with the matter and in the effort even overstayed by a day its sessions at St. Matthew, Milwaukee. All that could be accomplished was to dismiss the so-called "Peace Committee" and turn the problem back to the Western Wisconsin District.[1] Delegates no doubt hoped that Brenner, who had been on the Northwestern board in 1924 and had then been shown some measure of confidence by the first protesters, would be able to apply the healing touch.

The hindsight of history suggests that both reasons for the retirement of the old regime were not all that valid. If Bergemann failed to settle the Protes'tant problem, so did his successor and successors. Already in the earliest years of Brenner's leadership the conflict worsened in Wisconsin districts and spread across the Mississippi. The valiant peace effort during Naumann's regime fizzled, as was noted in earlier accounts.[2] Even President

Mischke's years saw pastoral and congregational defections to the Protes'tants.

How much the Karl Koehler charge that Bergemann misrepresented the facts in a report to the Wisconsin-Chippewa Valley Conference was a factor is hard to tell. By this time that whole issue has been clouded and shrouded by the mists of history past.[3] In 1933, however, it may have loomed large.

The debt issue, the other reason for Bergemann's fall from synodical grace, also merits some explanation and exculpation. Valiant efforts were made to avoid a major debt situation. Build-as-you-pay resolutions were enforced for the seminary relocation even though there was a relaxation when New Ulm needed its administration building.[4] What counted much more was a synodical willingness to tolerate annual and biennial shortfalls in the regular treasury. These had a way of mounting while sporadic debt retirement efforts were under way.[5]

In any event, Bergemann would have wanted to push forward despite any budgetary deficits. In the Lord's work of gospel proclamation he was the original and incurable optimist. A favorite sermon introduction of his flatly declared: "The Christian is an optimist. I do not say that he should be an optimist. I simply state that he is an optimist."[6] Given the times, the 1920s and early 1930s, one can sympathize with a synodical president who could remind the 1931 convention: "The preaching of the Gospel was and is and ever will be the one great and peculiar mission of the Church. Not until the Church has gone into all the world and has preached the Gospel to all creatures has it performed its mission."[7] With deep regret Bergemann reports to the 1933 convention: "Under prevailing circumstances there could be no thought of an enlargement of our work. No additional mission programs could be undertaken. The number of parish schools also did not increase. Therefore the majority of this year's candidates for the pastoral and teaching ministry are without a call; even several from the past year are still on the waiting list."[8]

In this situation the convention voted for a change in the presidency. Bergemann would remain at his pastoral post in Fond du Lac another fourteen years and still serve his synod as elder statesman and as head of the seminary board even longer. As a board member and synodical president he participated in the calling of thirteen seminary professors. The first of these was John Schaller in 1908, seminary president from 1908 to 1920, and the twelfth was Carl Lawrenz, president from 1957 to 1978. Bergemann's influential service to his synod, especially in helping shape its theological stance, certainly did not end in 1933.

The presidential election of that year, however, has tended to diminish his synodical reputation. He deserves better. Bergemann was an able administrator at a time when the church body needed that gift as never before or since in its history. Even more important, his ministry and his administration, his theology and preaching were thoroughly gospel oriented and permeated. Those who worked with him and those who learned from him agree that this commitment to the gospel was the driving force in this synodical leader.

The successor, John Brenner, was already fifty-nine years old at the time of his election to the synodical presidency. He was the son of one of the pioneer teachers of the Wisconsin Synod who served at Hustisford. It's a small world when it's the world of Wisconsin Synod history. The two men who would lead the church body from 1908 to 1953 were both sons of the same congregation in the little village of Hustisford on the Rock River some dozen miles north of Watertown.

By 1933 Brenner had acquired a considerable reputation for ability and energy in the work of his congregations and of the synod. His first parish was in Cudahy (1896-1908) where, among other things, he learned enough of the Slovak language to be able to preach to Slovaks in the neighborhood who as yet had no pastor of their own. He was one of the four founders of the original Milwaukee Lutheran High School in 1903. In 1908 Brenner was called to be Bading's successor at Milwaukee's St. John, then one of the largest congregations in the synod.

The busy pastorate did not prevent Brenner from putting his talents to use in other efforts. In 1914 he began a forty-year stint as a contributing editor to our *Northwestern Lutheran* that he helped found in that year. For thirty-five years he was on the staff of the *Junior Northwestern*, the now defunct youth periodical.

Brenner served on the Northwestern College board for twenty-four years, including those during which the "Watertown Case" occurred. For fifteen years he was a member of the seminary board. In World War I Brenner represented his synod on the Army-Navy Commission of the Synodical Convention. In the 1920s he headed the special committee whose task it was to gather building funds and retire the debt.

The latter task would carry over into the presidency. President Brenner and Board of Trustees members Leonard Koeninger and Paul Pieper had the unenviable assignment of overseeing synodical fiscal problems in the Great Depression. The grim experience left Brenner forever wary of any rapid expansion, especially the kind that did not accord with strict synodical protocol.

Brenner ran a tight synodical ship, tight in the fiscal sense and also from the administrative viewpoint. He mastered the facts and knew the details. Let a personal anecdote make the point. In 1948 this writer called Brenner from Fond du Lac to ask for an appointment to discuss a call he had received to a congregation involved in the Synodical Conference "Detroit Case." Without moving from the phone Brenner rattled off the long and complicated history, citing membership and findings of a dozen committees and concluding, "Is there anything else you want to know? I hope I've spared you a trip to Milwaukee." Pity the convention delegate who tried to challenge Chairman Brenner on the facts in the case!

As the quotation indicates, Brenner viewed travel with a jaundiced eye. He hated the waste of time involved. Pastor A. Hertwig, a Missourian with a great love for the Synodical Conference brethren, put it facetiously but also somewhat apropos when he said back in the 1950s, "The Synodical Conference would be in much less trouble if we could get Brenner to travel or could schedule more meetings in Milwaukee." The allusion is of course to the long conflict within the Conference between Missouri and Wisconsin over fellowship. This is the second major *leitmotif* in the story of the Brenner presidency. Its treatment must be deferred to the next chapter. The other theme, synodical management in the Great Depression, is given attention in the next section, *A Debt and Its Retirement*.

A Debt and Its Retirement

At the synodical convention in August 1929, just ten weeks before "Black Friday" ushered in the Great Depression, the treasurer, Theodore Buuck, reported these items:

	1929	**1927**
Notes Payable to Banks	$256,000.00	
Notes Payable to Others	$450,055.29	$275,354.68[9]

The annual budget for the next biennium was set at $575,000, an increase of almost 30% over the previous budget. The synodical debt in 1929 was well over the annual budget. That was the predicament the Wisconsin Synod was in when the Depression began.

Where had that huge debt come from? Major building programs at Wisconsin Lutheran Seminary and Doctor Martin Luther College, each costing over $300,000, are often viewed as the main reasons for the $700,000 debt. This is not even a half truth. It will be recalled that the seminary building was subject, not only to cash-on-the-barrelhead requirements, but also to the added stipulation that the synodical debt must first be liquidated. Chairman

Brenner's collection committee worked hard to get all congregations to do their bit and for the most part succeeded. Money was on hand when the building operation began at Thiensville, now Mequon. The 1929 financial report also credits the collection committee with almost halving the "old debt" of $290,000 and supplying almost $100,000 for the New Ulm building.[10]

The terminology, "old debt," tells its own story. While an "old debt" was being reduced by special collections, current deficits were creating a "new debt." The synod was growing throughout most of its years, but somehow never seemed able to meet the added expenses through a concomitant growth in the stewardship of giving. Heroic special efforts would be attempted in time of crisis and seemed to succeed, but the end result would often be at the expense of the regular synodical offerings that had a way of lagging and sagging badly during and after the special drives.[11] This was the case in the fiscal efforts at the turn of the century and it was also the case in the 1920s.

In the sad story of the debt attention must be turned to the 1927 convention at St. Lucas in Milwaukee. As has been previously recounted, that convention tried unsuccessfully to break new ground in worker training. It did succeed in establishing new fiscal patterns for the synod. It scrapped the old "pay-as-you-build" stipulations, allowing the borrowing of $650,000 to be paid off in ten years.[12] This was 1927, a boom time for everybody except Florida land investors. The result after two years was an increase of over $400,000 in the "notes payable" column. The 1929 *Proceedings*, however, contains this optimistic note in the next biennium's budget: "With the liquidation of most of the outstanding Accounts Receivable (Seminary Bldg. Com.) the present debt will be reduced to approximately $650,000.00 and upon this basis the retirement of debts is based viz. $65,000.00 annually."[13]

Subsequent financial reports tell a different story. No Depression budget allowed for a $65,000 item for debt retirement. Paying the interest was enough of a problem. The worst aspect of all was the wet-blanket effect the awesome debt had on every effort to extend and even maintain the church's mission program. Any proposal of the sort was countered with the old refrain, "We are in debt already."

The debt had to be retired if the Wisconsin Synod wanted to continue to do the church's work. It was retired. Let a main participant tell the story in his own words:

> The members of the Southeastern Michigan Conference were greatly encouraged in their stewardship efforts by the positive,

forward-looking address of our synodical president [Bergemann to the 1931 convention]. It encouraged them to set up a systematic method for disseminating information, for motivating greater concern for the synod's work program in the congregations, and for applying evangelical discipline to achieve a more equitable assumption of the financial burden of the synod's budget. . . .

Remember that in 1931 one half of our Seminary graduates were without a call and many New Ulm graduates fared no better! The "Every Member Canvass" debt reduction effort produced only a modest result. The debt which stood at $752,649.69 at the close of 1931 was still $597,863.35 on April 30, 1932, and hovered at that staggering amount, consuming almost $30,000 for interest payments annually. . . .

The convention [Michigan District, 1932] approved the program of the Southeastern Conference and urged its introduction in the other two Michigan conferences. During the same year President John Gauss encouraged the Southeastern Conference to prepare a memorial for the 1933 synod convention with a view to making the program applicable to the other districts also. It was adopted and known thereafter as "the Michigan Plan." It is printed in full in the 1933 Synod Report, Pages 91-93. . . .

By this time the program had been refined in Michigan to provide a monthly informational bulletin in addition to the original monthly posters which presented the institutions and missions of the synod. Current information was presented in a one-page, printed bulletin which also brought pictures of interest and graphs of the synod's performance. Pen sketches were added occasionally to underscore certain items of interest.[14]

Perhaps the most valuable of the latter was a pen sketch of the synod, depicted as a steam locomotive pulling a string of cars marked missionaries but prevented from reaching the mission fields by a deep wash-out of the right-of-way. As the debt was gradually reduced, the wash-out was being filled with the legend, "Help us get rid of the debt so the synod can get going again."

The synod praesidium now authorized the distribution of these monthly bulletins gratis to those who ordered them from the bulletin secretary. A complete report is found in the 1935 Synod Proceedings pages 97-99. During the remaining 17 months of the biennium 693,920 bulletins and 11,900 posters were ordered at a cost of about $2,500 to the synod. During the biennium the contributions of the eight districts increased at an average rate of 14%.—But the trustees reported to the same convention that the synod debt had increased and on July 1, 1935, stood at $638,067.70! . . .

Repeatedly irritation was expressed [at the 1935 synodical convention] over the fact that every proposal which might involve an outlay of funds was quashed with the objection that we could not incur the expense since the interest payments on the debt had to be given priority consideration.

After six days of this it should have come as no surprise when, on this last morning of the convention, a young pastor asked for the floor with the proposal, "Inasmuch as we have seen from the beginning of this convention that our debt and its interest payment is standing in the way of progress in every area of our synod's endeavor and, as our president stated in his opening report that we ought to expand our mission endeavor, I would like to make the motion that we retire our debt without delay!"[15]

President Brenner smiled at the speaker and said, "I appreciate your spirit, but I feel that it is too late for this convention to take any action on your motion." Back near the door of the Dr. Martin Luther assembly room a gentleman who already had his hat in hand and was about to leave asked for the floor. The president granted him the floor, although the time for adjournment was fast approaching. The man was a highly respected member of the synod, a New Ulm hardware man, Mr. Frank Retzlaff. He spoke very briefly: "I like what that young man has proposed and I want to second the motion."

The motion had to be called and to the surprise of President Brenner it was passed with a large majority![16]

The vignette from the 1935 convention, interesting enough in its own right, was also a harbinger of history to come. In the years ahead, as in 1935, Edgar Hoenecke would repeatedly push for mission expansion, President Brenner would seek to maintain synodical protocol, and there would be concerned laymen serving their synod according to their abilities.

In 1935, however, the result was an urgent and determined debt retirement effort, Depression or not. The successive Proceedings tell the story in numbers. The 1937 report points to $249,162 in debt retirement subscriptions from 331 congregations. At the same time President Brenner could report, "Taken as a whole, our regular collections show a gain for which we have every reason to be thankful. Though the salaries of our workers were increased, we have been able to meet all our obligations and to close our books with a surplus of $4,000."[17]

By the time of the 1939 convention the debt had been reduced to $320,799.04. The regular contributions had exceeded the expenses of the biennium and "allow for the payment of a $5000 loan."[18] It was much the same story in 1941. There was a $7000 balance in the general treasury and the debt was under $250,000.[19]

In the World War II convention held in 1943 at Watertown the debt figure could finally be reported in five figures, specifically at $97,682. Both the general and the church extension treasuries showed balances, the former of almost $60,000 and the latter of almost $250,000.[20] A favorable financial forecast for 1945 could be risked. By then there was no longer any debt and the balancing of the biennial books showed black figures.

During the waning years of World War II those who had been frustrated so long in efforts to further mission efforts and synodical growth had their moments of joy. A mission effort in new overseas areas, brought into the synodical ken by the far reaches of the armed conflict, could be envisioned and was. The details remain for later narration.

Meanwhile the synodical training schools were showing the effects of almost twenty years of standstill and neglect. Building operations were long overdue, especially at Watertown where library needs were crying for attention, and at New Ulm where housing for women students had to be provided, and at Saginaw where a previously small school was beginning to bulge at all seams.

An expansion era was in the offing even before the debt was fully retired. It was a heady moment when for the first time in synodical circles a *million* was used when speaking of a single collection or an annual budget. Those with the gray hairs of wisdom and experience said that it could not be done. It was soon done and actually done twice over. That too is another story after the war years receive attention.

World War II Problems

In 1945 the synodical convention at New Ulm adjourned on August 6, the day the first atomic bomb was detonated over Hiroshima. The delegates could not know that another such bomb three days later would call a halt to World War II. In a matter-of-fact manner they expressed "complete confidence in the Spiritual Welfare Commission" and encouraged "it to continue in its well-known spirit."[21]

The "complete confidence" in the "well-known spirit" of the synodical arm entrusted with the care of members in the armed services, the Spiritual Welfare Commission, calls attention to the very individualistic stance the Wisconsin Synod took in its World War II activities as contrasted to that of other church bodies, including the sister Missouri Synod in the Synodical Conference. In summary, the Wisconsin Synod sought to care for its some 22,000 members in the armed services by a mailing program, by camp pastor arrangements, and eventually by sending out its own chaplains, without any involvement in the government's chaplaincy program. This requires explanation.

IN THE GREAT DEPRESSION AND WORLD WAR II

Well in advance of the country's involvement in the hostilities but while war clouds were already gathering over Europe, the Wisconsin Synod took a hard look, then another, and then others at the armed forces chaplaincy system that the government had developed. Every look from the first in peacetime to those later on while World War II was raging found the government's Military Chaplaincy a program that a confessional Lutheran church body would have to avoid. Among other doctrinal concerns regarding the call and church and ministry, it mandated a unionistic ministry, requiring "Protestant" services and Christian burials for all.

The chaplaincy question came to the floor of the 1937 convention, first through an item in John Brenner's presidential report. This is his explanation:

> Requests have come to District Presidents and to me to recommend ministers for chaplaincies in the service of the Government. My stand has been that we have no authority to do this as long as our Synod has not included such work in its program. If the Synod decides to take up this work, a Commission will have to be created to issue calls to men and to supervise their work, as faithfulness to a divine call would, as I see it, forbid that a minister on his own initiative look about for a new field of labor. We should not act hastily in the matter. The committee to which this matter will be referred should answer these three questions:
> 1. Is there need for this work?
> 2. Is such service in the employ of the Government compatible with Scripture principles?
> 3. Would it not be more expedient to pay the salaries of such missionaries ourselves?[22]

President Brenner, it will be recalled, had intimate acquaintance with World War I chaplaincy matters as the Wisconsin Synod's chief representative in working with the Missouri Synod's official agency. He was determined that the church body should reach its decisions in the important question in an orderly and unhasty procedure.

The convention committee was of the same mind. It begged off committing itself in 1937 as not being "in a position at this time to familiarize itself thoroughly with all the details."[23] It did, however, urge a new committee to report to the 1939 Convention. It then added the significant caution: "Your committee holds that any pastor entering into such service is doing so without the sanction of the Synod until the Synod has definitely decided in this matter."

Two years later the Michigan-based committee of Chairman Al. Maas, O. J. R. Hoenecke, G. L. Press, F. Soll, and A. Wacker presented a three-point report the synod accepted.[24] The first point, with its statement that "any ordained pastor is at liberty to minister unto the men in service" was of course suggesting the use of regular pastors stationed near military camps. This would eventually become a major part of the program of the Spiritual Welfare Commission that was eventually established.

The second point dealt with the call and ministry problems of a pastor chosen, placed, and salaried by the government. The conclusion was that "the fundamental principle of the separation of Church and state is thereby violated."

The third point concerned itself with doctrinal and confessional principles and voiced the fear that, on the basis of the official manuals, it would "become a practical impossibility" to uphold them.

A final paragraph on "the advisability of calling and supporting our own chaplains" suggested a "comprehensive survey of Army camps and Navy zones." Eventually such a synodically supported camp pastor was sent into the cluster of military camps in Louisiana. This was Erwin Scharf, who would also serve later in Vietnam.

The 1939 convention adjourned less than a month before the *Blitzkrieg* in Poland began. New war threats for the country practically required further study—better, restudy—of the chaplaincy question. The 1941 convention adopted the new committee's report and again rejected synodical participation in the government's chaplaincy system. The reasons were the familiar three: conflicts with the divine call, violation of the separation principle and the doctrinal indifference of the chaplaincy's ministry.[25]

A much-debated decision ran the risk of becoming a much-opposed decision when four months after the 1941 convention Pearl Harbor brought us into the war. With church members now in military service in sizable numbers and with some of them dying in that service, the chaplaincy debate continued and heated up. The 1943 convention received the report of the synod's Spiritual Welfare Commission that pointed to a mailing program of over 15,000, additional attention to "Contact Pastors" located near training camps, and the possibility of actually calling and sending our own chaplains. In the interest of fortifying the faithful and convincing the wavering, the convention also ordered synod-wide dissemination of President Carl Schweppe's writing on the subject, the best of its kind.[26]

In contrast to this deliberated and repeated chaplaincy study in Wisconsin circles, the sister synod, Missouri, committed itself promptly and never looked back. Missouri at its 1935 convention, meeting only every three years, was concerned about the real threats of war posed by the Ethiopian invasion and the resultant oil embargo effort. Not being able to visualize what the 1938 international scene would be, that 1935 Missouri convention empowered its Army and Navy Commission to deal with emergencies as it saw fit. By the next convention in 1938 the Missouri convention found that it had bought the government's military chaplaincy lock, stock, and barrel.

The result was that, when war came to the country in 1941 and even before that, sister synods in the Synodical Conference were reacting to a major problem from two opposing viewpoints. An even greater problem arose for Wisconsin Synod pastors and members when the latter were sent into war zones in considerable numbers. The question for members in the armed forces and for their spiritual advisors was: Should the services of chaplains of the sister synod be utilized, especially in battle zones and for rare communion opportunities?

With most of the synod agreeing on the principles, as demonstrated by a unanimous vote on the 1941 resolution, the application of those principles in actual war conditions caused some difference in pastoral advice. No polls have ever been taken but it is a fair assumption, based on some interchange of experiences, that some answered the question: Use the service of the Missouri chaplain.

Beyond these difficulties loomed another. Here was a clear indication of a divergence of the pathway of Wisconsin and Missouri within the Synodical Conference. By the end of World War II there were a number of others. These should receive careful consideration.

CHAPTER EIGHTEEN

Break with Missouri

For those who were Wisconsin Synod members in the middle years of the twentieth century and lived through the long struggle to maintain the Synodical Conference on its historic confessional foundations, the loss of the battles and of the war will always remain the most significant and traumatic episode in their own personal version of their church body's history. The struggle was long, stretching over a quarter century. The losses in cherished fellowships were large, touching personally most pastors, teachers, and lay families of the synod. The results could have been tragic in the extreme, as dire prophecies of the time from without and within loudly and repeatedly proclaimed. That they were not was because the Lord of the church once again did all things well.

It all began in 1938 and 1939 when Missouri issued its church union resolutions and our synod in the following year reacted sharply. It ended when the Wisconsin Synod in its 1961 convention broke fellowship with the Missouri Synod and when two years later it withdrew from the Synodical Conference.

The dates, 1938-1963, need underscoring at the outset. The stretch between them plays its role when an answer is sought to the important and still relevant question: Was Wisconsin's action in 1961 and 1963 hasty or was it tardy? A viable church body, the Church of the Lutheran Confession, came into being on Wisconsin Synod turf basically because it opted for the latter answer.

Note the year 1938 again. At the time of this writing 1938 is already a half century ago. There is danger that this crucial event in Wisconsin history will be misinterpreted by those who live much later. From their vantage point it would be easy for them to conclude, "The fathers were surely slow in catching on to what was happening in the Synodical Conference back in the 1940s and

1950s. Couldn't they see that Missouri was on a unionistic track and that a break was inevitable, the sooner the better?"

The view in 1938 was not all that clear. This was just six years after the Missouri Synod accepted the *Brief Statement,* a doctrinal position paper Wisconsin approved of wholeheartedly, even if not officially by synodical resolution. The points on Scripture inerrancy and biblical fellowship were just what Wisconsin wanted to hear while those points were under attack, also in Lutheran circles. Today the Missouri Synod has been revealed as a church body misguided by its "moderate"—better, liberal—wing and still struggling to right itself after ridding itself of some of that liberal wing. In 1938 Missouri was viewed as the champion of the Synodical Conference's Lutheran orthodoxy.

A related factor that tended to blur one's viewpoint was the question of how much Missouri was changing and had already changed. Today few in or outside of the Missouri Synod would want to uphold the thesis that the Missouri of 1962 or even 1952 or 1942 was the Missouri of 1932. In fact, Missouri spokesmen from both sides will today freely acknowledge such change and regret that information about it was suppressed.[1] Back in days when issues like scouting and fellowship were being debated strenuously in Synodical Conference circles, an inordinate expenditure of time and discussion and ink had to be made in the interest of a point that today is a given and that then diverted attention from the real issue, the biblical relevance of the viewpoints in conflict.

Readers are being urged to try to put themselves into the fathers' shoes, to see the situation as it was then, not as it might seem to be much later. The first effort must be to cope with a half dozen or more individual issues that began to disturb the peace of the Synodical Conference.

Divisive Issues

The very first such issue, as has been indicated previously, was the effort to find doctrinal unity between Missouri and the fledgling first American Lutheran Church. In 1938 the American Lutheran Church declared at its Sandusky convention: "We are firmly convinced that it is neither necessary nor possible to agree in all non-fundamental doctrines [doctrines revealed in Scripture but not absolutely necessary for saving faith]."[2] Earlier that year the Missouri convention had resolved that its 1932 doctrinal position paper, the *Brief Statement,* "together with the Declaration of the representatives of the American Lutheran Church and the provisions of this entire report . . . be regarded as the doctrinal basis for future church-fellowship."[3]

In its 1939 convention the Wisconsin Synod registered a prompt protest. It termed unacceptable "the doctrinal basis established by the Missouri Synod and the American Lutheran Church. "No two statements should be issued as a basis for agreement," it explained, "a single joint statement, covering the contested doctrines thetically and antithetically . . . is imperative."[4]

By 1944 the one joint doctrinal statement was produced by ALC-Missouri representatives. This "Doctrinal Affirmation" found little favor and by the end of the decade had been replaced by the better-known "Common Confession." Until new and different merger efforts by the American Lutheran Church put the "Common Confession" in a non-functioning status in 1956, the document was a major bone of contention between Missouri on the one hand and Wisconsin and its Evangelical Lutheran Synod ally on the other. The former viewed the "Common Confession" as an adequate settlement of past doctrinal disagreements. The latter contended that a "common" confession had been achieved only by ignoring real points of controversy and soft-pedaling important doctrinal positions of the Synodical Conference.

By 1956 other issues had arisen to complicate the situation. As has been described, the Missouri and Wisconsin synods disagreed about having pastors serve in the country's military chaplaincy.[5] After Pearl Harbor this disagreement assumed larger and larger proportions.

At its Saginaw convention in 1944 the Missouri Synod abandoned its long-standing position on the Boy Scouts. Its individual congregations could now decide for themselves whether or not to have troops in their midst. Serious disturbances soon resulted in Wisconsin parishes where the old Synodical Conference position still held sway and Scouting was deemed objectionable because it undermined the truth of salvation by grace alone. In the eyes of many lay members Scouting was the main issue in the intersynodical debates and differences.

In that same 1944 Saginaw convention the Missouri Synod sought to justify a growing practice of premature prayer fellowship by assuming without Biblical warrant that so-called "joint prayer" with those not in doctrinal agreement was under certain conditions proper and God-pleasing. The ill-fated synodical resolution claimed that "joint prayer at intersynodical conferences, asking God for his guidance and blessing upon the deliberations and discussions of his Word" did not militate against its previous stand of no prayer fellowship with errorists, "provided such prayer does not imply denial of truth or support of error."[6]

There would be serious repercussions from this obvious departure from a long-standing Synodical Conference position.[7] It became a sharply debated issue in the next years and finally provided the "impasse" that halted Synodical Conference doctrinal discussions and paved the way for the body's dissolution.

By 1944 the "cooperation in externals" issue had also surfaced. The problem was not with cooperation in what was really external. No one would object to pooling statistics or sharing a common address for relief shipments. The problem arises when "cooperation in externals" actually involves the church body in joint religious work with church bodies not in fellowship.

The record indicates that in the Synodical Conference such a distinction had long prevailed. As late as 1940 a Missouri spokesman put it this way for the Synodical Conference, "The A.L.C. has relations toward other Lutheran bodies, some of which we would call cooperation in externals only while others we judge to be cooperation in the religious field."[8]

But under the tensions that came with the onset of World War II the Missouri Synod entered into agreements with the National Lutheran Council calling for cooperation in the work of aiding dislocated missions and of serving men in the military training camps. Other synods in the Synodical Conference, the ELS and ours, refrained on principle. Joint service centers paved the way to the NLC-LCMS communion agreement, according to which a chaplain could in an emergency situation commune those belonging to synods not in fellowship with the chaplain's synod.

Soon there were any number of other instances that one side viewed as legitimate cooperation in externals and the other as unionism or as President Brenner liked to put it, "numerous instances of an anticipation of a union not yet existing."[9] By 1950 there were issues enough to be dealt with on the floor of the Synodical Conference.

The Conference developed two committees for the dealing. The first was the Committee on Intersynodical Relations, consisting of the four synod presidents and two more representatives from each of the four synods. The Wisconsin men who served with President Brenner were Edmund Reim and Arthur Voss. The committee was called into being especially because of our 1944 protest overture to the Synodical Conference.

A request of the Twin Cities Mixed Pastoral Conference for a study of army and navy chaplaincies led to the establishment of a special "Interim Committee" given the task of investigating this issue and "all other matters relating to the doctrine of the call, the ministry, and the church where there has been disagreement with the aim of achieving complete unity."[10]

Neither Synodical Conference committee achieved any notable success in healing the breaches. Usually the committees themselves split along synodical lines and often issued dual reports. Synodical Conference conventions tended to reflect the same division.

In the early 1950s a large-scale pamphlet war was going on. Professor Edmund Reim, secretary of the synod's Standing Committee in Matters of Church Union, outlined the Wisconsin position in "Where Do We Stand?"—in the main a collection of his *Northwestern Lutheran* articles. The synod also issued eleven tracts on the "Common Confession" and issues in controversy.

In the meantime the "Fraternal" exchange went on, set off by the Missouri Synod's "A Fraternal Word." Wisconsin replied with "A Fraternal Word Examined." Next came Missouri's "Another Fraternal Endeavor" and its "A Fraternal Reply," a response to the eleven tracts of Wisconsin.

Crucial Conventions

The Synodical Conference's difficulties were vividly demonstrated by its first conventions in the 1950s. Meetings at Fort Wayne in 1950 and the Twin Cities in 1952 reached new lows in strife. Bitterness divided reports and there was bloc voting. Positions had hardened, mostly along synodical lines with Wisconsin and the Norwegians lined up against the Missouri and the Slovak Synod.

So bleak had the scene become that immediately after the St. Paul convention the Wisconsin delegation resorted to an *in statu confessionis* declaration. The reason for the action was set down this way, "Because the confessional basis on which the synods of the Synodical Conference have jointly stood so far has been seriously impaired by the Common Confession, we continue to uphold our protest and to declare that the Missouri Synod by retaining the Common Confession and using it for further steps toward union with the ALC is disrupting the Synodical Conference."[11]

The state of protest was then explained, "While we await a decision of our Synod in this grave situation we continue our present relationship with the Missouri Synod only in the hope that it may still come to see the error of its ways."

The 1953 Wisconsin convention recessed from August to October in order to have adequate time for the burning controversy. In August it had before it a recommendation to declare the fellowship with Missouri ended. This was from Winfred Schaller, synod secretary. The floor committee urged that the 1952 protest be approved and that the adoption of the "Common Confession" and the persistent adherence to unionistic practices by the Missouri Synod be recognized as the cause for the break in relations threatening the existence of the Synodical Conference. It also requested that the next Synodical Conference convention devote all its sessions to a consideration of the issues in controversy.[12] The recessed convention accepted the substance of the floor committee report.

The 1954 Synodical Conference convention recessed from East Detroit in August to Chicago in November in order to carry out the Wisconsin Synod's request. Delegates heard presentations on the "Common Confession," one by a Missouri, one by a Wisconsin, and one by an ELS representative, two presentations on scouting and military chaplaincy, and two others on remaining issues, in both cases by a Missouri and a Wisconsin representative.

The presentations run to almost a hundred closely printed pages.[13] Wisconsin's newly elected president, Oscar Naumann, appointed two young and obscure Michigan District pastors as Wisconsin essayists, no doubt in an effort to disprove the common notion that the Michigan District and younger pastors did not really share their synod's position. Along with them Naumann appointed President Kowalke of Northwestern College.

The whole 1954 effort merely served to indicate once more, at the cost of over 50,000 printed and who knows how many spoken words, that the Synodical Conference was a house divided. Yet that 1954 effort does demonstrate that every God-pleasing avenue was being followed in the endeavor to heal the breaches, no matter how bleak the prospects of any success seemed to the human eye. That was the situation as 1954 drew to a close and the 1955 Wisconsin Synod convention loomed on the horizon.

One would have to go back as far as 1868 for a synodical convention to equal that of 1955 in significance for the inter-church scene. By convention time our allies, the ELS, had formally declared fellowship ties with Missouri broken. Leading the ELS to this action were men who would soon play leadership roles in the Missouri Synod.[14]

Two realities, to a certain extent at war with one another, faced the 1955 Wisconsin convention. The unsatisfactory state of affairs, against which Wisconsin's 1953 admonition spoke so strongly, had deteriorated rather than improved during the biennium. It was hard to advance in admonition without declaring fellowship broken. Nobody wanted to back off from the earnest word of warning of 1953. Many felt that a break would have to be declared, if Wisconsin did not want to make itself guilty of that same sin of unionism that it was protesting against.

On the other hand, there was the calendar and the timetable. No Missouri synod convention had as yet had our 1953 admonition on its agenda. In those days Missouri had conventions every three years with meetings scheduled for early July. The 1953 Missouri convention met before ours did. Missouri would not meet again in convention until 1956. But it was now 1955 and the Wisconsin synodical convention needed to act.

What eventuated was the much-debated 1955 resolutions. In a preamble Missouri's unionism was rebuked and identified as the cause for a break in relations. That preamble was adopted unanimously. Then by a two-to-one vote it was decided to "hold in abeyance," until a Missouri convention had met, the final vote on the proposition, "Whereas the Lutheran Church—Missouri Synod has created divisions and offenses by its resolutions, policies, and practices not in accord with Scripture, we in obedience to the command of our Lord in Romans 16:17-18, terminate our fellowship with the Lutheran Church—Missouri Synod."[15]

Some fifty convention delegates formally protested the vote postponement to a special convention to be held in 1956 after Missouri's had met. Among them was Professor Reim, who tendered his resignation as secretary of the Standing Committee in Matters of Church Union and also put his resignation as seminary president at the disposal of the synod and its seminary board. The convention voted unanimously to ask him to continue to serve on the committee. It also urged the board not to accept the resignation.

One other resolution should be mentioned. It called for the drafting of a "single, concise confession of our doctrine and practice in theses and antitheses pertinent to present-day controversies." The response was the pamphlet *This We Believe*, which has been widely used and often reprinted down to the present.

When the special Watertown convention assembled, it had before it the report of the Standing Committee on Church Union urging the synod to continue "to hold the judgment of our Saginaw resolutions in abeyance."[16] Professor Reim spoke strongly in support of that report. No one argued that all problems were solved. But at its earlier 1956 convention the Missouri Synod had declared that the troublesome "Common Confession" would no longer function as a union document, since the ALC was by then taking steps to merge with American Lutheran Conference bodies into a second and larger ALC. Missouri had also gratefully acknowledged our concerns and admonitions. By a five-to-one margin the special convention resolved "to hold in abeyance." It also endorsed participation in a proposed "conclave of theologians" which would bring overseas brethren into a discussion of the unresolved issues.

This placed the burning interchurch relations issue squarely before the 1957 New Ulm convention. That convention was nearly equally divided on the question. One group insisted that a break be made. The other declared that not enough had happened for the worse between 1956 and 1957 and that therefore it would be, at a minimum, inconsistent to break in 1957. The Standing Committee did not make a recommendation. Its report simply described the sad situation that prevailed.[17]

By a four-to-one margin the floor committee brought out a recommendation to break. There was long and strenuous debate with speeches soon limited to a few minutes. The convention did not follow the lead of its floor committee. By a vote of sixty-one ayes to seventy-seven noes it rejected the break proposal and then resolved to "continue our vigorously protesting fellowship" and urged a continuation of efforts to restore full unity.[18]

Two Separations

The efforts to restore full unity involved two avenues of approach. One of these was the so-called "Conference of Theologians" at which representatives of overseas churches in fellowship with the Synodical Convention joined the discussion. The first meeting was at Oakland in June 1959, the second at Mequon just prior to the 1960 Synodical Conference convention. Regarding this Mequon meeting our Commission on Doctrinal Matters—a new name for an old committee—reported, "We sincerely regret that the earnest wrestling with the problem on the part of the Thiensville [now Mequon] Conference of Theologians has not resolved the impasse. Therefore we plead with our brethren at the Synodical Conference convention to give this matter their prayerful consideration by evaluating this sad situation in the light of God's Word."[19]

The "impasse" referred to in the previous quotation had developed in the second avenue of approach to the Synodical Conference division. This was a proposal of the 1956 Synodical Conference convention by which its joint union committee should draw up a common doctrinal statement that would reflect the Conference's position. It was a test to determine whether doctrinal unity was still present or not.

The procedure involved studying three categories of doctrines with related special problems serving as test cases. This was the plan:

1. Atonement, Justification and the Dynamic of the Christian Life (Scouting);
2. Scripture (Revelation, Inspiration, Principles of Interpretation, Open Questions) and Eschatology (Antichrist);
3. Grace, Conversion, Election, and Church and Ministry (Fellowship, Unionism, Chaplaincy, Discipline).

Discussions began early in 1957. By the time of our 1959 convention an excellent statement on Scripture was at hand. It was accepted unanimously. The other three synods likewise accepted the statement. It was a fitting swan song for the Synodical Conference. No more doctrinal statements were fully accepted. The Antichrist statement was not voted on by the Missouri Synod on the dubious grounds that the Synodical Conference as a whole had not yet acted.

A more serious problem had developed in the study of the third category. This was the impasse. The issue was fellowship. Each synod drew up its own statement on the subject.[20] Wisconsin and the ELS produced statements that echoed the historic Synodical Conference position of no fellowship without full doctrinal unity and espoused it under the term "unit concept." The Missouri statement, with which the Slovaks were in basic agreement, upheld joint prayer beyond the confessional fellowship and contended for an obligation to express a so-called "growing edge" of fellowship in a limited way toward those outside the confessional-organizational grouping.

Wisconsin viewed fellowship as a "unit concept" with pulpit fellowship, altar fellowship, and prayer fellowship being manifestations of the same unity of faith and consequently all on the same plane. Missouri, without using the term in those days, was pressing for "levels of fellowship." In May 1960 the impasse was declared.

Our representation was working under instructions of the 1957 convention to "continue its efforts on the Joint Union Committees until agreement in doctrine and practice has been reached, or until an impasse is reached and no such agreement can be brought about."[21] Accordingly, the impasse was reported to the 1960 Synodical Conference convention and to the 1961 Wisconsin Synod convention.

In that tense situation several last-ditch efforts were made to keep the Synodical Conference together. The delegation of overseas brethren was given one more hearing, even though its proposal to begin discussion anew from the perspective of the doctrine of the church had to be rejected because it called for retracing steps over ground previously covered. The recessed 1961 Synodical Conference convention meeting in Milwaukee May 17-19 was not able to find a solution to the fellowship disagreement. In fact, doubts about Missouri's stand on Scripture had to be read into the record.[22] All avenues had been attempted that could be attempted by a church body serious about the application of Scripture's fellowship teaching.

The 1961 synodical convention, meeting in Milwaukee August 8-17, reacted to the impasse by voting 124-49 to suspend fellowship with the Lutheran Church—Missouri Synod and called for an orderly termination of joint projects.[23] It expressed a willingness to discuss the issues "under proper conditions." This was the termination of a cherished fellowship in existence for over ninety years.

Synodical Conference membership required special attention. The first approach was to request that the Synodical Conference dissolve itself at its 1962 convention. When this did not happen, in 1963 the Wisconsin Synod formally withdrew with the ELS from the Synodical Conference. The Conference then struggled on for four more years before passing out of existence in 1967. In 1963 a membership that had brought the Wisconsin Synod so much joy and so many blessings for over ninety years had to be ended.

From 1938-1939 to 1961-1963 is a long time to carry through brotherly admonition. It was a quarter century that brought its share of frustration and heartache. But it was worth it because it was an endeavor to keep the unity of faith alive in the Synodical Conference.

Because the effort lasted a quarter century, another painful separation occurred. There was a series of withdrawals from the Wisconsin Synod because of the continuation of fellowship with the erring Missouri Synod. This began slowly already in 1953, grew more frequent after the 1955 convention, and increased sharply in 1957. These were the men who for conscience' sake resigned their synodical membership and then formed a new fellowship in 1960, the Church of the Lutheran Confession. The 1962 statistics of the National Lutheran Council supply these numbers for the new church body: 62 pastors, 60 congregations, 8992 souls.

Soon after Wisconsin terminated fellowship with Missouri, efforts were made to find agreement between the two bodies since there was no longer any Missouri fellowship to cause disagreement. No such agreement could be found. What few discussions there were usually broke off over the issue of admonishing an erring church body. The CLC contended and still contends that this can only be done, once the error is marked, outside the framework of fellowship. Wisconsin always contended and still contends for the duty to admonish the brother that is erring as a weak brother while that is possible. The necessity to break when such admonition is no longer possible confronted the Wisconsin Synod in 1961. The members of the CLC judged that to be too late.

While this is being written, prolonged discussions are going on with the CLC. All in the Wisconsin Synod fervently hope and pray that this separation may be ended by a reunion in doctrine and practice of former allies in the struggle to maintain the Synodical Conference on its old foundations.

CHAPTER NINETEEN

Into All the States

It was a singular blessing of the Lord for the Wisconsin Synod that the ongoing effort, from the first caution to the Missouri Synod in 1938 to the withdrawal from the Synodical Conference twenty-five years later, did not have to be one long exercise in the negative. It was during just those years that the Lord of the Church was leading and luring, sometimes compelling and impelling, the Wisconsin Synod into a period in its history marked by progress and growth.

There was advance on all fronts, in educational endeavors, in mission outreach, in evangelism efforts, and in stewardship improvement. Events contradicted the craven fears from within and dire predictions from without that, as the Wisconsin Synod withdrew from its larger sister synod, it was laying itself open to spiritual isolationism, legalism, and stagnation. The obvious example is the growth and spread of home missions. A land-locked, midwestern church body was able in not too long a time to see the dream of "Into all the States" transformed into reality.[1] In the process, actually before the process could fairly begin, there had to be some change and enlargement in mission thinking and planning.

Enlarging Horizons

External forces played their part, creating a secular environment that all but cried out for outreach and expansion on the part of the church body. Like it or not, the Wisconsin Synod had to trade in its original, confined viewpoint of synodical purpose and mission outreach for a newer, larger model.

Sometime during that quarter century from 1938 to 1963—in fact, very close to the beginning of the era—the Wisconsin Synod changed from a predominantly German church body to one that fully adopted the language of the land. One World War with Germany spurred the change and a second completed the process. Certainly, the church body continued to minister to the language preferences of the elder generation, but those "senior citizens"—to use a phrase not yet invented at the time—were a dwindling minority. Whatever language problem there was, it was soon buried. The church body was more ready and able to gather non-Germans and non-Lutherans into its ranks.

There were more and more of those to be gathered. The old synodical purpose of ministering to immigrant German Lutherans had become anachronistic. The door, previously wide open to such immigrants, had been less used in the early decades of the century and was tightly closed in the 1920s. The church body could not continue to concentrate on gathering its "own kind of people." There just weren't all that many of them around anymore. More names like "Smythe" and "Smith" were appearing on our congregational rolls and on our pastoral rosters.

Already in 1941 the synodical General Mission Board was wrestling with such changes. In that year Chairman W. Roepke alerted the synodical convention to new needs when he stated in his report: "Let us free ourselves from the thought that our Home Mission work is done with the same kind of people that were available a generation ago. Then this type of mission work was done almost exclusively around those of the household of faith. Today it is different." As a case in point Chairman Roepke cited confirmation statistics of the Dakota-Montana District that showed adult and children confirmations to be almost equal, and a forty-sixty relation prevailing synodwide.[2]

These years also brought with them a marked increase in national mobility. Job opportunities, climate preferences, economic resources, and transportation advances put America at midcentury on wheels and wings. To be born, live, and die in one place—once the general rule—had become the rare exception. The members of the Wisconsin Synod began to move away from Wisconsin and its neighboring states into areas far beyond the synod's original ken.

Before midcentury the few moves of this sort had not caused great problems. The place moved to may not have had any Wisconsin Synod church in the vicinity or the state, but a Synodical Conference sister congregation could always be found nearby. Transfers were made without reservation or hesitation.

After midcentury it was a different matter. It was becoming more and more obvious that the Synodical Conference synod, with the most far-flung borders and wide-spread congregations, was marching to a different drummer and in a different step than the Conference had always moved previously.

This was especially the case in the coastal districts of the Missouri Synod and these were the areas that were especially luring Wisconsin Synod members. It was inevitable that a reluctance to provide automatic transfers would engender hopes for mission expansion and plans to carry this out.

In these circumstances it was likewise inevitable that there would be alteration and innovation in the church body's mission aims and operations. A cautious first step was the calling of so-called "general missionaries" for larger areas that seemed especially ripe for harvest. This was not an entirely new concept. It simply broadened the old *Reiseprediger* position that reaches far back into the early history of the old Wisconsin, Michigan, and Minnesota Synods. There was even the later example of such roving missionaries as F. Stern and R. Fenske in the Pacific Northwest in the early decades of the merged synod.

That was the setting for the 1939 synodical convention's resolution to approve the calling of such "general missionaries" for both Arizona and Colorado.[3] Called to the Arizona field was a veteran in the work, Pastor F. Stern, who had previously served in such a capacity in the Pacific Northwest. For the Colorado area, Pastor I. P. Frey was called. Not too much later Pastor R. Scheele became general missionary for Michigan.

Results were not slow in making an appearance. The Depression may have been over but the war was taking its place as a barrier to mission growth. Even so, in the four war years from 1941 to 1945 a total of eighty-eight new mission fields were opened on a trial basis. Not all of them passed the test and survived, but the old mission stagnation of the Thirties was a thing of the past.

The next step in the direction of mission expansion was the establishment of so-called "mission districts," special areas that were promising fields but geographically removed from the mother district. By the summer of 1942 Colorado, a part of the Nebraska District, and Arizona, then a part of the Southeastern Wisconsin District, were such mission districts operating under their own boards.[4]

In 1955 came the division of the old General Mission Board into separate boards for home and world missions. Eight years later a full-time executive secretary for the General Board for Home Missions was called to oversee the rapidly expanding work.[5] The man called to fill that post was Pastor Raymond Wiechmann coming who had been serving Milwaukee's St. Lucas. In 1968 he was succeeded by President Norman Berg of the Michigan District. Until the time of his retirement in 1988 Secretary Berg headed the synod's home mission operation and expansion.

The same 1963 synodical convention that called for the full-time executive secretary for home missions also furthered the work by dividing the whole country into areas of mission responsibility and assigning them to the district boards. A practical effect of this resolution was to render null and void a 1953 restriction that "the General Board for Home Missions shall be required to obtain specific authority from the Joint Synod whenever it desires to establish missions in areas . . . which lie outside of the general area served by the Joint Synod."[6] The 1963 resolution made it possible to leap-frog into non-adjacent states and opened the whole United States to mission expansion.

Meanwhile, additional planning for that expansion had to provide for two necessary ingredients: an efficient church extension fund and added manpower to serve in the new fields. Details of these two developments, which certainly are a part of the story of home mission growth, will be supplied in subsequent sections on fiscal matters and worker-training efforts.[7]

Into Sun-and-Sea States

The states are Florida and California. They receive special attention both because they are "firsts" in the story and because they typify subsequent efforts in other areas. They both represent breaks with old mission modes of operation. Up to midcentury California had been viewed as Missouri turf, with Arizona as its Wisconsin counterpart. Florida was far from the mission-reach of a synod that frowned on leapfrog ventures and chose to expand for the most part only into states adjacent to those in which it already had holdings. Because of the Apache field Arizona was an exception. In the East the limits were Ohio congregations in Jenera, Findlay, and Kenton. By 1955 there were Wisconsin Synod missions in both California and Florida.

Florida, especially, typifies the new outreach in home missions. California was at least "adjacent" to a state with Wisconsin Synod holdings, while Florida was four states and almost 1000 miles away. The "leap" into Florida took more than a little doing and even some unorthodox practices.

Mr. Louis Ott, a veteran member of the Michigan District's mission board, played a key role in this venture. He had a winter home in Florida and his heart was set on a Wisconsin Synod mission in the state. He was a member of the team that did the original mission exploration of the state in February 1954. Later that year he opened his winter home to the first missionary sent into the states, his old Michigan neighbor, Pastor William Steih. He continued his efforts until the dreams were realized in December 1954. If it could be said of any human being that he led the Wisconsin Synod into Florida, that person would be Louis Ott.

The venture into Florida took persistent effort. About the same time that the Michigan District mission board was beginning to give serious thought to going into Florida, the 1953 synodical convention was passing the "no leapfrogging" resolution referred to previously. The February 1954 exploration had to be undertaken without official blessing and funding. The report to the district states:

> No funds had been appropriated for an exploration of that State, and the matter could not wait until the next general convention might do so. After serious deliberations the pastor members of the Board [K. Vertz of Owosso, H. Zink of Stevensville, and A. Baer of Adrian] agreed to approach their congregations to see if they would be willing to bear the expense of a mission survey in Florida. Without hesitation they too consented, and the exploration took place February 8 to 17.[8]

The same report hints at opposition to the effort when the board defensively justifies its action by declaring: "The members of the Board resent the inferences, not all of which were made in jest, that the trip was an expense-paid vacation in Florida. St. Paul explored mission fields too on expense money provided by the church at Philippi and no one thinks he was on vacation. One does not relax and rest while traveling 1400 miles in eight days and checking city after city for mission possibilities. This survey was made in all earnestness."

In Florida events moved rapidly after the General Synodical Committee and the General Mission Board gave the Michigan District's mission board the green light to send one man to Florida. No provisions for a chapel, however, could be made. Pastor William Steih of Kawkawlin was called to serve in "Florida in general and St. Petersburg in particular." He came to Florida in September 1954; a parsonage was built before the year was out. In December Faith Church organized and on January 9, 1955, the first public service was held in a school auditorium. In March ground was broken for the chapel on 49th Street North and dedication day was July 24.

Since these necessary constructions had not been officially authorized, some special funding had to be provided. Individual Michigan congregations gathered funds for the distant daughter congregation even though the district itself acknowledged "that present Synod regulations make our District's financial support of this project an impossibility."[9] Some $15,000 dollars were collected to keep the wolf from the door until in August 1955 Faith Church became a member congregation of the synod and its parsonage and chapel were taken into the synodical Church Extension Fund.

The work in Florida spread rapidly. Soon there were three sister congregations of Faith Church. Mount Calvary of Tampa was organized in 1957, Peace of Bradenton in 1958, and Bay Pines of Seminole in January 1959. Three missionaries also joined Pastor Steih in the work. James Vogt came to Tampa in 1956 and in the next year added Bradenton to his field and eventually moved there. Edward Renz took over the Tampa field in 1959. In the previous year Howard Kaiser had begun work in Seminole. By 1962 all four congregations had erected chapels and parsonages. Within three years after dedicating its chapel Faith Church in St. Petersburg became self-supporting. The growth was for the most part real mission growth, not just a service to transplanted Wisconsin Synod members. At Bay Pines after eight years the congregation's roll contained only one family in ten that was of Wisconsin Synod background.

The four Florida congregations have become thirty-four. In addition, the work has spread into neighboring states. Already in 1973 the area was strong enough to become the South Atlantic District of the Wisconsin Synod, less than twenty years from the time Florida was entered with enthusiasm by a few and with reservations by many.

Across the continent, in the meantime, a similar development was taking place. Serious consideration was given to opening a California mission from the end of World War II on. By that time the old "Missouri in California—Wisconsin in Arizona" arrangement had given way. In 1938 Missouri began work in Arizona, the last of the forty-eight states it entered. By 1950 Wisconsin was ready to venture into California.

It had been there before, but only briefly, in the aborted Indian mission venture of 1876-1877.[10] It had come close at the turn of the century when there were appeals from Salt Lake City and Pasadena that were heard but not heeded. Finally, in 1950, a firm beginning was made when two missionaries were sent in response to urgent requests from Wisconsin Synod transplants in the area. Perhaps the most insistent of all the pleading voices was that of Mr. Carl Loeper, a Californian but also a son of the long-time Whitewater pastor. The role Louis Ott played in the Florida opening in 1954 was acted out on the West Coast by Carl Loeper at midcentury with his repeated requests for a missionary, his enthusiastic service on the mission board, and his work on the church council of the second of the California mission congregations, St. John of Tarzana.[11]

Two missionaries were sent to California in 1950. The one was Pastor Armin Keibel, called from his high school post in Milwaukee. He began work in the Mar Vista area in northwest Los Angeles, holding the first public service in a rented store building on December 24, 1950. The other was Pastor Frederick Knoll of Tucson, a veteran member of the Arizona Mission Board. His area was Tarzana, also in northwest Los Angeles and on February 4, 1951 he conducted St. John's first public service. Both men would remain at these posts for long stretches of duty, Keibel until 1966, when he accepted a call to Concord in the same state, and Knoll until his retirement in 1973.

The first synodical reports on the historic California openings are of the low-key, matter-of-fact type. The 1951 synodical proceedings present this summary of the Arizona Mission District, the responsible agency: "After long and much urging from our circles a beginning has been made by our Synod for Mission work in this State under the supervision of our District. After spending much time on surveys, acquisition of property and buildings for worship, two missionaries were sent to Tarzana and Mar Vista, located in greater Los Angeles."[12]

The report speaks of "spending much time on surveys, acquisition of property. . . ." It could also have spoken of "much money." When property was acquired for the Mar Vista mission less than an acre of land was priced at $8,600, a new high for the synod's trustees. This was a portent of things to come. Land cost, building permits, and zoning restrictions would be features of the history of subsequent mission plantings in California.

There was another problem in the early years. California then did not sound the siren song in synodical circles that it does for many today. When the time came in 1954 to find a third man for the growing field, the call practically went begging for over three years. In the second year a call was accepted but then quite promptly declined when the man was recalled by his former congregation.

Finally, in 1957, Paul Heyn became the third man in the California field. He was stationed at Pomona but remained alert to other promising fields in the area, even beginning work in San Francisco. Two years later Robert Hochmuth came to nearby Santa Clara. These two men, Paul Heyn and Robert Hochmuth, would work energetically for mission expansion in both the southern Los Angeles and the northern San Francisco areas. Soon there were congregations in such places as Garden Grove, Sacramento, and San Jose.

This growth soon spurred and then was in turn spurred by the creation of a California Mission District of the Arizona-California District. This took place in 1961 when the mission board was organized with Pastor Heyn as chairman, Mr. Carl Loeper as secretary, and Pastor Hochmuth as treasurer, all familiar names in this mission story.

At the time of this writing there are nineteen congregations in the northern area and twenty-nine in the southern field. One congregation, Citrus Heights' St. Mark, has passed the 1000 baptized membership count.

Into the Other Thirty-six States

At the time World War II ended in 1945 the Wisconsin Synod had congregations in fourteen states, stretching for the most part across the northern states from Ohio and Michigan to Oregon and Washington. There were also holdings in the area reaching from Nebraska southwest across Colorado to Arizona. Besides these seven states mentioned the synod was represented in Wisconsin, Illinois, Iowa, Minnesota, North and South Dakota, and Montana, a total of fourteen. Thirty-four were left; and after 1959, thirty-six. There was also a home mission in Canadian Sault Ste. Marie.

During the years when the California and Florida fields were opened, 1950-1954, three other states had their first organized Wisconsin Synod congregations. In Arofino, Idaho, Peace Church organized in 1950 and in Cheyenne, Wyoming, Redeemer did the same in 1952. Missouri entered the list of states with WELS congregations when Orthodox Church was organized in 1954. The distinctive name is a reminder of ties to the old Orthodox Lutheran Conference, the first organization of Missouri dissidents that soon disbanded. That left twenty-nine or thirty-one states.

During the five years from 1955 to 1960 no advance into new states occurred. There was an acute shortage of pastoral manpower. The Church Extension Fund could not begin to respond to the numerous requests for chapels before it. These were also the years when so much time and energy was being given to the worsening fellowship problems of the Synodical Conference. What few mission openings could be made in those years were made in familiar territory.

These negative factors were in the process of dissolving with the advent of the decade of the 1960s. A Manpower Committee began operations in 1959. In 1961 borrowing for the Church Extension Fund was made a matter of policy and soon the treasury swelled to $4,000,000. The break with Missouri in 1961 made it all the more necessary that Wisconsin have holdings throughout the country. The push was on.

Using the annual statistical reports and the synodical annuals as guidelines, one finds five new states appearing on the lists from 1961-1965. They are Kansas in 1962, Virginia in 1963, New Jersey and Texas in 1964, and Pennsylvania in 1965. The count of unrepresented states was down to twenty-six. In addition, the Canadian province of Alberta was added when a mission in Edmonton was organized in 1963.

The five years from 1966 to 1970 were a boom time for mission openings in new states. There were new missions in 1966 in Huntsville, Alabama; and Baltimore, Maryland. Anchorage, Alaska; Albuquerque, New Mexico; and Guymon, Oklahoma had missions in 1967. The next year found East Hartford, Connecticut and Indianapolis, Indiana on the Wisconsin mission map. In 1969 there was a new mission in Slidell, Louisiana, and in the next year there were openings in Honolulu, Hawaii; Pittsfield, Massachusetts; and Columbia, South Carolina. This five-year period brought a total of eleven new states on the home mission list. In addition, the work in Canada spread into British Columbia in 1968. By the end of 1970 the number of states without Wisconsin Synod churches was down to fifteen.

The work continued at a fast pace from 1971 to 1975. In 1971 missions were opened in Little Rock, Arkansas; College Park, Georgia; Las Vegas, Nevada; and Hendersonville, Tennessee. The next year Wisconsin's mission spread reached Schenectady, New York in the East and Salt Lake City, Utah in the West. New states for 1973 were Delaware, Kentucky, North Carolina, and Rhode Island when mission work was undertaken in Wilmington, Louisville, Raleigh, and Providence. In 1975 there was a mission in Nashua, New Hampshire. It should be mentioned that Idaho and Wyoming were re-entered after earlier mission closings. Also, another Canadian province, Quebec, had a Wisconsin Mission in 1971, and in 1975 we inherited the Antigua, West Indies, mission from the disbanding Federation for Authentic Lutheranism. The eleven new states for 1971-1975 left only four with no synod missions.

By 1983 that number had been reduced to zero. In 1980 Beckley, West Virginia, had a mission and in 1981 work began in Barre, Vermont. Finally, in 1983, all fifty states had Wisconsin Synod congregations. In that year there were plantings in Portland, Maine, and Columbus, Mississippi.

The long list of places and dates can serve to complete the record. But it cannot begin to describe all the trial and patience and experience and hope involved in every one of those mission openings and those that came later in the area. It could take years from the time transplanted Wisconsin members first sought home mission help until the first public service was held in the mission chapel.

There were trials also for the sponsoring mission boards. Hard choices and agonizing decisions had to be made as likely fields competed with one another. Limited resources in missionaries and chapel funds often could not begin to match all the opportunities and challenges. Worst of all, for one reason or another an exploratory field might have to be shut down.

Several men were especially involved in this often difficult decision making, the chairmen of the General Mission Board and after 1963 the executive secretary of the Home Mission Board. William Roepke, long-time pastor at Menominee, Michigan, headed the synod's mission board through the 1940s and into the next decade, serving long enough to see the California venture under way. Until 1961 his successor, Karl Gurgel, brought his boundless enthusiasm to the supervisory task, even when expansion opportunities were severely limited.

For most of the 1960s Raymond Wiechmann carried on the assignment. His tenure spanned the changes in the structure of the mission board. He was both the last of the chairmen acting as executive officers of the board and the first of its executive secretaries.

In 1968 Wiechmann's successor, Norman Berg, began a long service that lasted until his retirement in 1988. He brought with him to the office administrative skills developed as Michigan District president. Even missionaries in the field who chafed under his barrage of questionnaires on goals and accomplishments and brethren in the work who could not always warm up to his latest slogan, would not hesitate to testify to Norman Berg's ability and dedication as for two decades he headed the synod's home mission ventures. He even had the opportunity to help train his successor.

When mission expansion enlarged the work load at the office, a second man was called in. The first man to fill the position was Larry Zwieg. The second was Harold Hagedorn, who in 1988 succeeded Berg in heading the home mission effort that had in a relatively brief span of the synod's history transformed the church body's look from merely midwestern to truly national. The synod had completely outgrown its name. At the time of this writing, in fact, a synodical convention is considering the possibility of a name change.

CHAPTER TWENTY

Into All the World

At midcentury, when most American mainline churches were drastically cutting back their foreign mission efforts in quantity and, even more, in quality, the Wisconsin Synod undertook its first overseas outreach efforts to a nonchristian area. It wasn't that there was no interest in such work earlier in the history of the synod. After all, the founders themselves had been trained for such work and they gathered funds for *Heidenmission* (heathen missions) from the start.

When more direct involvement was desired toward the close of the previous century, a Japanese mission was seriously considered. A stateside effort, however, was substituted, the Apacheland evangelism effort previously described.

Beginning in the 1920s Wisconsin worked overseas in Poland, but this was not strictly speaking an outreach to unbelievers. It was rather an effort to help German-speaking fellow Lutherans carry on church work in a predominantly Roman country with a declining official Lutheran church. World War II drastically altered this effort.

Wisconsin also shared in the work in Nigeria but that was a joint project of the Synodical Conference. The bulk of the support came from the large Missouri Synod, even though Wisconsin contributed more than its fair share of missionaries to the cause.

That is why a new chapter in synodical history began to be written when the 1951 synodical convention passed the resolution: "We recommend that our Synod enter into foreign heathen mission work in the Northern Rhodesia field in Africa."[1] It was further resolved "to place a man in Tokyo: (a) to care for our service men, (b) to investigate mission opportunities in Japan."

Pathway to Decision

Those resolutions did not come as easily as it might appear on paper. Quite the contrary! For six years it was touch and go whether an overseas mission would be undertaken as two differing points of view developed and vied with one another.

It began at the 1945 synodical convention at New Ulm, during the waning weeks of World War II. In fact, the convention closed on August 6, the fateful day for Hiroshima and for the world. When the report on the Indian Mission was presented, it concluded by offering this resolution: "Resolved that the President appoint a committee to gather information regarding foreign fields that might offer opportunity for mission work by our Synod. When ready, this committee shall report the results of its study, first to the General Mission Board and then to the Synod."[2]

The proceedings tersely add "Adopted" to the printed resolution. The one word covers a convention episode, crucial in Wisconsin's history. When the resolution was offered, Chairman President Brenner ruled, "Out of order." His ruling must have been based on the fact that a routine report had introduced new business, big new business. The convention reacted by speaking for the resolution and passing it by a large majority. Appointed to the Commission on Foreign Missions were: Arthur G. Wacker, member of the General Mission Board; First Vice President E. Benjamin Schlueter; Henry C. Nitz, Waterloo pastor and Chairman of the Northwestern board; Leonard H. Koeninger, of the Board of Trustees; and Prof. Edmund R. Bliefernicht of Dr. Martin Luther College.

This committee's efforts and reports became the battleground for those urging mission expansion overseas and those, headed by President Brenner, who opted for a more cautious and conservative approach. It is assumed that nobody was actually anti-mission in his viewpoint.

The first group emphasized that beginning an overseas mission was the need of the hour. The old barriers had fallen. The war was over; the debt was liquidated. A synod nearing its centennial should want to participate actively in fulfilling the Lord's Great Commission. The spokesmen for the cause liked to recall a 1935 word of Professor John Meyer in the aftermath of an earlier World War:

> Until very recently there was always a shortage of men for our work. Why? Many people withheld because there was more material success luring them to other professions. What did God do? When we withheld our sons from His service, He sent the World War and we had to let our sons go to the shambles of foreign battlefields! God showed that He can—very painfully too—take our sons if we refuse to give them to Him willingly.
>
> After the war we gradually got more men. Yet, although our country, and our Christians along with the rest, was practically wallowing in money, contributions toward missions were far

from keeping step with the general prosperity. We withheld our money from God. He sent us the Great Depression and many lost practically all they had. God *can* get at our money, if we withhold it from Him, get at it so that it hurts, while we might have enjoyed the pleasure of giving for his saving cause.[3]

On the other side were those who urged a cautious approach in any mission expansion. They also recalled the 1930s Depression but with emphasis on the painful cuts in synodical salaries and in mission plantings. They warned against hasty overexpansion in outreach, rosy overenthusiasm in the Lord's work. On the theological level they believed that a church body should wait for a specific call to mission service, rather then seek out opportunities on its own. They claimed as their ally the veteran synodical leader, President John Brenner.

President Brenner's personal mission commitment was not in question. Earlier in his career he had learned the Slovak language in order to be able to minister more faithfully as a vacancy pastor. He wanted to save souls. But President Brenner had personally presided over Depression salary cuts and mission cutbacks. He had battled to liquidate the old pre-Depression debt and provide funds for the seminary relocation. He hated red—red figures in a synodical fiscal report. His idea of sound financial planning was a strict pay-as-you-go policy. He did not want to let any new undertakings hamper an honorable discharge of old commitments. As chief synodical officer he wanted to run a tight ship and to that end liked to operate through the Synodical Council which he was able to influence and often dominate.

This was the setting for a prolonged struggle regarding foreign missions that disturbed the synodical waters from 1945, when the proposal for a foreign missions committee was made and adopted, to 1951, when it was decided to work in Africa and place a man in Tokyo.

At the first meeting of the Commission on Foreign Missions a dispute developed over what the assignment "to gather information regarding foreign fields" really meant. One side, headed by Pastor Arthur Wacker, contended that this obviously implied an active search for mission opportunities. The other side insisted that the assignment was to receive and gather information, in line with waiting for a direct call for mission involvement. When an impasse developed, a special arbitration committee was appointed to settle the dispute. The committee, Carl Lawrenz, Harry Shiley, and Gerald Hoenecke, ruled for the broader meaning of "gather information" but cautioned that no personal, on-the-spot investigation of fields had been authorized. It further ruled that, after study of the fields in relation to the synod's abilities, a report should be made to the General Mission Board and then to the synodical convention.[4]

When the Commission on Foreign Missions reported to the 1947 synodical convention at Northwestern College it offered three resolutions: (1) dismiss the committee, (2) authorize expansion into foreign mission fields, and (3) instruct the General Mission Board to explore the most promising fields and report to the General Synodical Committee for further instruction.[5]

The resolutions were debated during several sessions with all the old and some new pro and con arguments heard and reheard. Finally, in a moment of high drama Arthur Wacker moved the question. The convention sided with him and then passed the resolutions. The synod wanted to work in a foreign mission field. It was not any longer a question of whether or not but of where.

The General Mission Board's original plan was to investigate two areas, China and Africa. In China, however, there was a sudden and complete political turnover from 1947 to midcentury that canceled any projected mission exploration. Two men were to be sent to Africa. One was Arthur Wacker. It took over a year to find the companion. Finally, Edgar Hoenecke and his Plymouth congregation were convinced that he should be the second member of the exploratory team. In Easter week 1949 the members of the Southeastern Conference of the Michigan District bade their two brothers Godspeed at a special service at Scio, Wacker's congregation and the oldest in the Wisconsin Synod.

The record of the exploration is a history in itself. It need not be retold here, for one of the explorers, Edgar Hoenecke, has written "The WELS Forty-niners" for the *WELS Historical Institute Journal* and it can be read there.[6] The expedition finally found a most promising field in Zambia (then Northern Rhodesia) in the Hook of the Kafue area west of Lusaka. That was the heart of the report Wacker and Hoenecke submitted to the General Mission Board upon their return to the states just before the 1949 synodical convention in August.

The report was not acted on there. Instead it was first discussed at the fall Mission Board meeting. Then a special seven-man committee was appointed to study the whole matter. After the passage of a year this committee, in October 1950, requested additional time to prepare a report for the General Synodical Committee. Ultimately the mission question came before the 1951 convention where the General Mission Board recommended sending two men to Africa and two to Japan. The convention endorsed the African venture but whittled down the Japan part of the proposal, as previously indicated, to one man caring for servicemen and investigating mission opportunities. Just past its centennial, the Wisconsin Evangelical Lutheran Synod finally was in the foreign heathen mission business.

The First Two Fields

The man sent to Japan to minister to servicemen and to investigate mission opportunities there, Pastor Frederick Tiefel of Spokane, Washington, sailed for his outpost in February 1952. This was a full year and more before the African Mission team of Pastor and Mrs. Albrecht Habben and the lay helpers, Mr. and Mrs. Paul Ziegler, all of Hastings, Nebraska, arrived at Lusaka in Zambia, Africa, on June 5, 1953. For reasons that will become obvious, however, the African venture will be given first place in these overseas mission annals of the Wisconsin Synod.

The delay in getting missionaries to Africa was caused by a regrettable series of declined calls, nine in all. The tenth call was finally accepted by Pastor A. Habben. Accompanying him was his parishioner, Paul Ziegler, skilled in building trades, who was to get the mission buildings off the ground. The second missionary was a 1953 candidate, Otto Drevlow, completing his studies at Bethany Seminary, Mankato, Minnesota, and able to leave for Africa only in the summer.

As indicated, there were some adjustments made in the original site projections. The "Hook of the Kafue" area, almost a mission shibboleth by that time, was lost to others because of the long delays. Instead, work began in and about Lusaka, in the city proper, in the native suburb of Matero, and in nearby Sala Land.

The first report to the 1953 synodical convention offered these cautious comments on the work of the mission team: "We may not expect tangible results from their labors for some time. During the full year that will be consumed in building their base and learning the native language they will be unable to do any actual mission work. The most we may hope for is that during this time they will win the natives' confidence and pave the way for the Gospel to reach their hearts."[7]

The next report two years later, however, indicated that more was accomplished than had been expected.[8] The white mission in Lusaka was drawing twenty-five people to its regular services. In Matero almost 100 natives were gathering for the services and there were instruction classes for both children and adults. In Sala Land four preaching stations were opened with attendance ranging from 150 at Cuyaba to 400 at Lumano.

There was a setback in the work when Missionary Drevlow returned to the states. He was replaced by Pastor John Kohl, who took up the work in Matero in December 1954. Meanwhile a modest building program had been begun and schools were operating under the control and supervision of the colonial government's Department of Education.

A key paragraph in this 1955 report reads: "We have planned an indigenous African Church. As the natives are brought into the church, they will begin to share in the responsibility of supporting it. We are planting good seed; and good seed bears fruit after its kind." Missionary Habben predicted, "After ten years, we should be out of our infant stage and be able to walk almost alone."

By 1957 Missionaries Harold Essmann and Richard Mueller had been called to replace Mr. Ziegler and Missionary John Kohl, whose health problems forced his return to the states. The staff was enlarged when the fourth missionary was added, Edgar Greve. He was called from the Synodical Conference Nigerian field.

Medical work as a mission arm was undertaken. Mrs. Arthur Wacker, who accompanied her husband on a six-months visit to the field in 1955, was the pioneer in this phase of the work that was sponsored from the start by ladies' societies of WELS congregations. In 1961 a dispensary staffed by two American nurses was set up at Lumano on the Sala Reserve.

At the tenth anniversary milestone in 1963 the synod had every reason to be grateful to the Lord for leading it to this field of labor and for richly blessing the efforts there. There were new names on the roll of expatriate missionaries, among them some that loom large in the synodical mission story. Dr. William Schweppe, the Nigeria veteran, was an invaluable addition to the staff until his death in 1968. Theodore Sauer served as field superintendent for three years in the early 1960s and gained valuable experience for his work as the second executive secretary for the synodical foreign mission board. Ernst H. Wendland came to the field in 1962 and three decades later is again serving there after an eight-year tour of duty at Wisconsin Lutheran Seminary from 1978 to 1986. He succeeded Superintendent Sauer when the latter returned to the states but is best remembered for his work in establishing the Lusaka Bible Institute and the seminary that grew out of it. A son, Doctor Ernst R. Wendland, joined the father in the mission effort, working especially in providing translations of religious materials for the field. Among those who joined the work in the early 1960s was Raymond Cox, who succeeded E. H. Wendland in the superintendency in 1978.

Soon after the tenth anniversary important steps were taken on the road to an indigenous mission planting. In the fall of 1964 the Lutheran Bible Institute was opened in Zambia in the Lusaka area for training native workers for the field. The two-year course prepared students for intern service and seminary study. At the present time seven graduates are serving as national pastors alongside fourteen expatriate missionaries.

In 1965, twelve years after the work began, African congregations joined together in organizing the Lutheran Church of Central Africa. The missionaries from America were still lending their services but the church was becoming more and more an African Church.

As the mission celebrated its silver anniversary in 1978, it could count 7000 souls and 3300 communicants in 106 congregations and preaching places served by 5 national pastors, 12 expatriate missionaries, 2 vicars, and 32 evangelists. The total number of baptisms was almost 1000—992, to be exact. By that time work had expanded from the original Zambia field into neighboring Malawi and also into Cameroon. "God made it grow."

On the other side of the globe the Japanese mission venture, authorized by the same 1951 synodical convention, presented a different kind of story. In this highly cultured and industrial land no rapid growth was achieved, nor was any expected. In the pattern of the first American overseas missionary a century and a half earlier, who took six years to win his first Asian convert, the work in Japan moved forward slowly. Progress could not be counted by villages and preaching stations, not even by families, but by single souls, won one at a time.

What was accomplished in the first years in Japan, had to be done over. The first planting was lost to the Wisconsin Synod when the first missionary, Frederick Tiefel, broke ties with it over the fellowship issue. These were the years when dissatisfaction with the synodical actions—nonaction, some would say—was coming to a head and would soon result in the formation of the Church of the Lutheran Confession.

Missionary Tiefel was among the dissatisfied. When he arrived in Japan in 1951, he soon encountered rank departures from Synodical Conference fellowship practices on the part of Missouri Synod missionaries. Problems that disturbed parishes in this country loomed all the larger in a mission field in a heathen land. It is understandable that Missionary Tiefel would be in the forefront of the ranks of those who deplored delay in taking decisive action.

This is not to say that he neglected his assignment. On the contrary, the first reports showed good results. By 1953 the church body was ready to view the work in Japan as gospel outreach, more to the unbelievers than to the Wisconsin Synod servicemen stationed there. The pertinent resolution reads: "We recommend that Synod begin mission work in Japan immediately . . . that two men be called to the Japan field (Tokyo, Yokohama) . . . that these two men also care for the spiritual needs of our men in the armed forces." A first-year budget of $54,400 was also adopted.[9]

The 1955 report calls attention to three confirmations, two baptisms, catechism translation, Bible classes, worship services, a printing room, and the acquisition of two houses. On the negative side, the second missionary had not yet been sent. Seven calls to the post were declined.

What was far worse, Missionary Tiefel's dissatisfaction with the synodical relations with Missouri increased. He and his Japanese Christians viewed the action of the special synodical convention in 1956 as a violation of biblical fellowship principles. Efforts were made to prevent the calling of the second missionary, so that the field might not be unduly disturbed.

Meetings stateside in early 1957 between the missionary and the Japan mission board could not resolve the clash in views. The missionary presented his resignation, withdrew it and then renewed it. A field visit planned already before the resignation was attempted in April. President Naumann, Chairman Hoenecke, and Pastor Shiley, newly appointed chairman of the Japanese mission board, flew to Japan but could achieve nothing more with the missionary than a telephone conversation broken off by him. What they were able to do was to welcome the second—now actually the one man on the field. This was Richard Seeger, a 1956 graduate of Wisconsin Lutheran Seminary who had been assigned to the field the previous May.

The property, consisting of the two houses, was lost to the Wisconsin Synod. The trustees of the synod stated in their section of the 1957 *Reports and Memorials,* "The Japanese property situation is no cause for alarm in the Board of Trustees room. At the time of investment the Board of Trustees made a thorough study of possibilities. . . . It was advised to choose and also chose the course it did because at the time [that] was the wiser."[10] The synod convention, however, was urged by the Japanese Board to resolve, "That we request the Board of Trustees of Synod with the cooperation of the General Board for Foreign and Heathen Missions to take immediate steps to repossess our mission property in Japan."[11]

This could not be done. Japanese law at that time allowed a church body to incorporate only after three missionaries were on the field. Consequently the property was legally held by the missionary and his congregation and they retained ownership.

The same synodical convention that heard these discouraging reports also resolved that in Japan "mission work be continued and expanded."[12] This was done promptly. Soon Richard Poetter, a former Missouri Synod missionary, joined Missionary Seeger in the field. By the end of 1959 he was performing the first WELS baptisms of a notable Japan mission service that eventually stretched into a fourth decade.

The 1961 synodical convention that severed fellowship with the Lutheran Church-Missouri Synod had the more joyful opportunity to ponder favorable reports from the Japan field. A third missionary, Luther Weindorf, joined Pastor Poetter in Mito and was already reaching into Hitachi. The convention voted $50,000 for parsonage grants and chapel loans.[13]

In February 1965 the fourth missionary, Norbert Meier, began language study. The report of that year could also call attention to the invaluable service of Pastor Yamada and to the one student at "our 'seminary'" in Japan.[14] In July 1969 Harold Johne, a former Twin Cities pastor, was commissioned for the Japanese field with the special assignment of heading the growing seminary located at Tsuchiura.

Let excerpts from one 1982 *Northwestern Lutheran* article by Ernst H. Wendland, "Praising His Grace: 25 Years in Japan," summarize and carry forward the story:

> This year another of our Synod's world mission fields is celebrating 25 years of the Lord's gracious guidance and blessing; 1982 has been designated as Japan's year of "Praising His Grace." Special services will be held in our stateside churches on September 12 commemorating this happy occasion, and in Japan the Lutheran Evangelical Christian Church (LECC) will culminate its celebration on September 15. . . .
>
> In 1971 funds were made available from the WELS World Mission Building Fund to construct and dedicate a multipurpose church facility at Tsuchiura. This center of LECC activity now houses a church for the Nozomi congregation, seminary classrooms, a library, an elementary school for missionaries' children and a printshop. . . .
>
> At present there are eight Japanese congregations in the LECC with adequate chapels and parsonages. Two others use rooms provided by Japanese church members, and another congregation worships in rented facilities. Radio work was initiated by Pastor Poetter in 1963. . . .

Expatriate missionaries in Japan now number seven with Richard Poetter serving as superintendent, Kermit Habben as assistant superintendent, Harold Johne as seminary head, and Roger Falk, David Haberkorn, John Boehringer, and Elwood Fromm completing the staff. Other WELS pastors who have served in Japan during its 25 years include Richard Seeger, Luther Weindorf, Norbert Meier, and Herbert Winterstein. . . . National pastors presently serving are Fukuichi Oshino, Tadashi Yoshida, Menuhide Nakamoto, and Wakichi Akagami. Deacon Igarashi continues his literary work.

Although church growth in the LECC is slow, there has been a steady increase in membership in spite of the difficulties connected with reaching out to a people with an ancient culture and a long heritage of religious beliefs.[15]

Statistics supplied at the time of the anniversary list for the field 600 souls under care, 283 souls, 183 communicants; average attendance in church services 159, in Sunday School 278, in weekly Bible class 100; enrolled in membership classes 55; and total contributions of $55,224.[16]

Other Mission Fields

Once the first mission steps were taken, the third and fourth and fifth came that much more easily, relatively speaking of course. Especially those who bore the heaviest assignments in charting the course, in selecting and entering the fields, in meeting the special needs encountered there, would emphasize that it was never easy. Worthwhile, joy-bringing it was, but never easy. Each foreign field has its own story of ups and downs, gains and cares that cannot and need not all be related here.[17]

In the cursory look at other world mission fields that is being presented, some special note should be taken of the three men who especially provided leadership in the endeavor. They are Edgar Hoenecke, Theodore Sauer, and Duane Tomhave. During the last half of the century they filled the executive role for the synodical board entrusted with the task of overseeing our efforts to go into all the world.

Service as head of the Apache mission board prepared Edgar Hoenecke for the larger tasks. Elected in 1955 to head the newly established separated "General Board for Foreign and Heathen Mission," he was especially involved in laying the foundations of the synodical foreign mission efforts. When in 1959 the synod convention called for the creation of the full-time post of chairman of the Board for World Missions on a temporary basis, Edgar Hoenecke was chosen for the post.[18]

How necessary this "temporary" step had become and why it soon acquired a permanent character, is indicated by the report to the 1961 convention:

> The chairman took over the full-time work in January of last year, and within less than a month he was on his way on a five and a half month's assignment in Rhodesia and Germany. By the grace of God peace and confidence were restored in Rhodesia and, after visiting the work in Nigeria and in Germany, he returned to the States. A month later the board authorized him to accompany the executive secretary of the Japanese Mission to that field to help in formulating policy and strategy for the work in the Ibaraki Prefecture. On the same journey the request of an independent missionary at Hong Kong was investigated and subsequently referred to the Missouri Synod to which the missionary belonged.[19]

As the following sections will indicate, the pace never really slowed down, even when Chairman Hoenecke became Executive Secretary Hoenecke in a restructuring of the mission organization in 1965. In his 1977 report Edgar Hoenecke concluded with a "Swan Song" that aptly summed up a memorable service with the words, "'We all have our exits and our entrances.' The work must and will go on. That is the important matter. It has been the keenest pleasure of a lifetime to have been a part of the team of pioneers who broke the trail and of the faithful workers who followed."[20]

One of those "faithful workers who followed" was the successor, Theodore Sauer. He brought to his executive tenure that lasted until his retirement in 1984 a wealth of experience in long service in the African field and in the synodical mission board. His replacement was the present incumbent, Duane Tomhave.

Latin American missions of WELS have roots that are long but slender. At the century's midpoint Pastor Venus Winter of Tucson was conducting Spanish services. Later, similar work was carried on at El Paso. Plans to enter Mexico and use it as a jumping-off place for regions to the south were set back by governmental regulations that severely limited the work that missionaries from the United States could do in the neighboring country.

Work in Mexico was initiated through contacts with a Mexican Lutheran pastor, David Orea Luna, who brought several other pastors and a number of laity into our fellowship. Eventually a program was developed that called for Mexican missionaries to man the congregations and preaching places, with supervision and assistance supplied by a three-man team based at El Paso. There the seminary for Latin America was also established.

In a sense, Latin American work as we know it began through a "missioner corps" that was synodically authorized in 1961 and that began to function in Puerto Rico in 1964. The first men in the field were Roger Sprain and Rupert Eggert. On the eastern end of the island, congregations and preaching stations were established. After a score of years some 100 communicants could be counted.

Meanwhile, Puerto Rico had served as the stepping stone into South America. This was the first fruits of the "missioner" goal of planting the seed of the Word in one place and then reaching out from there to new fields. In 1974 three missionaries were sent to begin work in Medellin, Colombia, and a fourth man was authorized the next year. When the first national pastor was ordained in 1985 for service in Medellin, the work could expand into Bogota.

Early on in the South American mission venture attention turned inevitably to Brazil. In fact, from early on there had been a WELS Brazilian connection. Back in 1975 contact was established with the small one-congregation Orthodox Lutheran Church near Porto Alegre. For ten years stopgap measures kept the contact alive and supplied some service. This small, seemingly unimportant venture would eventually prove to be a great blessing. When finally the Brazil mission survey, authorized already in 1977, could be undertaken, it was this Porto Alegre congregation that provided an open door through legal technicalities and government restriction.

That visitation was reauthorized in 1983 with the stipulation that there be a report for the 1985 convention.[21] The encouraging report moved that convention to send a team of five missionaries into Brazil. The first three, Charles Flunker, Bruce Marggraf, and Richard Starr, began work in October 1987. Soon they were joined by Charles Gumm and Kenneth Cherney. The field, first established in the Porto Alegre area, soon reached out to Dourados 800 miles to the northwest.

As the last decade of the century began, twelve WELS missionaries were preaching the gospel in Southeast Asia: four in Hong Kong, five in Taiwan, and three in Indonesia. The story of this mission begins at Hong Kong in 1960 when Peter Chang, an ordained ex-businessman, asked for help in caring for the three congregations that he had gathered through mission schools. On apartment rooftops these schools were used by Pastor Chang to teach children the gospel along with the English instruction that was what first attracted them.

The help that Peter Chang received from the synod consisted for the most part in "friendly counselors," WELS pastors sent over for limited terms of duty. In 1964 President Frey of Michigan Lutheran Seminary was the first such "friendly counselor." Needed financial assistance was also provided for the growing Christian Chinese Lutheran Mission.

When in 1972 Peter Chang left Hong Kong for San Francisco, our mission staff was able to carry on the work in the congregations and in the schools. A dozen years later the Hong Kong field reported some 200 souls under care in three congregations. The veteran missionaries, Gary Schroeder, Gary Kirschke, and Roger Plath, together with Mark Sprengeler, a teacher in charge of outreach through education, are working with an eye to 1997, when Hong Kong reverts to mainland China.

Radio work in Hong Kong drew Taiwan into the synodical mission sphere. Pleas for more pastoral service by listeners to Pastor Chang's "The Voice of Salvation" broadcast brought to the island from Hong Kong a Chinese pastor, Timothy Lee, and a vicar, both trained in the Hong Kong schools. For a decade the nationals carried on the Taiwan work. Three congregations were formed. When in 1979 our first missionaries, Marcus Manthey and Robert Meister, arrived, they found a little church of some 100 baptized members on the island.[22]

Since then the field has enjoyed modest growth in souls and staff. In 1990 the gospel was being spread by four missionaries, one of them the veteran Robert Meister, one national pastor, and four national evangelists. The Bible Institute for training workers had seven students.

In 1979 WELS missionaries arrived in Indonesia. They were Bruce Ahlers and Howard Festerling, who formerly taught in the Hong Kong mission and subsequently completed theological training. A third missionary, Robert Sawall, a veteran of the African field, arrived later.[23]

The original point of contact with this field was through a Chinese Lutheran pastor, Martinus Adam. He was found to be in fellowship with us, although those ties were subsequently severed.[24] The work, however, continued and in a 1990 report these figures were included: 216 souls, 200 others under care, 3 missionaries, 1 national pastor, 7 evangelists, 9 seminary students.

India, although distant from Southeast Asia, is for administrative purposes a part of that field. From about 1970 our church body has been in contact with T. Paul Mitra, leader of a Lutheran gospel mission in the Madras area. Soon after the ties with Paul Mitra were cemented, our synod brought him and his wife to the United States so that he could deepen his Bible knowledge by some one-on-one study at Mequon. Two decades later the Mitras are still one of the few connections we have with India, a country that has shut its doors tightly against foreign missionaries.

Our mission board is making strenuous efforts to establish additional ties with this large and populous country. Professor Valleskey of Wisconsin Lutheran Seminary and Pastor John Kurth, World Mission Counselor, made two exploratory trips to India in the early 1990s to investigate two promising mission enterprises.

Fellowship Ties

This chapter will conclude with a brief discussion of fellowship ties we have with confessional Lutheran church bodies in other parts of the world. Strictly speaking, they are not missions to those who do not yet know Christ, as are the outreach efforts previously described. But since these ties reach out across the seas into foreign countries, we include them here in "Into All the World." The sister churches overseas include the Lutheran Confessional Church (Sweden and Norway), the Evangelical Confessional Church (Finland), the Evangelical Lutheran Free Church in Germany, and the Evangelical Lutheran Church of Australia.

The last-named overseas fellowship comes to us via the Evangelical Lutheran Synod. At the two-congregation parish the pastor is Daniel Schroeder, a pastor member of the ELS. These fellow believers in Australia stood aside for conscience's sake when other Lutherans in the land formed their merger.

The Evangelical Lutheran Confessional Church (Finland) has one pastor. It also stands alone because it wants to stand foursquare on the Scriptures.

In 1975 the WELS declared itself to be in fellowship with a small and very young Lutheran Confessional Church of Sweden, which could no longer live under the kind of Lutheranism provided by the state church.[25] In those years it was especially Dr. Siegbert Becker of Wisconsin Lutheran Synod who most actively fostered our Swedish connection. He learned the language and made frequent trips to Sweden to encourage the beleaguered believers in their difficult confessional stand. To that end he also lectured on several occasions at their Bible institute.

When the effort expanded and reached into Norway, the official name became Lutheran Confessional Church (Sweden and Norway). In 1990 there were in that church seven active pastors serving seven congregations, two of which are in Norway.

Our fellowship with the Evangelical Lutheran Free Church of Germany has roots reaching back to the first decades of the twentieth century and to our Polish mission that came into being then.[26]

World War II uprooted and dispersed that mission. When it was regathered there had to be western and eastern sections.

In the West a number of Lutheran free churches, some in our fellowship and some outside of it, began merging. The results were that most of our former Polish mission became entangled in a church body that differed with us in the doctrines of Scripture, creation, and church and ministry.

A further difficulty arose when the old Synodical Conference split apart and created so-called "triangular fellowship situations." Old Synodical Conference partners in Germany, as well as in France and Belgium and South Africa, maintained fellowships with both our church body and the Lutheran Church-Missouri Synod, even though we and the latter had gone our separate pathways. Eventually this untenable development had to be regularized by unilateral action on the part of our church body.

The one group that remained in confessional fellowship with us was the remnant of the mission in Poland that was located behind the Iron Curtain in East Germany.

When that barrier fell these staunch believers could begin endeavors to reclaim what had been lost on the other side. At the time of the reunification this Evangelical Lutheran Free Church in Germany had seventeen active pastors and some fifty preaching stations, one in Wittenberg. It also operated a theological seminary in Leipzig with a teaching staff of five.

A footnote to this section on ties with Germany might well be the mention that our church body has always tried to provide some pastoral service for members serving in the NATO forces and stationed in Germany. This usually took the form of maintaining civilian chaplains in Germany. The first was Edward Renz, who went there in 1973. These chaplains, usually two, led services at bases and hospitals and provided individual pastoral care to our fellow believers in the armed services overseas.

A final note to this chapter might mention that efforts are under way to bring into being a *redivivus* Synodical Conference.[27] If the hope becomes a reality, the federation will have little chance, humanly speaking, of ever resembling its predecessor in numerical strength. There is every reason, however, to hope that like-minded church bodies mentioned in this chapter could form a larger body that would resemble exactly the doctrinal position of the old Synodical Conference. The Wisconsin Synod, other Lutherans, and, for that matter, the world would be well served by such a future development.

CHAPTER TWENTY-ONE

Three Decades of Progress and Problems in Education

In the last half of the twentieth century the one area of church activity in the Wisconsin Synod that caused the most concern was education. This applies to both parish and synodical ventures in that field. It was an era of ups and downs, of progress and problems, of much expansion and some contraction. In the first decade of that last half of the century elementary enrollment jumped over fifty percent in parish day schools and a mad scramble was on to provide teachers for the added schools and classrooms.[1] Not too long thereafter there were surplus classrooms and unused candidates for the teaching ministry.

In 1950 a building boom began on the campuses of the synodical worker-training schools. Not too much later there was such concern about underutilization of schools and their building plants that moving and closing synodical schools became a major part of synodical convention planning and resolving every other year.

All this does not point to any undue overreaching or indolent foot-dragging on the part of the leadership or the members. As the oft-repeated folksong of the era had it, "The times they were achangin'." Sometimes the changes simply came too unexpectedly and too rapidly to be addressed in ordinary fashion. And often the changes forced actions that were all to the good.

Elementary Education and Teacher Training

In 1950, the synod's centennial year, on June 8 the cornerstone for a new dormitory on the Doctor Martin Luther College campus was laid. This was the first fruits of the post-war "Million

Dollar" building collection authorized by the eventful synodical convention of 1945.

This was a "first" in another respect—the first housing for women on any WELS campus. That is not to say that the synod was ahead of the times in providing "equal facilities." The church body was simply facing a fact of synodical life: the career male teacher, viewed by many in those days as the absolutely indispensable ingredient for a successful parochial school, was in short supply, if not yet an endangered species. More and more women teachers were manning the congregational classrooms.

Some with good memories will recall the—for some—ominous announcement of the secretary of the Wisconsin Synod State Teachers Conference in 1950, "For the first time in the history of our conference there are more women teachers than men." His count was 224 male and 242 women teachers. Very soon a new category began to appear in the statistical listings, the married women teachers. By 1960 almost 200 of the 500 women teachers were in that category.

Pupil enrollments were skyrocketing in that post-war era from 15,410 in 1950 to over 24,000 in 1960. Older parochial schools added classrooms. New schools were opening at a fast pace. Soon teachers were hard to come by and heroic efforts were being made to find them. One of those efforts was the ill-advised "six-weeks" crash program to get teachers ready in a hurry.

This is the place to recall a much more professional and productive effort, teacher training on the junior college level in Milwaukee. This school, named Wisconsin Lutheran College or Lutheran Teachers' College-Milwaukee, began operations on the grounds and in the buildings and with the teaching staff of Wisconsin Lutheran High School. The 1959 synodical convention supplied the authorization, and the operation began in September 1960.[2]

For a decade the school aided the synod in coping with the teacher shortage. Already in 1962 the graduation of thirty-five sophomores was a step in the right direction. All of them either began to teach or transferred to New Ulm for the four-year course. Two years later the enrollment passed the 150 figure and in another two years the count was over 200.

Naturally such student growth caused plant and staff problems. In the fall of 1963 Robert Voss became the school's president, and Siegbert Becker and Alfons Woldt filled faculty posts. A year later the dedication of a synodically funded addition to Wisconsin Lutheran High School could be held. The construction was necessary to alleviate the strain on the high school plant that 200 college students were exerting. A temporary dormitory facility was acquired in Elm Grove. An adequate site for future buildings was acquired in Brookfield, part of metropolitan Milwaukee, in the Bluemound-Sunny Slope roads area.

The site was never used for that purpose. It was becoming apparent that the synod would soon have two teachers' colleges on its hands when really only one was needed, provided it was adequately supplied and maintained. The 1969 synodical convention wrestled with this problem, especially with the location of the one teacher-training school. It was a problem that had been debated in synodical circles over and over again during those years. A so-called "Blue Ribbon Committee," ordered by the 1962 special convention, submitted a detailed report of twenty-four pages for consideration by the 1964 district conventions, which essentially urged a switch of the junior and senior teachers' colleges from their respective locations.[3]

The 1969 convention spoke the final word on the issue. It produced one last five-hour debate on the where question. By a vote of 150 to 65 the decision was to concentrate teacher education on the New Ulm campus and merge the Milwaukee school with Dr. Martin Luther College by September 1970.[4]

For the Milwaukee school the future seemed bleak as the resolution was carried out. Nothing dies harder than a school, even if it has lived only ten years. A new Wisconsin Lutheran College, however, soon arose in its place, this time not as a synodical worker-training school but as an all-purpose Lutheran college. Its story belongs in the final section of this chapter.

The synodical convention of 1969 would not have reached the decision it did, had not two developments taken place in the previous years. One was the decline in the number of new teachers required for WELS schools. From a projected high of 200 the number had already shrunk to 175 by 1969. And New Ulm had been putting its best foot forward.

There were heroic building ventures, the details of which will be supplied in a subsequent section. More important were steps in the upgrading of the whole educational program.[5] A major development was the addition of a fourth year to the course. The class that enrolled in the fall of 1950 was offered the choice between a three-year and a four-year course. Nine opted for a 1953 graduation; the other fourteen preferred to be members of the first DMLC graduating class to be awarded the Bachelor of Science in Education degree. A school report to the districts in 1952 described the procedure in this way:

> Our college freshman class is now proceeding in the four year course. This June we shall have to split our second-year class. This will be done on the basis of volunteers, some for the three-year course, so that we shall have a graduating class in June 1953, and some for the four-year course, so that we shall have graduation and teacher-candidates in 1954. Naturally, both of these graduating classes will be small, the one for 1953 very small. It may not be larger than 7 or 8, but this is the only way in which we can put the four-year course into operation. It will mean, of course, that we shall have to rob the lower classes for several more years in order to take care of our schools. But there is no other solution for this problem.[6]

Seventy years after its founding the New Ulm school was a college in the fullest sense of the word. The "very, very small" classes soon were swelling in number. The 1962 special synod convention voted that "Dr. Martin Luther College be retained as a four-year college for the preparation of elementary-school teachers" and that it "be developed to serve in this capacity for a minimum enrollment of 500 college students" and that it "be directed and enabled to incorporate a beginning program for the training of secondary-school teachers."[7]

The school met this challenging assignment by embarking on a "Venture of Trust," a self-study that looked long and hard at such basics as curriculum, staff organization, plant needs, and recruitment. Professor T. Hartwig coordinated the effort that reshaped the school's structure and enabled it to cope with the needs of the times.

As the enrollment climbed, enough teaching posts and campus buildings were added so that by 1970 Dr. Martin Luther College could absorb the relocated Milwaukee school without undue stress. In the process fourteen men were installed as professors in an October 5, 1970, service, a number that almost tripled previous highs and will very likely not be equaled for some time to come.

In 1970 the college enrollment at New Ulm passed the 800 mark with 226 men and 582 women enrolled. By that time President Conrad Frey was well into the work he had undertaken in 1966 and would not relinquish until 1980. In that year the student number peaked at 850.

The year before, the New Ulm preparatory department had moved to the Prairie du Chien campus, and there was ample room on the hill in New Ulm for the record number of college students. Building planning had for some time been working with a goal of 1000 students.

That number was not achieved. Instead, a sharp decline set in. By the school's centennial year 1984, the enrollment was already down to 629, a drop of over one fourth. The next year brought another decline, to 555. The school report to the 1984 district meetings explained: "There is no doubt that the economy of our day is a cause for the enrollment decrease. . . . But perhaps the greatest single cause for the drop in enrollment is the fact that 95 eligible candidates from the past three graduating classes received no assignment in May 1983.[8]

Elementary school enrollment had begun to level off in the last years of the 1970s. Few new schools or classrooms were being added. Dr. Martin Luther College had been so successful in meeting the synod's teacher needs that it brought a decline on its own campus. Should other educational growth-decline cycles appear in the future, the hope must be that the DMLC of that time will be as energetic and resourceful in facing problems as was the school in the 1960-1980 years, an era that must be reckoned as DMLC's "shining hour."[9]

Building at the Worker-Training Schools

The long Depression and then World War II severely hampered efforts to maintain and enlarge the schools at Watertown, Thiensville, New Ulm, Saginaw, and Mobridge. The 1920s saw the last major building operations on synodical campuses. The seminary in Thiensville (now Mequon) was dedicated in August 1929 with funds gathered in a long and energetic special collection. The year before, the Administration Building at New Ulm had been built largely with borrowed monies, monies difficult to repay with hard-to-come-by Depression dollars. As far as campus construction was concerned that was it, for two decades. There were building needs and even building plans. From his high school years at Northwestern in the early 1930s the writer recalls an architect's sketch of a proposed library building prominently displayed.

The building was not erected until 1951. Similarly, on other campuses plans for critically needed building had to be put on hold. In the waning years of World War II plans were made for gathering funds for building when restrictions would be lifted. The result was a synodical worker-training building boom in the 1950s.

Michigan Lutheran Seminary's long-overdue classroom and administration building was put into use in 1951. The cost was over $400,000. The enlargement in classroom space enabled the school to grow from 175 students in 1951 to around 300 in just four years. By 1954 a new dining room was needed.

As has been mentioned, in 1951 Doctor Martin Luther College erected its first dormitory for women students. That was its share in the first phase of synodical campus construction in the post-war era.

At Northwestern College the long-awaited combination library-classroom structure was dedicated in June 1951. A thirty-year dream became a reality.

Northwestern Lutheran Academy at Mobridge in South Dakota was almost left behind in the process. For a long time the only tangible and visible evidence of any new building was of the infrastructure sort. As the 1951 board report has it, "The smokestack which rises above the basement plant has been a source of encouragement to all who are interested in the Academy, for it gives promise of better days when the new building (Administration-Auditorium) will rise at that spot to the glory of God and for the cause of Christian Education."[10] Two years later that board could report: "On April 26, 1953, Northwestern Lutheran Academy was privileged to dedicate the last monument to the two 'Million Dollar Collections'—an Administration-Gymnasium building. With thankful hearts, one of the largest Wisconsin Synod Lutheran crowds ever to gather in the Mobridge area helped consecrate this building to the Triune God for educational purposes."[11]

The 1953 synodical convention at Watertown received this report from the treasurer of the Wisconsin Synod Building Fund Collection, covering the period from January 1945 to June 1953:

Disbursed for New Buildings:

Northwestern College	578,310.96
Dr. Martin Luther College	347,515.55
Michigan Lutheran Seminary	422,656.36
Northwestern Lutheran Academy	371,179.95
Total Expended for New Buildings	$1,719,662.82 [12]

All this represented a major effort and a major step forward in the synodical worker-training program. New facilities encouraged increased enrollment and they in turn produced new needs in facilities. Before the dust had fairly settled more of them had to be supplied. Already in 1953 the synodical convention authorized a new million-dollar collection for additional buildings: a dining hall at Saginaw and at Watertown a dormitory, a new classroom building, and a new dining hall.[13]

As previously mentioned, Saginaw needed and received a new dining hall in 1954. Construction problems delayed the fall school opening for two weeks, but not too many students minded.

At Watertown the dining hall and kitchen were completed just one day before the 1955 fall term began. Meanwhile construction of the first of three dormitories began. The project was completed in January 1956. When it was time to plan the new classroom building, a handsome bequest of just under $100,100 was available for a chapel, a gift from Mrs. Meta Kilgas Michelson of Manitowoc. The result was a combination chapel seating 400 and a classroom complex joined together by an attractive entrance.[14]

The fast pace of campus construction during the 1950s did not slacken in the next decade. All the synodical schools except Mobridge participated. So pressing were the needs in the 1960s that a committee on teacher-training facilities described the situation in this way: "The expansion and renovation program necessary at our synodical schools now was considered a matter of such urgency that a special convention of the Synod was called in November 1962. The delegates assembled with an air of expectancy. The theme of the convention was 'Arise and Build.'"[15]

Build the synod did. At Northwestern the first of the twin dormitories, Wartburg and Wittenberg, was ready for occupancy in 1967.

At Wisconsin Lutheran Seminary the library wing was added to the main complex. Under the direction of Professor Martin Lutz, the seminary's first called librarian, the book collection was moved into its well-appointed new home in 1968. In the process the seminary gained badly needed classrooms in the old and new areas.

On April 19, 1964, Michigan Lutheran Seminary dedicated a wrap-around addition to the main building constructed in 1951. By this time the school's enrollment had reached 321 and upgraded and enlarged facilities for library quarters, science laboratories, music rooms, and general classrooms had become necessary. To make this addition possible, Old Main, the original 1887 building, had to be razed.

Doctor Martin Luther College at New Ulm added four major facilities to its holdings during the decade. First came two women's dormitories with four stories to house about 225 students in each. Hillview Hall was ready for the 1964-1965 school year and its twin, Highland Hall, was completed two years later.

In 1968 the New Ulm school dedicated two more buildings. The first was Luther Memorial Union, providing dining-kitchen and gymnasium-auditorium facilities along with student lounges. The second project was a major addition to the 1928 main building. This supplied tiered classrooms, science laboratories, and especially a chapel seating 999.

The building continued apace at New Ulm in the early 1970s. In 1971 the original campus building, Old Main, as old as the school itself, was given a second life when it was extensively remodeled into an administration building. There was some agonizing debate over the proposal to demolish and replace the structure with a more functional and more modern-looking version. Efficiency factors aside, the school's thousands of alumni and alumnae are always happy to see familiar Old Main when they visit their alma mater. It is now well into its second century and links the modern teachers college with its venerable predecessor, the all-purpose worker-training school of the Minnesota Synod established in 1884.

No such links with the past are associated with the DMLC library completed in 1971. This was the first building of the kind on the campus. Previously whatever library there was had to make do with whatever inadequate quarters it could find. The library, especially before its enlargement, stood out. Cost factors dictated a white look that did not match the traditional red brick of the campus. But for the librarian, the recently called Professor Gerald Jacobson, and the students it was a most welcome campus addition nevertheless.

At Saginaw, on February 1, 1976, the dormitory complex was dedicated. To make fullest use of scarce space on the grounds, the two wings of the dormitory rose to a fifth level. About 250 students could be accommodated.

Before the decade ran its course, the synod resolved to make major changes on the map that located its five schools. In brief, it removed one name, Mobridge, and added in its place Prairie du Chien. After citing facts and figures on schooling costs and building needs, the 1979 synodical convention resolved "that the Synod, with deep regret, discontinue the operation of Northwestern Lutheran Academy as a synodical institution, effective immediately."[16] At age fifty-one the school that had earlier played a very useful role in the worker-training system closed its doors. Faculty and students were invited to move to Prairie du Chien, Wisconsin.

There a recently closed Jesuit boarding high school was available for purchase. And at New Ulm Martin Luther Academy was being crowded out of the Doctor Martin Luther College plant. Back in 1963 the New Ulm college and high school separated administratively but both remained on the one campus. The plan was to relocate the high school in the vicinity. Suitable land on the hill was purchased, and housing for the teaching staff was provided.

Before any major building was undertaken, the Prairie du Chien opportunity surfaced. A rare special synodical convention convened at New Ulm in July 1978 to reach final decisions. After long debate it resolved to buy the Campion campus at Prairie du

Chien as a new home for Martin Luther Academy and to give it the new name, Martin Luther Preparatory School. Costs involved were to be $2,800,000 as the purchase price and $560,000 for refurbishing and remodeling. On September 5, 1979, the relocated school began operations in its new home.[17]

The MLPS move to Prairie du Chien rounded off thirty years of intensive effort to bring the pre-Depression worker-training system into line with the needs of the 1980s. It was on the whole a heroic effort for a small synod and required the joint effort of a host of synod members.

Many of them merit special mention. There is only room for a few who planned the projects and pushed for their completion. When the 1969 synodical convention authorized the position of full-time executive secretary for the Commission on Higher Education and at the same time merged the teachers' colleges, it had at hand a ready and able candidate for the executive post, the former head of Wisconsin Lutheran College, Robert J. Voss. From then on until he assumed the presidency of Northwestern College on July 1, 1987, Robert Voss played a key role in the development previously described.

Before 1970 the synod's worker-training system was in the hands of an Advisory Committee on Education (ACE) consisting of board chairmen and presidents of the schools plus a few other representatives of agencies with educational concerns. Before ACE the synodical conventions would receive reports and recommendations from a "Heads of Institutions" committee, which was exactly what it was called, given the customary identification of worker-training schools as institutions.

The ACE operation rendered valuable service, especially during the building decades from 1950 to 1970. It was, however, unwieldy and lacked a central head who had no special interests of his own and could coordinate the efforts on a half dozen campuses.

This coordination Robert Voss provided for almost a score of years, years that were extremely important in the history of the synod's worker-training planning and doing. Without such leadership it is doubtful that schools could have been so efficiently nurtured and purchased and moved and closed. In 1987 Wayne M. Borgwardt became his successor, bringing to the post long and broad classroom and administrative experience at Doctor Martin Luther College and area high schools in Appleton and Milwaukee.

During these building decades there were men at each of the schools who played key roles. At Wisconsin Lutheran Seminary Carl Lawrenz served as school head from 1957 until 1978, when Armin Schuetze succeeded him. Armin Panning succeeded Schuetze in

1985. Edward Zell joined the seminary's board in 1969, became its chairman ten years later and served long enough to participate in the calling of nineteen seminary professors.

At Northwestern E. E. Kowalke served as president until 1959 when he turned the office over to Carleton Toppe, who filled it until 1987. Together with Doctor Ernst, Kowalke's predecessor, the Northwestern presidency was for 117 years in the hands of just three men. Members of the Northwestern board with long tenures as chairmen during the growth decades were Pastors Walter Zank of Newville, Wisconsin, and Pastor Reginald Siegler of Bangor, Wisconsin.

The Doctor Martin Luther College story has already been told in detail. For purposes of rounding out this listing it could be reported that the school heads during its time of great expansion were President Schweppe, completing thirty years of service in 1966, and Conrad Frey, who succeeded and held the post until 1980. Pastor Otto Engel of Danube was board chairman through the sixties and seventies and became quite efficient in functioning at ground-breaking, cornerstone-laying, and ribbon-cutting ceremonies.

At Michigan Lutheran Seminary, the grand old man, Director Otto Hoenecke, a son of Adolph Hoenecke, was succeeded by Conrad Frey in 1950, who in turn served as school head through the main growth era until 1966. Then came Martin Toepel (1966-1978) and after him John Lawrenz. Pastor Emil Kasischke of Bay City was board chairman for almost twenty years during the busy 1950-1970 era.

Out in Mobridge the school head from 1939 to 1966 was President R. A. Fenske. The really veteran faculty member was Professor K. Sievert, who began with the school and served forty-three years almost to its end.

Area Secondary Schools

At the Centennial of another church body, the motto was developed: "The first century for Christian elementary education—the second century for Christian secondary education." The Wisconsin Synod never officially adopted such a slogan but in actual practice that is the way it worked out. By the end of the first century there were almost 200 Wisconsin Synod elementary schools. There was at the time, strictly speaking, only one area high school in the synod, Winnebago Lutheran Academy, opened in 1925. There were also two joint Missouri-Wisconsin high school ventures, the Milwaukee Lutheran High School, operating from 1903 on, and Racine Lutheran High School, begun in 1944.[18]

Forty years later the elementary school count had more than kept pace with synodical growth. The great upsurge, however, was in area secondary education. The number of Wisconsin area high schools stood at twenty. It is the purpose of this section to sketch in broad outline this remarkable growth, this singular evidence of God's continuing work of motivating and blessing his believers.

During the 1950s five area high schools were begun and a sixth should also be counted, the Wisconsin part of the joint Milwaukee Lutheran High School that separated in the 1950s.

This Wisconsin Lutheran High School began operating as an entity of its own in 1955. Already three years earlier the sponsors of the old Milwaukee Lutheran High School had divided into Wisconsin and Missouri sections. Growing enrollments and building needs, added to the mounting intersynodical problems, occasioned this step.

Wisconsin Lutheran High School began with 350 students and within three years mushroomed to over 500. In March 1957 $1.25 million was gathered in more than thirty Wisconsin congregations in the Milwaukee area for building purposes. This made possible the erection of a $2 million building to hold 750 students at the Bluemound Road area site. Plans included additions to bring enrollment up to 1000, a number that was surpassed in 1967. Overseeing this school founding and growth was Robert Krause, a veteran teacher of the joint high school who would remain principal until his retirement in 1985.

In the fall of 1953 Fox Valley Lutheran High School in Appleton began teaching an entering class of eight.[19] An association had been formed already in 1948. The building was dedicated in November 1957. Additions in 1965 and 1977 brought the school to an enrollment capacity of 750. Harold Warnke, the first principal, served in that post from 1954 to 1974.

In the La Crosse area a high school association began working in 1944. After a decade and more of spade work Luther High School, Onalaska, opened its doors in 1957. The building, a three-unit structure, was built as the school grew, one unit at a time in successive years. The early school head was Wayne Schmidt, later at Concordia Seminary, St. Louis. One of his successors was David Kuske, who later served at Wisconsin Lutheran Seminary.

One year before Onalaska's opening Manitowoc Lutheran High School began teaching its first class, which graduated with seventeen members. The present property was acquired in 1963. The building was dedicated on April 23, 1967. At that time the school had graduated just over 200 students and had just under 200 enrolled. The pioneer principal was Loren Schaller.

Lakeside Lutheran High School in Lake Mills and near Rock Lake opened its doors to its first class of forty-one in the fall of 1958. In its beginning stages it appears in the records as Jefferson County Lutheran High School and the first teaching was done in Fort Atkinson. The Lake Mills property was purchased in 1959 and the building there was dedicated on Reformation Sunday in 1963. Lloyd Huebner, who later became school head of Doctor Martin Luther College, was the first principal. At dedication time the school already had 261 students in the building constructed for 450.

St. Croix Lutheran High School was the first of such schools outside the boundaries of the state of Wisconsin. Located in West Saint Paul, St. Croix Lutheran began teaching in 1958. The principal, Morton A. Schroeder, was a veteran and able elementary teacher, the second Lutheran High School principal from the teachers' ranks. The first was T. W. Zuberbier, who became acting principal of Winnebago Lutheran Academy some years earlier. St. James Church provided the temporary facilities and Emanuel donated land for the permanent building readied by February 1960.

There had been just one exclusively Wisconsin Synod area high school in 1952, Winnebago Lutheran Academy. Just six years later it had six sister schools. A large step forward in Christian education had been taken, so large that a time for breath catching was needed. No more Lutheran high schools were opened for over a decade.

A special paragraph needs to be included on another Wisconsin Synod high school, neither a worker-training preparatory school nor an area high school in the usual sense of the term. This is East Fork Lutheran High School on the Apache reservation in Arizona, providing Christian training for Apache high-schoolers but operated by the synodical World Mission Board. At East Fork the elementary school quite naturally developed a high school program.

The mission report to the 1949 synodical convention describes the development in this way: "Keenly aware of the necessity of granting the Indian children high school training, the force at East Fork began a ninth grade with 12 eager boys and girls in attendance. A tenth grade is planned for this fall."[20] It was not until 1978, however, that East Fork Mission High School found a listing in the synodical Annual. Arthur Meyer was the long-time head of the school. It will hereafter be included in this account of area high schools.

During the 1960s there was for the most part steady growth in the existing high schools. The total enrollment at the beginning of the decade stood at 2111. By 1969 that figure had grown to 2847, without the addition of any new schools. Such additions, however, became quite commonplace in the 1970s.

The first new school was at St. Joseph in Michigan, serving the Benton Harbor area. Named Michigan Lutheran High School, it went on from small beginnings to a building program, accomplished in 1972. The first school head was Elmer Dobberstein.

Shoreland Lutheran High School in the Kenosha area at Somers was the Wisconsin section of the joint Racine Lutheran High School. The separation was finally completed and in 1971 the school opened with freshman and sophomore classes in facilities provided by Friedens Church. In 1979 the building at Somers was dedicated. Edgar Greve, a veteran at Racine Lutheran, was installed in 1971 as the first principal, along with science teacher Gerald Mallman.

The eleventh high school was Kettle Moraine Lutheran High School, northwest of Milwaukee and south of Jackson. After a brief year and a half of planning, much of it under the direction of Principal James Fenske, the school began teaching in 1974 in rented rooms in the village of Jackson. The first building unit was dedicated in the fall of 1977.

The year after Kettle Moraine's opening Huron Valley Lutheran High School began instructing its first two small classes, totaling only seventeen. Huron Valley, located in Westland, Michigan, aimed to serve the teens of the southeast area of the state. The early school head was Carl Peterson, installed July 27, 1975. Until its building was completed, Huron Valley Lutheran rented classrooms from St. Mary's Catholic School in what was then called Wayne.

Now the scene moves west, far west. The next three Lutheran high schools were established by WELS congregations in the western districts, Pacific Northwest and Arizona-California. The three schools are California Lutheran High School in Garden Grove, Arizona Lutheran High School in Phoenix, and Evergreen Lutheran High School in Kent, Washington. All three were established in the 1977-1979 biennium.

The February 18, 1978 *Northwestern Lutheran* cover has a picture of the small temporary facility of California Lutheran High, the even smaller student body of ten, and the principal, Milton Burk. The story has the title, "First WELS Lutheran High West of the Missouri River." While the portable classroom building nestled on the property of King of Kings Church in Garden Grove, the difficult search for a more permanent site went on. After a sojourn in Tustin the school returned to Garden Grove.

Arizona Lutheran Academy opened with the first two high school grades in 1978. The two teachers were Principal Robert Adickes, called from Lakeside Lutheran High, and Victor Fenske.

This development culminated a long-standing desire for Christian secondary education in Arizona. Older synod members may recall the high-powered but fruitless pitch for the purchasing of an Arizona Desert School, presented to the 1955 synodical convention. More ancient lore has it that such hopes were already being voiced at meetings in the 1930s. At the 1978 school opening there were forty-four students, some from areas over 150 miles from Phoenix.

That same year up in Tacoma, Washington, Evergreen Lutheran High School enrolled its first two classes totaling twenty-seven. The staff consisted of Principal Wayne Baxmann and Instructor Richard Wiechmann. Before they were installed Larry Joecks had served as coordinator of the school promotion. The original location was at DuPont, a Tacoma suburb.

Four more Lutheran high schools opened in one year, 1979. A *Northwestern Lutheran* article in the December 9 issue of that year reports the story under the heading, "New Area High Schools." The article describes the beginning at Nebraska Ev. Lutheran High School at Waco; Northland Lutheran High School in Merrill, Wisconsin; West Lutheran High School at Rockford in the Twin Cities area, and Minnesota Valley Lutheran High School in New Ulm.

The *Northwestern Lutheran*'s title for the Nebraska item is "A Thirty-year-old Dream Come True." For some of those years many synod members assumed Nebraska would be the place where the next synodical academy would be built. It did not work out that way. Instead, interested members of the district worked to open an area high school at Waco. There was dormitory planning from the start. At the opening, there were twenty students from four states in the first two classes. Karl Blauert, the administrator, was aided by Richard Everts, Dean Dawson, and by part-time teacher, Pastor Paul Reede.

The first part of the name, "Northland Lutheran High School", was well chosen. The school could move from its temporary Merrill setting to Wausau, its present location, with no name change needed. Administrator John R. Schultz, assisted by a full-time teacher, Delbert Draeger, and six part-time instructors, began teaching twenty-four students enrolled in the first two high school years.

The sprawling Twin Cities area felt the need for more than just the one area high school, St. Croix Lutheran. In 1979 West Lutheran High School acquired its temporary location in the western suburb of Rockford, where the school remained until the move to Hopkins. The planning in the latter stages was aided by the consultant, Principal Karl Peterson, then of Huron Valley Lutheran and later at Manitowoc Lutheran. Adair Moldenhauer was the first principal.

THE WISCONSIN SYNOD LUTHERANS

Also on the staff were one full-time and four part-time instructors. In the first year there were twelve students.

Lutherans in the Minnesota Valley thought of the possibility of a Lutheran high school before 1979, but it was the transfer of Martin Luther Preparatory School from New Ulm to Prairie du Chien in that year that was the catalyst that transformed thinking into action. In that fall Principal Jerome Birkholz, two other full-time teachers, and five part-time teachers began instruction in temporary facilities provided by St. Paul Lutheran Church in New Ulm. The opening enrollment of forty-five indicated that more permanent facilities would have to be secured in the near future.

By the end of the 1970s the area Lutheran high school count had been brought to nineteen by the addition of the eleven schools opened during that decade. The next ten years would see only one more such opening. In 1987 the two congregations in Crete, Illinois, in partnership began Illinois Lutheran High School. Zion opened its school to some of Trinity's elementary students and Trinity was able to provide room for high school instruction. The present principal is Richard Bakken.

For ready reference a list of the twenty area Lutheran high schools, including East Fork, is supplied with the beginning year and the 1988-89 enrollments:

School	Location	Founding Year	1988-89 Enrollment
Wisconsin LHS	Milwaukee WI	1903 (1955)	881
Winnebago L Academy	Fond du Lac WI	1925	337
East Fork LHS	East Fork AZ	1948	86
Fox Valley LHS	Appleton WI	1953	520
Manitowoc LHS	Manitowoc WI	1956	240
Luther HS	Onalaska WI	1957	235
Lakeside LHS	Lake Mills WI	1958	354
St. Croix LHS	West St. Paul MN	1958	213
Michigan LHS	St. Joseph MI	1970	138
Shoreland LHS	Somers WI	1971	199
Kettle Moraine LHS	Jackson WI	1974	249
Huron Valley LHS	Westland MI	1975	78
California LHS	Garden Grove CA	1977	67
Arizona L Academy	Phoenix AZ	1978	186
Evergreen LHS	Kent WA	1978	46
Minnesota Valley LHS	New Ulm MN	1979	191
Nebraska LHS	Waco NE	1979	100
Northland LHS	Wausau WI	1979	63
West LHS	Hopkins MN	1979	65
Illinois LHS	Crete IL	1987	35
		Total	4283[21]

In the fall of 1988 there were in the 20 area high schools 323 teachers, 66 of them women. While there are of course distinguishing characteristics in the story of the different area high schools, there are also marked consistencies. Long concerns for Christian secondary education would eventually give birth to a Lutheran high school. The founding body would usually be an association of congregations, if not immediately, then soon thereafter. The beginnings were in temporary quarters with small enrollments. Soon came the need for a major building effort. Financial resources were always a problem at the beginnings or a later stage, at the large school and at the small school. No school, however, up to the time of this writing, has had to close its doors. This we can fairly attribute more to the fact that the Lord loves those schools than to the educational ability of Wisconsin Synod high school teachers and administrators and the generous contributions of members to the cause.

This chapter's final paragraphs are set aside for the one Wisconsin Synod area Lutheran college, Wisconsin Lutheran College. This college, as has been previously indicated, grew out of another school with the same name, the Wisconsin Lutheran College that had a place in the worker-training program of the synod during the 1960s and was merged with the New Ulm teachers' college in 1969. The synodical convention decision of that year set the wheels in motion to open a second Wisconsin Lutheran College, not synodically funded or operated for worker-training purposes.

The beginning was as a junior college in Wisconsin Lutheran High School facilities in 1973. Advancement came rapidly under Dr. Gary Greenfield's direction. Grounds and buildings on Milwaukee's Bluemound Road, previously used by a Roman Catholic nunnery, were dedicated in April 1978 after extensive remodeling. The full library of the defunct Milton College, Wisconsin's oldest private senior college, was acquired—60,000 volumes for less than a dollar per book.

Soon the school was ready to advance to senior college status. The first bachelor's degrees were awarded to 1987 graduates. Generous gifts, especially from Mr. Marvin Schwan, made possible the erection of a library. The chapel was enhanced by the installation of a new pipe organ. The curricular offerings were broadened year by year and the staff grew to number some thirty full-time instructors and administrators by 1990.

There is still much room for growth at Wisconsin Lutheran College despite the good beginnings. The school could enroll many more students. The school needs college students interested in Christian and Lutheran college instruction and they, in turn, need the college.

CHAPTER TWENTY-TWO

Synodical Administration

It is only late in its history that the Wisconsin Synod began to show proper regard for the gift of administration. It tolerated good administrators, to be sure, re-electing them again and again. In only one synodical convention, that of 1933, was an incumbent candidate in the presidential election unseated. That was when in the Depression doldrums John Brenner was chosen over G. E. Bergemann.

But all that time the synod indicated quite plainly that it was most pleased when its administrative officials administered the least. In his brief presidential tenure in the 1860s William Streissguth made a valiant effort to provide the synod with some centralization in its operation but was frustrated in the effort.[1] He resigned his office a year ahead of time.

President Bergemann had completed a superb job of administration when he spearheaded the transformation of the 1892 federation into the merger of 1917. That, however, is quite completely forgotten in the collective synodical memory. Bergemann is rather thought of as the leader whose tenure was marred by Depression cutbacks and Protes'tant controversies and who deserved to be voted out of office.

There is more truth than caricature in a description of the Wisconsin Synod's ministerium as a collection of "rugged individuals." This holds true for most of the century and a half of its history. The record is dotted with instance after instance of declining to establish full-time executive posts. As late as 1959 it took a massive effort to persuade the synod and the incumbent in the presidency to make the latter's office a full-time position.[2]

It is all the more surprising, therefore, that in the last quarter century there has been a marked growth in the synodical bureaucracy, without much opposition, except for individual opinions expressed here and there. In all likelihood the hinge event in spurring this change in synodical thinking was an administration seminar at Madison on five days of November 1967. It had been set up with synodical authorization, but without funding, by the Administration Survey Committee that was at work in the late 1960s. It assembled some fifty synodical officials. The committee's report explained, "The purpose of the seminar was to put the men into formal touch with a very respectable body of thought called 'administration.' During the five day seminar the participants considered the meaning and application of planning, objectives, goals, organization, direction, leadership, control, coordination, and commemoration."[3]

The results of the seminar were far reaching. In its "Final Remarks" the committee stated, "If the visible results of the Commission's work over four years appear to be meager, it must be remembered that in administration the most necessary change is in people, not in formal organization. The Commission likes to believe that it has implanted the fundamentals of good management among the many administrators who will guard with exceeding care the stewardship of love's gift the Synod's people bear to it."

At Synodical Headquarters

At the time the Administration Survey Committee was making its study and recommendations, the synod headquarters were on North Avenue at Thirty-Seventh Street. This building, occupied in late 1948, was actually the home of the Northwestern Publishing House. Because there was room for office space, the synodical boards and agencies found a gathering place for really the first time in the synod's history.

Before 1948, synodical headquarters meant office space and an extra desk in the parsonage study of the synod president. That could be at Helenville or Watertown or Winona or Fond du Lac or Milwaukee or St. Paul. The establishment of the full-time synodical presidency naturally spurred the centralization of the synod's administration. Soon 3512 North Avenue was bulging at the seams, even after the acquisition of two nearby buildings.

The crowding and a deteriorating neighborhood caused separate moves of the Northwestern Publishing House and synodical offices. The new synod office center was located at 2929 Mayfair Road. The remodeled facility was dedicated on October 7, 1984. The bulk of the $3 million purchase and remodeling costs was a gift of the Schwan Sales Enterprises, Inc. At this "nerve center for the Wisconsin Synod to carry out its work," as dedication speaker, Board of

Trustees Chairman Carl S. Leyrer, referred to the building, the day-to-day operation of the Wisconsin Synod is carried on in accordance with the direction of the biennial synodical conventions.[4]

In the hierarchy of synodical boards and agencies the top rank must be assigned to the Conference of Presidents, the synodical praesidium meeting with the district presidents. The districts are responsible for right doctrine and practice and their presidents play key roles in maintaining and enhancing the well-being of the church body as a whole. There are twelve district presidents, all pastors serving congregations.

The merged synod began with six districts, three in Wisconsin and one each in Michigan, Minnesota, and Nebraska. Two more were quickly added, the Pacific Northwestern in 1918 and the Dakota-Montana in 1920. A third of a century passed before a ninth district, the Arizona-California, was created in 1954. The tenth district, the South Atlantic, formed in 1973. The eleventh district was the North Atlantic and the twelfth the South Central. Both were organized in October 1983, the first on October 10 and the second on October 19.

There have been major shake-ups in the synodical administrative structure. One came in the late 1950s, the result of the work of the Administration Survey Committee mentioned a few paragraphs earlier. The second study came in the early 1980s with the final report being accepted by the 1985 synodical convention. Such reorganization was long overdue and so big a task that it required two efforts to complete it. The first Administration Survey Committee pointed out the grim facts. "In 1953 there were 26 standing boards, committees and commissions reporting to the convention. In 1967 the number had grown to 53 standing boards, commissions and committees. . . . If the growth continues the Synod will not only need coordinating councils, but coordinating councils to coordinate coordinating councils."[5]

What was enacted in 1969 was to create a "Coordinating Council" made up of representatives of the Board of Trustees and of the five areas into which the synodical work was divided: worker-training, home missions, world missions, benevolences, and administration. The duty of the Coordinating Council was to present to the synodical conventions a balanced program of immediate and long-range undertakings of the divisions. Planning was to stretch over a six-year period.

One of the few survey suggestions that was declined by the 1969 convention was the proposal to terminate the old Synodical Council, a creation of the 1917 merger. Some 100 synodical officials would assemble once or twice a year to discuss the church body's affairs. It was an unwieldy and inefficient way of doing business, but the convention chose to keep it alive, citing useful service "as a discussion forum for doctrinal issues and other matters" and the need to retain some "wide horizontal structure" at a time when "vertical growth . . . is tending toward centralization of authority and control."[6]

By the time the second phase in administration reorganization was being undertaken in the early 1980s the Synodical Council was no longer an issue. The 1981 convention faced the fact that synodical restructure had made this body an anachronism, leaving it little to do except for editing *Reports and Memorials.* The result was an official demise for an agency that for more than 60 years had made Wisconsin Synod history.[7]

The 1990 *Annual* lists 38 men at the headquarters at 2929 Mayfair Road. The 1990 *Statistical Report* counts fifteen full-time pastor administrators and four more teachers in a similar status. It adds nine pastors in the "social services" category.

After four years of consideration, the synod in its 1961 convention adopted the pre-budget subscription system.[8] What was replaced was the "quota" system, the "quota" being the average amount of synodical giving needed from the individual member to keep the synodical books in the black. The total budget divided by the number of communicants supplied the "quota."

The new arrangement called for a synod-wide presentation of needs and programs, after which congregations would ascertain what they could do in the way of funding the efforts. This would enable the synodical boards and conventions to plan the synodical work program realistically.

It was hoped that the new approach would insure against deficits and special offerings. It never quite worked out that way. Congregations' subscriptions had a way of falling short and the growth needs of the synod kept mounting. Major expenditures still required special offerings, as they had in the past.

Building needs at the worker-training schools and mission opportunities sparked the *Missio Dei* offering. It was inaugurated by the 1965 convention with a goal of $4 million.[9] James P. Schaefer headed the effort and also the concurrent "Called to Serve" home visits. By the end of 1969 receipts stood at $5.3 million.

A *Northwestern Lutheran* piece in 1963 reported, "In seven different Lutheran synods the average total contributions per communicant ranged from a high of $119.18 to a low of $72.27. The $72.27 figure was the Wisconsin Synod's." A follow-up writing in

1974 reported that the synodical all-purpose figure had more than doubled to $148.81 to rank respectably very near the middle of the Lutheran column. Progress was being made but problems still remained.

Congregational subscriptions did not keep pace with inflation and a 100 percent return on them was only rarely achieved. Too often there were what President Brenner used to call "shortfalls in brotherly cooperation." When such large districts as the Northern and Western Wisconsin lagged behind the synodical average in all-purpose and mission giving, the results could be a crisis at North Avenue and a halt in expansion efforts.

Soon another special collection was needed to cope with mission needs and school expansion. The "Reaching Out" story, however, belongs in the next chapter.

Publication

The Wisconsin Synod has been in the business of publication since 1865, when it began to issue its official periodical, the *Gemeinde-Blatt.* In 1891 it ventured into the actual printing of its materials when a print shop was added to the synodical bookstore. This was housed in a rented two-story building at 310 North Third Street in Milwaukee. After several Third Street moves the Northwestern Publishing House constructed its own building, this time on downtown Fourth Street in 1913-1914. There it remained until ousted by a city building project in 1948. Presiding over the Publishing House for most of these early years was Julius Luening, manager from 1898 to 1945.

There were important happenings during the thirty-four Fourth Street years. In 1914 the *Gemeinde-Blatt's* little sister began to appear, called the *Northwestern Lutheran.* Soon the Wauwatosa Seminary men, J. P. Koehler, August Pieper, and John Schaller, were writing their theological works for publication by the Northwestern Publishing House. Koehler's *Kirchengeschichte* appeared in 1917 and the first part of his synodical history, the German *Geschichte der Allgemeinen Evangelisch-Lutherischen Synode von Wisconsin und andern Staaten,* in 1925. August Pieper's *Jesaias II* was published in 1919 and Schaller's *Biblical Christology* in 1919. *Jesaias II* was translated and *Biblical Christology* was updated in more recent times.

In 1909 there was a posthumous publication of Adolph Hoenecke's *Dogmatik,* edited by two sons, Walter and Otto.[10] Never again would the Northwestern Publishing House publish such excellent theological writing in such a short span of time.

Naturally the Fourth Street operation concerned itself with the special and official periodicals of the synod. The *Gemeinde-Blatt* reached a high of almost 15,000 subscribers in 1923. For obvious reasons that periodical was discontinued in 1959. The last editor was Professor Henry Vogel of the seminary. By that time circulation had dropped to about 2,300.

The *Northwestern Lutheran*, like the *Gemeinde-Blatt* a semi-monthly periodical, did not immediately replace its German counterpart. It was only in the late 1930s that its subscription list was longer than the *Gemeinde-Blatt's*. The editorship is associated in the minds of the older generation with Wm. J. Schaefer, pastor of Atonement and the father of the present editor. The father was editor from 1936 to 1957. Successors were Werner Franzmann (1957-1968), Harold Wicke (1970-1982), and James P. Schaefer (1982-).[11]

Another synodical periodical was the *Junior Northwestern*, a youth periodical, begun in January 1919. It survived the Depression era but fell victim to a budget crunch in 1981, just four years after the synodical convention met under the motto, "Publish and Conceal Not."

There are professional journals for both teachers and pastors. The *Theological Quarterly* began in 1904 with a German name, of course. It has always been edited by the seminary faculty. The current managing editor is Wilbert Gawrisch.

For the teachers there is the *Lutheran Educator*, subtitled "The WELS Education Journal." Its Volume 1, Number 1 is dated October 1960. The immediate predecessor was the *Lutheran School Bulletin*, edited by F. W. Meyer. It ran from 1930 to 1960.

The January 1, 1989, *Northwestern Lutheran* has an article by Northwestern Publishing House editor-in-chief at that time, Mentor Kujath, with the title, "The Story of a Best Seller." The "best seller" is *Meditations*, the quarterly daily devotional booklet published by Northwestern Publishing House since 1957. The "best seller" epithet is no exaggeration. The first press run of 23,000 sold out. Now the issues are printed in 90,000 copies and 2,000 more in large print. In volume *Meditations* far surpasses any other synodical publication. The quantity is the best proof that quality is also involved. Werner Franzmann was the founding editor.

Back in 1923 the periodical, *Apache Scout*, now *Apache Lutheran*, began to appear and is still being published at the time of this writing. Its purpose is to promote the interest of our veteran mission in Apacheland.

Among the many Northwestern Publishing House projects there have been several that call for special mention. There is the theological series with such titles as *No Other Gospel*, the Formula of Concord anniversary essays, *Luther Lives*, by the seminary faculty at the time of the anniversary of the reformer's birth. There is the widely used set of Bible class materials with some forty titles. Day and Sunday and vacation Bible school materials have always been big items in the publishing house's catalog.

Important publications in 1989 include *Concordance to the Book of Concord* and *Bible History Commentary, New Testament* in two volumes, a companion to the earlier Old Testament commentary, both by Werner Franzmann.

Special attention should be called to what is without doubt the most ambitious undertaking of the Publishing House in its long history, *The People's Bible*, popular commentaries on the Bible books for laity and clergy. Several volumes have come out each year since publication of the series began in 1984.

Synodical and Parasynodical Agencies

The busy 1961 synodical convention that voted the break with the Missouri Synod managed to find time and energy to inaugurate programs that are still operative. Those actions may not have had the large theological implications of the break resolution, but they do to this day add their part to the orderly functioning of the church body.

That 1961 convention heard and received the first reports from a pension study commission created by resolution of the Synodical Council and by appointment of President O. J. Naumann.[12] The result was the creation of the synodical pension plan currently in operation. The intention is to supplement other income of retired workers with a modest pension. For the worker with a lifetime of service this pension amounts to some $400 monthly. There were naturally some difficulties in getting such a huge program into smooth operation but in time that was accomplished.

The 1961 convention also passed the resolution, "Resolved, that the Praesidium of Synod appoint a Group Insurance Study Committee composed of at least three (3) men to study this matter; and that this Study Committee report its findings and make recommendations to the synod at its convention of 1963."[13] What eventually resulted was the now familiar VEBA. The acronym stands for Voluntary Employees' Beneficiary Association. The full-time administrator is Mr. Richard Sonntag.

Believe it or not, the 1961 convention made another contribution to this chapter's treatment of parasynodical agencies. It acted on a report of a committee authorized by the previous convention "to study the Lutheran Girl Pioneers and their place in the life of Synod and that its findings be reported to the next regular session of the Synod."[14] The report contains this history of the organization:

> The Lutheran Girl Pioneer movement had its beginnings in the fall of 1954 as an outgrowth or extension of the Pioneer movement for boys. In September of that year when the parent organization was three years old, a girls' club was organized by Mrs. W. J. Masewicz and Pastor Harold Backer of Mt. Calvary Lutheran Church in La Crosse, Wisconsin, with the idea of "completing a youth program for Christian fellowship." On May 4, 1955 a meeting of six congregations (from La Crosse, Wisconsin, Fountain City, Wisconsin, and Winona, Minnesota) was held at Mt. Calvary Lutheran Church to draw up a formal constitution for Lutheran Girl Pioneers. This constitution was adopted on June 22, 1955, and on the same day the first national council was elected. The first Girl Pioneer manual was printed in 1956 and the same year the first national convention was held in Winona, Minnesota.

At the suggestion of the committee the convention resolved not to give official sanction to the organization as a matter of policy, but it did "encourage those congregations and pastors who feel the need for the Lutheran Girl Pioneer program." At its thirtieth anniversary in 1985 the program had 324 caravans and just under 6800 members.

If the La Crosse-Winona area is the place associated with the origins of Lutheran Girl Pioneers, then for the counterpart, Lutheran Pioneers, the roots are found in Burlington, Wisconsin. Pastor Reuben Marti and his energetic lay member, Bruce Thompson, brought the organization into being, as the report quoted above indicates, in 1951. From then until now the story of Lutheran Pioneers has been one of growth and development. In 1976 a combination administration-warehouse building was built in the Burlington area.

While campus ministries go back much farther, it was in 1965 that the first annual convention of Lutheran Collegians was held in Whitewater, Wisconsin. The organization, later known as WELS Lutheran Campus Ministry, sponsored rallies and retreats for our youth enrolled at secular schools and colleges.

WELS Lutherans for Life came into being on May 14, 1983 at West Allis, Wisconsin. A predecessor organization had been in operation since 1980 in the northern Illinois area and had set up a pregnancy counseling center at Palatine, Illinois. Mr. Larry Marquardt, as chairman, spearheaded the effort. Since 1983 WELS

Lutherans for Life has been able to grow rapidly and widely. Numerous pregnancy counseling centers are in operation. A full-time director, Pastor Robert Fleischmann, is headquartered at a national office located at 2401 N. Mayfair Road, Milwaukee.

Along with such synodical committees for relief and for special ministries, there are a number of synodically related charitable efforts. The East Fork Nursery has roots going back to the 1920s. As then, so now it provides physical and spiritual care for neglected Apache children on the Arizona reservations.

The Lutheran Home for the Aged and Retarded at Belle Plaine, Minnesota, was the earliest such home in our circles. Beginning in 1896 it became a concern of the merged synod in 1917. In more recent years Pastor Robert Schlicht has been the administrator. Other such homes are St. Michael's at Fountain City, Wisconsin; Martin Luther Memorial Home with facilities in four Michigan communities, South Lyon, Holt, Saginaw, and South Haven; and Arizona Lutheran Retirement Center, Phoenix.

In the Milwaukee area there are Luther Haven, a retirement community, and the Wisconsin Lutheran Child and Family Service with its social services and health care divisions and outposts in Appleton, Eau Claire, Fort Atkinson, La Crosse, Wausau, and Morton Grove, Illinois.

Owls, Organization of Wisconsin Lutheran Seniors, was begun in 1984. Its name describes its function. There are annual national get-togethers and activities for local groupings.

In 1979 the synod authorized the Commission on Higher Education to bring about the WELS Historical Institute as an official synodical agency but without year-to-year funding. The first meeting was in the fall of 1981 and since then there have been spring and fall gatherings at different places. The *WELS Historical Institute Journal* has been published twice a year under the editorship of James P. Schaefer. The society has been active in restoring old Salem Church, dating back to 1863, as a museum site and shared in the work of establishing the synodical archives on the seminary campus. Roland Cap Ehlke was the first president.

In the financial field the Wisconsin Lutheran Synod Foundation is an official arm of the synod. It has been operating since 1965. LACE, acronym for Lutheran Association for Church Extension, may be less official but it has been most helpful to congregations needing building loans. WELS Kingdom Workers is a group that pools the resources of its members to help shoulder undertakings that need help but cannot find it through ordinary channels. An example is the four-year funding of the fourth Taiwan missionary in 1988.

A final note calls to mind the Lutheran Women's Missionary Society already described in a previous chapter on overseas missions. Two medical missions in central Africa, the Mwembezhi Lutheran Dispensary in Lusaka, Zambia and the Lutheran Mobile Clinic based at Lilongwe, Malawi, are sustained by this society.

This listing of "Synodical and Parasynodical Agencies," which cannot claim to be complete, is strong evidence that a church body that eschews the social gospel can maintain wide-ranging and sorely needed endeavors in social services, human concerns, and charitable efforts. The objects of concern range from the aged to the young to the unborn. Those who love the Lord love their neighbor.

CHAPTER TWENTY-THREE

The Mischke Years and Beyond

The same issue of the *Northwestern Lutheran* that contained an announcement of the 1979 synodical convention also carried the obituary of President O. J. Naumann.[1] The convention theme, which President Naumann had helped choose, was, "I know whom I have believed."

President Naumann was busy to the end, which came on June 18. That month he traveled to Minnesota twice, once to participate in the assignment of graduating seniors at New Ulm and the other time to help Emanuel of Fairfax celebrate its centennial. He was still catching up on day-to-day chores when he died.

Earlier that year in his *Newsletter* he had written, "I feel that I should inform you that I am asking the convention to elect someone else as their president this summer. My health is such that I could be stopped from functioning properly at any time and I wouldn't want the Synod to suffer in any way or be hindered or delayed in carrying out its God-given work by an unexpected inability of its executive officer to function."[2] There was no hindrance or delay in the transfer of the presidential post from Oscar Naumann to Carl Mischke. For only about six weeks the latter was acting president. He won election on the first ballot and chaired the convention like a veteran.

He was that in a way. For fifteen years as pastor of St. John at Juneau he had been president of the Western Wisconsin District. For ten of those years he was first vice president of the church body and before that the second vice president. His administrative abilities gained him those posts and prepared him for 1979.

260

Before considering that year and those that followed, it might be well in this closing chapter to review President Mischke's predecessors briefly. Counting both elected and acting presidential years, the roster looks like this:

President	Term
Johannes Muehlhaeuser	1850-1860
John Bading	1860-1863 and 1867-1889
Gottlieb Reim	1863-1865
William Streissguth	1865-1867
Philipp von Rohr	1889-1908
Gustav E. Bergemann	1908-1917 Original Wisconsin Synod
	1917-1933 Merged Wisconsin Synod
John Brenner	1933-1953
Oscar Naumann	1953-1979
Carl Mischke	1979-

The synod was founded by Muehlhaeuser. It was led to its confessional position by Bading, spelled briefly by Reim and Streissguth while he was overseas collecting building funds. Cooperation with neighboring synods was the highlight of von Rohr's term of office. Bergemann turned the federated into the merged synod we know today. Brenner shepherded the synod through the lean Depression decade to the first post-war growth and into the serious problems with the Missouri Synod.

At Oscar Naumann's funeral his successor, Carl Mischke, referred to the former's presidential service in this way: "So what do you say at the funeral of a man whom God used mightily to lead a Synod in remaining faithful to the Word of God and the Lutheran Confessions while at the same time mounting a vigorous thrust to share that Word with a dying world that is hopelessly lost without it? And how do you say it? How do you say it in a way that gives all glory to the God of grace and mercy?"[3]

Carl Mischke was born in Hazel, South Dakota on October 27, 1922. He was graduated from Martin Luther Academy, Northwestern College, and Wisconsin Lutheran Seminary, finishing his ministerial studies there in 1947. For two years he was assistant pastor at First Lutheran in La Crosse. Then came a pastorate at the dual parish at Goodhue, Minnesota. In 1954 he moved to St. John at Juneau, Wisconsin, to begin a pastorate of twenty-five years. That ended when the synod presidency became his work.

Finances in the Mischke Years

It isn't the most important issue but it has loomed large from 1979 on to the time of this writing. Some in fact erroneously assume that synodical deficits and cutbacks in the post-World War II era began during and continued throughout the Mischke years. That is not the case.

Deficits did not begin in 1979. A commentator at the time put it this way:

> Professor Lawrenz in his opening sermon to the delegates hailed the latter part of the "Naumann era" as a period of unprecedented expansion as the Synod sought to share the Gospel with the world of the lost. Year after year, he pointed out, the expansion continued: 25 new missions per year, country after country penetrated with the Gospel till we had 13 mission fields all over the world we were supporting.
>
> In each of those years there were budget difficulties, but each year after some pruning and cutting we did not need to interrupt our forward movement. But several years ago there were changes: a small deficit, then a larger one, and finally a deficit that no amount of pruning could eliminate.[4]

That was the situation that confronted the 1979 synodical convention and its new president, Carl Mischke. The first step taken was to make an unmanageable deficit manageable by casting it into a six-year fiscal cycle and thus spreading out its stifling effects. There would be six years to work at deficit reduction instead of just one. There was some success. The 1984-85 fiscal year ended in the black, but only by $3,737.

Meanwhile "Reaching Out" was underway. The 1981 convention resolved "that the Conference of Presidents plan and initiate a capital funds offering with a minimum goal of $10 million" and "that this offering be divided as follows: 50% Educational Institution Building Fund (EIBF), 40% Church Extension Fund (CEF), 10% World Mission Building Fund (WMBF)."[5] To augment its resources the 1981 convention transferred the cost of the pension plan from the synodical budget to the congregations.

"Reaching Out," directed by Daniel Malchow, more than doubled the goal of $10 million. Some $23 million was contributed. The sums beyond the goal were subjected to the same division formula that had applied to the original goal. Overseas and home missions could begin to catch up with chapel and parsonage construction. Fifty-five new parsonages, twenty-six worship-education-fellowship units, nineteen chapels, and thirty-five land acquisitions could be reported to the 1985 convention. There was a new boom in building on worker-training campuses, as has been previously described. It was an unprecedented response on the part of the synod to a plea for funds.

The joy that was engendered was dampened by concerns about "Reaching Out" methodology. An outside fund-raising firm had been engaged at the cost of $400,000 and some of its targeting practices had had a bitter aftereffect in a number of instances. A few protests were so loud and long that disciplinary action had to follow.

The 1985 convention responded by passing the twin resolutions that "we thank the Director and everyone involved in the program for their fruitful labors" and "we thank those whose evangelical concern led them to suggest areas of improvement in the program."[6] A prophecy that could be risked in this connection would be to suggest the Wisconsin Synod will not in the foreseeable future seek the services of professional fund-raising firms.

The 1985 convention also acted favorably on the suggestions of an *ad hoc* committee on "Special Giving and Designated Giving."[7] What is attempted is to augment short budget receipts by obtaining large and special donations for the common cause or for special purposes. Fifty years ago President Brenner would have opposed such a step. He did not want to seek to gain the one big gift and in the process risk losing the many small gifts. In this day and age, however, such special and designated giving is becoming more and more a part of the synodical financial scene.

A factor in that scene that has caused concern in recent years is the shrinkage in the synodical share of the all-purpose giving. How much shrinkage there is will depend on how one figures pension costs and special offerings, but what is obvious in any set of figures is that there is such shrinkage and enough of it to create budget crunches.

A 1987 special Lenten offering provided some temporary relief. At the time of this writing a major "Lift High the Cross" special offering is underway.

The 1991 convention was confronted by a suggested cutback in worker-training campuses to cope with a huge projected deficit in that division. So serious the financial problem has become. The outcome remains to be seen. One thing is certain, and that is the need for major improvement in the synodical giving bracket. Another sound conclusion is that the picture would be much worse had less able administrative skill been available at the top.

Other Highlights of the Mischke Years

Doctrine aside, a feature of the Mischke era has been change when change was useful and desirable. Cases in point are the books used most in the parishes at church, school, and home: the Bible in translation, Catechism exposition, and the hymnal. A change in even one of these is a major event and can bring on strong repercussions. Changes in all three are a part of the Mischke years.

The 1979 convention, the first that President Mischke chaired, passed these resolutions:

> That as a Synod we still concur with the 1977 resolution of the Synod, namely "That we commend the New Testament of the NIV [New International Version] to our people as a faithful contemporary translation that may be used with a high degree of confidence". . . .
>
> That we also commend the Old Testament of the NIV to our people as a faithful contemporary translation. . . .
>
> That the BPE [Board for Parish Education] may use the Old Testament of the NIV in its instructional materials. . . .
>
> That for the sake of uniformity the publishing agencies of the Synod choose the New International Version for their printed material. . . .
>
> That we still concur with the 1977 resolution, "That this action should not be construed as the adoption of the NIV as the Synod's official Bible. . . ."[8]

There were some objections from King James Version admirers and from some proponents of that version's basic Greek text. One congregation made this one of its reasons for dropping out of the synod. On the whole, however, this major step was received with good grace or hailed enthusiastically.

In 1982 the long-awaited Catechism revision appeared in its now-familiar blue cover. Professor David Kuske, of Wisconsin Lutheran Seminary, prepared this "Small Catechism of Dr. Martin Luther and an Exposition for Children and Adults Written in Contemporary English," as the title page explains. The book was widely used from the start. Soon it acquired the nickname of "Kuske Catechism" in teacher and ministerial circles and "blue Catechism" among the learners and their parents.

Then in 1983 the convention, acting on a recommendation of the Commission on Worship, voted that "The Synod now begin work on a new/revised hymnal of its own, one that under the blessing of God will be Scripturally sound and edifying, welcomed and judged to be highly satisfactory for purposes of devotion and worship by a majority of our members, in harmony with the character and heritage of our church body and will reflect the larger perspective and mainstream of the worship of the Christian Church."[9]

Soon work on the proposed hymnal got underway. Kurt Eggert accepted a six-year call to head the project. A committee, composed of men with the necessary background and judgment and representing a cross section of the church body, began to prepare liturgies and the lists of hymns to be included. Field trials were undertaken. At the time of this writing the project has not yet been completed.

When the current drive for the ordination of women infiltrated the Wisconsin Synod enough to cause a study of God's roles for men and women, the result was by no means a matter of changing with the times. Here it was a matter of standing firm on the Bible's teaching.

Synodical action began when the Commission on Higher Education submitted a set of theses on "The Role of Man and Woman According to Holy Scripture" to the 1979 convention.[10] That Commission had been discussing the place of women teachers in synodical preparatory schools and area high schools. The discussion soon moved from a narrow practical question to basic Bible principles. The theses were largely the product of Professor Carl Lawrenz, seminary president and Genesis specialist. In brief, the theses stress that the Bible gives man a headship and woman a helper role and that this role relationship, as part of God's immutable will, holds for all men and women for all time.

The synodical convention asked for study of the theses "by congregations and conferences" and by "the 1980 district conventions."[11] The results of these studies caused the 1981 synodical convention to call for a special committee to act for it, especially in the matter of preparing a study pamphlet.[12] The 1981 volume of the *Wisconsin Lutheran Quarterly* published exegetical articles by its New Testament teachers on the key passages, Galatians 3:28; 1 Corinthians 11:3-16; 1 Corinthians 14:33b-36; 1 Timothy 2:11-15; and 1 Peter 3:1-7.

The districts received the first reports of the study committee in 1982 and gave the committee their reactions. The 1985 synodical convention, after noting that the desired pamphlet had been issued and that a more elaborate study document was in preparation, resolved that "the Synod thank the COP [Conference of Presidents] and the committee for their work on the report which has been released" and "we urge the members of the Synod to continue the study and discussion of this report and the additional tract when it is released."[13]

In content the committee's studies reiterated what the original "Theses" proposed. This was a position that clashed with most modern thinking on the subject but it agreed with the Bible's statements. A follow-up study was readied for the 1991 convention.

A special concern that came to the fore during the Mischke years was evangelism. The 1981 synod convention in fact authorized the calling of an executive secretary for evangelism "subject to funding by the Coordinating Council."[14] In those bleak fiscal times, however, no funding could be granted. The 1983 convention reactivated the resolution and this time there was funding. On June 11, 1984 Paul Kelm was installed as the synod's first full-time evangelism executive.

Three months later David Valleskey was installed at Wisconsin Lutheran Seminary to teach New Testament and evangelism. This was the first time that evangelism was made a special assignment for a Mequon professor. David Valleskey began his evangelism training already in the Detroit parsonage where he grew up. His father, Wilmer, was an early spokesman for evangelism in our church body. The emphasis on evangelism demonstrated in 1984 was long overdue. Has there been a great upsurge since then? If adult baptisms are any kind of measure, then immediate results have not been achieved. In 1984 there were throughout the synod 667 such baptisms but in 1990 the number was 612.

In 1987 the synodical convention resolved that "the board for Parish Services be authorized to create the position of Project Director for Spiritual Renewal." It then urged that "the filling of this position be given a high priority" and that "a progress report be offered to the 1989 convention."[15]

The 1989 synodical convention had before it two related statements, one on "Mission Objectives" and the other titled "Vision 2000."[16] The latter statement set goals of 1500 congregations, 10 cross-cultural urban missions, 70 world missionaries, 60% church attendance, 30% Bible class membership, doubled synodical offerings, 60% of the membership involved in opportunities for ministry, and 100% enrollment of children in Christian education. Both statements were adopted.

In 1990 the Spiritual Renewal Project Director, Paul Kelm, gave the district meetings a substantial report on the first stages of the effort. Four essays on basic issues, the report said, were prepared by Forrest Bivens, Saginaw pastor; Richard Lauersdorf, synodical vice president; and John Jeske and James Tiefel, seminary professors. The report then pointed to its goals of "adult spiritual growth and revitalizing congregations."[17] Surprisingly, the subject was not a major item of synodical convention business in 1991. Yet this comprehensive effort at spiritual renewal continues to hold its ideals before the synod as goals for which to aim.

The restructuring project of the mid-1980s has already been described. Add this to "Other Highlights of the Mischke Years" and to many another development that could not be included, and the conclusion is inescapable that the Wisconsin Synod from 1979 on has been exceedingly busy both in administrative matters and in larger issues.

What has given President Mischke the most regrets as he has presided over the synodical conventions from 1979 on? A likely candidate for that dubious distinction might well be the closing of Mobridge in his home state by the very first of his conventions. What convention has given him his greatest joy? One might venture the guess that it was the 1985 convention that heard final "Reaching Out" reports and voted a five-man missionary team to Brazil.

The Years Ahead

Synod members certainly hope some of those "years ahead" will also be "Mischke Years." There are a number of unfinished items on the synodical agenda. Humanly speaking, they will fare better in veteran, skilled hands. But it is not beyond the realm of possibility that the incumbent president might not see fit to enter a new term after passing his seventieth birthday and might not be moved by pleas that he stay on.

But whether Carl Mischke or someone else is chief executive officer of the Wisconsin Synod in the years ahead, certain aspects of those years are fairly predictable. Others are even more certain.

The Wisconsin Synod will have to find a way to make the twenty area high schools more useful to the worker-training system. The high schools are there; we hope they will not go away. Sound economics and sound stewardship suggest that they be used more fully as a source for worker-training, especially when a severe shortage of pastors and teachers looms a few years down the road.

This could mean cutting back the number of synod schools. It could mean some modern version of the old 1927 "Moussa Plan." It could be some combination of steps or some entirely new proposal. The collective synodical wisdom will have to settle on what the procedure should be in the years ahead.

All trends point to a pastor-teacher shortage. Steps are already being taken to find more pastor and teacher students and to devise what is being called "alternative forms of ministry." This is a practical problem with important doctrinal implications. Church-ministry doctrinal discussions are nothing new for the synod.

In the years ahead much thought, time, energy, and prayer are going to be devoted to carrying through on "Vision 2000." Even if only some of the goals are achieved, and that only partially, great changes for the good will be effected in the Wisconsin Synod. At the same time its members will have to approach "Vision 2000" with the viewpoint Luther expressed long ago in 1518 at Heidelberg: "He, however, who has emptied himself [Philippians 2] through suffering no longer does work but knows that God works and does all things in him. For this reason, whether God does work or not, it is all the same to him. He neither boasts if he does good works, nor is he disturbed if God does not do good works through him."[18]

A pending venture that will reach fulfillment in the next years is the introduction of the new hymnal. It will bring blessings in our worship for decades to come. The hymnal being replaced bears the copyright date of 1941. It has already had a lifetime of fifty years. One can only hope that its replacement makes its way into the hands and hearts of the worshipers as easily as did the 1941 hymnal.

On the larger Lutheran scene, it seems, the years ahead will not bring all that much change for the Wisconsin Synod. The synod will remain a small minority of the Lutherans in the land. Its theological position of faithfulness to the Scriptures and to the Lutheran Confessions will keep it in that minority position.

If God wants to bring others to this confessional position, we will rejoice. Whether or not that happens, we will want him to help us maintain the position in any event and at any cost.

Amid all the hypotheticals of this look into the "years ahead" one thing is certain. It is the truth that the Lord God of all history will guide the history of the church body that trusts in him. In over 140 years of Wisconsin Synod history, in the 100 years since the Wisconsin Synod federated with other synods, in the 75 years of the merged Wisconsin Synod history, he has always proved himself to be the Lord God who has done all things well. In the years ahead he will continue to do the same.

ENDNOTES

Chapter 1. Roots That Reach the Rhine

1. See the first paragraph of the original constitution. The document, as well as the early proceedings up to 1869, are available in one volume, *Verhandlungen der Versammlungen der Evangelisch-Lutherischen Synode von Wisconsin.* References to these and later synodical proceedings will be cited simply as *Wisconsin Synod Proceedings* with the appropriate date. The first constitution is printed with the 1850 *Proceedings*.

2. J. P. Koehler was uniquely qualified to write this history. He grew up in a pioneer Wisconsin Synod parsonage, studied under Doctor Walther, was a colleague of Doctor Hoenecke, taught at Northwestern College and Wisconsin Lutheran Seminary, and was assigned the task of writing both the golden and diamond jubilee histories of the Wisconsin Synod. The first appeared in Volume 35 of the Wisconsin Synod's *Gemeinde-Blatt*. The second has the bibliographical entry: Koehler, J. P., *The History of the Wisconsin Synod*. St. Cloud, Minn.: Sentinel Publishing Company for the Protes'tant Conference, 1970 and 1981. An earlier and incomplete German version is *Geschichte der Allgemeinen Evangelisch-Lutherischen Synode von Wisconsin und andern Staaten*, Milwaukee: Northwestern Publishing House, 1925. Reference will be to *History of the Wisconsin Synod* and cited simply as Koehler, *Wisconsin Synod*.

3. Koehler, *Wisconsin Synod*, has a lengthy description of such mission societies and schools on pp 19-24 and 27-30.

4. Koehler, *Wisconsin Synod*, provides biographical material on Muehlhaeuser, as well as on Weinmann and Wrede, in the "Barmen Missionaries" section, pp 34-36. For an evaluation of Muehlhaeuser's influence see also Armin Schuetze, "Muehlhaeuser, Founding Father of the Wisconsin Synod" in *Wisconsin Lutheran Quarterly*, 72 (July 1975), pp 194-210.

5. Koehler, *Wisconsin Synod,* p 29. Koehler had access to the Langenberg records and copied many of them during his sabbatical in Europe in 1924-1925. He does not, however, identify these sources.
6. J. Nicum, *Geschichte des Evangelisch-Lutherischen Ministeriums vom Staate New York und angrenzenden Staaten und Laendern* (Reading, Pa.: Theodor Wischau Press, 1888), pp 169-170.
7. J. Muehlhaeuser was requested to write a history of the synod's first decade as a tenth anniversary project. He read it at the 1860 convention and "the synod heard with great interest the history," as the minutes say. The unprinted manuscript is in the Northwestern College Archives. A copy is available at the library of the Wisconsin Lutheran Seminary. The quotation runs from the manuscript's first page to the second.

Chapter 2. First the Stalk

1. Wisconsin's second president, John Bading, finished at Barmen but received the major part of his training at Hermannsburg.
2. Koehler's *Wisconsin Synod* quotes this November 1853 letter on pp 43-44. The Weitbrecht argument in the next paragraph is also to be found in this location.
3. See Note 1 of the previous chapter for the location of the synod's first constitution.
4. Koehler's *Wisconsin Synod* discusses this matter on p 41.
5. Koehler's *Wisconsin Synod* has a colorful account of Fachtmann's journeys on pp 53-56. Armin Engel's "Ernst August Gottlieb Fachtmann: WELS First Traveling Missionary" in *WELS Historical Institute Journal,* 1 (Fall, 1983), pp 9-20, covers both the journeys and also the sad expulsion chapter of the story.
6. Moldehnke's own accounts are found in his *Fuenf Jahre in Amerika* articles in Hengstenberg's *Evangelische Kirchen-Zeitung* from October 1868 to February 1870. A copy of the articles is available at the Wisconsin Lutheran Seminary library.
7. See *Wisconsin Synod Proceedings,* 1866, p 30. Moldehnke eventually became a leading member of the New York Ministerium and a president of the General Council.
8. Ibid., 1860, p 14.
9. Ibid., 1863, pp 23-24. Kowalke's *Centennial Story* (Milwaukee: Northwestern, 1965) summarizes the site debate on pp 19-23.
10. Koehler, *Wisconsin Synod,* p 89.
11. Bading himself describes at length the Russian tour in the first *Gemeinde-Blatt* volume under the title *Reise-Erinnerungen,* beginning in 1, 3, p 3, and continuing through Iambic, 6. At the time the account was published Bading was serving as one of the original co-editors of the *Gemeinde-Blatt.*

12. Koehler, *Wisconsin Synod* p 89.

Chapter 3. Good Neighbors

1. Schmid himself tells the story in the letters of report he sent back to Basel on a regular basis for most of the rest of his life. A large number are reproduced in "Selected Letters of Friedrich Schmid" in *Michigan Memories* (Saginaw: Michigan District of the Wisconsin Synod, 1985), pp 1-157.
2. *Michigan Memories* also includes a translation by G. Struck of the golden jubilee history, *Kurzgefasste Geschichte der Evangelisch-Lutherischen Synode von Michigan u. a. St.* (Saginaw: F. and C. Reitter, 1910), titled "A Brief History of the Evangelical Lutheran Synod of Michigan and Other States." The demise of the "Mission Synod" is described on p 161 of the translation.
3. "Brief History" in *Michigan Memories,* p 162.
4. Ibid., p 184.
5. A General Council side of the story can be found in *Memoirs of Henry Eyster Jacobs* (Edited and printed by Henry E. Horn, 1974) 2, pp 276-277.
6. "Brief History" in *Michigan Memories,* pp 190-191.
7. In an unpublished essay, "The Negative Effects on *Stephansgemeinde,* Adrian, Michigan, of Building Michigan Lutheran Seminary," Daniel Drews, an Adrian vicar, presents the congregation's side of the story. His essay is on file at the library of Wisconsin Lutheran Seminary.
8. An interesting description of the school can be found in Thomas L. Ziebell's "The Michigan Synod and Its 'School of the Prophets' " in *WELS Historical Institute Journal,* 1, 2 (Fall 1983), pp 21-35.
9. Not much Minnesota History has been written. In 1910 a golden anniversary publication appeared, *Geschichte der Minnesota Synode und ihrer einzelnen Gemeinden* (St. Louis: Louis Lange, 1910). A district golden anniversary in 1968 produced *Golden Jubilee History of the Minnesota District* (Minneapolis: Ad Art, 1969). Its pages 15-30 carry a condensation of a thirty page pamphlet, *The Minnesota District's First Fifty Years,* written by E. C. Fredrich and printed by the District.
10. When Heyer died in 1873 the General Council ordered a biography to be written. The resolution that remained unfulfilled at that time was finally enacted in 1942 when E. Theodore Bachman wrote *They Called Him Father: The Life Story of John Christian Frederick Heyer* (Philadelphia: Fortress, 1942).
11. *Geschichte der Minnesota Synod,* p 4.
12. Carl E. Schneider, *The German Church on the American Frontier* (St. Louis: 1939), p 439.
13. *Minnesota Proceedings,* 1870, pp 42-43. The *Gemeinde-Blatt* reports the matter at length in the July 15, 1872, issue.

14. *Minnesota Proceedings,* 1867, p 5. These *Proceedings* also supply the data for the two resolutions referred to in the next paragraph.
15. Biographical material on Sieker is provided by P. Roesener, *Ehrendenkmal des weiland ehrwuerdigen Pastor Johann Heinrich Sieker* (West Roxbury, Mass., 1905) and by Ella Hesse Fick, "Young John Henry Sieker" in *Concordia Historical Institute Quarterly,* 57-3 (Fall 1984), pp 100-108.
16. Often the $300 Muehlhaeuser received from Pennsylvania and distributed to the most needy in those early years made the difference between sink or swim for some Wisconsin pastors and congregations.
17. *Geschichte der Minnesota-Synode,* pp 16-17.
18. Morton A. Schroeder wrote the centennial history of the school under the title, *A Time to Remember: An Informal History of Doctor Martin Luther College* (New Ulm, Minnesota: Dr. Martin Luther College, 1984).
19. See *Missouri Proceedings,* 1847, pp 10-11 in the 1876 reprint.
20. There is a dearth of Nebraska District and Synod history writing. Only a few items can be mentioned. One is "History of the District of Nebraska" in *Centennial Story,* M. Lehninger, editor (Milwaukee: Northwestern, 1951), pp 111-119. Koehler's *Wisconsin Synod* has Nebraska material on pp 178-179.

Chapter 4. Turn to the Right

1. See p 11.
2. See pp 12,13.
3. *Wisconsin Synod Proceedings,* 1862, p 6.
4. A representative *Lutheraner* article, one of many others, is found in 16 (Dec. 27, 1859), 78. For a Buffalo example see W. Wier in "Huelferuf aus Wisconsin," *Kirchliches Informatorium,* 2 (July 15, 1852), p 6.
5. *Kirchliche Mittheilungen aus und ueber Nord-Amerika,* 1854-1. In an October 1861 report in the same periodical, Deindoerfer reiterates and intensifies his characterization by calling Wisconsin *dik uniert* (thoroughly unionistic).
6. *Wisconsin Synod Proceedings,* 1854, p 3.
7. A. Kuhn, *Geschichte der Minnesota Synode und ihrer einzelnen Gemeinden* (St. Louis: Louis Lange, 1910), pp 167-168. Back in 1854 at Granville Goldammer, with a prophetic voice, had also argued that using both bread and wafers was to be avoided because thereby "a cause for division was being supplied to future generations."
8. Koehler's *Wisconsin Synod,* pp 46-47, lists the questions the absent Weinmann at Baltimore posed in order to rouse and raise the confessional thinking of the synodical body to which he still belonged.
9. Bading, whom Koehler knew intimately, plays a large role on the pages of the latter's history. The citations are too numerous to be listed.

An autobiographical *vita* of Bading is in the essay file of the library of Wisconsin Lutheran Seminary. The April 1975 issue of *Wisconsin Lutheran Quarterly* has a pertinent writing, "Bading and the Formative Presidency of the Wisconsin Synod," pp 110-128.

10. *Hermannsburger Missionsblatt,* 1 (January 1854), p 6.
11. George Haccius, *Hannoversche Missions-Geschichte,* 3 Vols. (Hermannsburg, 1909-1920). The point is discussed in the opening pages of Vol. 2.
12. See Koehler's *Wisconsin Synod,* p 45.
13. *Wisconsin Synod Proceedings,* 1860, pp 11-13. Actually the original constitution limited the president to two two-year terms but in 1854, 1856, and 1858 the Wisconsin conventions simply set that provision aside on the grounds of Muehlhaeuser's indispensability.
14. Ibid., 1861, p 6, and 1862, p 13.
15. Ibid., 1862, p 21.
16. Ibid., 1861, pp 14-19 carry Reim's essay verbatim and on pp 23-24 report on the discussions.
17. Prime reading material is available in autobiographical material by Philipp Koehler that *Faith-Life* supplies in the issue of 45, 3 (May - June 1972) and sporadically thereafter.
18. See *Wisconsin Synod Proceedings,* 1858, p 12, for a typical instance.
19. Ibid., 1856, p 2.
20. Ibid., 1860, p 9.
21. Ibid., 1859, p 11.
22. Ibid., 1862, p 28.
23. See pp 15-17.
24. Koehler's *Wisconsin Synod* has a long section on this matter on pp 97-104.
25. *Wisconsin Synod Proceedings,* 1867, pp 22-23, presents both reports and describes the debate they triggered.
26. Ibid., 1868, p 26.

Chapter 5. Early Interchurch Relations

1. *Wisconsin Synod Proceedings,* 1869, p 14.
2. Ibid., p 11.
3. Ibid., 1863, p 24.
4. Koehler discusses this matter on p 85 of *Wisconsin History.* See also the 1862 *Proceedings,* p 29.
5. *Wisconsin Synod Proceedings,* 1866, p 9.
6. The amended constitution and "Fundamental Principles" can be found in the General Council's 1867 *Proceedings,* pp 20-26 and also in R. C.

Wolf's *Document of Lutheran Unity in America* (Philadelphia: Fortress, 1966), pp 143-145.
7. See *General Council Proceedings*, 1867, pp 16-17, for the reply to Ohio and p 19 for the resolution on Iowa and the subsequent recording of negative votes.
8. See *Wisconsin Synod Proceedings*, 1868, pp 14-17 and 27, for the report on these discussions.
9. Ibid., 1868, p 19.
10. *General Council Proceedings*, 1868. The adopted majority report is found on pp 22-25. The minority's declaration is on p 25.
11. *General Council Proceedings*, 1869, pp 32-34.
12. *Wisconsin Synod Proceedings*, 1869, p 11.
13. Ibid., 1857, p 4.
14. G. Fritschel, *Geschichte der lutherischen Kirche in America* (Guetersloh, 1896), 2, p 412.
15. *Wisconsin Synod Proceedings*, 1862, p 17.
16. Ibid., 1867, pp 13-15.
17. Ibid., 1862, p 17.
18. Ibid., 1864, pp 7, 11, and 14.
19. Ibid., 1868, p 18.
20. For Wisconsin's reasoning see its *Wisconsin Synod Proceedings*, 1870, p 34 and for Sieker's analysis see *Minnesota Proceedings*, 1870, p 9.
21. The two test questions appear in *Minnesota Proceedings*, 1870, pp 11-12, and in Wolf's *Documents of Lutheran Unity*, pp 167-168.
22. *Minnesota Proceedings*, 1871, pp 41-42.

Chapter 6. In the Synodical Conference

1. Wolf, *Documents*, p 186.
2. Koehler's *Wisconsin History* discusses the polemics on pp 79-86 and 115-118.
3. Ibid., p 45.
4. *Wisconsin Synod Proceedings*, p 9. Attention might be called in this connection to the article, "A Few, Faithful in Few Things: Our Synod's Fathers and the Formation of the Synodical Conference," in *Wisconsin Lutheran Quarterly*, 69 (July, 1972), pp 154-173.
5. *Wisconsin Synod Proceedings*, pp 27-28. Frequent reference is made to this section of the *Proceedings* in the material which follows.
6. *Proceedings of the Northern District of the Missouri Synod*, 1868, pp 28-29.
7. See *Wisconsin Synod Proceedings*, pp 22-23 or Wolf, *Documents*, pp 181-182.

8. H. Meyer, *Pflanzungsgeschichte des Minnesota Districts der Ev. Luth. Synode von Missouri, Ohio und andern Staaten* (Minneapolis, 1932), p 51.
9. *Gemeinde-Blatt*, 7 (Jan. 1, 1872), p 8.
10. Ibid., (Feb. 1, 1872), p 7.
11. Ibid., (April, 1872, and three subsequent issues). Koehler's *Wisconsin History*, p 133, has a variant listing, dividing Thesis 2 and including Thesis 5 with Thesis 3. This is the arrangement of material used by the Minnesota Synod in its subsequent deliberations at its 1872 convention.
12. H. Fick and E. A. Bauer, "*Bericht ueber das mit der ehrwuerdigen Synode von Minnesota abgehaltene Colloquium,*" *Lutheraner* 28 (July 1, 1872), pp 149-150.
13. *Minnesota Proceedings*, 1872, pp 11-26.
14. The *Denkschrift* was ordered to be published by Ohio in both German and English versions. It is often included with the published 1872 *Wisconsin Synod Proceedings* of the Synodical Conference. A printing, along with the proposed constitution, was put out at Columbus, Ohio, in 1871. See also Wolf, *Documents*, pp 187-196.
15. *Synodical Conference Proceedings*, 1912, p 5.
16. Wolf, *Documents*, p 196.
17. This is the chief argument A. Kuhn makes in a pro-state synod article that appears in the May 1, 1877, *Gemeinde-Blatt*. The next *Gemeinde-Blatt* issue carried an *Entgegnung*.
18. *Synodical Conference Proceedings*, 1876, pp 44-53. The state synod resolution is on p 47 and the school plan that follows on pp 48-53.
19. See *Wisconsin Synod Proceedings*, 1877, pp 26-30, for such sentiments of District President Strassen and Pastor Allwardt of the Missouri Synod.
20. Ibid., pp 19-30. The subsequent resolutions are included in the latter pages.
21. "Reminiscences from Professor August Pieper" in *WELS Historical Institute Journal*, 1 (Fall 1983), 54. The next Pieper quotation is found on p 56.
22. *Missouri Proceedings*, 1878, pp 33-34. Koehler, *Wisconsin History*, p 148, supplies information about Walther's *widergoettlich*. He could have been present at Missouri's convention since he was a Concordia student from the fall of 1877 on, or he could have heard this from Bading, who with Adelberg represented Wisconsin at the convention. The Missouri resolution quoted in the next sentence is found on p 34 of the *Proceedings*.
23. See especially the issues of the free-lance *Theologische Monatshefte* put out in Allenton, Pennsylvania, by Pastor Brobst. A comment on

Luther's election views in a footnote of an article on usury touched off a series of articles, with Iowa men on one side and Missouri men on the other.

24. Koehler's *Wisconsin History*, pp 157-158, describes the incident and names the witnesses.
25. Koehler's *Wisconsin History* supplies detail on pp 158-159. See also Carl Meyer, ed., *Moving Frontiers* (St. Louis: Concordia, 1964), pp 273-274.
26. Both the theses and their discussion and Hoenecke's election presentation are to be found in *Wisconsin Synod Proceedings*, 1882, pp 13-63. The description of the subsequent session in the next paragraph rests primarily on pp 34-35.
27. *Synodical Conference Proceedings*, 1882, pp 4 and 29-30.

Chapter 7. Silver Anniversary Perspective

1. The statistical table on p 44 of the 1875 *Wisconsin Synod Proceedings* says, 119 congregations. Bading's concluding remarks on p 48 put the total at 130. Perhaps he was including a number of preaching places that he knew were nearing organizational status. Since almost all the material in "Jubilee Convention" rests on *Wisconsin Synod Proceedings*, 1875, no additional citations will be provided. The p 6 designation of Psalm 108 as the text for Bading's jubilee sermon is obviously a misprint for Psalm 138.
2. The need for clarification is indicated by a May 2, 1976, *Northwestern Lutheran* item that states flatly: "As a separate synod the Wisconsin Ev. Lutheran Synod had four presidents: J. Muehlhaeuser, 1850-1860; J. Bading, 1860-1889; Ph. von Rohr, 1889-1908; and G. E. Bergemann, 1908-1917." Even the official synodical publication writes as though neither Reim and Streissguth ever existed nor that synodical conventions in 1864 and 1866 held elections. The centennial publication, *Continuing in His Word*, likewise pictures Bading as 1860-1889 president (p 18).
3. *Wisconsin Synod Proceedings*, 1865, p 17. This page also contains the quotation in the next paragraph.
4. This may be the place to refer to an amplification of this and the subsequent section on Streissguth found in the July 1978 *Wisconsin Lutheran Quarterly*'s article, "Two Forgotten Wisconsin Presidents: Reim and Streissguth," pp 188-198.
5. *Wisconsin Synod Proceedings*, 1865, p 16.
6. This rests on the conclusions of a research paper by a seminary student from Helenville, Lynn Wiedmann. His writing, "The Helenville Problem," is deposited in a special file of the library of Wisconsin Lutheran Seminary.
7. Before the Wisconsin Synod established its Northwestern Publishing House, Brumder did much of its printing, including the hymnal for

which the synod received five cents per copy sold. The 1872 sales netted the synod $124.75. In the following years Brumder voluntarily doubled the synod's take.
8. *Wisconsin Synod Proceedings*, 1866, p 20.
9. Ibid., 1867, p 6.
10. Ibid., p 5.
11. Ibid., p 10.
12. Ibid., 1868, p 6.
13. Ibid., 1867, pp 11-13.

Chapter 8. Fifteen Good Years: 1876-1891

1. Bading's report is on p 13 of *Wisconsin Synod Proceedings*, 1876. The synodical reaction is described on pp 30-31.
2. Funds for the venture were to come from the mission festival offerings that customarily had been going to Hermannsburg. The minutes point out that that mission society was at the time "in very favorable financial circumstances." It was not a case of "robbing Peter to pay Paul" but of applying monies to the most pressing need.
3. Bading's report is on p 12 of *Wisconsin Synod Proceedings*, 1877. The synodical action is reported on p 37.
4. *Synodical Conference Proceedings*, 1877, pp 50-51.
5. *Wisconsin Synod Proceedings*, 1883, p 54.
6. Koehler had to be designated as "senior" because his son John Philipp had been admitted to synodical membership in 1881. The latter is the great synodical historian.
7. *Wisconsin Synod Proceedings*, 1884, p 56. This location also supplies the basis for the subsequent quotation.
8. Ibid., 1891, p 65.
9. A most important record of these happenings and others in the first forty years of the seminary is contained in a little and very rare pamphlet of 26 pages: A. Hoenecke, *Das Ev. Luth Seminar zu Wauwatosa, Wisconsin* (Milwaukee: Northwestern, 1903). The pamphlet's pp 9-12 form the basis for this writing.
10. *Wisconsin Synod Proceedings*, 1878, pp 36-38.
11. The most memorable of the often differing tales begins with Inspector Notz's discovery of a Paul-at-Damascus type of elevator to smuggle back into the dormitory those who overstayed their leave from campus. He noted the signaling set-up and then employed it one evening to trap the culprits. Unfortunately for him, the haulers recognized the rider when he was halfway up. They stopped the elevator pronto. In the ensuing dialog the Inspector pledged eternal silence in exchange for a safe landing. He broke that pledge at one of his anniversaries, but not before securing the consent of the human elevators in attendance—one of them soon to be a synodical school head.

THE WISCONSIN SYNOD LUTHERANS

12. E. E. Kowalke, *Centennial Story* (Milwaukee: Northwestern, 1965), p 129.
13. See a letter in which Dr. Walther sought to remove Sihler's concern in *Selected Letters*, translated by Roy Suelflow (St. Louis: Concordia, 1981), pp 155-158.
14. Loren H. Osman, *W. D. Hoard* (Fort Atkinson: Hoard Company, 1985), p 106. Four pages later is found the wording of the bill quoted in the same paragraph.
15. Quoted from Osman, *W. D. Hoard*, but with punctuation improved.
16. *Wisconsin Synod Proceedings*, 1889, supplies Bading's last presidential address on pp 9-14. Convention action, described in subsequent paragraphs, is reported on pp 59-63.
17. Ibid., 1890, pp 14-50.
18. Ibid., pp 67-70.
19. *Reports and Memorials*, 1963, pp 33-35 and *Wisconsin Synod Proceedings*, 1963, p 141.
20. Koehler, *Wisconsin History*, pp 184-185.
21. *Wisconsin Synod Proceedings*, 1887, p 16.
22. Ibid., 1890, p 70.
23. Ibid., 1891, pp 63-64.
24. Ibid., 1889, p 18.
25. The best writing on President von Rohr is Richard Balge's "Von Rohr: A Beloved Brother and Faithful Minister" in *Wisconsin Lutheran Quarterly*, 72 (July 1975), 211-234. The July 1960 issue of *Concordia Historical Institute Quarterly* supplies informative family reminiscences in Philip von Rohr Sauer's "Elfrieda von Rohr Sauer," pp 33-55.

Chapter 9. The Federation Years: 1892-1917

1. See the third "Good Neighbors" chapter in this volume for details.
2. A chapter in *Michigan Memories*, "Haste Makes Waste in the Story of the Michigan Synod's Division," pp 215-242, makes the "too rapidly" point.
3. *Federation Proceedings*, 1892, pp 12-17. This will be the first and last reference to the brief protocol of the constituent convention, from which the material in subsequent paragraphs is drawn.
4. That cornerstone can be seen in the archway of the present Mequon Wisconsin Lutheran Seminary.
5. *Federation Proceedings*, 1893, pp 124-125(6-7). In the printing process Federation minutes were often simply attached to synodical minutes. Hence the three-figure page numbers with the actual page numbers in parentheses. There were only 12 pages in the 1893 Federation minutes and these included the constitution in final form. This is the form of the constitution that will be quoted in the next paragraphs.
6. *Wisconsin Synod Proceedings*, 1892, pp 69-70.

7. See *Federation Proceedings,* 1893, p 123, for the constitutional paragraph on missions and p 127 for the resolve to undertake the Indian mission.
8. See note 6 for location.
9. Today these terms must of course be taken with the proverbial grain of salt. In 1892 the New Ulm school, for example, actually provided only a three-year preparatory and a two-year college course, five years instead of today's eight.
10. There is naturally a considerable literature. A house periodical began to appear as *Apache Scout* in 1923 and from 1952 on as *Apache Lutheran.* Koehler's *Wisconsin History* devotes pp 198-206 to the subject. *Continuing in His Word* has a section, "Apache Indian Mission," pp 229-250. Too numerous to cite are *Gemeinde-Blatt* articles on the subject.
11. *Wisconsin Federation Proceedings,* 1899, p 18. The previous report of 1897, p 8, refers to school collections for a bell but not to a gathering of individual gifts.
12. Ibid., 1893, p 127 (9).
13. Koehler, *Wisconsin History,* p 201, reports that this Missionary Cook in the early 1900s scotched a Presbyterian effort to start a mission on the Apache reservation.
14. *Wisconsin Federation Proceedings,* 1899, p 16.
15. Ibid., 1901, p 64.
16. Koehler's *Wisconsin History* describes the event on pp 204-205.
17. The same point is made by Karl Krauss in "Our World Missions" in *Wisconsin Lutheran Quarterly,* 72 (October 1975), pp 274-293.
18. Some of this perhaps oversimplified viewpoint Koehler espouses in *Wisconsin History,* pp 198-199. See also the essay review of the *History* in I. Habeck's "J. P. Koehler's History of the Wisconsin Synod," *Wisconsin Lutheran Quarterly,* 68 (October 1971), pp 217-227. The Protes'tant response is found in *Faith-Life,* 45 (March-April 1972), pp 24-26.
19. *Michigan Synod Proceedings,* 1893, p 35.
20. *Federation Proceedings,* 1893, p 126 (8).
21. Ibid., 1895, p 5.
22. *Michigan Synod Proceedings,* 1899, p 39.
23. Ibid., 1900, pp 62-64.
24. These are the main points agreed to at an April 24-25, 1906, peace conference. See Ibid., 1906, p 9.

Chapter 10. Doctrinal Concerns at the Turn of the Century

1. *Wisconsin Synod Proceedings,* 1900, p 11. The following statistics are found on p 110 of those *Proceedings.*

2. See Ibid., 1899, pp 103-104 for the establishment of the committee and p 99 of the 1900 *Proceedings* for the first report.
3. Ibid., 1904, p 106.
4. Basic historical material is gathered in "The Situation in Cincinnati, Ohio," *Proceedings of the Missouri Synod's Middle District*, 1904, pp 80-112. Koehler, who participated energetically in the Wisconsin Synod's handling of the matter, describes the developments in *Wisconsin History*, pp 233-234 and beyond.
5. Koehler, who was on the scene and actively involved, makes the point that there was a great deal of such impure motivation. See the previous reference.
6. *Wisconsin Synod Proceedings*, 1906, p 78.
7. Ibid., 1907, p 121.
8. Ibid., 1908, pp 32 and 127.
9. Ibid., 1909, p 135.
10. Ibid., 1910, p 101.
11. Koehler's *Wisconsin History*, p 234.
12. Koehler, a participant in some of those first discussions, describes them in the *Amtslehre* section of *Wisconsin History*, pp 230-233.
13. The *Quarterly* articles, with volume number supplied, are: *Menschenherrschaft in der Kirche* (8), *Die Suspension noch einmal* (8), a review of Walther's *Die Stimme unserer Kirche in der Frage von Kirche und Amt* (9), *Die Lehre von der Kirche und ihren Kennzeichen in Anwendung auf die Synode* (9), and *Abschluss der Diskussion ueber die Lehren von der Kirche. etc.* (10)
14. *Der Lutherische Herold*, the New York Ministerium periodical, at the time published a series of articles on the 1903-1904 free conferences by Dr. Nicum that supply the most thorough press coverage these conferences received and form the basis for much that is included in this writing, especially in the matter of the Detroit prayer debate. The Detroit conference is described in the May 7 and 14 issues of the 1904 *Herold*.
15. The most significant of the writings is Professor Bente's *Warum koennen wir keine gemeinsame Gottesdienste mit Ohioern und Iowanern veranstalten und abhalten?* in *Lehre und Wehre*, 51 (March 1905), pp 97-115. In answer to his theme question, "Why Can We not Set up and Carry out any Common Worship Services with Ohioans and Iowans?" Bente argues (pp 110-111), "If we become one with the Ohio men in prayer, we will also have to invite them to our altars." It is an argument for a "unit concept" of fellowship even if that term is not used.
16. *Theologische Quartalschrift*, 3 (April 1906), 120.
17. *Wisconsin Lutheran Quarterly*, 37 (April 1940), 122, and *Wisconsin Synod Proceedings*, 1975, p 172.

18. A February 22, 1920, *Northwestern Lutheran* obituary supplies the biographical details that follow.
19. See Note 2 of the first chapter for details on these writings.
20. *Wisconsin History* describes the assignment on pp 188-191.
21. Joh. Ph. Koehler, *Lehrbuch der Kirchengeschichte* (Milwaukee: Northwestern, 1917).
22. E. E. Sauer, trans., T*he Epistle of Paul to the Galatians: A Commentary by Joh. Ph. Koehler* (Milwaukee: Northwestern, 1957).
23. *Wisconsin Synod Proceedings,* 1959, pp 120-164. The first of these pages identifies the origins of the essay.
24. See note 21 of chapter 6. Additional biographical material can be found in "Reminiscences from Professor August Pieper" in *WELS Historical Institute Journal,* 1 (Fall 1983), p 48-56, and an introduction to E. E. Kowalke's translation of Pieper's *Isaiah II* published by Northwestern in 1979.
25. After some twenty years the writer still vividly recalls an instance of this approach. When Doctor Martin Luther College in the mid 1960s began its accreditation studies, a basic article on the divine call seemed in place. The essayist declared at the outset that he would simply take his hearers through the New Testament, passage for passage that cast light on the subject. The refreshing result was a wealth of motivation and a dearth of regulations and bylaws we normally attached to the doctrine of the call. The writer, incidentally, was happy to see that essayist of long ago join him on the seminary faculty in 1986.

Chapter 11. From Federation to Merger

1. *Nebraska District Proceedings,* 1903, pp 37-39.
2. *Nebraska Synod Proceedings,* 1916, p 72.
3. Ibid., 1917, p 55.
4. A. Kuhn, ed., *Geschichte der Minnesota Synode und ihrer einzelnen Gemeinden* (St. Louis: Louis Lange, 1909), p 38.
5. *Geschichte der Minnesota Synode,* pp 49-50.
6. See *Wisconsin Synod Proceedings,* 1867, p 6.
7. *Minnesota Proceedings,* 1915, p 34.
8. *Wisconsin Synod Proceedings,* 1959, pp 24-28, 35-37.
9. *Michigan Proceedings,* 1911, pp 33-35. This location also supplies the three theses of the essay.
10. Ibid., 1912, pp 28-58.
11. *Wisconsin Synod Proceedings,* 1913, pp 114-115. See also "Carl Gausewitz: Churchman and Catechist" in *Wisconsin Lutheran Quarterly,* 76 (April 1979), 146-153.

12. It is interesting to note that when finally another synodical catechism was developed in the early 1980s, this was from start to finish basically the work of one man, Professor David Kuske of Wisconsin Lutheran Seminary.
13. J. Schaller, *Dr. Martin Luther's Kleiner Katechismus* in *Theologische Quartalschrift*, 14 (April 1917), 165-170.
14. *Federation Proceedings*, 1901, p 74.
15. E. E. Kowalke, *Centennial Story* (Milwaukee: Northwestern, 1965), pp 132-138.
16. See for example *Federation Proceedings*, 1899, pp 21-24.
17. Ibid., 1899, p 7.
18. Ibid., 1905, p 36.
19. A.L. Graebner, *Geschichte der Lutherischen Kirche in America* (St. Louis: Concordia, 1892). The book only carries the story to 1820 but is especially valuable for its treatment of the early Dutch beginnings in New York. Graebner learned Dutch to be able to include in his account first-hand records of early New York Lutheranism in this country that already then were two and a half centuries old.
20. *Federation Proceedings*, 1901, p 69.
21. See *Centennial Story*, pp 157-159.
22. *Federation Proceedings*, 1903, pp 67-68.
23. Ibid., 1905, pp 42-43.
24. Ibid., 1907, pp 35-36.
25. Ibid., 1911, pp 57-58.
26. Ibid., 1913, pp 48-51.
27. See Koehler's *Wisconsin History*, pp 234-241.
28. *Synodical Conference Proceedings*, 1920, p 47.

Chapter 12. Merger Beginnings in War Years

1. *Wisconsin Synod Proceedings*, 1919, pp 187-285. The subsequent remark about "woman suffrage" is from the parochial report of the Pacific Northwest District to be found near the middle of the 100 pages.
2. *Wisconsin Synod Proceedings*, 1921, p 196.
3. Ibid., 1919, p 12.
4. Ibid.
5. A lengthy biographical and evaluative writing is Armin Engel's "The Bergemann Era—1908-1933" in *Wisconsin Lutheran Quarterly*, 72 (October 1975), 294-308.
6. *Wisconsin Synod Proceedings*, 1919, p 160.
7. *Michigan District Proceedings*, 1918, pp 75-77. The secretary who summarized President Bergemann's report in this fashion was John Gauss.

8. President Brenner's letter is to be found in the seminary's vertical file in the folder with the title "Chaplains."
9. Morton Schroeder elaborates in the chapter "The Triumphant and Tragic Years" in his DMLC centennial history, *A Time to Remember*, put out by the school press in 1984.
10. One of the board members at the meeting related the incident to the writer, quoting Ackermann as saying at the finale, *Recht muss Recht bleiben!*
11. The striking story is described in Theodore Aaberg's *A City Set on a Hill* (Mankato MN: Board of Publications ELS, 1968).
12. There is of course no hard statistical evidence, but in 1930 the writer enrolled at a synodical preparatory school and found that in German studies the novices outnumbered the knowledgeable in a divided program. He may be reading too much into a single instance.
13. One instance of many is Professor August Pieper, who was vociferous in sounding the warnings to which reference is made. He could also urge wider use of English in the church's work. See his lengthy *Unser Uebergang ins Englische* in *Wisconsin Lutheran Quarterly* beginning in the October 1918 issue.
14. This is the Soll whose pericope booklet was widely used. Synodical lore has it that he did much of the pericope development on the long train trips from Yakima to Milwaukee as a substitute for sleeping on the way.
15. *Northwestern Lutheran*, August 25, 1918, p 134.
16. A Dakota veteran, Pastor E. R. Gamm, recounts several such incidents in his 1970 unpublished Minnesota District essay, "Our Daughter District's Golden Jubilee - 1970," pp 6, 7.
17. *Federation Proceedings*, 1918, p 46.
18. *Minnesota Proceedings*, 1920, p 101. This location, along with the following pages, supplies the data in the next paragraph.

Chapter 13. Focus on Education

1. These and subsequent school data are drawn from records gathered at DMLC. They can, however, be no more reliable than the rather hit-and-miss statistics on which they rest. Time after time such statistics are accompanied by an appeal for more ample and accurate records.
2. *Federation Proceedings*, 1893, p 12 (130). The statistical table carries the notation that the Wisconsin and Michigan reports are complete but that Minnesota's is not.
3. E. E. Kowalke's *Centennial Story* barely mentions the normal department at Northwestern. A little more information (p 50) is supplied in the golden jubilee memoir *Soli Deo Gloria* by Doctor Arthur Hoermann. Northwestern does not regard its temporary "normal" department as a skeleton-in-the-closet but prefers to stress its commitment to pre-seminary training.

4. *Soli Deo Gloria*, p 50.
5. *Centennial Story*, pp 118-119, provides more details.
6. The lengthy report covers pp 85-111 in *Wisconsin Synod Proceedings*, 1919. The proposals are on pp 107-109.
7. See *Wisconsin Synod Proceedings*, 1921, pp 58-59 for the enabling resolution.
8. An interesting history of that new property going back to Indian days was written by Daniel Balge. The paper is on file at the library of Wisconsin Lutheran Seminary.
9. *Wisconsin Synod Proceedings*, 1921, p 58.
10. Ibid.
11. Ibid., 1923, pp 98-99.
12. Ibid., 1927, p 35.
13. Ibid., 1929, p 57.
14. Ibid., 1919, p 110.
15. The story of the Kenosha high school venture is recorded in the Friedens centennial booklet, pp 46-47.
16. See the eightieth anniversary history of St. Peter and the closing section, "History of Winnebago Lutheran Academy," p 25.
17. *Wisconsin Synod Proceedings*, 1927, pp 41-47. This location supplies the data in subsequent paragraphs dealing with the issue.
18. The 1850 *Wisconsin Synod Proceedings* state, "Resolved that every pastor who joins our church body should especially make himself responsible for the youth and conduct day schools, Bible hours, mission hours, etc."

Chapter 14. Protes'tant Controversy

1. See his account of his *Gemeinde-Blatt* protest regarding the announcement of the decision in the Cincinnati case in 1911 in his *History*, p 234.
2. See *Faith-Life*'s "Is this Really True," March 1930 through June 1930 for an account of the discussion.
3. The Beitz paper, "God's Message to Us in Galatians: The Just Shall Live by Faith," was recently reproduced in the 1978 September-October issue of *Faith-Life*.
4. For details see the May-June 1973 issue of *Faith-Life*, pp 12-15.
5. Strangely President Kowalke's *Centennial Story*, p 180, speaks of a March 31 faculty meeting "at which the tutors reported that during the night they had learned of a large number of thefts." All other reports indicate that the theft investigation began already on March 28.
6. *Time* issues of Dec. 12, 1942, and Jan. 25, 1943, describe the Agricultural Department activities of Herbert Parisius.

7. See the *Faith-Life* supplements from July to September 1940 for the "Watertown Transcripts." They were reprinted in the July-August 1985 *Faith-Life*, pp 11-30.
8. *Western Wisconsin District Proceedings*, 1927, pp 31-34.
9. At the time of this writing the most readily accessible reprint of the Beitz paper is to be found in *Faith-Life* September-October 1978. The golden anniversary of the Protes'tant Conference was observed in that year.
10. *Western Wisconsin District Proceedings*, 1926, p 34.
11. On the occasion of the tenth anniversary of the formation of the Protes'tant Conference *Faith-Life* published Claus Gieschen's "Ten Lively Years," an annals-type account of the controversy's first decade. This item is found in *Faith-Life*, January 1938, p 5.
12. August Pieper and John Meyer in August 1929 put out a pamphlet, *Antwort*, in the interest of refuting the *Beleuchtung* Koehler had addressed to the 1929 synodical convention. The quotation is found on p 8 of the *Antwort* pamphlet.
13. For details see "The Parting of Professor J. P. Koehler and the Wisconsin Lutheran Seminary" in *WELS Historical Institute Journal*, Fall 1983, pp 40-41 and the less readily available *Antwort*, pp 9-10.
14. *Antwort*, p 9.
15. J. P. Koehler, "Witness, Analysis, and Reply." *Faith-Life*, 3 (July 1930), Supplement, p 6.
16. *Western Wisconsin District Bericht*, 1927-28. See especially pp 20-23.
17. The "Elroy Declaration" is found in *Faith-Life*, 2 (July 16, 1929), 8 pp 4-5.
18. *Wisconsin Synod Proceedings*, 1929, p 35.
19. *Minnesota District Proceedings*, 1928, pp 48-49.
20. Ibid., 1930, pp 32-35.
21. Ibid., 1932, pp 72-73.

Chapter 15. Missions Old and Missions New

1. *Wisconsin Synod Proceedings*, 1923, p 60.
2. Ibid., 1925, p 68. The previous pages contains the declaration in the next paragraph and also provide the basis for what follows.
3. See Koehler's *Wisconsin Synod* for the section on "Indian Mission," pp 198-203.
4. *Wisconsin Synod Proceedings*, 1925, p 67.
5. See for example Koehler's *Wisconsin Synod*, pp 196-198.
6. *Wisconsin Synod Proceedings*, 1925, p 68.
7. M. Lehninger, ed., *Continuing in His Word* (Milwaukee: Northwestern Publishing House, 1951), p 254.

8. At the time of this writing the Spring 1986 *Quarterly* carries an obituary of Armin Schlender, pp 147-148, that merits citation and reading.
9. For more on the Nigerian mission see a brief paragraph on the first page of Ch. 20.
10. A colorful biography of the latter, a colorful missionary in his own right has been written by John F. Nau, *Nau! Mission Inspired* (St. Louis: Clayton, 1978).
11. The *Lutheran Witness* reports the action on p 252 of its July 18, 1935, issue.
12. *Wisconsin Synod Proceedings*, 1935, p 105.
13. *Synodical Conference Proceedings*, 1936, p 112.
14. In the Fall 1984 *WELS Historical Institute Journal*, pp 33-44, Edgar Hoenecke pays an eloquent and interesting tribute to Alfred Uplegger and Henry Rosin and their associates in "The End of an Epoch on the Apache Indian Mission."
15. *Wisconsin Synod Proceedings*, 1912, p 32.
16. The quotation is from p 44 of the article cited in note 14.
17. Good additional reading on this point is found in Norman Berg's "Home Mission Moods and Modes—125 Years in WELS" in the October issue of the 1976 *Wisconsin Lutheran Quarterly*, pp 250-265.
18. *Wisconsin Synod Proceedings*, 1929, pp 67-69.

Chapter 16. Significant Intersynodical Developments

1. Peter Schlemmer, a participant as pastor of Fort Ridgley's St. John, describes in detail the first events in the effort that would eventually produce the Chicago or Intersynodical Theses in an essay for the Minnesota District's second convention entitled "Current Unity Endeavors in the Lutheran Church." See *Minnesota District Proceedings*, 1920, pp 18-62.
2. *Minnesota District Proceedings*, 1920, p 34.
3. *Minnesota Synod Proceedings*, 1917, pp 10-11. The same *Proceedings*, p 69, carries the synodical resolutions that follow.
4. *Wisconsin Synod Proceedings*, 1919, p 159.
5. For a full print-out of the "Chicago Theses" see the 1929 October issue of *Wisconsin Lutheran Quarterly*, pp 250-273. For the rejection of *intuitu fidei* in the next paragraph see pp 272-273.
6. This may be written down in some place that allows for proper citation but the writer recalls it only from class lectures of John Meyer, who was a participant at the discussions and whose recollection of past events was always accurate.
7. See the footnote to the Note 5 citation.
8. See the *Lutheran Witness*, July 9, 1929, pp 231-232.

9. This is an after-the-fact verdict of a member of the Intersynodical Commission, John Meyer, reviewing a book in *Wisconsin Lutheran Quarterly*, 33 (July 1936), p 219.
10. This is a reference to the historic "Minneapolis Theses," Wolf, *Documents*, pp 340-342.
11. *Wisconsin Synod Proceedings*, 1929, pp 86-87.
12. These papers can be found in the respective *ULCA Proceedings*. Wolf, *Documents* presents them on pp 346-359.
13. *ULCA Proceedings*, 1934, pp 415-417. Wolf, *Documents*, pp 356-357.
14. The essay appears in *Wisconsin Synod Proceedings*, 1935, pp 17-46.
15. A collection of these articles that appeared originally in *Northwestern Lutheran* were put out in pamphlet form under the title, "Where Do We Stand?"
16. The convention resolution is found in *Wisconsin Synod Proceedings*, 1935, pp 107-109.
17. This translation of the "Thiensville Theses" is from Koehler, *Wisconsin Synod History*, p 239. He was not a participant and is unenthusiastic in his description, pp 238-239. Valuable background material is available in "Basic Documents in the Church and Ministry Discussions" in *Faithful Word*, 7, 1 (pp 23-31) and 2 (pp 10-21), a report that is obviously from the other side of the Synodical Conference backyard fence.
18. The reference is to the first section of Chapter 10.

Chapter 17. In The Great Depression and World War II

1. *Wisconsin Synod Proceedings*, 1933, pp 111-114.
2. For this and the next item see chapter 14, pp 162-163.
3. A strong case for Bergemann can be made in the matter. If the issue involved reporting about parental access to the original faculty expulsion meeting, as the writer assumes, he deems it significant that at the follow-up Conference meeting Pastor Bergemann brought as his witness a pastor and parent involved. This is not to accuse Karl Koehler of misrepresentation of his own. He heard a report and may have reacted most honestly. Bergemann's witness, however, dealt directly and privately with President Kowalke who does not discuss the issue in his book.
4. See chapter 13, pp 148-149.
5. The WELS monetary stewardship is described in the first issue of the *WELS Historical Institute Journal*, pp 24-40.
6. The writer heard President Bergemann use that sermon introduction on several occasions.
7. *Wisconsin Synod Proceedings*, 1931, p 9.
8. Ibid., 1933, p 14.

9. Ibid., 1929, p 121.
10. Ibid., pp 56-57.
11. See pp 30-31 of the writing cited in note 5 for details.
12. *Wisconsin Synod Proceedings,* 1927, p 51.
13. Ibid., 1929, p 104.
14. The historically oriented writer could tear his hair and gnash his teeth at the thought that there is no full collection of the bulletins available. Some of his seminary classroom notes are written on the clean back page of the bulletins but unfortunately they are all of a single issue of the series of 17 bulletins. Even the writer, Edgar Hoenecke, does not have a full set.
15. The "young pastor" was of course Edgar Hoenecke, whose account is being quoted extensively. Like John, Edgar Hoenecke does not like to mention his own name. After service on the debt retirement committee he served on the board for the Apache mission and eventually became the first executive secretary of synod's board for world missions.
16. The long quotation comes from an unpublished article by Edgar Hoenecke with the title, "The Development of the Information and Stewardship Program in the Michigan District." The quotation is on pp 5-7 of the mimeographed copy in this writer's files.
17. *Wisconsin Synod Proceedings,* 1937, p 14. The debt retirement report is on p 20.
18. Ibid., 1939, p 53.
19. Ibid., 1941, pp 12 and 67.
20. Ibid., 1943, pp 49 and 56.
21. Ibid., 1945, p 38. This is the location for statistics that appear in the next paragraph.
22. Ibid., 1937, p 16.
23. Ibid., p 55.
24. Ibid., 1939, pp 67-68.
25. Ibid., 1941, pp 43-44.
26. Ibid., 1943, pp 30-31 and 71. The Schweppe pamphlet is "The Government Chaplaincy: An Appraisal."

Chapter 18. Break with Missouri

1. Missouri's Vice-President R. Wiederaenders was making this point already in a 1963 paper to Missouri's Council of Presidents and Seminary Faculties. See the 1.24.74 - 9 release from the Missouri Public Relations Department. *No Room in the Brotherhood,* the apology for the 1974 Concordia Exile, approves, p 354.
2. *American Lutheran Church Proceedings,* 1938, p 255.
3. *Missouri Proceedings,* 1938, pp 231-233, contains the full report. Many

regard this action of the Missouri Synod as marking a sharp turning point in its long history.
4. The full report is found in *Wisconsin Synod Proceedings*, 1937, pp 59-61.
5. See chapter 17, pp 195-197.
6. *Missouri Proceedings*, 1944, pp 251-252.
7. See Chapter 10, p 112, for an earlier discussion of the issue.
8. *Synodical Conference Proceedings*, 1940, p 91.
9. Ibid., 1944, pp 99-104.
10. Ibid., 1946, p 61.
11. This quotation and the one following are from *Wisconsin Synod Proceedings*, 1953, p 104 note.
12. Ibid., 1953, pp 102-106.
13. *Synodical Conference Proceedings*, 1954, pp 17-111.
14. The reference is of course to Drs. Jacob and Robert Preus.
15. *Wisconsin Synod Proceedings*, 1955, pp 85-88.
16. Ibid., 1956, pp 52-61.
17. Ibid., 1957, pp 130-136.
18. Ibid., p 144.
19. *Synodical Conference Proceedings*, 1960, p 46.
20. The four fellowship statements are attached to the 1960 *Synodical Conference Proceedings*. The Missouri statement referred to in the next paragraph is on pp 15-47 of the attachment.
21. *Wisconsin Synod Proceedings*, 1959, p 195.
22. *Synodical Conference Proceedings*, 1961, p 15.
23. The historic 1961 resolutions are found in *Wisconsin Synod Proceedings*, 1961, pp 197-200.

Chapter 19. Into All the States

1. A more complete treatment of this subject can be found in Norman Berg's "Home Mission Moods and Modes—125 Years in WELS" in *Wisconsin Lutheran Quarterly*, 73 (October 1976), 250-267.
2. *Wisconsin Synod Proceedings*, 1941, p 24. It is interesting to note that in our day with its decline in birthrate and emphasis on evangelism the ratio of adult to children confirmations is not as high as the instances cited for 1941.
3. Ibid., 1937, pp 59-60 and 1939, pp 12 and 20.
4. Ibid., 1941, pp 78-79.
5. Ibid., 1963, p 232.
6. Ibid., 1953, pp 50-51.

7. See chapters 21 and 22.
8. *Michigan District Proceedings*, 1954, p 67.
9. Ibid., p 99.
10. See chapter 8, pp 1-2.
11. Much of the detail in this California section was researched by Frederick A. Voss for his paper, "A Study of the WELS in the California Mission Field," in the Seminary Library's vertical file.
12. *Wisconsin Synod Proceedings*, 1951, p 35.

Chapter 20. Into All the World

1. *Wisconsin Synod Proceedings*, 1951, p 54.
2. Ibid., 1945, p 34.
3. The writing of John Meyer is contained in the Debt Retirement Bulletin series in Bulletin 20, dated July 1935.
4. This committee report is found in unpublished writings of Edgar Hoenecke and Arthur Wacker that supply background for much of the material in these paragraphs.
5. *Wisconsin Synod Proceedings*, 1947, p 51.
6. Edgar Hoenecke, "The WELS Forty-niners" in *WELS Historical Institute Journal*, 3, 1 (Spring 1985), 3-67.
7. *Reports and Memorials*, 1953, p 36.
8. See *Wisconsin Synod Proceedings*, 1955, pp 43-49.
9. Ibid., 1953, pp 50-51.
10. *Reports and Memorials*, 1953, p 36.
11. *Wisconsin Synod Proceedings*, 1957, p 41.
12. Ibid., pp 63 and 65. The same *Proceedings*, pp 70-72, provides a lengthy discussion of the problem in the Japanese field.
13. Ibid., 1961, p 62.
14. *Reports and Memorials*, 1965, p 75.
15. *Northwestern Lutheran*, 1982, pp 120-121.
16. *Report to the Ten Districts*, 1982, p 80.
17. A special and complete history of the WELS world mission fields is: Theodore Sauer, ed., *To Every Nation, Tribe, Language and People* (Milwaukee: Northwestern, 1992).
18. *Wisconsin Synod Proceedings*, 1959, pp 37-39.
19. Ibid., 1961, p 42.
20. *Reports and Memorials*, 1977, p 85.
21. Ibid., 1985, pp 87-92.
22. Ibid., 1979, pp 122-123.
23. Ibid., p 123.

24. Interesting detail is supplied in Edgar Hoenecke's report in *Reports and Memorials,* 1969, pp 74-76. Background for the next paragraph on India is found on pp 76-78.
25. *Wisconsin Synod Proceedings,* 1975, p 95.
26. See an earlier chapter, "Missions Old and Missions New," pp 164-168.
27. See Duane K. Tomhave's "Synods of Mission-Minded Confessional Lutherans" in *Wisconsin Lutheran Quarterly* 86 (Spring 1989), pp 105-130.

Chapter 21. Three Decades of Progress and Problems in Education

1. In 1962 school problems forced the calling of a special synodical convention. As the foreword of the *Wisconsin Synod Proceedings* of that convention put it: "The delegates searched diligently for a God-pleasing solution to the problem confronting the Synod regarding the need for expansion in our worker training schools."
2. *Wisconsin Synod Proceedings,* 1959, pp 104-105.
3. The lengthy report is contained in *Report to the Nine Districts,* 1964, pp 26-49.
4. *Wisconsin Synod Proceedings,* 1969, pp 108-109.
5. Informative and very interesting descriptions of these developments are supplied in pertinent chapters in Morton Schroeder's informal history of DMLC, *A Time to Remember* (New Ulm MN: Dr. Martin Luther College, 1984).
6. *Report to the Eight Districts,* 1952, p 53.
7. *Wisconsin Synod Proceedings,* 1962, p 57.
8. *Report to the Twelve Districts,* 1984, p 17.
9. A growth part of such a cycle may already be underway. The National Center for Health Statistics reported, in a *USA Today* front page story of April 9, 1991, that 1990's 4.2 million births surpassed the total of 1964, the last year of the previous baby boom. The report suggests that the 1957 high of 4.3 million births will soon be equaled.
10. *Reports and Memorials,* 1951, pp 45-46.
11. Ibid., 1953, p 54.
12. *Wisconsin Synod Proceedings,* 1953, p 132.
13. Ibid., pp 82-86.
14. For more details see E. E. Kowalke's *Centennial Story* (Northwestern College, 1965), pp 205-210.
15. This report of the so-called "Blue Ribbon Committee" is included in the 1965 *Wisconsin Synod Proceedings,* pp 109-131. The quotation is on the third page of the report.
16. *Wisconsin Synod Proceedings,* 1979, p 77.
17. *Northwestern Lutheran,* August 6, 1978, p 257.

18. There was also very limited Wisconsin involvement in the Detroit Lutheran High School, but so limited that it is not included in the count.
19. Much of the detail for this and subsequent material is found in two articles in *Lutheran Educator,* December 1960 (pp 9-10) and February 1961 (pp 11-12). The first, "The Lutheran High School in Our Synod," was written by Principal Harold Warnke of Fox Valley Lutheran High School and the second, "Lutheran High Schools," by Walter Hoepner of the Winnebago Lutheran Academy faculty.
20. *Wisconsin Synod Proceedings,* 1949, p 55.
21. *Reports and Memorials,* 1989, p 107.

Chapter 22. Synodical Administration

1. Long before its time, President Streissguth was advocating a full-time office combining presidential and visitor duties. See *Wisconsin Synod Proceedings,* 1867, p 6.
2. Ibid., 1957, p 22 and 1959, pp 24-28 and 35-39.
3. *Reports and Memorials,* 1969, p 114. A search for a notice or report on the seminar in the *Northwestern Lutheran* turned up nothing. The subsequent quote is found on p 125.
4. *Northwestern Lutheran,* November 15, 1984, p 333.
5. *Reports and Memorials,* 1969, p 124.
6. *Wisconsin Synod Proceedings,* 1969, pp 165-166.
7. *Northwestern Lutheran,* September 27, 1981, p 314.
8. *Wisconsin Synod Proceedings,* 1961, p 209.
9. Ibid., 1965, p 374.
10. An English version is presently being prepared.
11. The periodical celebrated its own seventy-fifth anniversary in 1989 by running a series of historical articles by Professor Morton Schroeder in the issues of March 15, May 1, June 15, September 1, October 15, and December. In the interim between the editorships of Franzmann and Wicke, Professor Wilbert R. Gawrisch was the acting editor.
12. *Wisconsin Synod Proceedings,* 1961, pp 259-262.
13. Ibid., p 261.
14. Ibid., pp 263-265.

Chapter 23. The Mischke Years and Beyond

1. *Northwestern Lutheran,* July 22, 1979, pp 230, 232-233 and 246.
2. President's *Newsletter,* dated June 1979, p 2.
3. *Northwestern Lutheran,* July 22, 1979, p 233.
4. "The Money Convention," by James P. Schaefer in *Northwestern Lutheran,* September 16, 1976, p 302.

5. *Wisconsin Synod Proceedings*, 1981, p 138.
6. Ibid., 1985, p 47.
7. Ibid., pp 43-48.
8. Ibid., 1979, p 93.
9. Ibid., 1983, p 90.
10. These theses are to be found in *Reports and Memorials*, 1979, pp 5-16.
11. *Wisconsin Synod Proceedings*, 1979, p 87.
12. Ibid., 1981, p 59.
13. Ibid., 1985, pp 50-51.
14. Ibid., 1981, pp 77-78.
15. Ibid., 1987, p 95.
16. Ibid., 1989, pp 55-59.
17. *Report to the Twelve Districts*, 1990, pp 119-124.
18. *Luther's Works*, 30:55

INDEX

Aaberg, Theodore, 283
Accreditation, 281
Ackermann, Adolph, 129, 138, 151, 283
Adascheck, George, 80, 98, 99
Adelberg, Reinhold, 39, 44, 54, 62, 275
Adickes, Robert, 246
Adrian, MI, 8, 21, 84, 213, 271
Africa, 5, 30, 72, 73, 75, 101, 168, 169, 219, 221-225, 229, 231, 233, 259, 286
Ahlers, Bruce, 231
Ahnapee, WI, 13
Akagami, Wakichi, 228
Alabama, (state), 217
Alaska, (state), 217
Alberta, 217
Albrecht, Christian J., 4, 25, 29, 84, 94, 311
Albrecht, Immanuel, 168, 177
Albrecht, Richard, 125, 130, 147
Albuquerque, NM, 217
Allenton, PA, 275
Allwardt, Henry A., 59, 61, 111, 275
Altes und neues, 60
Althoff C., 60
American Lutheran Church (ALC), 119, 179, 185, 199, 200, 202, 204, 208, 288
Amling, W. H., 98

Amtslehre, 110, 280
Analogy of Faith, 111, 112, 116, 117
Anchorage, AK, 217
Andrespol, Poland, 165
Angerstein, Pastor in Poland, 165
Antichrist, 181, 206
Antigua, 217
Apache, 38, 97, 98, 100-128, 166, 167, 170-172, 212, 219, 228, 245, 255, 258, 279, 286, 288
Appleton, WI, 152, 242, 244, 248, 258
Archives, 258, 270
Arizona Lutheran Academy, 246-248, 258
Arizona-California District, 140, 216, 246, 252
Arkansas, (state), 217
Arlington, 176
Armed forces, 135-137, 143, 194, 197, 226, 233
Armstrong, MN, 60
Arofino, ID, 216
Ashford, WI, 14, 31, 71
Asia, 5, 101, 225, 230, 231
Atonement, 182, 206, 255
Aufderheide, Herman, 151
Augsburg Church, 165, 167
Augsburg Confession, 12, 40, 44, 101, 180, 182
Augsburg Synod, 104

Augustana Synod, 22
Australia, 10, 232
Austria, 4, 7
Ave-Lallemant, R., 141

Bachelor degree, 236, 249
Bachman, E. Theodore, 271
Backer, Harold, 257
Baczanski, Nell, v
Bading, John, 3, 13, 15, 16, 27, 29-31, 34, 35, 37, 40-42, 44-47, 50-52, 54, 55, 58, 60, 62-65, 67, 68, 70, 79, 87-91, 101, 125-127, 134, 135, 138, 187, 189, 261, 270, 272, 273, 275-278, 314
Baer, A., 213
Baer, George, 169, 213
Bailiwick, 159, 187
Bakken, Richard, 248
Balge, Richard, 278, 284
Baltimore, MD, 7, 8, 70, 179, 217, 272
Bangor, WI, 243
Baptisms, 64, 90, 99, 168, 225-227, 266
Barington, WI, 70
Barmen, 3-8, 10, 27, 32, 68, 72, 157, 166, 269, 270
Barre, VT, 217
Basel, 2-4, 10, 11, 15, 18, 19, 27, 70, 71, 103, 157, 166, 271
Bauer, E. A., 275

295

Bauer, Wm., 177
Baumann, J. R., 122, 123, 147, 177
Bavaria, 18
Baxmann, Wayne, 247
Bay City, MI, 134, 135, 214, 243
Bay Pines, MI, 214,
Beamtentum, 155
Beaver Dam, WI, 66, 71, 72, 103, 156-158, 161
Becker, Siegbert, 232, 235
Beckley, WA, 217
Beitz, William, 156, 158-162, 284, 285
Beleuchtung, 160, 161, 285
Belgium, 233
Belle Plaine, MN, 127, 258
Beloit, WI, 61, 111
Bennett Law, 81, 85-89, 144
Bennett, Michael, 85
Bente G. Fr., 280
Benton Harbor, MI, 246
Bequest, 127, 240
Berg, E., 120
Berg, Norman, 212, 218, 286, 289
Bergemann, Gustav E., 83, 94, 109, 125, 126, 131, 134-136, 138, 141, 146, 147, 150, 187-189, 192, 250, 261, 276, 282, 287
Berlin Mission Society,, 10, 14, 15, 30, 32, 33, 36, 37, 71, 102, 157, 166
Berlin-Zehlendorf, 165, 167
Bernhausen, Germany 7
Betbrueder, 141, 142
Bethany, 223
Bethel Church, Milwaukee, 105
Bethesda, 165
Bible, 2, 3, 7, 13, 59-61, 64, 86, 99, 107, 109, 111, 117, 140, 155, 156, 224-226, 228, 231, 232, 256, 263-266, 284
Biblical, 36, 51, 114, 126, 199, 200, 226, 254

Birkholz, Jerome, 248
Bivens, Forrest, 266
Blacks, Mission to, 55, 80, 129, 168, 169
Blauert, F., 177
Blauert, Karl, 247
Bliefernicht, Edmund R., 129, 147, 220
Bloomfield, WI, 71
Blue Ribbon Committee, 236, 264, 291
Bluemound Rd., 236, 244, 249
Blumer, 23
Bocler, O. C., 168
Bodamer, William, 94, 103, 147, 159, 167, 177
Boehner, C. F., 94, 103
Boehringer, John, 228
Boessling, Sophia, 127
Boettcher, C., 141
Boettcher, H., 177
Bogota, Columbia, 230
Bohemia, 4
Bolle, C., 130
BORAM, 135
Borgwardt, Wayne, 242
Boundaries, 27, 53, 56, 97, 128, 131, 137, 184, 245
Bowdle, SD, 142
Bradenton, FL, 214
Braeuer, I., 94, 120
Brandt, 22
Braska, 121
Braun, C., 71
Brazil, 230, 267
Brenner, John, 125, 126, 138, 147, 148, 180, 181, 187, 189-191, 193, 195, 201, 220, 221, 250, 254, 261, 263, 283, 314
Brenner, Ph., 34, 80, 98
British Columbia, 217
Brobst, Samuel, 275
Brockmann, J., 34, 65, 73, 80
Brohm, Theodore, 58, 84
Brookfield, WI, 236
Brumder, George, 66, 88, 90, 276
Buehren, W., 70

Bues Farm, 148
Buffalo Synod, 9, 10, 21, 22, 26-28, 45, 91, 177, 179, 272
Bunge, Martin, 111
Burk, G. T., 129
Burk, Milton, 246
Burlington, WI, 14, 50, 70, 257
Burr Oak, WI, 13, 70
Buuck, Theodore, 190

Caledonia, WI, 7, 69, 70
California, 80, 101, 212, 214-216, 218, 246, 248, 290
Callicoon, NY, 8
Calumet, WI, 30, 31, 50, 70, 71
Calvinists, 176
Cameroon, 225
Campion School, 241
Cape Girardeau, MO, 114
Carlsson, Erland, 22
Casadora, Chief, 99
Catechism, 31, 99, 125, 168, 180, 226, 263, 264, 281
Catholic, Roman, 6, 27, 70, 85-88, 124, 165, 180, 219, 246, 249
Centennial, 220, 223, 234, 237, 243, 260, 270, 272, 276, 277, 282-284, 291
Chang, Peter, 313
Chaplain, 135-137, 194-197, 200, 201, 203, 206, 233, 283, 298
Cherney, Kenneth, 230
Cheyenne, WY, 216
Chicago, IL, 9, 22, 26, 54, 89, 128, 178, 179, 203, 286
China, 100, 103, 168, 222, 231
Chorales, 73
Chrischona, Saint, 2-4, 20, 23, 72, 94
Christgau, F., 177
Christmas, 62, 97, 166
Church of the Lutheran Confession (CLC), 198, 207, 208, 225

INDEX

Church-state, 89, 167
Cincinnati Case, 107, 108, 280, 284
Clausen, Claus, 22
Collinsville, IL, 128, 129
Colloquy, Iowa-Missouri, 46, 47
Colombia, 230
Colome, SD, 120
Colorado, (state), 211, 216
Columbia, SC, 217
Columbus, MI, 217
Columbus, OH, 275
Columbus, WI, 31, 70-72, 98
Concord, CA, 215
Concord, WI, 72
Concordance, to Book of Concord, 256
Concordia Seminary, St. Louis, 56, 82, 244, 275
Condemnation, 35, 162
Confessionalism, 10-13, 15, 20, 24, 28, 29, 31, 32, 34, 38, 40, 41, 49, 50, 55, 66, 68, 78, 126, 134, 138, 165, 181, 195, 196, 198, 202, 206, 232, 233, 261, 268, 272, 291
Confessions, 12, 13, 19, 20, 27-31, 40, 41, 44, 46, 55, 63, 78, 101, 120, 121, 180-183, 198, 201-204, 207, 225, 261, 268
Confirmations, 64, 210, 226, 289
Connecticut, 217
Conrad, J., 28, 29, 62, 70
Constitution, WELS, 12, 13, 27, 28, 32, 41, 42, 66, 96, 128, 131, 142, 269, 270, 273, 279
Contribution(s), 3, 6, 24, 60, 114, 115, 117, 126, 186, 192, 193, 221, 228, 249, 253, 256
Conversion, 55, 59, 60, 82, 107, 111, 112, 119, 121, 175, 176, 178, 179, 206
Cook, Missionary, 98, 279
Coolidge Dam, 170
Coordinating Council, 252, 266
Cornerstone, 95, 234, 243, 278
Counselors Friendly, 230-232
Cox, Raymond, 225
Cracy, 251
Craemer, Fr., 18
Crete, IL, 248
Cronenwett, G., 18
Cross-cultural, 266
Cudahy, WI, 189
Curzon Line, 97, 164
Custer, George A., 79
Cutbacks, 221, 250, 262, 263
Cuyaba, Africa, 224

Dakota, 32, 120, 122, 128, 141, 142, 149, 152, 216, 239, 261, 283
Dakota-Montana District, 140-142, 152, 210, 252
Dam, 66, 71, 72, 103, 117, 156-158, 161, 170
Damann, 52
Danube, MN, 243
Dasler, A., 167
Dawson, Dean, 247
Debt-retirement, 6, 106, 122, 131, 134, 186, 191
Deficits, 25, 106, 107, 188, 191, 253, 262, 263
Definite Platform, 40
Deindoerfer, John, 28, 272
Delaware, (state), 217
Delegates, 19, 20, 23, 29, 38, 41, 43, 60-62, 79, 95, 109, 121, 123, 130, 134, 135, 141, 142, 187, 190, 194, 203, 204, 240, 262, 291
Denkschrift, 54, 275
Denninger, A., 34
Depression, 3, 25, 63, 89, 134, 142, 148, 149, 151, 152, 170, 174, 185-187, 189-191, 193, 211, 221, 238, 250, 255, 261, 287
Detroit, MI, 19, 111, 112, 173, 174, 190, 203, 266, 280, 291

Diehlmann, C., 71
Discipline, 53, 66, 109, 144, 155, 156, 160, 162, 184, 192, 206, 263
Dispensary, Medical, 224, 259
Districts, 26, 93, 119, 131, 132, 140, 142, 149, 155, 187, 192, 211, 236, 246, 252, 254, 265, 274, 290, 291, 293
Dobberstein, Elmer, 246
Dodge Co., 31, 69, 70
Dohaschtida, 101
Dornfeld, E. G., 109
Doughboys, 136
Dourades, Brazil, 230
Dowidat, Ch., 61, 80, 98
Downer College, 82
Draeger, Gilbert, 247
Dreves, Missionary, 79, 80
Drevlow, Otto, 223, 224
Drews, Daniel, 271
Dr. Martin Luther College, (DMLC), 129, 145, 220, 236-239, 241, 272, 283, 291, 311
Duborg, H., 71
Dumser, Missionary, 19
Dupont, WA, 247

East Fork, AZ, 100, 171, 245, 248, 258
Eberhardt, Christoph, 3, 19, 21, 44, 85
Ebert, L., 4
Edmonton, AK, 217
Eggebrecht, 147
Eggert, Kurt, 264
Eggert, Ruppert, 230
Ehlke, Roland C., v, 258
Eickmann, Martin, 130
Eimermann Park, 82
Eitzen, MN, 129
Ekong, Jonathan, 168
Elberfeld, Germany, 4
Eldorado, WI, 72
Election-conversion debate, 59, 113, 175, 178
Elementary schools, 5, 86, 143, 227, 234, 237, 238, 243, 245, 248
Elkhorn, WI, 63

297

El Paso, TX, 229
Elroy, WI, 161, 162, 285
ELS, 201, 203, 206, 207, 232, 283
Emanuel Church, Fairfax, MN, 260
Emanuel Church, St. Paul, MN, 245
Emmel, Ludwig, 4, 47
Engel, Armin, 270, 282
Engel, Otto, 165-167, 243
English, 1, 2, 6, 11, 15, 23, 39, 46, 55, 56, 76, 81, 83, 85, 86, 88, 98, 101, 108, 114, 115, 125, 139, 140, 146, 230, 264, 275, 283, 292
Enrollment, 82-84, 100, 104, 123, 129, 133, 148, 151, 234, 235, 237-240, 244, 245, 248, 249, 266
Ephesians, 46, 111
Episcopalians, 103
Erdmann, Illinois Synod President, 54
Erlangen, 5
Erline, 23
Ernst, August, 16, 26, 39, 54, 83, 88, 94, 106, 110, 112, 125, 126, 128, 130, 145, 147, 184, 243, 310
Eschatology, 206
Essmann, Harold, 224
Europe, 3, 16, 44, 65, 83, 91, 101, 136, 164, 165, 195, 270
Evangelical, 1, 4, 7, 8, 10-13, 18, 19, 23, 29, 40, 46, 61, 119, 131, 139, 142, 178-180, 192, 200, 223, 227, 232, 233, 263, 271
Evangelism, 3-5, 14, 67, 72, 79, 123, 165, 167, 168, 172, 174, 209, 219, 225, 231, 266, 289
Evergreen LHS, 246-248
Evolution, 155
Excommunication, 53, 107-109, 184
Exegesis, 110, 116, 117, 265
Expatriate Missionaries, 224, 225, 228
Extension, Church, 173, 194, 212, 214, 216, 257, 258, 262

Fachtmann, George, 13-15, 23, 24, 33, 46, 52, 71, 270
Fair, 158, 197, 219
Fairfax, MN, 260
Faith-life, 161, 162, 273, 279, 284, 285
Falk, Roger, 228
Farmington, WI, 35, 72
Federation, 1, 3, 18, 21, 24-26, 47, 54, 55, 78, 91-99, 101-107, 111, 117, 119-123, 125-131, 134, 135, 137, 144, 217, 233, 250, 278, 279, 281-283
Fellowship, v, 11, 20, 21, 24, 29, 34-36, 42-45, 47, 49, 53, 59, 61, 66, 68, 91, 106, 107, 112, 138, 156, 158, 162, 163, 180-183, 185, 190, 198-207, 216, 225-227, 229, 231-233, 257, 280, 289
Fenske, James, 211, 246
Fenske, R. A., 243
Festerling, Howard, 231
Fick, Herman, 54, 272, 275
Fidei, (see *intuitu),* 286
Finance, 6, 16, 24, 25, 39, 81, 121, 133, 149, 150, 167, 186, 189-192, 194, 214, 221, 231, 249, 258, 261-263, 266, 277
Findlay, OH, 212
Finland, 232
Fleischmann, Robert, 258
Flint, MI, 123, 173
Florida, 191, 212-214, 216
Flunker, Charles, 230
Fond du Lac, WI, 67, 69, 71, 103, 135, 150, 152, 188, 190, 248, 251
Fords, Model T, 137
Forest, WI, 34, 178

Fort Atkinson, WI, 71, 72, 156, 157, 160, 245, 258, 278
Fort Wayne, IN, 20, 41, 42, 52, 54, 83, 84, 111, 112, 116, 202
Fortress Press, 271, 273
Forty-niners, 222, 290
Fountain City, WI, 34, 257, 258
Fox Valley LHS, 244, 248, 292
France, 136, 233
Francke, August H., 101
Frank, H., 147
Frankenhilf, MI, 28
Frankenmuth, MI, 18
Franzmann, Werner, 255, 256, 292
Fredrich, Edward, vi, 271
Freistadt, WI, 9
Fremont College, IA, 146
Fremont, WI, 163
Frey, Conrad, 231, 237, 243
Frey, I. P., 211
Frick, Ella Hesse, 272
Friedens Church, Kenosha, WI, 149, 150, 246, 284
Friesland, WI, 159
Fritschel, G., 46, 274
Fritschel, S., 46
Fromm, Elwood, 228
Fuerbringer, Ottomar, 50, 51
Fund-raising, 3, 16, 263
Fundamental Principles, 20, 41, 42, 44, 273

Galatians, 115, 158, 265, 281, 284
Galena, IL, 60, 61
Gallant, 186
Gamm, E. R., 283
Garden Grove, CA, 216, 246, 248
Gausewitz, Carl, 94, 109, 121, 122, 125, 127, 281
Gausewitz, Carl, (father), 13, 52
Gauss, John, 166, 192, 282
Gawrisch, Wilbert, 255,

292
Gaylord, MN, 175, 176
Gemeinde-blatt, 2, 24, 48, 50, 53, 66, 72, 96, 109, 139, 254, 255, 269-271, 275, 279, 284
Genesis, 73, 265
Gensicke, Traugott, 74
Georgia, 217
Gerberding, G., 20
German, 1-5, 8, 9, 12, 15, 18, 22, 23, 28, 37, 39, 40, 46, 55, 57, 67-69, 76, 80, 89, 114, 125, 135, 138-141, 144, 147, 164, 172, 209, 210, 254, 255, 269, 271, 275, 283
Germania, 88
Gettysburg School, 15, 24, 39
Geyer, 26
Ghana, 169
Gibbon, MN, 138
Gieschen, Claus, 146, 285
Gieschen, Waldemar, 116
Globe, AZ, 100, 170, 171
Globe, WI, 159
Goldammer, Carl, 13-15, 29, 62, 70, 101, 272
Goodhue, MN, 122, 123, 131, 261
Gospel, 8, 27, 35, 73, 86, 89, 99, 110, 113, 117, 118, 125, 136, 140, 171, 173, 178, 181, 186, 188, 189, 223, 226, 230, 231, 256, 259, 262
Gossner, John, 30
Grabau, John, 10, 91
Grace Church, Milwaukee, 8, 31, 64, 68-70, 106, 122, 125, 127, 142, 144, 167
Graebner, August, 60, 81, 82, 88, 114, 129, 282
Grand Rapids, WI, 173, 243
Granville, WI, 1, 8, 11-13, 24, 28, 29, 39, 46, 69, 70, 106, 272
Grasshopper Plague, 25
Greensboro, NC, 168
Greve, Edgar, 169, 224,

246
Griebling, O., 98
Grossmann, G. M., 46
Gruber, G. F., 120
Gruber, J., 60, 61
Gruber, R., 120
Guenther, Carl, 99, 100
Guenther, Edgar, 170, 171
Guenther, Martin, 58
Guetersloh, 274
Gumm, Charles, 230
Guntur, India, 22
Gurgel, Karl, 218
Gutachten, 158-162
Guymon, OK, 217

Haak, 74
Haase, Henry, 100, 177
Habben, Albrecht, 223, 224
Habben, Kermit, 228
Habeck, I., 279
Haberkorn, Daniel, 228
Haccius, George, 273
Hagedorn, Harold, 218
Halle University, 3, 14, 17, 35, 82, 101, 102, 129
Hammond, MN, 71
Harders, Gust. A, 100, 101, 170, 171
Harms, Ludwig, 10, 30, 37
Hartford, CN, 217
Hartwick Seminary, 16
Hartwig, Th., 237
Hartwig, Th. (father), 98
Hattstaedt, W., 18
Hauge Synod, 119
Hausandachten, 116
Haven, Luther, 258
Hawaii, 217
Haymarket Riot, 89
Hazel, SD, 261
Headship, 265
Heathen, 3, 73, 80, 165, 219, 223, 225, 226, 228
Hebnken, Meta, 74
Heidelberg, 268
Heidenmission, 219
Heimerdinger, George, 21
Heins, John, 121
Helenville, WI, 14, 37, 44, 52, 65, 66, 70-74, 98,

251, 276
Henderson, MN, 71
Hendersonville, TN, 217
Hengstenberg, Ernst W., 270
Henkel, William, 147, 159, 161
Hennicke, F.,71
Hensel, Oswald, 159
Hermannsburg, 10, 15, 20, 30, 31, 37, 38, 45, 70, 75, 79, 270, 273, 277, 308
Herrmann, William, 128
Hertwig, August, 175,
Herzer, John, 53
Heyer, J. C. F., 14, 22, 23, 42, 46, 47, 52, 271
Heyn, Paul, 215, 216
Highland Hall, 240
Hillview Hall, 240
Hilpert F., 4
Hinnenthal G., 131
Hiroshima, 194, 220
Historical-critical, 117
Historical-grammatical, 117
Hitachi, Japan, 227
Hoan, Gov. Dan, 89
Hoard, Gov. William D., 85-87, 89, 278
Hochmuth, Robert, 215, 216
Hoeckendorf, J. M., 26
Hoelzel, Ph., 120
Hoenecke, Adolph, 13, 17, 34, 35, 41, 42, 46, 47, 51, 52, 54, 58-60, 63, 81, 82, 84, 90, 102, 105, 111-116, 126, 129, 243, 269, 276, 277, 310
Hoenecke, Edgar, 171, 193, 222, 226, 228, 229, 286, 288, 290
Hoenecke, Gerald, 123, 221
Hoenecke, Otto, 105, 147, 243, 254, 311
Hoenecke, Walter, 254
Hoepner, Walter, 292
Hoermann, Arthur, 283
Hoffman, Julius, 71
Hoffmann, Fredrich, 47

299

Hofius, G., 121
Holt, MI, 258
Homiletics, 17, 90, 113, 126
Hong Kong, 229-231, 312
Honolulu, HI, 217
Hook of the Kafue, 222, 223
Hopkins, MN, 247, 248
Horn, Henry E., 271
Hoyer, Prof. O., 95
Hubbard, Town, 51
Huber, D., 70
Huber, Director, 94
Huebner, Lloyd, 245
Hungary, 4
Hungry, 186
Huntsville, AL, 217
Huron Valley LHS, 246-248
Hustisford, WI, 71, 134, 189
Huth, William, 130
Hymnal, 67, 90, 263, 264, 268, 276

Ibaraki, Japan, 229
Ibesikpo, Africa, 168
Idaho, (state), 216, 217
Igarashi, Japan, 228
Illinois, (state), 15, 20, 25, 45, 49, 54, 60, 128, 216, 248, 257, 258
Immigrants, 2, 46, 68, 79, 80, 141, 172, 210
Impasse, 201, 205-207, 221
Inbusch, H., 41
India, 22, 101, 168, 231, 232, 290
Indiana, (state), 20, 217
Indianapolis, IN, 217
Indians, 14, 18, 19, 79, 80, 96-99, 101, 135, 214, 220, 245, 279, 284-286
Indonesia, 230, 231
Inerrancy, 181, 199
Infant Baptism, 168
Informatorium, 28, 272
Inspiration, 127, 206, 286
Interchurch Relations (see Intersynodical), 3, 36-39, 41, 43, 45, 47, 48, 50, 78, 180, 203, 205, 273
Intersynodical Relations (see Interchurch), 3, 68, 78, 111, 116, 121, 174, 175, 177-181, 183, 200, 201, 244, 286
Intuitu, (see *fidei*), 286
Iowa Synod, 20, 41, 42, 45, 46, 60, 79, 111, 112, 176-179, 274, 276, 280
Iowa, (state), 28, 216
Iowa-Missouri Colloquy, 46
Iron Ridge, WI, 71
Isaiah, 73, 95, 116, 281
Isogogics, 114
Isolationism, 38, 55, 58, 179, 209

Jaalann, 101
Jackson, WI, 246, 248
Jacobs, E. C., 150, 271
Jacobs, Henry Eyster, 271
Jacobson, Gerald, 241
Jaekel, Theodore, 65, 122
Jaenicke, John, 30
Japan, 219, 223, 225-228, 290
Jefferson, WI, 14, 70, 72, 73, 151, 245
Jenera, OH, 123, 212
Jens, Rudolph, 100
Jerusalem Church, Milwaukee, 100
Jesaias II, 116, 254
Jeske, John, 266
Joecks, Larry, 247
Johl, Missionary Z., 141
Johne, Harold, 227, 228
Journal, 88, 96, 115-117, 145, 222, 255, 258, 270, 271, 275, 281, 285-287, 290
Juneau, WI, 260, 261
Junior Northwestern, 189, 255
Justification, 11, 50, 59, 109, 113, 160, 206

Kaiser, Howard, 214
Kalamazoo, MI, 173
Kannenberg, F., 177
Kansas, (state), 217
Kasischke, Emil, 243
Katzer, Archbishop, 86, 88
Kawkawlin, MI, 213
Keibel, Armin, 215
Kelm, Paul, 266
Kenosha, WI, 67, 70, 71, 149, 150, 246, 284
Kent, WA, 246, 248
Kenton, OH, 212
Kentucky, 217
Kettle Moraine LHS, 246, 248
Keturakat, M., 128
Kewaunee, WI, 116
Keyl, Ernst, 9
Kingston, WI, 167
Kionka, P., 94
Kirchengeschichte, 115, 254, 281
Kirschke, Gary, 231
Kittel, Hermann, 43, 60
Kleinhans, H., 181
Kleinlein, 60
Klindworth, J., 60
Klingmann, J., 94, 109
Klingmann, Stephan, 3, 4, 19
Knubel, F. H., 180, 184
Koch, Gerda, 157
Koch, H. W., 159
Koch, O., 98
Koehler, J. P., 1, 15, 50, 83, 89, 90, 109-111, 114-117, 125, 126, 130, 148, 155, 156, 159-162, 166, 177, 254, 269-282, 285, 287, 310
Koehler, Karl, 115, 156, 162
Koehler, Kurt, 166
Koehler, Philipp, 31, 51, 52, 71, 80, 134
Koeninger, Leonard, 189, 220
Koerner, Chrs., 88
Koester, C., 70
Kohl, John, 224
Kothe, John, 121
Kowalke, Erwin E., 130, 203, 243, 270, 277, 281-284, 287, 291
Krause, J. F., 9
Krause, Robert, 244
Krauss, F., 94, 103

Krauss, Karl, 123, 279
Krauth, Charles P., 41, 47
Kropp School, 20
Krueger Aileen, 169
Krug, L. C., 141
Kuhn, A., 4, 25, 47, 272, 275, 281
Kujath, Mentor, 255
Kurth, John, 232
Kusel, Daniel, 41
Kuske, David, 244, 264, 282
Kutz, 100

Lace, 258
LaCrosse, WI 14, 23, 43, 47, 60, 61, 70, 71, 161, 244, 257, 258, 261
Lahme, G., 141
Laity, 7, 21, 41, 106, 122, 129, 131, 151, 177, 193, 229, 256
Lakeside LHS, 244, 246, 248
Lange, A., 21, 34, 51, 58
Lange, Louis, 271, 272, 281
Langenberg, 4, 5, 7-9, 11, 15, 30, 32, 33, 36, 70, 71, 270
Language, 6, 46, 55, 56, 81, 85, 86, 97-100, 114, 117, 125, 139, 140, 146, 147, 164, 165, 171, 189, 209, 210, 221, 223, 227, 232, 290
Lansing, MI, 123, 173
Las Vegas, NV, 217
Latin, 150, 229, 230
Lauersdorf, Richard, 266
Law, 81, 85-89, 138, 144, 146, 160, 175, 180, 227
Lawrenz, Carl, 188, 221, 242, 262, 265
Lawrenz, John, 243
Lebanon-Ixonia, 25, 70
Lederer, C. A., 4, 94
Lee, Tmothy, 231
Leeds, WI, 71
Legalism, 116, 209
Lehninger, M., 120, 121, 177, 272, 286
Lehre und Wehre, 50, 113, 280
Leipzig, 233
Leyrer, Carl, 252
Library, v, 2, 33, 83, 147, 149, 194, 227, 238 241, 249, 270, 271, 273, 276, 284, 290
Lilongwe, Malawli, 259
Linsenmann, W., 4, 104
Lithuanians, 128, 129, 135
Little Rock, AR, 114, 217
Lochner, Fr., 18
Lodge, 20, 24, 42, 182
Lodz, Poland, 165-167
Loehe, J. K. W., 10, 18, 19, 114
Loeper, Carl, 214-216
Lomira, WI, 34, 70
London, 13
Louisiana, 196, 217
Louisville, KY, 217
Loy, Matthias, 49
Luebbert, E. L.,141
Luening, Julius, 254
Lukas, Paul, 43
Lumano, Africa, 224
Luna, David, 229
Lusaka, Africa, 222-225, 259
Luth, 274, 277
Luther, Martin 25, 80, 126, 129, 142, 144, 145, 147, 152, 159, 190, 193, 220, 227, 228, 234, 236-245, 248, 256, 258, 261, 264, 268, 272, 275, 281, 282, 291, 293
Lutheran Evangelical Christian Church (LECC), 227, 228
Lutheran-Reformed, 10, 24
Lutheraner, 28, 50, 52, 53, 272, 275
Lutz, Martin, 240

Madison, WI, 86, 176, 251
Madras, India, 231
Magdeburg, 7
Maine, 217
Malawi, Africa, 225, 259
Malchow, Daniel, 262
Male, 99, 144, 235
Mallison, W., 23
Mallman, Gerald, 246
Manchester, MI, 21, 84
Manitowoc, WI, 13, 14, 69-71, 115, 152, 240, 244, 247, 248
Mankato, MN, 54, 130, 142, 223, 283
Manthey, Marcus, 231
Maple Grove, WI, 69, 72
Mar Vista, CA, 215
Marggraf, Bruce, 230
Marquardt, Larry, 257
Marshall, MI, 103
Marshall, WI, 71
Marshfield, WI, 157, 161
Marti, Reuben, 257, 261
Martin Luther Preparatory School (MLPS), 159, 242, 248
Maryland, 217
Masewicz, Mrs. W., 257
Massachusetts, 217
Mayer, 94
Mayerhoff, Paul, 80, 98, 100
Mayfair Rd., 251, 253, 258
Mayhews, 171
Mayo, Will, 91
Medellin, Colombia, 230
Meier, Norbert, 227, 228
Meiss, Paul, 8, 11
Meister, Robert, 231
Memorials, 134, 135, 172-174, 192, 226, 240, 253, 258, 278, 290-293
Menominee, MI, 218
Menomonie, WI, 116
Mequon, WI, 118, 148, 183, 191, 205, 231, 238, 266, 278
Merna, SD, 120
Merrill, WI, 247
Methodists, 10, 11, 70
Metzger, G. W., 18
Meumann, Theodore, 35, 51
Mexico, 217, 229
Meyer Arthur, 245
Meyer, F. W., 255
Meyer, H., 177
Meyer, J. (father), 74, 77
Meyer, John, 77, 113, 127, 147, 159, 161, 220, 285, 286, 290,

301

308
Meyer, Robert, 169
Meyer v. Nebraska, 146
Michelson, Mrs. Meta Kilgas, 240
Michigan District, 133
Michigan Lutheran Seminary, 4, 21, 34, 84-94, 96, 97, 102-105, 123, 129, 147, 194, 203, 231, 238-241, 243, 271, 311
Michigan (state), 71, 248
Michigan Synod, 1, 3, 4, 14, 18-21, 40, 44, 45, 78, 85, 92-95, 102-104, 119, 120, 124, 131, 136, 144, 155, 172, 173, 278, 279, 283
Millennialism, 20, 42, 44-46
Milton, WI, 246, 249
Milwaukee, WI, 1, 2, 7-9, 11-15, 28, 34, 39, 43, 46, 50-52, 54, 55, 58, 62-64, 66-72, 79, 81, 82, 87, 88, 90, 95, 100, 102, 105, 106, 111, 112, 122, 124, 125, 127, 134, 138, 142, 144, 145, 150, 165, 167, 187, 189-191, 206, 207, 211, 215, 235-237, 242-244, 246, 248, 249, 251, 254, 258, 269, 270, 272, 277, 281-283, 286, 290
Ministerium, 1, 4, 6-8, 17, 24, 38, 39, 41-44, 250, 270, 280
Ministry, 21, 22, 24, 29, 33, 39, 66, 68, 75, 107, 110, 111, 114, 117, 135, 140, 142, 151, 184, 187-189, 195, 196, 202, 206, 233, 234, 257, 266, 267, 287
Minneapolis, 71, 178, 271, 274, 287
Minnesota District, 138, 142, 162, 271, 275, 283, 285, 286

Minnesota (state), 1, 3, 4, 14, 18, 20, 22-25, 39, 40, 42, 44, 46-49, 52-54, 60, 61, 78, 81, 84, 92-96, 98, 112, 119-122, 125, 127, 129, 131, 138, 140-142, 144, 145, 155, 162, 175-177, 211, 216, 223, 241, 247, 248, 252, 257, 258, 260, 261, 271, 272, 274, 275, 281, 283, 285, 286
Minnesota Synod, 4, 14, 22-25, 34, 39, 44, 46, 48, 52-54, 60, 84, 93, 94, 121, 122, 125, 127, 140, 141, 145, 176, 177, 211, 241, 271, 272, 275, 281, 286
Minnesota Valley LHS, 248
Mischke, Carl, 4, 188, 260-264, 266, 267, 292, 314
Mishicott, WI, 63
Missionaries, 4, 5, 7, 8, 14, 16, 18, 19, 22, 23, 32-34, 72, 75, 79, 98-101, 103, 128, 141, 169-173, 192, 195, 211, 213-215, 218, 219, 223-232, 259, 266, 267, 270, 279, 286
Missions, 3, 14, 72, 79, 80, 96-98, 101, 102, 122, 128, 130, 135, 142, 164, 165, 167, 172, 173, 192, 201, 209, 211, 212, 217, 219-222, 226, 228, 229, 232, 252, 259, 262, 266, 279, 285, 288
Mission Synod, 18
Mississippi, 14, 18, 52, 187, 217
Missouri Synod (LC-MS), 8-10, 19, 26, 27, 34, 48, 50-54, 60, 72, 106-110, 129, 131, 136, 146, 168, 170, 178, 179, 184, 185, 190, 194, 195, 198-204, 206, 207, 209, 211,

219, 225, 227, 233, 243, 256, 261, 274, 275, 280, 289
Missouri-Wisconsin, 50, 52, 243
Missourians, 184
Mito, Japan, 227
Mitra, Paul, 231
Mobridge, SD, 32, 142, 152, 238-241, 267
Moldehnke, Edward, 13-17, 33, 82, 129, 270
Moldenhauer, Adair, 247
Monatshefte, Brobst's, 275
Monhardt, E., 120
Monroe, MI, 18, 20
Montana, 140, 142, 216
Montello, WI, 71
Mosel, Town, WI, 71
Motzkus, William, 159
Moussa, A., 98
Moussa, Hans Kollar, 150-153, 267
Muehlhaeuser, John, 3-15, 24, 27-30, 32, 33, 38, 39, 41, 62, 64, 65, 68, 70, 119, 122, 134, 261, 269, 270, 272, 273, 276, 314
Mueller, Richard, 224
Muhlenberg College, 39
Multanowski, 51
Mundstock, Kenneth, 169
Muskego, WI, 22
Muskegon, MI, 173
Mwembezhi Lutheran Dispensary, 259

Nakamoto Menuhide, 228
Nashua, NH, 217
Nau, H., 168, 169
Nau, John, 286
Naumann, Justus, 94, 122, 123
Naumann, Oscar, v, 187, 203, 226, 256, 260-262, 314
Navaho, 98
Navy, 136, 137, 196, 197, 201
Nebraska, (state), 1, 18, 25, 26, 93, 94, 97, 119-121, 131, 146, 149, 155, 177, 211, 216, 223, 247, 248,

INDEX

252, 272, 281
Nebraska LHS, 247, 248
Neenah, WI, 72, 74
Neillsville, WI, 115, 162
Nemoto, 313
Neuendettelsau, 10, 18
Nevada, (state), 217
Newton, WI, 67, 70, 71
Newtonburg, WI, 13, 69
New Ulm, MN, 24, 25, 29, 66, 71, 94, 127, 133, 176, 193, 194, 204, 220
New Ulm School (see also Dr. Martin Luther College), 84, 85, 95, 114, 129, 130, 138, 145-147, 149, 151, 152, 177, 178, 188, 191, 192, 235-238, 240, 241, 247-249, 260, 272, 279, 291
Newville, WI, 243
Nicolaus, A. F., 157
Nicum, J., 270, 280
Nigeria, Africa, 164, 168-170, 219, 224, 229, 286
Nikimi, WI, 61
Niles, IL, 71
Nitz, Alma, Henry, 101, 220
Norfolk, NE, 25, 26
North-America, 77
Northern Wisconsin District, 64, 119, 122, 132, 133, 181, 254
Northland LHS, 247, 248
Northwestern College (NWC), 26, 32, 39, 41, 43, 62, 80, 81, 83, 94, 114-116, 123, 126, 128-130, 134, 135, 144, 145, 149, 151, 156, 157, 187, 189, 203, 220, 222, 239, 240, 242, 243, 261, 269, 270, 282, 291, 309
Northwestern Conference, 14, 31
Northwestern Lutheran, 67, 139, 189, 202, 227, 246, 247, 253-255, 260, 281-283, 287, 292, 293
Northwestern Lutheran Academy (NLA), 32, 152, 237, 239, 241-243
Northwestern Publishing House, v, vi, 1, 2, 90, 101, 251, 269, 270, 272, 276, 277, 281, 292
Northwestern Preparatory School, 32
Norwegian, 22, 25, 49, 53-57, 60, 61, 71, 119, 139, 168, 176, 178, 202
Notz, Eugene, 39, 81, 116
Notz, F. W., 83, 144, 145, 277
Notz, William, 84, 88, 128
Notzingen, Germany, 3-5
Nozomi, Japan, 227
Null, 212

Oakland, CA, 205
Oakwood, WI, 7, 8, 11
Oarai, Japan, 313
Oconomowoc, WI, 148
Oertel, Max, 5, 6
Offerings, 37, 38, 74, 80, 121, 191, 249, 253, 263, 266, 277
Officialdom, 155, 159
Ohio (state), 22, 107, 123, 212, 216, 280
Ohio Synod, 19, 20, 25, 40-42, 45, 49, 54, 56, 60, 61, 72, 111-113, 137, 175-179, 274, 275
Oklahoma, (state), 217
Old-Lutheran, 11
Onalaska, WI, 244, 248
Opgjor, 176
Opitz, A., 73
Ordained, 5-7, 12, 13, 30, 70, 106, 166, 168, 196, 230
Ordination, 135, 166, 167, 181, 265
Oregon, (state), 104, 216
Orphanage, 127, 171
Orthodox, 38, 43, 52, 53, 57, 80, 173, 216, 230
Orthodoxy, 47, 48, 52, 54, 105, 181, 199
Oshino, Fukuichi, 228

Oshkosh, WI, 50, 60, 61, 64, 71, 72, 81, 166
Osman, Loren, 278
Osterburg, Germany, 7
Ott, J. Henry, 83
Ott, Louis, 212-214
Outreach, 14, 21, 55, 79-81, 97, 101, 128, 141, 168, 186, 209, 212, 219, 221, 226, 231, 232
Overseas, 7, 33-35, 38, 40, 42, 65, 97, 110, 164, 165, 167, 168, 194, 205, 206, 219, 220, 223, 225, 232, 233, 259, 261, 262
OWLS, 258
Owosso, MI, 213

Pabst Farm, 82
Pacific Northwest District, 132, 133, 140-142, 211, 246, 252, 282
Palatine, IL, 257
Pamphlet, 110, 136, 159, 202, 204, 265, 271, 277, 285, 287, 288
Pankow, E. A., 94, 122
Pankow, Michael, 26
Papacy, 6
Parisius, Herbert, 157, 284
Parochial Schools, 87, 88, 144, 149, 157, 184, 235
Parsonage, 15, 19, 33, 74, 75, 77, 91, 120, 121, 213, 214, 227, 251, 262, 266, 269
Pasadena, CA, 214
Passavant, William, 20, 22, 39
Pastorale, 114
Pennsylvania, (state), 22-24, 38-42, 45, 46, 128, 217, 272, 275
Peridot, AZ, 99, 100, 171, 312
Peters, Oscar, 173
Peterson, Carl, 246, 247
Pfister and Vogel, 82
Pfotenhauer, Frederick, 108
Philadelphia, PA, 42, 128,

303

129, 271, 274
Philippians, 268
Phoenix, AZ, 246-248, 258
Pieper, August, 58, 83, 88, 90, 106, 113, 114, 116, 125, 126, 146, 159, 161, 254, 275, 281, 283, 285
Pieper, Franz, 110, 111
Pieper, J., 177
Pieper, Paul, 189
Pietists, 101
Pilgermission, 3
Pima Reservation, 98
Pioneers, Boys and Girls, 257
Pittsburgh, PA, 20, 39, 40, 44
Pittsfield, MA, 217
Plath, Roger, 231
Platteville, WI, 13, 45, 71
Plocher, J., 80, 98-100, 151
Pluess, Kasper, 11, 12, 70
Plymouth, MI, 222
Poetter, Richard, 227, 228
Poland, 97, 133, 164-168, 196, 219, 233
Polemics, 274
Polk, Town, WI, 71
Pomona, CA, 215
Pontiac, MI, 173
Pope, 87
Portland, ME, 217
Porto Rico, 230
Port Washington, WI, 69-71
Poughkeepsie, NY, 6
Praesidium, 40, 67, 180, 192, 252, 256
Prairie du Chien, WI, 96, 152, 159, 237, 241, 242, 248
Prayer, 12, 74, 107, 112, 121, 142, 176, 200, 206, 267, 280
Preaching, 5, 13, 14, 18-21, 23, 25, 26, 30, 33, 44, 72, 106, 132, 140, 141, 158, 178, 187-189, 224, 225, 229, 230, 233, 276
Presbyterians, 20, 98, 279
President-visitor, 67
Preus, Jacob and Robert, 289
Prohibition, 123, 124
Protes'tants, 128, 156, 158, 161-163, 187, 188, 250, 279, 284, 285
Prussian Union, 9, 27, 29, 35
Psalms, 40, 63, 276
Puerto Alegre, 230
Pupils, 133, 144, 146, 235

Quartalschrift, 96, 107, 110, 112-114, 116, 117, 280
Quebec, Canada, 217

Raasch, Martin, 141
Racine, WI, 7, 8, 13, 42, 43, 50, 51, 68-72, 243, 246
Radio, 227, 231
Raleigh, NC, 217
Rauschenbusch, Walter, 7, 8
Reading, PA, 41
Rechtfertigung, 113
Redlin, E., 120
Reede, Paul, 247
Reedsburg, WI, 43
Reedsville, WI, 71
Reformation, 9, 130, 140, 158, 175, 177, 245
Reformed, 6, 9, 10, 27-29, 31, 35, 38, 43, 45, 124, 140
Reformer, 256
Reim, C. G., 34
Reim, Edmund, 181, 201, 202, 204
Reim, Gottllieb, 3, 13, 14, 31, 64-68, 71, 261, 273, 276
Reim, Norbert, 169
Reiseprediger, 14, 15, 19, 33, 79, 211
Reitz, F. W., 4, 47
Released-time, 99
Remus, MI, 21
Renewal, 266
Renville, MN, 25
Renz, Edward, 214, 233
Republicans, 86, 87
Resurrection, 69, 171
Retzlaff, Frank, 193
Reuter, Elizabeth, 157
Reuter, F. A., 129
Rhine, 1-5, 7, 8, 10, 14, 269
Rhode Island, (state), 217
Rhodesia, 169, 170, 219, 222, 229
Rice County, MN, 22
Richfield, WI, 71
Richter, 5, 10
Ridgley, Fort, MN, 286
Rochester, NY, 6-8, 68
Rochester, MN, 91
Rock River, 156, 157, 189
Rockford, MN, 247
Roell, J., 71
Roepke, William, 210, 218
Roesener, P., 272
Rohr, Heinrich von, 91
Rohr, Philipp von, 90-92, 94, 95, 106, 109, 126, 134, 135, 261, 276, 278, 314
Romans, 204
Rosin, Henry, 170, 171, 286
Ruediger, Gerhard, 156, 160, 161
Rueter, A., 72
Russia, 16, 34, 87, 141, 168, 270

Sacramento, CA, 216
Sacraments, 11, 35, 172
Saginaw, MI, 21, 84, 85, 94, 97, 102-105, 114, 123, 129, 147, 194, 200, 204, 238, 239, 241, 258, 266, 271
Sala Land, Africa, 223, 224
Salem Church. Milwaukee, 69, 258
Saline, 21
Salzburgers, 87
San Carlos, AZ, 99, 100, 170, 171, 312
San Francisco, CA, 215, 216, 231
Sanctification, 11, 160
Sandusky Convention, 199
Santa Clara, CA, 215
Sauer, Chr., 88
Sauer, E., 147
Sauer, Elfrieda von Rohr, 278

INDEX

Sauer, Elmer, 115, 281
Sauer, J. J. E., 28, 29, 31, 71
Sauer, Theodore, 224, 228, 290
Sauer, William, 147
Savannah Declaration, 179, 180, 183
Scandinavian, 15, 22, 179
Schaefer, James, 253, 255, 258, 293
Schaefer, Wm. J., 255
Schaeffer, C. F., 39
Schaller, John, 58, 83, 90, 110, 114-117, 125, 126, 145, 147, 177, 188, 254, 310
Schaller, Loren, 254
Schaller, Winfred, 202
Scharf, Erwin, 196
Scheele, Roland, 211
Schenectady, NY, 217
Schieferdecker, George, 46
Schlacht, J., 177
Schlemmer, Peter, 286
Schlender, A. and H., 167, 286
Schlesingerville, 8
Schlicht, Robert, 258
Schlichten, A. and E., 107
Schlueter, E. Benjamin, 220
Schmid, Friedrich, 3, 4, 7, 18, 19, 271
Schmidt, Fredrich A., 54, 60, 61, 111
Schmidt, Wayne, 244
Schneider, Carl E., 72, 73, 271
Schoenberg, Otto, 100
Schofield, WI, 158
Schoof, N., 41
Schroedel, A., 94, 122
Schroeder, David, 232
Schroeder, Gary, 231
Schroeder, Morton, 245, 272, 283, 291, 292
Schuetze, Armin, 242, 269
Schultz, John, 181
Schultz, J. R., 247
Schulzeitung, 85, 96, 145
Schwan, Marvin, 249, 251
Schweppe, Carl, 130, 142, 196, 243, 288
Schweppe, William, 169, 224
Schwertfeger, 313
Science, 145, 236, 240, 246
Scio, MI, 136, 222
Scouting, 199, 200, 203, 206
Scripture, 2, 10, 12, 19, 55, 88, 110, 111, 113, 117, 124, 156, 177, 180-183, 185, 195, 199, 204, 206, 207, 232, 233, 265, 268
Sectarian, 44, 62
Secular, 150, 209, 257
Seebach, 7
Seeger, Richard, 226-228
Segregate, 182
Seiss, Joseph, 42
Seminole, FL, 214
Servicemen, 137, 223, 226
Shakopee, MN, 23, 84
Sheboygan, WI, 11, 13, 70, 71
Shiley, Harry, 221, 226
Shoreland LHS, 246, 248
Sibley County, MN, 175, 176
Siegler, C. W., 120
Siegler, Reginald, 243
Siegrist, J., 60
Sieker, J. Henry, 15, 24, 39, 46, 47, 53, 54, 272, 274
Sievert, K. G., 152, 243
Sihler, Wm., 83, 278
Sioux, 79
Slavery, 49, 73
Sleepy Eye, MN, 122
Slidell, LA, 217
Slinger, WI, 8, 12, 28, 29, 31, 63, 71
Slovaks, 169, 189, 202, 206, 221
Sonderlehre, 110
Sonntag, Richard, 256
Southeastern, Wisconsin District, 119, 211
Spangenberg, Richard, 169
Spehr, O., 76
Spittler, Ch. F., 2-4
Spokane, WA, 223
Sprengeler, Mark, 231
Sprengling, Ph., 71
Springfield School, 26, 45, 84
Springfield, MN, 61
Sprinter, The, 309
Sputnik, 145
St. Croix LHS, 245, 247, 248
St. John Church, Milwaukee, 34, 55, 64, 67, 69, 90, 125, 126, 129, 138, 189
St. Louis, MO, 10-17, 52, 54, 56, 58, 79, 81, 82, 84, 114-116, 145, 244, 271, 272, 276, 278, 281, 282, 286
St. Lukas Church, Milwaukee, 150, 191, 211
St. Matthew Church, Milwaukee, 64, 102, 107
St. Paul, MN, 10, 22-24, 39, 46, 53, 104, 121, 123, 136, 176-178, 251
St. Peter Church, Milwaukee, 62-64, 144
St. Petersburg, FL, 213, 214
Starck, Christian, 45, 71
Starr, Richard, 230
State-synod, 26, 56
Statistics, 64, 85, 88, 89, 132, 133, 135, 144, 154, 172, 175, 201, 207, 210, 217, 228, 235, 253, 276, 279, 283, 288, 291
Statu Confessionis, in, 202
Stellhorn, F. W., 59, 60, 84, 111
Stern, F. E., 141, 211
Stevensville, MI, 213
Stewardship, 121, 168, 191, 209, 251, 267, 287, 288
Stillwater, MN, 22, 23, 60, 61
Stoeckhardt, Goerge, 111, 116
Strassen, Karl, 51, 275
Streissguth, Wm., 3, 40, 41, 64-68, 71, 122, 250, 261, 276, 292
Suelflow, Roy, 278
Suffrage, 133, 282
Sumser, Pastor, 71

305

Sweden, 22, 232
Switzerland, 2
Syncretism, 176
Synergists, 176
Syracuse, 6

Tacoma, WA, 140, 247
Taiwan, 230, 231, 258
Tampa, FL, 214
Tarzana, CA, 215
Tennessee, (state), 217
Theobald, A., 166
Theological, Quarterly, 96, 254-256, 265, 269, 272-274, 276, 278-283, 286, 289, 291
Theologische Quartalschrift, 96, 107, 110, 112-114, 116, 117, 280, 282
Theses, 53, 54, 60, 63, 88, 110, 124, 176-179, 183, 184, 204, 265, 276, 281, 286, 287, 293
Thiele, Gottlieb, 54, 65, 82, 114, 115, 129
Thiensville, WI, 110, 148, 149, 183, 184, 191, 205, 238, 287
Thirties, 5, 170, 171, 174, 184, 211
Thompson, Bruce, 257
Thompson, William, 22
Thuebingen, 70
Thurow, G. M., 160
Tiefel, Frederick, 223, 225, 226, 266
Toepel, Martin, 243
Tokyo, 219, 221, 226
Toledo, OH, 18
Tomah, WI, 135
Tomhave, Duane, 228, 229, 291
Toppe, Carleton, 243, 310
Trautmann, Ph., 18
Trenton, Town, WI, 70
Trustees, Board of, 149, 189, 192, 215, 220, 226, 252
Tsuchiura, Japan, 227
Tucson, AZ, 215, 229
Tustin, CA, 246
Tutors, 130, 284
Twenties, 135, 143, 146, 148, 170-172, 174

ULCA-WELS, 182
Unchurched, 4, 6, 14, 33, 173
Ungrodt, B., 72, 74
United Lutheran Church in America (Ulca), 119, 179-184, 287
Unionism, 27, 28, 31, 34, 51, 52, 182, 195, 199, 201, 203, 204, 206, 272
Unity, 29, 35, 47, 51-58, 63, 112, 120, 121, 123, 159, 175-177, 179, 182, 199, 202, 205-207, 273, 274, 286
Uplegger, Alfred, 170, 171, 286
Uplegger, Francis, 170, 312
Uplegger, Johanna, 171
Urbanization, 174
Usury, 275
Utah, 217

Valleskey, David, 232, 266
Valleskey, Wilmer, 266
VEBA, 256
Vermont, 217
Version, Bible, 264
Vertz, Kenneth, 213
Vicars, 225, 231, 271
Vice, 220, 260, 266
Vice-president, 3, 65, 66, 68, 122, 127, 135, 288
Vietnam, 196
Virginia, (state), 217
Vision-2000, 267, 268
Vogel, Henry, 255
Vogel, Henry, Sr., 46
Vogt, John, 214
Vollmar, J., 60
Vorberg, G., 43, 65
Voss, Arthur, 201
Voss, Frederick, 290
Voss, Robert, 235, 242, 310
Voss, 144

Wacherhagen, Pres., 6
Wacker, Arthur, 103, 123, 220-222, 224, 290
Waco, NE, 247, 248
Wafers, Communion, 29, 31, 272
Wagner, A., 167
Wagner, M., 130
Wallmann, John, 10
Walther, C. F. W., 52, 55, 56, 58-60, 91, 116, 269, 275, 278, 280
Walz, 144
Warnke, Harold, 244, 292
Wartburg Hall, 240
Washington D. C., 137
Washington Declaration, 179, 182
Washington, (state), 70, 216, 223, 246, 247
Waterloo, WI, 63, 220
Watertown, WI, vi, 3, 13-18, 23-26, 30, 31, 34, 35, 38, 39, 45, 46, 48, 50-52, 57, 59, 62-66, 70, 73, 79, 81, 83, 84, 88, 94, 96, 111, 112, 114, 126, 129, 130, 142, 144, 145, 147, 149, 151, 152, 156, 157, 160, 161, 189, 193, 194, 204, 238, 239, 251, 285
Waukesha, WI, 89
Wausau, WI, 158, 247, 248, 258
Wauwatosa, WI, 82, 83, 90, 95, 96, 107, 109, 110, 113-118, 125, 129, 148, 158-160, 165, 170, 254, 277
Weimar, William, 83
Weindorf, Luther, 227, 228
Weinmann, John, 7-9, 11-13, 28, 29, 62, 70, 119, 269, 272
Weitbrecht, Gottlieb, 10, 11, 70, 270
Weitbrecht, John, 4
WELS, 1, 32, 119, 132, 216, 222, 224, 227-232, 235, 236, 246, 255, 257, 258, 270, 271, 275, 281, 285-287, 289, 290
WELS Historical Institute, 258
Wendland, Ernst, 130
Wendland, Ernst H., 224,

225, 227, 313
Wendland, Ernst R., 224
Werre, Alvin, 169
Wesel, Germany, 4
West Allis, WI, 257
Westendorf, Bernhard, 123
Westendorf, G., 94, 103
Westerhaus, G., 130
Westerhaus, Martin, v
Western Wisconsin District, 119, 156-160, 162, 187, 254, 260, 285
Westland, MI, 246, 248
Whitewater, WI, 214, 257
Wicke, Harold, 255, 292
Widows, 64
Wiechmann, Raymond, 211, 218, 247
Wiederaenders, R., 288
Wiedmann, Lynn, 276
Wier, W., 22, 272
Wiese, Mrs., 75, 76
Wilmington, DE, 217
Wilton, WI, 158, 161
Wimzheim, Germany, 2
Winchester, WI, 60, 61, 74, 75, 77
Winnebago Lutheran Academy, 150, 151, 243, 245, 248, 284, 292
Winona, MN, 81, 91, 126, 144, 251, 257
Winter, Venus, 229
Winterstein, Herbert, 228
Winthrop, MN, 176
Wischau, 270
Wisconsin Lutheran College (WLC), 235, 236, 242, 249
Witt, J., 120, 121, 147
Wittenberg Hall, 240
Woldt, Alfons, 235
Woldt, Fr., 72
Wolf, F. A., 141
Wolff, Fred, 151
Wollbrecht, Pastor, 54
Wood Lake, 122
Worker-training, 15, 16, 20, 21, 25, 52, 56, 59, 65, 67, 84, 94-97, 129, 130, 133, 134, 144-146, 151, 152, 168, 186, 212, 234, 236, 238, 239, 241, 242, 245, 249, 252, 253, 262, 263, 267
Wrede, William, 7-9, 11-13, 28, 62, 70, 119, 269
Wuerttemberg, Germany, 2-5, 7, 68
Wuppertal, 4
Wyoming, (state), 216, 217

Yakima, WA, 141, 283
Yamada, Pastor, 227
YMCA, 136
Yokohama, Japan, 226
Yoshida, Iadashi, 228
Youth, 64, 89, 99, 144, 149, 152, 172, 189, 255, 257, 284
Ypsilanti, MI, 21

Zambia, Africa, 169, 170, 222, 223, 225, 259, 313
Zank, Walter, 243
Zaremba, E., 120
Zell, Edward. 242
Zich, August. 94, 122
Ziebell, Thomas, 271
Ziegler, Paul, 223, 224
Zielke, L., 167
Zimmermann, H., 120
Zink, H., 213
Zondervan, 2
Zuberbier, Traugott, 245

GERMAN ROOTS

The mission school at Hermannsburg, Hanover, Germany about 1870. A number of early Wisconsin Synod pastors were trained here.

Hermannsburg students. Among them is Johann Meyer (middle row, far right; see pages 74-77).

A more informal picture of the Hermannsburg students. (See if you can locate Johann Meyer.)

NORTHWESTERN COLLEGE

Northwestern University, Watertown, Wisconsin, in its early years.

Northwestern College, a typical study room in 1919.

The Sprinter, a campus landmark since the early 1900s.

The old kitchen at Northwestern College.

PASTOR TRAINING

Northwestern faculty in 1874. Seated front center is Pres. Ernst.

Pres. Carleton Toppe
1959-1987

Pres. Robert Voss
1987-

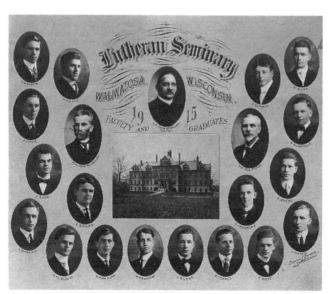

Wisconsin Lutheran Seminary class of 1915. Top center, Pres. John Schaller.

Adolph Hoenecke, long-time Seminary head

Pres. J. P. Koehler
1920-29

SYNODICAL SCHOOLS

Dr. Martin Luther College, Old Main, the original building still in service.

Michigan Lutheran Seminary's Old Main, 1887-1962.

Dr. Martin Luther College class of 1912.

Pastor C. J. Albrecht, Minnesota Synod president and founder of DMLC.

Otto J. R. Hoenecke, MLS president, 1910-1950.

APACHELAND

The Uplegger family with the Peridot mission chapel in the background.

Pastor F. Uplegger with Apache member San Carlos, Arizona.

An Apache brother.

WORLD MISSIONS

Evangelist Nemoto teaching confirmation class at Oarai, Japan, 1965.

Lutheran school children distributing tracts at Hong Kong fair with Mr. Schwertfeger and Pastor Peter Chang.

Superintendent E. Wendland and students, Zambia, Africa.

SYNOD PRESIDENTS

Johannes Muehlhaeuser
1850-1860

John Bading
1860-1863, 1867-1889

Philipp von Rohr
1889-1908

John Brenner
1933-1953

Oscar Naumann
1953-1979

Carl Mischke
1979-